A WHITE-BEARDED
PLAINSMAN

A WHITE-BEARDED
PLAINSMAN

The Memoirs of Archaeologist W. Raymond Wood

W. RAYMOND WOOD

THE UNIVERSITY OF UTAH PRESS
Salt Lake City

The Defiance House Man colophon is a registered trademark of the University of Utah Press. It is based upon a four-foot-tall, Ancient Puebloan pictograph (late PIII) near Glen Canyon, Utah.

15 14 13 12 11 1 2 3 4 5

LIBRARY OF CONGRESS CATALOGING-IN-PUBLICATION DATA

Wood, W. Raymond (Walter Raymond), 1931–
A white-bearded plainsman : the memoirs of archaeologist W. Raymond Wood / W. Raymond Wood.
p. cm.
Includes bibliographical references and index.
ISBN 978-1-60781-130-5 (cloth : alk. paper) 1. Wood, W. Raymond (Walter Raymond), 1931– 2. Archaeologists—United States—Biography. 3. Archaeologists—Great Plains—Biography. 4. Great Plains—Antiquities. I. Title.
CC115.W625A3 2011
978'.01092—dc22 2010051499

Cover photo courtesy of Tom Stromme
Index by Andrew L. Christenson

Printed and bound by Sheridan Books, Inc., Ann Arbor, Michigan.

For my children:
Stanley, Eric, and Marigene

Contents

Figures

Foreword

For five decades, Ray Wood's influence on the course of Great Plains archaeology has been pervasive. In pursuit of his interest in Great Plains prehistory, ethnology, ethnohistory, and fur trade history, he has authored 41 monographs, 17 book chapters, 110 journal articles, 8 book introductions or forewords, 50 book reviews, and 40 contract reports. He has edited 3 professional journals, served on 11 professional advisory commissions or committees, held membership in 10 professional organizations, and been honored 14 times for his professional accomplishments.

Throughout his career Ray devoted his intellectual energy to explicating and refining the theoretical principles inhering in culture history, an approach that was and remains the backbone of American archaeology. Despite the fads, fantasies, theoretical flourishes, and convoluted criticisms that fill so many pages of recent books and journal articles, neo-evolutionists, processualists, post-processualists, and landscape archaeologists all use the analytical, descriptive, classificatory, and sequencing practices developed by prehistorians for the study of culture history. To me this indicates that culture history produces useful results for both critic and practitioner. Ray was an outstanding example of the latter. He consistently achieved a masterful integration of carefully constructed research design with highly productive techniques of data extraction, analysis, and interpretation.

In his 1967 masterpiece, *An Interpretation of Mandan Culture History*, Ray demonstrated that military threat or conflict, amplified perhaps by drought, forced formerly scattered proto-Mandan populations into large towns, stimulating the development of the integrative devices seen among historic Mandans, such as the multiclan scheduling of ceremonialism, age-graded societies, and the Okipa ceremony. Trade with alien village groups and pedestrian nomads brought wealth to these large towns, providing new norms of and for manufacture and conduct that leveled some of the differences between the Mandans and their neighbors. This model was systemic in organization and intent. In this respect it was exemplary culture history at the cutting edge of the processual onslaught that dominated American archaeology for several decades.

While the ecologically oriented archaeological studies conducted during the 1960s used data supplied by experts in various fields, the interdisciplinary part of these ventures was largely confined to the laboratory. Ray and Bruce McMillan directed one of the earliest interdisciplinary field efforts, integrating the research of specialists in geology, palynology, paleontology, physical anthropology, and archaeology. This collaboration, focused on the lower reaches of the Pomme de Terre River, developed a fluvial and paleoenvironmental record covering the last 34,000 years. The archaeological contributors defined five adaptive patterns for the area's Archaic-stage inhabitants.

In 1967 I was privileged to address one of Ray's Plains Archaeology seminars, which dealt with the data generated by a field school held the previous summer. Ray and a cohort of his graduate students had excavated two house sites in the Central Plains and were in the process of integrating, describing, and interpreting the results. They had taken soil samples for pollen, conchological, and other purposes and had used recently popularized water-screen and flotation techniques on the fill from all features. The two house ruins, one Upper Republican and the other of Nebraska culture origin, were chosen to provide maximum geographic and environmental contrasts. From differences in the animal and plant remains, the group concluded that Upper Republican peoples were more mobile and firmly focused on bison hunting than their Nebraska culture compatriots, who were more committed to crop growing and solitary game animal hunting.

To interpret this evidence, Wood combined ethnographic with archaeological findings to suggest that Upper Republican and Nebraska culture peoples shared a common cultural heritage of matrilineal, matrilocal communities, or neighborhoods, composed of extended, polygynous households organized into bands led by men holding key kinship positions. The published results of this archaeological experiment were considered controversial by some, but in retrospect they marked a turning point in the conduct of Plains village research. *Two House Sites* generated hypotheses about Upper Republican and Nebraska culture social life that are still being tested. The seminar that produced them integrated fieldwork and classwork with intense tutorial guidance, a productive mix that became the hallmark of Ray's approach to graduate education. His students attribute his profound impact on Plains archaeology to his role in the graduate anthropology program at the University of Missouri–Columbia.

When I joined the staff at the University of Missouri in 1968, I experienced firsthand the vibrant interaction of graduate students and faculty that centered on a newly acquired research facility at 703 Missouri Avenue. From the street the building was an unimpressive two-story former student co-op. The first evidence that it housed something special came from the backyard parking lot, where a fleet of green carryalls, pickup trucks, and a station wagon were parked, all bearing the logo of the University of Missouri, Division of American Archaeology. The second story housed an ancient woodrat midden being carefully disassembled, and assuming some of its former olfactory glory, by David Madsen, who was extracting pollen and preserved Pleistocene flora from it. A perfectly preserved Pleistocene flower from one of the middens soon graced the cover of *Science*.

In another room on the second story Carl Falk managed the newly created and continually expanding comparative faunal collection, whose hunter-donated and roadkill specimens were being defleshed and fed to a colony of dermestid beetles in the rear of the basement. Rumor had it that this facility, formerly housed in the attic of Swallow Hall, had contributed to the speedy acquisition of the 703 Missouri Avenue co-op building because in its previous location the pungent defleshing operations of the dermestids were, to the disgust of maintenance workers, vented to the campus's Quadrangle.

The front portion of the basement was devoted to the storage of field equipment: water screens, dry screens, shovels, mattocks, picks, fire hoses, hose couplings, pumps, generators, alidades, transits, tripods, surveying rods, and ranging poles. J. Bennett Graham managed this equipment and the vehicle fleet from his office on the first floor.

In one of the offices on the first floor Stan Ahler studied the wear marks produced by using stone tools he had made. Additional offices, equipped with microscopes, illuminated magnifying devices, sorting trays, tables, and desks, were occupied by other graduate students, including Rain and Susan Vehik, Fred and Mary Jane Schneider, Marvin Kay, Gary Leaf, Francis Calabrese, and Kerry Lippincott, all conducting research sponsored by the Division of American Archaeology.

The first-floor parlor was the nerve center of 703 Missouri Avenue. It was where the graduate students met to discuss their research, seek the advice and aid of their compatriots, and interact with faculty and students in other subdisciplines of anthropology. In 1968 the anthropology department added an emphasis on quantitative analysis. Courses taught by

Michael Robbins and Robert Benfer, and the ideas forwarded by their graduate students, Richard Pollnac and Phillip Kilbride, became an integral part of informal graduate student seminars centered on the parlor at 703 Missouri Avenue. The synergy created there led the participants to identify themselves as the Missouri Mafia, a designation many of them celebrate to this day. Ray supervised these graduate student efforts with diligence.

During his tenure as a member of Missouri's graduate faculty, Ray served on 73 master's committees in anthropology, three in history, three in geography, and one in geology. He served on 32 doctoral committees in anthropology, three in history, and one in English. He directed 36 master's theses and 22 Ph.D. dissertations. Eight of the master's theses and 12 of the doctoral dissertations were subsequently published. He also served on doctoral committees at the Universities of Kansas, Colorado, and Alberta-Edmonton and on a master's committee at the University of Kansas. As Ray's advisees graduated, they assumed research and/or teaching positions in Arkansas, Missouri, Oklahoma, Kansas, Nebraska, South Dakota, North Dakota, Colorado, Utah, and Montana.

In sum, Ray has had a truly remarkable professional career. His influence made Plains archaeology what it is today. His students speak of him with respect and affection. His colleagues who disagree with him on issues of theory nonetheless respect his opinion. In contemporary parlance Ray both talks the talk and walks the walk. His work has become the "gold standard" of Plains anthropology. Though I have known him for fifty years, have admired his work, and have been impressed by the outstanding achievements of his students, I knew little about the rich array of experiences that shaped the life of this white-bearded plainsman until I read a draft copy of the pages that follow.

Richard A. Krause
Tuscaloosa, Alabama

Preface

From time to time friends have suggested that I write my memoirs. I paid little or no attention to such queries until some years ago. As you age and watch as your colleagues become older and older, you gain a new and less optimistic perspective on life, especially when you find that your early graduate students are beginning to take retirement or pass away. Another clue is when people begin to ask you to tell them about the "olden days," thereby casting you in the role of an "old fogey" (a euphemism for you-know-what). Many younger folks would like to know how it was "when dinosaurs roamed the earth," or their elders wish to refresh their memories of days gone by. I've done a number of such talks in recent years, from which I've shamelessly cribbed some of my present text. Archaeologists elsewhere in North America have published autobiographies—notably Michael D. Coe, Luther S. Cressman, Jesse D. Jennings, Neil M. Judd, Florence Lister, Stanley A. South, and Fred Wendorf—but the principal ones for Plains prehistorians have been the short essays first published serially in the *Kansas Archaeologist*. These began appearing in the 1990s with reminiscences by Carlyle S. Smith and Ralph Solecki, and I published my own background a little later. These essays later were collected, augmented, edited, and published in 2006 in the *Plains Anthropologist* as "Plains Archaeology's Past: A Collection of Personal Narratives."

Andy Rooney (1995:xiii) has written, "If you're pleased with the way you've been remembering some of the major events of your life, don't set out to write a book about them. The chances are, they weren't that way at all." He later observed that reporting "is far from an exact science and by the time the story of an event or the description of a person has been set down on paper, the truth about either is changed or distorted, even by the best reporter. It's a fact that accounts for the popularity of revisionist history."

I've written this narrative essentially from memory, but I have verified names and dates whenever possible by consulting relevant publications and manuscripts and by delving into the five file drawers that contain my correspondence. I've kept most of the letters I've received over the course of my professional career, as well as carbons or photocopies of most of the letters I've written, though unfortunately I didn't do the same for letters I wrote to family members. Admittedly, everyone's correspondence has been impoverished since the advent of e-mail, though I do print out and save most of those missives that I deem important or interesting. In addition, I've consulted my newspaper clippings, unpublished talks, and published papers, and I've drawn heavily on three autobiographical articles (Wood 1995a, 2006a; Wood and Hoffman 1995). Unfortunately, and perhaps inexcusably, I've never kept a personal field journal or even a diary, something I'd now recommend to any field investigator. Those looking for juicy tidbits here about my colleagues will be disappointed, however, for I include nothing (ah, but I could) that will embarrass or overly dismay any friend or acquaintance—at least, not living ones. Some of the best stories therefore remain untold. I've also eschewed rehashing the two emotional impediments I've endured in an otherwise generally cheerful and productive career. In any case, I have tried my best and can only hope that I've avoided "Rooney's Rule."

I set out to write this narrative about the turn of the century, when I began to enter into my computer some of the more interesting events of my life. In early 2005 I started to string them into a more or less coherent text and then into a consistent narrative. Since that text would have been of interest only to my family, I began to insert historical background so the product would have some merit as a history of my profession in the midcontinent and place my career in perspective. In the end I decided to include "insights" from some of my papers, not just to give them further exposure but to illustrate the changing paradigms that characterize our profession. For readers seeking greater depth and breadth to the story of Plains archaeology to enrich this admittedly personal and myopic offering, I recommend three excellent, though inevitably dated, overviews: George C. Frison's "The Plains" (1973), Waldo R. Wedel's "Toward a History of Plains Archeology" (1981), and Richard A. Krause's "A History of Great Plains Prehistory" (1998). But do not neglect Thomas Thiessen's *Emergency Archeology in the Missouri River Basin* (1999), for it details the role of the Missouri Basin Project and the Midwest Archeological Center in the Inter-Agency Archeological Salvage Program between 1946 and 1975; the introductory chapters in the Plains volume of the Smithsonian Institution's *Handbook of North American Indians* (DeMallie 2001); or Marlin F. Hawley's fine essay in the *Plains Anthropologist* (Hawley 2006).

This story is of course egocentric in that it deals with my own experiences through the years, but I did not work in a vacuum and what I did reflects to one degree or another the changes that took place in archaeology during my lifetime. It's for this reason that I've yielded to adding citations to the text—surely far too many, but after a lifetime of writing in this fashion, I can't abandon it, though I have not included all the trade books I mention in passing. I'm especially indebted to Marvin Kay, Richard A. Krause, R. Bruce McMillan, Michael J. O'Brien, Thomas D. Thiessen, and my wife, Carolee, for readings of the manuscript that proved to be invaluable; they caught numerous egregious errors. Lastly, I'm grateful to the two readers for the University of Utah Press, whose constructive criticism was so very helpful.

I thank the editors of the journals shown here for permission to incorporate the (somewhat revised) text published in them from the following articles: "The Missouri River Basin Surveys: Archaeology without the Middle 'A,'" from "Plains Archaeology's Past: A Collection of Personal Narratives," *Plains Anthropologist* 51(200):671–682 (2006); "Ecology and Great Plains Studies," *Review of Archaeology* 12(2):30–34 (1991); "Some Views on Great Plains Prehistory," *Review of Archaeology* 14(1):21–24 (1993); and "The Jaguar Gorget: 'The Missouri State Artifact,'" *Missouri Archaeological Society Quarterly* 16(2):8–11 (1999). I'm also grateful to Tom Stromme, of the Bismarck *Tribune*, for his permission to use the photograph he took of me at the interpretive kiosk at Fort Clark State Historic Site.

The book's original title was inspired by a flowering plant that I was told was native to the southern High Plains, the "Gray-Bearded Plainsman," but the title changed along with its author to "White-Bearded." The plant was pointed out to me by my friend Jack L. Hofman during a joint University of Missouri–University of Kansas field school that spent the first part of the summer of 2000 at the Waugh site, a Folsom camp in northwestern Oklahoma (though I have yet to find the plant listed in any compendium of the wild flora in the Great Plains). The narrative generally is chronological, though the interrelated nature of the events has made a strictly calendrical ordering of material as impractical as it would be undesirable. For this reason, a calendar of events is included as an appendix. I hope the result is more than an exercise in ego. For me, the effort answered the age-old question that so many of us ask ourselves from time to time: "What have I done with my life?"

W. Raymond Wood
Columbia, Missouri
June 30, 2010

1

Early Years

The Plains of this countrey are covered with a Leek Green Grass [Big Bluestem], well calculated for the sweetest and most norushing hay— interspersed with Cops [copses] of trees,... and nature appears to have exerted herself to butify the Senery by the variety of flours... which Strikes & profumes the Sensation, and amuses the mind [and] throws it into Conjecterng the cause of So magnificent Senery in a Country thus Situated far removed from the Sivilized world.

— William Clark at Independence Creek, near modern Atchison, Kansas, July 4, 1804, in Gary E. Moulton, ed., *The Journals of the Lewis and Clark Expedition*, 1986

Gordon, Nebraska

I was born in my parents' home in Gordon, Sheridan County, in the panhandle of extreme northwestern Nebraska, on May 18, 1931, in the second year of the Great Depression. (So was Don Martin, cartoonist for *Mad* magazine, though it's probably irrelevant.) I was named after my father's younger brother, U.S. Army private Walter Raymond Wood, who died at St. Amand Talland, France, of bronchial pneumonia two weeks before the armistice that ended World War I, never once having seen the front lines. He'd served as a telegrapher (his civilian job) for the 163rd Field Artillery Brigade, which had gone into training at Clermont-Ferrand and Bordeaux. His unit was destined never to see action, and it returned to the United States shortly after the armistice. Because he was called by his middle name by his family, so was I. But when I went away to high school during my sophomore year, the fact that most people go by their first name was rudely reinforced, and not caring to be called Walter by that time, I adopted the use of a first initial (though for many years I convinced some people it stood for Winthrop).

Gordon lies on the very margin of the northwestern rim of the Sandhills, the most distinctive physiographic unit in Nebraska. In mid-postglacial (Hypsithermal and later) times the ever-present Great Plains wind created that gently rolling to hilly terrain, composed of giant sand dunes that resemble the Great Sand Sea of the northern Sahara Desert. Today the Sandhills are mantled by a lush prairie of mixed grasses and constitute the largest sand dune area in the Western Hemisphere, equal in size to the states of Vermont and New Hampshire combined. In many areas one may gaze to the horizon without seeing any trace of trees; when they are in view, they likely line the floodplain of one of the few streams or surround the buildings of one of the widely spaced cattle ranches. The rapid absorption of rain into the sand results in poor drainage, and a high water table has created innumerable lakes, marshes, and fens surrounded by moisture-loving grasses, including wild rice. The water table, indeed, is easily identified, for ducks and geese paddle about on it! The land has been imaginatively but accurately compared with an open, rolling seascape, though lacking the regularity of ocean swells. Some dunes attain heights of four hundred feet and may be twenty miles long. The human population here is low, with cattle outnumbering people by a very large margin. Gordon was set in a shallow basin on the northwest rim of this stark but beautiful landscape.

My boyhood recollection of the Sandhills was one of unrelieved aridity, for one may drive for an hour or so through the dunes without crossing a stream or seeing a lake of consequence. It was not until I drove through the region many years later that I realized how ecologically diverse it truly is. When I was young, I'd seen a few of the hundreds of lakes that dot its landscape, but they'd not really registered because of their scarcity near my home. The revelation I experienced on that latter-day drive gave me a deeper appreciation of ecology and a determination to stress ecological principles in one of my favorite courses at the University of Missouri, a class in environment and archaeology.

The region's position in the middle of the continent leads to great variation in daily to annual temperature and precipitation. The weather is characteristically uncertain. Indeed, one bright morning on the Fourth of July in about 1968, when I was visiting former student John S. (Steve) Sigstad in Vermillion, South Dakota, I was awakened by a clock radio that

Figure 1. The author at age twenty-two months, on the railroad station platform in Gordon, Nebraska, 1933. *Author's collection.*

cheerfully announced that the outside temperature was 32 degrees. I shook my head and thought, "That can't be," but a few minutes later the radio repeated that astonishing fact. I shouldn't have been surprised, for North and South Dakota are capable of experiencing a freezing temperature on any given day of the year. Years later Alfred E. Johnson and I were to write, "Plains scholars have never ignored interrelationships between culture and environment, although the extent to which these relationships have been explored varies a great deal. Those of us who were born and raised in the continental climate that characterizes the Great Plains—no less than those who have been introduced to –40 degree F. temperatures and 100 mph winds, having come to the Plains from elsewhere—tend to be sensitive to ecological matters" (Johnson and Wood 1980:42). This sensitivity characterizes most students of the Great Plains: ignore it at your peril both in everyday life and in your historical studies.

I had two very fine, caring, and supportive parents, Vera Gladys (Hiatt) and Elbert Stanley Wood, plus an older brother, Elbert Stanley Jr. ("Bert" to his friends); an older sister, Marjorie Mary; and a younger sister, Dorothy Elaine. Dad was a station agent for the Chicago & North Western Railroad and a member of the Masonic lodge in Gordon. During my earliest years in Gordon we lived in the railroad station. Such stations, universally known as "depots," were designed to serve both as the local office for the railroad and as homes for the station agent. The quarters were adequate if plain, and one soon became used to sleeping in a room that shook with tremors that would be interpreted elsewhere as a major earthquake as freight and cattle trains rushed past in the night only a few yards from one's bed.

A tall man, and thin throughout his life, Dad was never without a hat, though I never knew him to be self-conscious about his baldness. He was born in his farm home in Montgomery County, northeastern Missouri, on October 26, 1887 (he died April 8, 1970), and Mother was born in the small town of Haddam, in northeastern Kansas, on April 16, 1901 (she died December 29, 1993). I found it easy to remember her birthday, coming the day after income tax was due. Dad grew up among neighbors who had served in the Civil War, and he was able to discuss that great conflict in detail, both from his reading and from drawing on the experiences of neighbors whose conversations were often devoted to reminiscences of that tragic event. But he had a wry sense of humor, surely more so than Mother, and I have no doubt that I inherited my own (sometimes distorted) one from him. We didn't pal around much, though we enjoyed listening together to the radio in the evenings. Dad's middle name of Stanley (which he never used) came from the then-famous African explorer, Henry M. Stanley. Among the books in my grandfather's home in Missouri that I devoured as a child was a tattered copy of James W. Buel's 1890 *History of the Dark Continent*, which introduced me not only to Stanley's exploits but to travel adventure.

Dad's father, Theophilus Benson Wood, had become a lawyer after graduating in 1859 from Williams College (Williamsburg, Massachusetts). When he found he could not practice law and remain honest, however, he abandoned his practice and moved to Missouri after the Civil War, where he became a prosperous farmer. Because of his legal background, he was called "Judge" by his neighbors and was a respected and formidable member of the local community. Neither of my parents had graduated from high school, but my mother nevertheless was a strong advocate of education. After my brother Elbert was born, Mother spoke to Dad about his going to college. But my grandfather's career had led Dad to believe

Figure 2. Elbert and Vera Wood, my parents, at their fiftieth wedding anniversary, 1969. *Author's collection.*

that you didn't need higher education to be successful in life, so he resisted the idea of college for his infant son. Mother is thereupon reputed to have told him, "Well, then, we don't need any more children." Dad changed his mind: both his sons would attend college.

Elbert was plagued by the colic during infancy, and after a time Mother decided she wanted some help around the house. In those days it was customary for ranchers to board their children in town during the school year, for many of the ranches were dozens of miles in the country over roads that often were impassable during the winter, so commuting daily was out of the question. In 1922 Mother advertised in the *Gordon Journal* for a girl to help with year-old Elbert. One day, she told me, a local rancher limped up to the door and, when she answered his summons, said abruptly, "Here's my girl. Take her," and stalked off, abandoning a bashful teenage girl at the door. The rancher was Jules Sandoz, best known as Old Jules, whom many folks in the community regarded poorly. The ranch of this often-brutal Swiss immigrant was in the Sandhills thirty-five air miles southwest of Gordon (it was far longer by road) near present-day Smith Lake, some miles south of the upper reaches of the Niobrara River.

The young woman that Sandoz left impressed my mother. She was Flora, a younger sister of Mari Sandoz, the Nebraska writer whose fame is perhaps equaled only by that of Willa Cather. Years later Sandoz would write *Old Jules*, a biography of her notorious father that arguably became her most famous work, at least in Nebraska (Sandoz 1935). When I contacted Flora in the 1980s to ask for information about my brother, she wrote me that she'd never been in town before meeting my mother and that she'd been brought to Gordon to attend high school. She went on to say that my mother (an excellent seamstress) had made the first dress she ever had that wasn't "countrified," by which I suspect she meant that it wasn't made from flour sacks. One of the reasons our family weathered the depression so well was the fact that Mother made many of our clothes, saving substantial sums by purchasing fabric so she could avoid store prices.

Many people retain excruciatingly detailed memories of their childhood, but I remember little of Gordon save for fleeting images of the several homes we lived in there. First was the railroad depot, then the two houses that my mother finally demanded as an escape from proximity to the trains, though many fragmentary glimpses of events flash back unbidden: snippets of Christmas scenes and of grade school. Some parts of one's life stand out in photographic clarity and minute detail, yet others vanish into some dark memoryless crevice and defy resurrection.

Life at the depot sometimes must have been onerous for Dad because he could never escape his job, for he lived next door to his office. Being a generous and obliging person, he was liable to be called back to his office even when he was not on duty, even on weekends, when a knock on the door might summon him back to work. Railroads enhanced their business by having station agents live on the premises, but they also knew that live-in agents discouraged burglars and, furthermore, reduced their fire insurance (Grant 1994:118). I spent many hours in Dad's office, pecking away with one finger on his Royal typewriter when it wasn't in use.

Dad was a homebody, with no great urge to travel, quite the opposite of my mother. It had to have been from her that I inherited my own love of travel, for his occasional answer to her request to go for the once-popular "Sunday drive" was "Fine. We need to go to the dump," a response that was poorly received. There was no garbage pickup: after we moved to the town of Cody, we burned what we could in a barrel in the backyard and carried the residue and other noncombustibles to a dumpsite over the hill and out of sight just east of town. Mother also was responsible for my fondness for classical music and was accomplished enough to play the piano for church services. To this day the only music I own, whether first on phonograph records or today on compact discs, is from the classical and romantic periods, especially by German and Russian composers; I can tolerate limited quantities of baroque. I enjoy music in the background as I work, for it effectively drowns out the distractions of nearby conversations and other unwanted sounds. The present fad for rap music is the cruelest prank played on the world of music since the invention of the guitar, at least as it is so often played today (excluding of course Andrés Segovia).

Three events that took place during my childhood are ingrained in my memory. First was the balloon that lifted off in the Black Hills in 1935 and floated into the stratosphere, across the greater part of South Dakota, taking the first photograph to show the curvature of the earth. Second, in 1936, was Shep, the renowned Montana sheepdog. A local sheepherder was taken in his casket to the railroad station in Fort Benton, still accompanied by Shep. After the train left, carrying his body back east for burial, Shep refused to leave the station. The faithful dog met every arriving train until old age claimed him and he slipped on the rails and was run over. His loyalty was national news, and the railroad employees refused all offers by dog lovers to adopt him. The dog is still celebrated in Fort Benton, where a heroic-sized bronze statue of him adorns the city park. (On my first visit to Fort Benton I made sure to visit his grave.) Finally, I recall best the parachutist who landed on the top of Devil's Tower, Wyoming, in 1941, and the effort it took to get him down after he spent a miserable week on its summit. Each of these events was remembered and talked about for years, usually prefaced with "Do you remember when…?"

Because Gordon was in cattle country and depended on the railroad to supply its necessities, Dad became acquainted with every rancher and businessman within a wide radius of town, including Clive Gildersleeve, the owner of the trading post at Wounded Knee, on the Pine Ridge Indian Reservation, twenty-six miles northwest of Gordon. I stopped by to see him many years later, before his store and the little museum he'd founded (the Crazy Horse Museum) were destroyed during the confrontation and hostilities that took place there in 1973, when members of the American Indian Movement occupied the town and defied federal agents. Gildersleeve had fond memories of my father's kindness.

The Great Depression occupied much of my childhood, though I remember little of it, for Dad's job with the railroad provided a dependable if not substantial income, and as far as I know we weathered the event without undue hardship. I'm sure my parents had other impressions of the era, though I cannot recall hearing them complain of hardships; perhaps they discussed them when we children weren't present. Dad's job meant that he had a steady paycheck, and the fact that we lived cost-free in the depot throughout those years—so desperate for so many others—meant there was no expenditure for rent. Indeed, Dad had saved enough money by the time I was a child to purchase a potato farm somewhere north of Gordon, but during the drought years of the 1930s he lost it. What I remember most about life in Gordon and Cody was my chore on Saturdays: dusting our living quarters in the depot. No sooner did I finish than the ever-present Great Plains wind would deposit another light layer on everything no matter how tightly the house was closed. It was a hopeless task. Cast-iron coal stoves heated the depots, and it was my duty to see to it there was sufficient coal on hand. On cold days the stove might become red hot, though it warmed principally the room it was in: on many a winter night I went to sleep in a frigid upstairs room with a carefully warmed flannel-wrapped brick at the foot of my bed.

My sister Marjorie sold tickets at the local movie theater in Gordon. When I had no money but I really, really wanted to see a special movie, she'd advance me the admission—one dime. However, one day when she wasn't selling tickets, two movies were playing in a double feature that I just had to see: the original versions of *Frankenstein* and *Dracula*. Somehow I managed to sneak in, but several times I fled quaking to the lobby when the drama became too intense. My illegal entry hadn't been wise. My bedroom at the depot was upstairs, and the light in the stairwell could be turned on only at the top. I couldn't explain to my parents why I'd been so terrified that afternoon that nothing on earth could convince me to walk upstairs into the darkness. Someone had to precede me and turn the light on for a very long time.

One of the few books I remember reading as a preteen in Gordon was a dog-eared, coverless copy of Gilbert L. Wilson's little book about the life of a Hidatsa Indian girl, *Waheenee* (Wilson 1921). Little did I realize that I'd become involved with Waheenee's relatives and with historic archaeological sites near her birthplace on the Knife River in North Dakota over much of the course of my career. Living as we did then so near Wounded Knee and the Pine Ridge Indian Reservation, I gained an early appreciation of American Indian culture, though I don't believe our location had any bearing on my later professional interests. One of my earliest memories is of an Indian dance on Main Street in Gordon, performed by residents of the nearby Sioux reservation.

Another book given to me by family friends was a slim, black-bound volume about dinosaurs that I treasured for years, and it inspired in me a fascination for those beasts I've never lost. After grade school I was also an avid reader and dedicated collector of the *National Geographic* magazine, though it was not as thrilling as Buel's *History of the Dark Continent.* The magazine introduced me to the outside world and to exotic peoples and cultures that I found compelling, and it may even have subtly preconditioned me for a career in anthropology. Books provided important recreation in those years before television, and I spent many evenings curled up on the couch reading. Later, after my family's move to Cody, I often worked at the town's diminutive Carnegie Library, and by the time I left for college I'd read the greater part of its contents, from *The Land of Oz* and the Hardy Boys series and all the holdings by Edgar Rice Burroughs and Jules Verne to more serious selections, such as a biography of Samuel Langhorne Clemens and some of the works of Winston Churchill. Among the most fascinating volumes were the adventurous travel books by Richard Halliburton, whose reckless conduct (he once dived into a Mesoamerican cenote at night) eventually led to his death. Though his books are today considered racist, they continue to be of interest for their romantic escapades.

Family traditions agree that I was an exceedingly hyperactive child, a trait that, fortunately, diminished as I aged. One afternoon when I was in the care of my older sister, Marjorie, I darted to freedom and sped into the local pool hall. In those days women simply did not enter such dens of iniquity, so she went to the depot to get Dad, who unceremoniously hauled me out, probably by one ear. I was also prone to play in settings around the depot that my father considered dangerous. One day I accompanied him down the railroad tracks some distance east of Gordon, where a hobo had been struck and killed by a train. I don't recall my mother's reaction to this event, though I'm sure it was adverse—but it had the desired effect, for I never played around the tracks again.

The Farm in Missouri

I never knew my dad's parents. His father died in Missouri on June 3, 1917, followed shortly after by his mother, and the farm was divided among their surviving children. By the time I was a child, Dad held half the farm and his sister Edith and her husband, George G. Maupin, owned the other

Figure 3. Aunt Edith's farm in Missouri, summer 1954. *Author's collection.*

half. That farm became a summer haven for the Wood children. Being convinced that the devil finds tasks for idle hands, my parents decided that it was less difficult to get into trouble on an isolated farm than in Gordon. Therefore, Elbert was shipped off to the farm at an early age, and I followed him into summer "camp" when I was four years old. I'm not sure how Aunt Edith and Uncle George felt about these waifs arriving annually on their doorstep, but they were unfailingly gracious to us. After Edith's husband died in 1938, we boys made ourselves useful by helping around the farm with milking and other chores. (I especially enjoyed catching the cats that lurked around the barn with a squirt of milk.) I continued to spend my summers there every year from 1935 until I graduated from high school in 1949, a seasonal migration that I greatly enjoyed. The nearly four years of rural summer months I spent there surely qualified me as a "farm boy," for during that time I participated in every farm activity suitable to someone my age.

The farm was at the junction of State Highway 161 and County Road CC, five miles south of the town of Middletown, in Montgomery County. The adjoining area was informally known as "Crossroads," and it was excellent farmland, its fertile soils having formed under the vast prairies that once blanketed this part of the state. Indeed, trees were so scarce on

Grandfather's farm that he'd purchased a tract of timber a few miles to the west from which he'd harvested firewood. One of my earliest introductions to ecological degradation, though certainly I was unconscious of it at the time, came as I accompanied my father down a farm road as he inspected his property. As we walked along the fencerow, he told me that the only grasses native to the area now grew in the right-of-way. I'm sure he did not know at the time that conservationists eventually would work to preserve the few pristine native prairie plots remaining in the state. It was not hard for me to envision prairie extending to the horizon across this gently rolling landscape, a vision that would return to me much later when my work in Missouri led me to investigate sites along the boundary between what is known as the Prairie Peninsula and the oak-hickory forests of the Ozark Highland.

A small intermittent stream locally called Possum Branch bisected the property, and beyond the farm it flowed into Elkhorn Creek, a tributary of the Cuivre River. It had a wonderful clay- and sand-bedded channel that provided great opportunities for sand sculpture, and moreover, it contained ephemeral pools of water after heavy rains from which I often harvested stranded catfish. My aunt's culinary arts transformed them into delicious alternatives to her other wonderful country-style menus.

The farm home was an old one: originally, it had been a two-story log house, though long ago large additions had been built to two sides, and the logs were visible only in what was called the "old upstairs." Grandfather Theophilus Wood had moved from New York to Missouri sometime after the Civil War and initially settled near Dardenne, not far from St. Charles, Missouri, where he taught school. Sometime after marrying one of his students, Mary Catherine Stevenson, he moved to Montgomery County and probably purchased the log cabin as it was. I have no idea when it was enlarged, but it was likely soon after he arrived, to accommodate his nine children, most of whom were born near Dardenne. After Aunt Edith's death in 1980 my cousin, Clifford W. Maupin, purchased the farm. He sold the logs in the building to a medical doctor in Columbia when he razed the old home and replaced it with a modern one.

Aunt Edith wrote a local news column under the heading of "Crossroads" for a local newspaper, the Wellsville *Optic-News*, and she gathered its contents by a method impossible today. She had an oak wall telephone with a bell that jingled with a code for each subscriber on the party line: hers was a long and two shorts. However, whenever the phone rang, she would listen in and thereby learn who was visiting and who was traveling, as well as details of births, illnesses, and deaths, all of which she faithfully transmitted weekly to the editor, receiving in turn a free subscription to the paper. My mother was mortified by the technique, but anyone familiar with a party line knew there was no such thing as a private conversation. Whenever you were on the phone, you were sure to hear a click as someone picked up the receiver—and not necessarily to make a call. There were other primitive aspects of the farm that I long took for granted: an outdoor privy several yards from the house (though "thundermugs" were available at night) and water that was hand-pumped into the house from a cistern that gathered runoff from the roof.

Sometime after the great influenza epidemic following World War I, Vera Singleton, one of George Maupin's cousins, now an orphan, came to live with him and Aunt Edith. Vera was deaf and could not speak, and she continued to live with Aunt Edith until a progressive case of Alzheimer's disease made it necessary for Edith to retire to a nursing home. I learned sign language to communicate with Vera, though I never became proficient. We often visited cousins and related kin in nearby Warrenton, Missouri, and had Sunday dinners with them. Two of the more ancient kin included one of Grandmother Wood's brothers, Michael Stevenson, who had lived in New Orleans, where he became a noted producer of queen bees; I still remember staring at a photograph of him wearing a "bee beard." A family rumor that a man named Wood had been involved with pirates I dismiss as myth. I once thought it would be great to verify the story, for there was no record of horse thieves, murderers, or other such riffraff to enliven the family's history.

Aunt Edith was quite self-sufficient, for every summer she and Vera and I tended a large garden that provided fresh vegetables, and the women canned great quantities of food to tide them over the winter, storing the jars in a partially buried root cellar near the house. Each Saturday Aunt Edith took the chicken eggs that I collected to town to exchange for "store-bought" items, including hundred-pound sacks of flour. The flour came in colorful cotton sacks that she chose carefully, for they provided the material from which she made her dresses and sunbonnets. In these clothes she was well known in Middletown and Montgomery City, two nearby towns where she did her shopping. When she shopped in Montgomery City, I sometimes went to the city library to check out books (they had most of Edgar Rice Burroughs's *Tarzan* and *Martian* series) or visited the "ice factory" to marvel at its technology. This chilly building contained rows of giant tin boxes holding three-hundred-pound blocks of ice, which could be purchased by individuals in twenty-five-pound blocks deftly ice-picked from the monolith. She'd pick me up when she finished shopping, and we'd take a block home to cool the icebox. Such items were a warm-weather necessity in the years before the Rural Electric Association brought the convenience of electricity to the countryside. It was many years before I managed to drop the term "icebox" for "refrigerator."

Some of our shopping was in Middletown, for Aunt Edith's daughter Verda and her husband, D. E. Bethel, lived there, and he taught at the Missouri Military Academy in the nearby town of Mexico. His father managed one of the town's grocery stores, and I recall the pungent aroma of the giant catfish that he purchased in Louisiana, a town some miles distant on the Mississippi River. I spent some of my time waiting for Aunt Edith in Ralph's Saddle Shop a few doors down, a fascinating place with mysterious odors, where Dad often visited old friends. The grown-up conversations there weren't as interesting as the jokes they sometimes told, which often were over my head. One Sunday at dinner I told the assembled family one of them I'd heard that, to me, had no salacious overtones. There was no laughter, only thunderous silence as a ring of stunned faces turned slowly toward me. After dinner I was taken aside and told, sternly and unequivocally, that I was never again, *never*, under any circumstances, to repeat *anything* I'd heard at Ralph's Saddle Shop. I don't recall being forbidden going there, but unquestionably that was part of the message I've forgotten. In any case, the local blacksmith shop was not far distant and provided an alternative attraction. I often stood in its door and marveled at the red-hot metal being hammered to the accompaniment of a fountain of sparks. It was reminiscent of a Norman Rockwell painting.

Until I was old enough to take the train to Missouri by myself, my parents drove to the farm, a move that also allowed Dad an opportunity to inspect his property and visit friends. We usually left about a week or so after school closed in the spring. Missouri at that season is a landscape dominated by magnificent greens; the grass and the ever-present trees are lush with the fresh growth of spring and reminded me of the Land of Oz, though the greens fade in intensity as summer progresses and age and dust dull their hues. In the Sandhills of Nebraska the grasses mantling the dunes were likewise bright green in the spring, but they soon matured to a uniform beige brown. When I first arrived in Missouri to begin work at the university in early April 1957, I was stunned by the gray drabness of the landscape, for the trees had barely begun to bud.

On rare occasions the family would pack a lunch, bundle into the car, and drive fifteen miles south to picnic at a secluded cave on the Loutre River. Today the overhang is the centerpiece of Graham Cave State Park, a location that became renowned in Missouri archaeology following excavations there that began in 1949. That work resulted in a master's thesis for Wilfred D. Logan, who obtained the first advanced degree bestowed in anthropology at the University of Missouri. Logan's subsequent career in the National Park Service eventually led to his position as archaeologist in the Omaha regional office of the service in 1962, where he replaced Paul L. Beaubien, and in 1969 he became the first chief of the Midwest Archeological Center, in Lincoln, Nebraska. For years, the results he published of the investigations at Graham Cave provided the best stratigraphic sequence for prehistoric cultures in the state, for the cave contained a cultural record that began about ten thousand years ago and lasted into the late prehistoric period. That enviable reputation endured for nearly two decades, but it eroded rapidly after the records at Rodgers Shelter in southwestern Missouri (discussed later at length) were published by a team that began under my direction, and after records from Pigeon Roost Creek in northeastern Missouri became available through the work of Michael J. O'Brien. The deposits in Graham Cave were shallow, and rodent activity had churned them badly, thereby blurring the archaeological record they contained.

I was free to run wild in the Crossroads neighborhood until I was old enough to milk cows and do farm chores. One chore I enjoyed was cranking the "separator," a device that separated the cream from fresh milk by centrifugal force. I roamed "the woods" (a pasture that contained abundant trees) and neighboring farms barefooted, stuffing myself on gooseberries and mulberries in season and invariably returning home with a healthy crop of chiggers. Aunt Edith once counted over three hundred of them on me. Fortunately, I managed to avoid serious injury, for Aunt Edith's remedy for cuts was to rinse them with alcohol and flood them with iodine: this burned so mightily that I often concealed my wounds. I became a self-taught and reasonably competent swimmer in shallow pools in Elkhorn Creek, playing with a neighboring boy of my own age, though I'm still uncomfortable in water over my head. I had a carefree existence, prowling the countryside with a dog named Buster, an apparent cross between a German shepherd and a collie. Edith's husband, George, would sometimes take sheep shears to Buster in the heat of the summer, leaving a mane around his neck and a tuft on the end of his tail like that of a male lion. Somehow Buster had learned on the word "Squirrel!" to race headlong to one of the giant oaks in the front yard and vainly attempt to claw his way up its trunk. I loved these vacations in Missouri and began packing a suitcase weeks in advance, making sure I'd remember to take everything I'd want there.

Brother Elbert had accumulated a fine collection of prehistoric chipped-stone tools from sites near the farm. I tried to do the same, though he died in World War II before I found where he'd obtained his collection, something that remains a mystery to this day. (On a later trip to New York City I donated his collection to the American Museum of Natural History.) I spent my evenings reading and playing board games (checkers and one called Carom) with Aunt Edith. For many years, kerosene lamps illuminated our nightlife. For all practical purposes, Aunt Edith became a surrogate grandmother to me, since my paternal grandmother and grandfather had died more than a decade before I had any chance to know them. My mother's father likewise had died before I was born, and her mother was a terror who (thankfully) rarely visited: she mercilessly criticized almost everything my mother did. Her first husband, my real grandfather, had been a railroad engineer, and on his death she'd married another engineer, the only "grandfather" I can remember. One of the highlights of my childhood was sitting on his lap in a locomotive and, with his hand tightly wrapped over mine on the throttle, driving it into the roundhouse in Douglas, Wyoming, something that my sister Marjorie remembered with equal pleasure.

My first employment away from Aunt Edith's farm was with a neighbor, Isaac Walton (really), during harvests. My job was to ride the binder, a farm implement drawn behind a tractor. It cut the grain and transported it on moving canvas belts to a complex mechanism that bound the stalks into bundles that dropped into a hopper at the side of the machine. I sat on a metal seat on one side of the device, watched for problems, and dropped the hopper to the ground at intervals so the bundles of grain weren't scattered across the field. Later, harvest crews roamed across the field and set the bundles upright in shocks of eight, capped with a ninth to shed water.

I remember well the next stage: threshing, when the entire rural community of Crossroads, men and women, collaborated in bringing in the crop of neighboring farms. Going to each farm in turn, the men threshed the grain—wheat, usually, or oats. This was in the years before combines, and the bundles of grain were carried by horse-drawn wagons to a giant stationary threshing machine and pitchforked onto a conveyor belt that carried the sheaves into its maws. A huge leather belt driven by a lug-wheeled tractor ran the thresher. The grain poured out of a spout on the side of the thresher into other horse-drawn wagons to be hauled away and hand-scooped into the granary. The straw was blown out one end of the thresher through a long tube that could be directed so the straw could be blown into the loft of a barn or deposited outside in a stack wherever the farmer wanted it. The noise was deafening, and the dust and chaff from the thresher filled the air and drifted into your clothes and down your neck, making threshing an altogether dusty and itchy experience. One didn't wait for Saturday night to bathe after the thresher left.

The women prepared the collective noonday meal, the memory of which still evokes great pleasure. Men carried great appetites in from the fields, and their wives each brought their specialty dishes. The table, as the cliché goes, literally groaned under the weight of the finest home recipes in mid-America. It was a labor-intensive time, but one that had deep social value for the participants. Neighborhoods lost some of their cohesion with the introduction of combines, and threshing bees became a thing of the past. Despite my short-term residence among the friendly folks of the neighboring farms, I remained a member of that community for the rest of my life. Such a feeling of belonging is unknown among the members of urban communities today.

Cody and Chadron, Nebraska

We lived in Gordon until July 1941, when we moved to Cody, in Cherry County, Nebraska's largest county, a bit larger than the state of Connecticut. I wasn't sorry to relocate, for it removed me from the attention of a particularly obnoxious bully who'd plagued me in Gordon. My father was approaching retirement, and the strenuous workload at Gordon was beginning to overwhelm him. When trains arrived, for example, he'd be responsible for loading endless twenty-gallon milk containers into baggage cars for transport to dairies, a duty that taxed the physical capabilities of a slim fifty-four-year-old man. He applied for and was given a less physically demanding and stressful assignment at the smaller station, something his seniority allowed him to do.

This was Dad's third and final duty station. He'd begun railroad work in December 1916 as a telegrapher for the Chicago & North Western Railroad, and in 1917 he was stationed at Orin (Junction), Wyoming, a nondescript locale some fifteen miles east of Douglas. It was there he met my mother when she came to visit one of her sisters who lived nearby. They were married on June 4, 1919, in Casper. In March 1920 Dad was promoted to station agent, and they moved to Gordon, where all four of us children were born. When he retired in 1953, he and my mother moved to California, though they are buried together in the Wellsville, Missouri, cemetery beside my brother Elbert, who died in aerial combat in World War II.

Cody is set in a low basin in the Sandhills very near their northern border yet well within them. Rolling dunes swept away from us in every direction. Out of sight of town the view instilled in one the feeling of being a solitary traveler on the desert, yet it has not always been so. It's hard to envision the land as it was at the end of the last glaciation, some nine to ten thousand years ago, when the spruce forests that mantled the countryside began to make way for this giant pasture. Travel in the Sandhills is a wondrous experience, the loneliness of the region offset by its stark beauty. But its true charm is in the late evening, when the harsh flat light of day fades and the angling rays of the sun cast interfingering shadows across the grass, which the wind ripples like water across the dunes. I was told that background scenes for the 1947 motion picture *The Sea of Grass* were filmed a few miles south of the town of Valentine, just east of Cody.

Cody had a population of about 250, and in a short time we knew everyone in town. And everyone knew everything about us. Life there gave me a clear appreciation of the important role that conformity and gossip play in the regulation of the affairs of a community in tribal societies—an early lesson in sociology and cultural anthropology. You behave and conform or the whole town knows about it. Main Street, just north of and parallel to the railroad tracks, was unpaved and was bordered by all the commercial buildings in town, all but one of them on the north side of the street facing the railroad. The town budget did not allow for the purchase of a new fire engine when the old one conked out, so it was pulled to fires behind a surplus army jeep.

It was eight air miles south (far more by road) over primitive roads to the deeply incised valley of the Niobrara River, though the Nelson-Cody Lake and a small stream, Hay Creek, were only a few miles north of town. The state line runs through the northern part of the lake; the bulk of it in Nebraska is named Nelson Lake, and that small fraction in South Dakota is Cody Lake. Seven miles to the east on U.S. Highway 20 the diminutive town of Nenzel nestled among the dunes, and Valentine, the county seat, was thirty-one miles farther east. Valentine, between the confluence of the Niobrara River and Minnechaduza Creek (said to be an Indian word meaning "murmuring water"), was the nearest goal of anyone needing either medical attention or a dentist. My teeth were never particularly good, so I learned early to be cautious of these white-gowned men. Perhaps the greatest pain I ever endured (years later) was having a tooth extracted without the benefit of Novocain; the dentist had given me three shots of it without deadening the tooth and could not safely administer more, so out it came. Need I say that this baneful event took place in the western Missouri Ozarks?

To the west there was no town of significance before Gordon, fifty-four miles distant. Nebraska's boundary with Todd County, South Dakota (that is, the Rosebud Indian Reservation), was only four miles north of Cody. Until automobiles became common for them after World War II, the Sioux came to town to shop in horse-drawn wagons. They'd camp overnight in tents on the east side of town before returning home. Despite its small size, the town offered conveniences that were not available for many miles, including a newspaper, hotel, drugstore, hardware store, barbershop, restaurant, and two groceries; a lumberyard and two gas stations graced Highway 20. The town was much smaller than Cody, Wyoming, where our mail was often erroneously sent before reaching us, days later. Well, after all, it had been named after the original "Buffalo Bill" Cody and ours had not; instead, ours was named for Thomas Cody, a railroad construction crew foreman who oversaw the construction of the water tower that fed the boilers of the locomotives. At one time Buffalo Bill had visited our town in the mistaken assumption it had been named for him.

For some time, we lived in the railroad depot, but we soon moved into a large two-story frame home a few blocks east of the station. It was indeed palatial, having been built by a former owner of the lumberyard. It was one of the grandest houses in town, with leaded windows and exquisite woodwork throughout. All it lacked was a fireplace. It was only one block to the center of the business district and the post office. Mother had a real house again, and I had my own room at last, with wondrous glass-fronted legal bookcases for my slowly growing collection of books. It was my last home before I left for college in the fall of 1949.

My parents regularly attended the Methodist Church, though I suspect that my father originally had been a Baptist, as were other members of his family in Missouri. They were dedicated but not fundamentalist churchgoers. Mother played the piano in the small church in Cody, and I was a regular attendee at Sunday school and church services until I left home. By that time my belief system had been seriously compromised by what I'd learned of biology and natural selection, and unlike my sisters, I became more than skeptical of religious matters and attended church only for weddings and funerals for the rest of my life. Watching the questionable activities of numerous practicing Christians over time furthered my schism with organized religion. My younger sister, Dorothy, learned to play the piano tolerably well, and sister Marjorie had played the bass viola in high school. Brother Elbert had mastered the clarinet to some degree, but I abandoned music lessons early when I discovered that the violin was more challenging than it appeared, and my piano lessons lasted for perhaps a year. Mother had been wasting her money on those lessons, for my ear for music was for listening, not performance.

World affairs rarely weigh heavily on the minds of those not yet in their teens, and certainly I was no exception. The news of the Japanese attack on Pearl Harbor that spread across town on the afternoon of December 7, however, abruptly reversed that state of mind. It was the first of several days that I can recall where I was and what I was doing, like the day my family was informed of my brother's death, that of President Roosevelt, and the dropping of the first atomic bomb on Hiroshima. I can still visualize the headlines of the newspaper declaring the war was over.

The arrival of trains carrying German prisoners of war to camps in Wyoming created major excitement in town during World War II. When the trains stopped, the Germans would lean out the windows (you could actually open them then) and ask, in English, "Is this where Buffalo Bill lived?" They were downcast to find it was not, for Germans are inordinately enamored of our American West and its Indians, largely thanks to the many novels by Karl May that he set in the American West. On the rare occasion when an Indian from the nearby Rosebud Reservation was on the station platform, so many heads appeared in windows it was surprising that the passenger car didn't tilt to one side. Indians of course frequently visited town to shop, and a few were temporary residents. One of them was a tall, distinguished-looking Sioux named Blue Horse who'd traveled with Buffalo Bill's Wild West Show and had performed before Queen Victoria when the troupe toured Europe.

The war had few day-to-day effects on Cody except for the troop trains that passed through town. We of course had no reason to fear being bombed, situated as we were in the middle of the continent, but nonetheless we had blackout curtains, though I don't recall we ever used them. One of our windows bore a blue star on a small banner, denoting that a member of the family—my brother—was in the military. After he died in action in 1943, a gold star replaced the blue one, though Mother never actively participated in the Gold Star Mothers, an organization that was formalized shortly after World War I; her loss was too devastating.

Elbert graduated from Gordon High School in 1939, but after a year at the University of Missouri and three semesters at the University of Nebraska, he enlisted in the U.S. Army on December 8, 1941. I saw him only a few times after that when he was home on furlough, and I well remember his last visit before he left for England, where he became a member of the 369th Squadron in the 306th Bomb Group of the 8th Army Air Force. Elbert was able to visit my sister Marjorie in New York City before he went overseas; she photographed him in Central Park. Knowing more than we did about his overseas duty, he told her, "I'm not coming back." And he did not. He died on October 14, 1943, as the navigator of the B-17 Flying Fortress *Wicked WAAC*, on its way to bomb the ball-bearing works in Schweinfurt, Germany. The number of bombers lost on that mission was so catastrophic that 8th Air Force personnel named the day "Black Thursday," though today it is called "Second Schweinfurt" by historians, for the losses on an earlier dual air strike on Schweinfurt and Regensburg had been equally devastating. Elbert was in one of the sixty American four-engine B-17 bombers that German fighters and anti-aircraft fire shot out of the skies on that clear October afternoon. It is reputed to have been the greatest air battle in history because of the high percentage of its losses, though later raids by far larger bomber fleets sacrificed greater numbers of aircraft. His body was returned to the United States after the war, and he was interred in the cemetery in Wellsville, Missouri. Eventually, Elbert would be joined there, first by our father and then our mother. My father, as the person who received all telegraph messages through the railroad, was of course the first person in town to know their contents throughout the war. I cannot imagine his grief as he tapped out first the telegram from the War Department that his first-born son was missing in action and later the one announcing that he was killed in action, for Dad had also lost a brother in World War I.

Elbert's death was a drastic loss to the family, and I spent days in deep depression, wordlessly contemplating life. One consequence was that it

Figure 4. Elbert S. Wood in Central Park, New York City, following his graduation from the San Marcos Air Force Navigation School, September 1943. *Author's collection.*

deepened my ambition to attend college and take up where this sibling role model had left off. The army never told us how he died, and eventually my curiosity led me to research his army career and publish a book about how he had died, a story I tell later in this volume. The ten-year gap in our ages meant that we pursued different activities, but I could always count on him to get me out of trouble out of sight of our parents. He was truly a big brother to me. I vividly recall one occasion when he took me to the Gordon city jail, where we viewed some of the miserable specimens incarcerated there. I cannot recall what he said to me, but the message was clear: "Stay out of trouble, or you might end up in here."

My older sister Marjorie left home after graduating from high school, and after spending some time at a business school in Lincoln, she moved to New York City, where she worked for the FBI during World War II. Later she moved to Ogden, Utah, and then to San Francisco, where she married John Behrens II and raised her family. John had been in the navy and had served on the destroyer USS *Caldwell* during the war. His destroyer was present in Leyte Gulf during the 1945 invasion of the Philippines, reputedly during the most savage naval battle ever fought. The sky swarmed with Japanese kamikaze aircraft, and fourteen of his mates were killed around him when the *Caldwell* was struck by one of them. This gave John strength in his final days with cancer, when he told his family, "I had forty-five years more than many of my friends." Younger sister Dorothy went to California after graduating from high school and lived with Marjorie until she married Richard Cowan; the two girls always lived near each other and were inseparable until Marjorie's death. It would be hard to envision two kinder and more pleasant sisters; Dorothy and I of course had childhood squabbles, but as adults neither she nor my sister Marjorie and I ever had any kind of falling-out. It was quite enough that we'd lost a brother, and we cherished a close relationship throughout life. Marjorie died after a lingering illness following chemotherapy, but Dorothy did it right, for she passed away in her sleep as she was returning home from a cruise to the Bahamas. I always enjoyed my visits with them, for both had a good sense of humor. Dorothy was fond of telling houseguests, "Would you like me to fix your breakfast, or can you peel your own banana?"

There were few jobs in Cody for teenagers, and I briefly held several, though only two of them were educational. During World War II I delivered the Omaha *World-Herald* newspaper across town on foot, learning the rudiments of managing a small business, and later I went to work as a clerk in one of the two grocery stores in town, the one operated by "Dusty" Rhodes. The store included a quick-freeze unit and a locker room in the basement. My duties involved every aspect of the store, from ordering groceries to pricing the goods as I shelved them. (How many of you can recall a loaf of bread selling for seventeen cents?) One summer Dusty believed I was experienced enough that he decided to take his wife on a well-earned two-week vacation. It gave me a deep feeling of accomplishment, for during his absence I did everything except issue checks to his creditors. Other opportunities to earn money were spare and included such jobs as shoveling a railroad gondola of sand into a trackside bin; stacking hay at a ranch on Hay Creek, north of town; raking up the leaves in the Cody town park; and mopping down the floors and tending the furnace as the janitor at the town bank. These chores did nothing to dim my enthusiasm for attending college.

There were few amusements in town: the local theater had movies every weekend; we could listen to the radio; and there was a skating rink, where I became reasonably proficient. The building also served annually as the site of the "White Elephant" Dance, where, I was later told, Dusty met his end when someone cut his throat. An occasional evangelist came through to save the town's sinners, and I witnessed at least one traveling exhibition and demonstration of a now-forgotten "Wonder Dog." I saved my money from chores and bought an antique radio that nevertheless worked well, and spent many evenings happily listening to Jack Benny, Edgar Bergen, Fibber McGee and Molly, the Lone Ranger, and other popular programs. There also were long hikes with friends in the surrounding Sandhills. We sometimes took cans of dog food with us for lunch, for I'd discovered that beneath the labels of one brand the cans were painted khaki. This concealed the fact they were actually surplus U.S. Army K-rations that were still perfectly edible (a serviceman would not have agreed). During the war I collected tin cans, rubber, and metal for various scrap drives, which netted me small change for sodas.

I was largely a loner throughout high school, for none of my cohort in Cody shared my academic interests, and if anyone of my general age ever attended either college or a university, I'm not aware of it. I had utterly no use for basketball, the sport that dominated the waking hours of the boys in school (we had football only one season, since there were too few boys large enough to make a team). The members of the basketball team prided themselves on their letter jackets with the school colors and a large letter *C* over the left breast that celebrated their participation in the sport. The school also awarded a letter for drama, and I was granted one for my participation in the freshman class play. I insisted that I'd earned it and persisted in wearing it, to the unmitigated disgust of the jocks.

World War II was an intensive lesson for me in many things, not the least of which was geography. Listening to the war news nightly and reading about it daily were rituals that my father and I attended faithfully. I had *National Geographic* maps of both Europe and the Pacific, by means of which I watched the progress of Allied troops as the war dragged on, and slowly I destroyed them both as my penciled erasure lines of the war fronts finally degraded them. I also had a huge wall map of the world on which I followed events. The result: there were few if any countries that I could not pinpoint by the war's end. I don't recall ever taking a course in geography (though I'm sure I must have), but in any event the political boundaries of our globe were no mystery to me by 1945.

The Chicago & North Western Railroad line that passed through Cody and Gordon began for us in Omaha and continued west into Wyoming. Known informally today as the "Cowboy Line" because of its emphasis on hauling cattle to the stockyards in Omaha, it was the subject of a 2009 book that also illustrated the line and the families of its employees. It includes photos of my parents and myself taken in the 1940s and 1950s (Terry 2009:37). Today the tracks are gone, and the rail bed between Norfolk and Chadron has been transformed into the Cowboy Recreation and Nature Trail, the longest rail-to-trail conversion in the United States. It passes through that part of Nebraska now known as the "Nebraska Outback" because of its low population density and its remoteness from urban centers.

Living as we did in the railroad depot meant that our living quarters were only yards from the tracks. Passenger trains of course stopped to pick up or discharge their transient occupants and freight. The many cattle trains, however, did not stop. Because cattle could not drink or feed in the cars during the haul to the Omaha stockyards, the trains would depart late in the day and race in the cool night air across Nebraska without stopping, running at night so the cattle would not overheat in the crowded cars. The house would rumble and dishes rattle as they passed through town at breakneck speed, usually after dark. Nonetheless, the sound and feel of trains passing in the night was so common that I routinely slept through their passage. Ah, that I could do so today!

Cattle were of course a fact of life in the Sandhills, and some of the ranches in the vicinity were enormous. One fall sister Marjorie and her husband, John, drove out from California to visit us. Though my brother-in-law had been in the navy and had seen action in the Pacific during World War II, he'd never traveled east of Lake Tahoe, and as they drove he began teasing my sister, "Are we there yet?" On a sightseeing trip to the neighboring hamlet of Nenzel we stopped for coffee at a small cafe, where John spotted an elderly man in bib overalls and wearing shoes but no stockings. He looked so destitute that John wanted to buy the old fellow a cup of coffee, but Dad told him, "Don't bother. He's one of the richest cattlemen in the county." Cattle ruled: needless to say, sheep were rare and poorly appreciated in this country. A western term for them, at least in some areas, is "range maggot."

Since shopping options were limited in both Gordon and Cody, my mother often went to shop in Omaha, and normally I'd accompany her. We'd ride overnight in a Pullman sleeping car, arrive early in Omaha, shop, and board the train that evening for another night's travel home. This great city was a monumental change from my small-town experiences, and its immense buildings and incessant bustle led me to realize how different the outside world could be. I'd usually haunt the book sections of the department stores while mother shopped for the material she'd turn into home-crafted clothing. My first experience with non-midwestern home-cooked meals came at King Fong's, a long-lived Chinese restaurant we often visited. I was of course accustomed to seeing Indians around town because of our proximity to the Rosebud and Pine Ridge Indian Reservations, but the only African Americans I met for many years were railroad porters. One day in Omaha when I was very young I saw a black woman with a small child and excitedly called out, "Mom, look, there's a baby porter!" I was hushed immediately. Later in life I concluded that my parents were racially prejudiced, though to what extent I never knew, for it was a topic they did not discuss with us. I deeply respect them both for the fact they never once tried to instill any form of ethnic superiority in their children, despite the fact my father had grown up in Missouri in what is called, for very good reason, "Little Dixie." My mother certainly displayed no emotion when I introduced her to one of my black friends from Omaha on one of her visits to me in Lincoln years later, nor did she comment on it.

Winters in western Nebraska were something to write home about, but the Central Plains winter of 1949 was special, for it featured the worst blizzard the region had endured since the famous and catastrophic one of January 1888, which all but destroyed cattle herds across the Great Plains. It began snowing in late December 1948, and conditions rapidly deteriorated as the New Year literally blew in. It was not long before snowdrifts of awesome size began to build, and eventually drifts hundreds of yards long and twenty feet deep filled many of the railroad cuts. A locomotive wedge plow attempting to bully its way through one of them by brute force derailed not far west of town. Another wedge plow was immediately dispatched from Chicago, but it too derailed. A wrecker locomotive eventually restored both of them to their tracks, and when a rotary snowplow appeared, it was finally successful in boring its way through the massive drifts.

Meanwhile, the rails had been blocked for nearly a month, and Cody became for a time the western terminus of the Chicago & North Western

Railroad. The entire storage room at the depot was piled to the rafters with sacks of U.S. mail. Towns west of Cody were suffering from the lack of supplies: I was told that yeast was flown into my hometown, Gordon, so people could bake bread. Cattle were dying by the hundreds because of the cold, and Indians on the Rosebud Reservation regarded the frozen carcasses as manna. The National Guard was called out, and in short order military vehicles capable of traversing the snow-covered surface were transporting supplies and hay to isolated ranches and cattle. The young soldiers driving them were having the time of their lives bouncing over the drifts.

One morning it was necessary for me to climb onto the roof of our front porch, jump into a snowdrift in the yard below, and shovel my way into the house, for drifting snow had wedged the doors shut. One bright afternoon I walked to the edge of town, where I saw a railroad cut filled to its rim with snow, and I stepped over the wires of telephone poles that barely broke the surface along the adjoining highway. I have a photograph of the scene that shows a snowplow cutting through a drift with the top of its smokestack level with the surrounding snow. There were drifts on Main Street twenty and more feet high; from the crest of one of them we could peer into its central cavity and see the roof of a car. Eventually, the snow began to melt and matters returned to normal, but residents of the region will never forget the Winter of '49, for it moved across the region slowly and featured nearly two days of blizzard conditions with temperatures in the single digits. I understand, however, that a blizzard in 1993 approached the severity of the one I experienced.

During my high school years I discovered that I was somewhat skilled in drawing and began to do some passable sketches, enough so that in 1945 my mother was contacted by the superintendent of schools in Cherry County, who encouraged her to have me become a portrait painter. The superintendent had been contacted by one of my teachers, who had seen my classroom "doodles." For a time, Mother contemplated having me take lessons. One possible teacher was the wife of a former governor of Nebraska, Samuel R. McKelvie, who lived in a ranch south of Valentine, Nebraska. However, the distance (more than fifty miles) and other considerations (principally the cost) eventually frustrated the plan. I never took a course in art during my university career, though I'd always planned to do so. Elbert had been a reasonably talented cartoonist, and he often drew cartoon sketches for me—another reason he'd been the role model I tried to emulate—although, as my older sister Marjorie told me, he wasn't necessarily a model child away from parental eyes.

Jesse D. Jennings, in his delightful autobiography, *Accidental Archaeologist* (1994), tells how opportunistically his life developed, a theme I've heard in many variants from my friends over the years. Michael D. Coe, in his 2006 autobiographical *Final Report* (what a magnificent title for an archaeologist!), also mentions random, unforeseeable events. Certainly I never planned to become an archaeologist. An early ambition was to remove the strip of engine oil that cars of the era left along the center of road lanes, but if I had fulfilled the first realistic childhood fantasy that I can recall, I'd have become an arctic explorer, for I'd read about Admiral Richard Byrd and his exploits in Antarctica. Matters went so far that one winter, about 1940, when a deep fall of snow mantled our yard in Gordon, I prepared a primitive igloo in which I intended to sleep overnight—a plan my mother firmly quashed. Later readings about dinosaurs, paleontologists, and explorers led me to tell one of my cousins, when he asked me what I planned to do when I grew up, that I wanted to become "another Roy Chapman Andrews," a response that he understandably told me lacked realism. (Andrews had headed the American Museum of Natural History's five expeditions to Mongolia in the 1920s and was the most famous explorer of the time, save perhaps for Admiral Byrd.) Whatever else I may have dreamed came to naught. Most of us probably have much the same story. I have no recollection of wanting to be a firefighter, a pilot, or any of the other things that so attract the fascination of children. One of my early book purchases was *Daily Life in Bible Times*, but it had nothing to do with an interest in archaeology—I valued it because it was ancient history, which certainly did attract me. History still appeals to me and accounts for my interest in the history of the American West, my postretirement abandonment of archaeology, and my forays into writing history itself.

I can, however, pinpoint the precise event (but not the date, though it was about 1942) that attracted me to the field of anthropology. My junior high school had an encyclopedia that I often consulted in the small library in the back of the room, and one day I was riveted by the short entry on *Pithecanthropus erectus*. I still recall with photographic accuracy that small library and even holding the book in my hands. Eventually, I committed that article to memory, and I began to read whatever I could on fossil humans, then of course called "fossil man." There was nothing in the Cody library or our high school that was of any use in my quest for such esoteric knowledge. However, I discovered a unique and very personal source in my brother Elbert's class notes for introductory anthropology, which he took when he was a sophomore at the University of Nebraska in 1941 (he got an A).

Elbert had graduated from Gordon High School in the spring of 1939, and that fall he enrolled at the University of Missouri in Columbia, intending to pursue a premedical curriculum. He rented a student apartment on Hitt Street, just across the street from the Memorial Tower, an imposing, Gothic cathedral–style structure that was to become the centerpiece of the Student Union after World War II. The apartment house in which he lived was razed in 1958 to provide a building site for the present Fine Arts Building. Although I was unaware of its history at the time, during my first stint at the University of Missouri in 1957 I helped a friend, Joe Pat Kennedy, dismantle the building, and he sold the used but well-seasoned lumber.

In the fall of 1940 Elbert transferred to the University of Nebraska, for it was too difficult for Dad to come up with out-of-state tuition during these last years of the Great Depression. The fact that Dad owned a farm in Missouri meant nothing as far as Missouri residency was concerned, so Elbert transferred to Lincoln, where in-state tuition was affordable. He lived there, as did my older sister Marjorie for a time, at the Proudfit boardinghouse in the south part of town, as I also did during my freshman year at the university. As a premed student, Elbert enrolled in introductory anthropology, and he had as his instructor John L. Champe, who in later years was to become my own undergraduate and graduate adviser through my master's degree. Elbert took very good class notes, and he sent his effects home when he enlisted in the army and went off to war. When I discovered his notes during my grade school years, I was fascinated, for they included information I simply couldn't get locally on fossil humans. Poring over his notes, I found a reference to a book by Earnest Albert Hooton with the provocative title *Up from the Ape*. With a bit of research I somehow gained the publisher's address and ordered a copy of it at what was, for me at the time, great expense. Elbert's library also included a biology textbook that was far superior to anything I could find in town, and a magnificent volume that I also consumed: H. G. Wells's *The Outline of History*. It continued to whet my appetite for history.

Pursuing my reading, in 1947 I wrote to Robert Broom, at the Transvaal Museum in South Africa, who provided me with references to the Australopithecinae. In 1948 I went so far as to write to the Peiping Union

Medical College, and its librarian, T. F. Chao, sent me copies of Davidson Black's "Asia and the Dispersal of Primates" and Franz Weidenreich's "On the Earliest Representatives of Modern Mankind Recovered on the Soil of East Asia" and "The Drifts of Human Phylogenetic Evolution." Chao also gave me Weidenreich's address at the American Museum of Natural History, and I soon obtained a copy of his 1948 book, *Apes, Giants and Man*. Two other books I purchased were Earnest A. Hooton's *Apes, Men and Morons* and Roy Chapman Andrews's popular review of human evolution, *Meet Your Ancestors*. I naively sent both these latter books to the authors, and both of them graciously autographed them and mailed them back to me at their own expense. These and other sources provided me with many long hours of difficult reading, but they provided a running start on my first course in anthropology at the University of Nebraska, taught by John Champe. My brother must have made an impression on John (or was it a reflection of Champe's near-total recall?), for when I mentioned during my first meeting with him that Elbert had taken general anthropology from him, Champe remembered him in detail, including the fact that he was blond. This was not a chance guess, for unlike Elbert, I sported long shocks of nearly jet-black hair.

One day in about 1947 the community was abuzz with news, for strangers were in town. A vehicle bearing a government license plate had arrived carrying a U.S. Geological Survey team. They rented quarters in a modest motel—the only one—on the west side of town and proceeded to conduct whatever fieldwork they were directed to do that was required to help complete the work on the Cody East, Nebraska, 7.5-minute United States Geological Survey quadrangle (a preliminary copy of which was not issued until 1985). These men stood out in the community, for in a town of two hundred fifty people no one's business was unknown, and I soon found an excuse to talk to them as they ate at the only restaurant in town. They were exciting strangers, especially the portly leader of the group, a man whose name I could not now possibly recall. He represented a way of life and a professional interest that I found compelling, and I made every excuse to talk to him and his crew. He must have found this small-town boy, constantly underfoot, intriguing as well, for he responded patiently to my endless questions and uninvited attention.

I was ecstatic when he invited me to accompany his team one night to a high and distant dune where they were to "shoot the stars" for a celestial reading necessary for map calibration. It was a dark and starry night, far from the lights of town, and I helped unpack the transit and its tripod and watched in fascination as he set up this intricate device and proceeded to take, with great but to me mysterious care, the requisite readings. I cannot now recall the source for my purchase, but a few months later I used part of my small savings to buy a spirit level and practiced running transects from downtown Cody across the railroad track to Highway 20. I was learning something that, unbeknown to me at the time, would be of value in later years. I was saddened when the team moved on to another duty station, but for the space of a few weeks they'd revealed to me a professional way of life far removed from those I witnessed in my small town.

Cody High School was extremely limited in resources, and there was no such thing as college preparation courses. Since my going to college was a given, my parents agreed that I'd attend Chadron Preparatory, a high school that was part of Chadron State Teachers College (later upgraded to Chadron State College), where course offerings were aimed at college-bound students. Chadron, 103 miles west of Cody, was built on the prairie below the north rim of the Pine Ridge Escarpment, a range of hills that parallels the course of the White River as it arcs to the northeast out of the state of Nebraska into South Dakota. Nebraska National Forest mantles the escarpment south of Chadron and provided a new and exciting environment for me to explore.

I went to Chadron Prep for my sophomore and junior years, first living as the sole boarder in the home of a widow a few blocks from the school and the following year taking up residence with another widow who lived across the street from Roy and Thelma Petree; Thelma was one of my mother's sisters. School in Chadron permitted me to accumulate hours that went a long way toward satisfying some of my prerequisites when I entered college, especially mathematics. I'm reasonably sure that if I'd had to master math in college I'd have ended up as a ranch hand in Nebraska or a farmer in Missouri: the subject was never my strong point. Among other things, I took two full years of typing, permitting me to type effortlessly, a wonderful skill that I treasured in my college and later years and that morphed into use on computer keyboards.

Living away from home, not with relatives, was a new experience. I lived in Chadron during the week and spent weekends at home in Cody. I rode the train to and from school at no cost because Dad had free family railroad passes as a railroad employee. Every Sunday night I took the train to Chadron and returned home on Friday after school. I usually sat in a seat

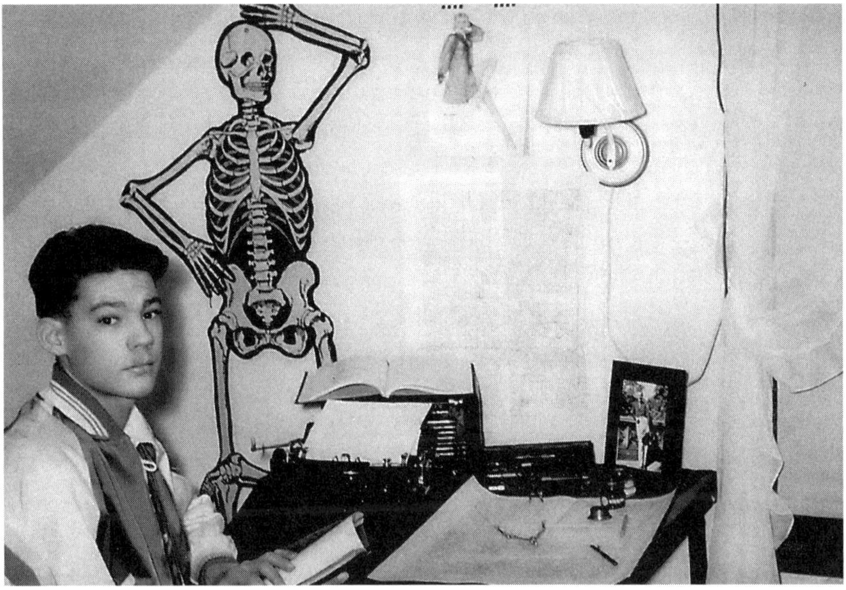

Figure 5. A posed view of my rented room during my sophomore year at Chadron Preparatory School, fall 1947. *Author's collection.*

facing backward, somehow caring more for the view of where I'd been than where I was going. Perhaps I took a perverse joy in ignoring comments by people that sitting backward would make you dizzy, or some foolish comment in a similar vein. The seats, of course, could be reversed when the train reached the end of the line and changed direction, but many of them were left in their former orientation.

The classes at Chadron were more demanding than the ones at Cody, and I made great friends with my history teacher, who convinced me that American history was as interesting as ancient history. I was doing A work in her class in ancient history but C work in American history. When she called me into her office, I tried to explain that the one was truly interesting, dealing as it did with the distant past, whereas American history was lackluster. Somehow she convinced me that both subjects were important, and I henceforth tried harder, not only because she was my favorite teacher but also because she stressed the importance of grades for getting into college, a move I was determined to make.

I also was befriended by a professor of geography at the college, and my first taste of higher education came when he allowed me to sit in on a seminar that he taught on geopolitics. Among the many insights I gained in those sessions was an introduction to the concepts of the German geographer Karl Haushofer and the role he played in the development of Nazism. Among Haushofer's students was Rudolf Hess, who introduced Haushofer to Hitler, who in turn was deeply influenced by his ideas. It was an intriguing introduction to a college-level class and to the background of World War II, which had ended only five years before. A new world also opened up to me in the college library; though it was small by university standards, it was a veritable Library of Congress for me in comparison with the one in Cody. I spent many evenings there and in the Carnegie Library downtown. One topic I studied was Folsom points, for one of my classmates had found one of them in the countryside near his home in Crawford, a town some miles west of Chadron. One weekend I visited him there and we hiked out to the locale where he'd found it, though we managed to find nothing of interest. On our way back to town it began snowing heavily, and just as we reached the highway we discovered that we were circling back into the hills. It was a narrow escape from what could have been a greatly uncomfortable if not life-threatening situation.

I avoided taking shop in Chadron by convincing the instructor that I could better use skills in drafting, so he permitted me to make maps of varying kinds, and I learned the use of drafting equipment and how to make blueprints. The experience built on my inherent love of maps, and I developed skills that were increasingly useful as I passed through college. I later produced maps and artifact illustrations for my own reports and even had a position for a time as the draftsman-cartographer for the Smithsonian Institution's Missouri River Basin Surveys office in Lincoln. I successfully avoided playing football in Chadron, though this deeply irritated the coach and gym teacher. I suspect that may be the reason this sadist decided to teach me boxing, and after a few futile attempts to hit him, I gave up and stood there until he decided I was not only sports-shy but also a coward. Our contempt was mutual.

Chadron State lies on the south side of town at the base of a high ridge of hills composed of Arikaree sandstone, behind which the land was then wholly undeveloped. On many occasions I hiked over that ridge and through the hills, looking for fossils and exploring the country. One evening I found a beautiful agate; only when I was in college did I discover that it was a neatly flaked Indian artifact, an end scraper. The second year in Chadron I bought a blue Schwinn bicycle that gave me far greater range. One evening as I rode north of town, in the valley of a small tributary of the White River, I spotted a glint of white as I passed an exposure of the fossiliferous Brule formation in an adjoining road cut. On investigation I found the palm-sized fossil skull and jaw of an oreodont (*Merycoidoden*), one of a group of Oligocene epoch (34 to 29 million years ago) grazing ungulates that are distantly related to camels or pigs. I removed the skull and carried it back to Cody, where I carefully exposed it by placing drops of water on the surrounding stone, softening the sediment so it could be easily scraped away without damaging the fossil. The skull turned out to be complete and perfectly preserved. This find encouraged me to look at some roadside exposures near Cody, and I managed to find a few small bones in one of them about a mile north of town. I sent them to the Denver Museum of Natural History, and a kindly curator responded with their identification as some Oligocene mammal.

Eventually, I donated the oreodont skull to the University of Nebraska State Museum through its director, C. Bertrand Schultz, when I took a two-semester course in vertebrate paleontology from him in my junior year. The class was in the afternoon, just after lunch, and because the room was on the west side of this brick building, it warmed appreciably in the afternoon. It required monumental effort to remain awake as Schultz lectured in his dry voice and showed slides in the darkened room. He seemed to like me, despite his long-standing feud with some of Nebraska's archaeologists, particularly John Champe, my academic adviser. He'd often make a deprecating remark in class about archaeologists, then look at me and smile, though he never tried to recruit me into paleontology. Years later, when I visited him in Lincoln during our excavations at the mastodon-bearing spring bogs in Missouri, I had to gently parry his pointed requests to become a member of our research group.

I also did some volunteer preparation of fossil specimens in the museum under the direction of Henry P. Reider, the famed staff member who prepared and mounted most of the museum's fossil skeletons. Discovering the resonating sound of the ribs of a fossil rhinoceros, he prepared an instrument resembling a xylophone which he called the "bonophone" but which had softer tones. He gave performances for school children for what he said was "only a small phenomenal fee." His favorite tunes were "Let's All Sing Like the Birdies Sing" and "Chopsticks." My least favorite task under his direction was exposing the skeleton of a small snake from the hard sediment in which it was encased. I'm sorry I never met Loren Eiseley, a friend and associate of Schultz and of archaeologists in the era before my arrival. He was universally admired by his contemporaries, and not simply for the stunningly imaginative but scientifically astute and readable essays he wrote. Perhaps his most popular essays are in *The Immense Journey*, a volume that is well worth reading—and rereading.

Several institutions had investigated the extensive Miocene mammal fossil beds south and west of Chadron along the Niobrara River on the "O4," or the Agate Springs Ranch. When I learned of them, I decided to visit the locale, and in February 1948 I wrote to Harold J. Cook, owner of the beds, asking if I could visit and obtain information from him on paleontology and fossil preparation. I was also curious about the tooth of *Hesperopithecus haroldcooki* ("Harold Cook's western ape") that had been found there (it was later discovered to be the molar of a fossil peccary). Cook was far more than a rancher, for Erwin H. Barbour had trained him in geology and paleontology at the University of Nebraska. He replied apologetically two months later, inviting me to visit and offering to give me advice on preparation. I had no transportation at the time except my bicycle, so I left Chadron early one Saturday morning and tried my hand at hitchhiking to his ranch. I was not successful, and by mid-afternoon I was standing in the hot sun on a gravel road halfway to my destination, so I wisely accepted a ride back to Chadron by a passing motorist. I was not to visit the beds for more than a half century, by which time they had been incorporated into Agate Fossil Beds National Monument, maintained by the National Park Service. This monument surely is in the most desolate part of Nebraska, for it is set in the center of the fifty-six-mile-long road between Harrison and Mitchell, which contains not a single town or gas station, an ideal setting for an isolation ward.

Not all my spare time in Chadron was spent on educational or exploratory pursuits. The only paying job I had there was as a pinsetter at the downtown bowling alley. Now those were the days before automatic pinsetters. You stood behind the rack and sent the ball back to the player, then picked up the pins by hand and set them in a tray that you lowered onto the alley. Then you hopped up on a bench while the bowler rolled his best. It was risky business, especially on the second ball, if the bowler rolled it before you'd finished picking up the first downs. I was fortunate that the only time I was struck by a ball it glanced off the muscular side of my tibia or I might today be wearing an artificial leg. Though we could bowl free when the lanes were empty, I never became more than an indifferent bowler. One of my fellow pinsetters had a friend who worked in a bakery just across the street, and when we got off work at midnight he'd bring with him a sack full of fresh doughnuts for a late-night snack.

It was in Chadron that a classmate named Wiggins introduced me to smoking. In retrospect, I should have strangled him on the spot, but there would have been many other times and temptations to take up this revolting habit, one that I retained for twenty-two years. Many evenings after school I spent perfecting snooker and eight-ball in a smoke-filled pool hall on Chadron's main street, honing skills that I also practiced in the pool hall in Cody on weekends, to my dad's intense displeasure. The pool hall there was owned and managed by a diminutive Japanese (known only as Tommy) who somehow managed to avoid being either interned or ostracized throughout the war years. His ability to perform sabotage apparently was too unlikely to merit consideration. A cigar-smoke-filled back room held a table and chairs occupied by local poker players, about whose habits and winnings or losses I never had a clue. Eventually, I became more than casually proficient at pool, and occasionally I later surprised some of my more staid academic companions at the game. Dad was as contemptuous of pool halls as he was of saloons, the latter of which he called "Halls of Mirth." Needless to say, he was a teetotaler, as was my Aunt Edith, for she would not even use alcohol-free cooking wine in her recipes.

There were two bars on Cody's Main Street, and if that wasn't enough for two hundred fifty people, the local chapter of the American Legion had another one in a back room, at least for a time. One of the occasional Saturday afternoon jobs that I neglected to tell my parents about was in Stotts' Bar, carrying cases of liquor from its basement and stocking the bar. (I also used this opportunity for my first experiments with some of the stock.) Behind the bar was a small building used to store ice, its contents shared by the bar and the adjoining drugstore, run by a related man named Stotts, part of a family that owned much of the town, including the hotel and a grocery store. On occasion in winter I helped the bar owner stock the ice house with blocks that were cut from the lake north of town and buried in the building under a thick layer of insulating sawdust that allowed the ice to last well into the fall. Cody was a true cowtown, and on several occasions I witnessed a rowdy cowpuncher ride his horse in the front door of Stotts' Bar, though the owner found many reasons to object and rapidly evicted them. Today a sign on the edge of town proudly proclaims, "Cody: A Town Too Tough to Die," though the community is no longer as robust as it once was.

I graduated from Cody High School on May 19, 1949, the day after my eighteenth birthday. It was a small class, for there were only four of us, all boys. This meant that each of us was a class officer: I was the president, and the others were the vice-president, secretary, and treasurer. (The next-smaller senior class had been about a decade earlier when one boy graduated.) There were so few of us we became known as the "do-nothing" class, and the larger junior class assumed the burdens normally taken on by the seniors: the senior play, dance, and the like. None of us seemed to care. The school at Kilgore, fifteen miles to the east, merged some years ago with the one in Cody, and the town's students today are bused to the Cody-Kilgore school.

Dad took me to visit the East Coast as a graduation present, though scheduling somehow made it necessary for us to go when I was a junior, not a senior. It was a dual trip, for Dad had numerous relatives on Long Island he'd not visited for many years. We first stopped at the farm in Missouri and then went by train to Washington, D.C., where we toured the several museums of the Smithsonian Institution, the Washington Monument (we took the elevator up but walked down) and other attractions on the Mall, and Ford's Theater, where President Lincoln had been shot: to my father it was a shrine. Then it was on to New York City, where we gazed at the Statue of Liberty from across the bay, took a tour bus through the downtown area and the Bowery, and marveled at the vast fleets of taxicabs visible from the top of the Empire State Building. I took my first roller coaster ride on our visit to Coney Island, though its other attractions have fled my memory. On the afternoon of June 4, 1948, we visited the American Museum of Natural History, where I admired its dinosaur skeletons and the famous dinosaur eggs found by Roy Chapman Andrews in Mongolia's Gobi Desert in 1923. I also donated my brother's collection of Missouri chipped-stone artifacts to the museum through its secretary, Clarence L. Hay.

We went on to visit Dad's relatives (and associated cemeteries) in and around the towns of Hauppauge and Port Jefferson, in central Long Island. Grandfather Wood had been born near Hauppauge, and because his family had been in residence on the island since about 1720, there were many of them to visit. I was, unfortunately, not interested in genealogy at the time or I could have accumulated much interesting family information, though a great-uncle, Simeon Wood, published *A History of Hauppauge* that contained an abbreviated story of the family's early years in New England

(Wood 1920). I was never to return to these ancestral haunts, though Long Island is now crowded with members of the Wood family.

On our return to New York City we took a Hudson River day steamer up the river to Albany, passing West Point and Hyde Park, and then proceeded by rail to Niagara Falls. Like typical tourists, we viewed it from the American side, descended to the drenched rocks at their base by elevator from Goat Island, and later stared up at the cataracts from the *Maid of the Mist*. And on home. It was a marvelous trip, one of the few in which I had Dad to myself, and we thoroughly enjoyed this father-and-son excursion. I sent numerous postcards home to Mother and signed them “The boys.”

2

Undergraduate Years at Nebraska

The outline of these prairies is grand and majestic in the extreme. They are rarely perfectly level. As you advance, one immense sea of grass swells to the horizon after another, unbroken for leagues by rock or tree. They are the home of the bison.

—John C. Van Tramp, *Prairie and Rocky Mountain Adventures*, 1860

Lincoln, Nebraska

I spent the summer of 1949 on Aunt Edith's farm as usual, but in the fall I returned to Cody, and Mother escorted me by train to Lincoln to enroll in the University of Nebraska. Going away to school for many people can be traumatic, but my many summers spent away from home in Missouri and my two years at school in Chadron had preconditioned me not to be homesick. Mother introduced me to the Proudfits, a couple who lived some two miles south of the campus, at 1747 Sewell Street. Mr. Proudfit was a watch repairman, and his wife ran their home as a boardinghouse for a variety of working people. Normally, they didn't take in freshman college students because of their often frisky activities, but my brother and my sister Marjorie had stayed with them when Elbert was at the university, so I was a "legacy," accepted because they had been model boarders, and I was expected to be the same (I believe I was). I had breakfast in their kitchen (invariably hot oatmeal with raisins) and delicious family-style dinners. I ate lunch downtown, usually a fifteen-cent hamburger and milk or coffee at a popular but tiny diner on 12th Street just south of a university building known as the Temple. After school I'd catch a ride home with Mr. Proudfit if I planned to eat dinner there. My roommate was a middle-aged postal employee with whom I had only fleeting contact.

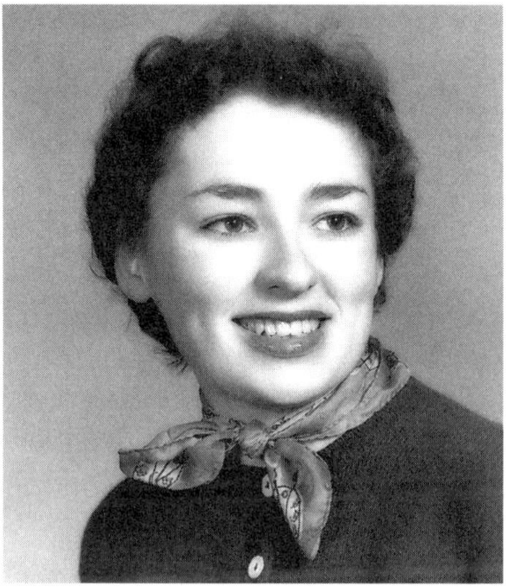

Figure 6. Carolee Kay Ramey at the University of Nebraska, 1954. *Author's collection.*

Among the first people I met at the university were the officers of the Palladian Literary Society, a social group that met monthly in a room on the top floor of the Temple, south of Love University Library. A room there was reserved for their activities and recreation, and I became for a time quite proficient at Ping-Pong. I was quite active in the society for my first two years in Lincoln. It was through one of its members that I met a young woman named Carolee Kay Ramey, who was writing a term paper on the Pawnee Indians who had lived not far from her hometown of Red Cloud, Nebraska. I was able to help her with a source, Waldo Wedel's 1936 *Introduction to Pawnee Archeology*. Soon we were dating regularly, and she was the only woman I seriously dated during my years in Lincoln. We had much in common, for her father also worked for the railroad. For a time, she roomed with Louise Pound, a retired professor of English at the university and a nationally renowned scholar, writer, and lecturer.

A variety of classes were taught in the Temple, though the building itself has changed dramatically in recent years through renovations enabled by an endowment from the Johnny Carson estate. Carson was a student while I was there, and no, I don't recall ever having met him. I took a class in the basement of the Temple in radio writing and broadcasting (I got especially good grades for my commercials). On the first floor I took a class in music appreciation—one that I loved and in which I excelled, for I owned a number of 45-rpm records and was familiar with virtually all the classical examples used in the final exam.

My mother had introduced me to classical music, and I learned more about it in Lincoln. There was a music room on the second floor of the Student Union replete with a large, well-cataloged library of 78-rpm disks of great music. It was a perfect place to study, and when someone was not playing his or her favorite, you could make your own choice from the catalog, pull the disk from the shelf, and enjoy your selection. There was no attendant; you replaced the disks in their sleeves and otherwise left the room as you found it. No other space on the campus was as congenial a place to relax. Needless to say, it is now used for some other purpose.

I often went to the room to study with a close friend, Robert L. Spale, an engineering student from Clarkson, a small town in eastern Nebraska in a part of the state that is dominated by the descendants of Czech settlers. Bob and I shared many interests besides music, and we spent much time together—so much, indeed, that we became known as "Bob and Ray," after a nationally popular comedy team of the day. We double-dated and otherwise were all but inseparable. We also resembled one another to a degree that total strangers often greeted me with a "Hi, Bob," as I crossed campus. Bob introduced me to one of eastern Nebraska's favorite Bohemian treats, the kolache, a type of eastern European pastry consisting of a bread roll stuffed with fillings ranging from fruits to cheeses. He often shared with me kolaches his mother had mailed to him in Lincoln. Because of our friendship, I associated largely with engineering students, including Harry Brindley and his buddy DeVries. He persuaded me to attend a Nebraska home football game (the first of two I ever attended anywhere), notable principally because Nebraska's star player, Bobby Reynolds, scored stunning, crowd-standing points that day. However, as I describe later, the Lincoln Bob-and-Ray team flunked out of school at the end of the sophomore year, and Bob went into the army. After his stint in the army in Europe he returned to the university and completed his degree in engineering; I continued in night school, for I was determined to overcome this obstacle.

For an aspiring anthropologist, 1949 was an exciting time to arrive at the University of Nebraska in Lincoln. At the invitation of John Champe, the headquarters for the Smithsonian Institution's Missouri River Basin Surveys (hereafter MRBS) of the Inter-Agency Archeological Salvage Program had been established in 1946 in what had formerly been the

Department of Sociology and Anthropology. The brand-new Department of Anthropology was then housed in the basement of the newly built Burnett Hall (weren't they all in basements back then?).

The department initially was in the basement of the Sociology Building. When Champe arrived in 1940, he set up the Laboratory of Anthropology as an agency to obtain Works Project Administration (WPA) contracts (since there was as yet no separate anthropology department). Champe gave all twenty-two courses in the department, for which he was paid $1,000 the first semester. The WPA lab operated with up to thirty people. In July 1946 the MRBS set up camp in the Social Sciences basement at Champe's invitation, but things quickly became crowded. When the U.S. Air Force gave up its barracks in Love Library after the end of World War II in 1946, the Laboratory of Anthropology and the MRBS expanded into its basement there. When they asked for additional space, they were told to look for other quarters. The basement of Burnett Hall had a dirt floor in 1946, and it too had been used as a barracks during the war. Champe thought it would do nicely, but Maintenance also wanted the space. When Champe finally got the news that he had secured Burnett, he had a day and a half to submit plans, and no blueprints to work from. He drew up plans, and the facilities there resulted.

When I arrived on the scene, the anthropology faculty consisted of chairman John L. Champe and instructor E. Mott Davis. John was a former insurance agent who'd been seduced into archaeology by his association with William Duncan Strong when the latter was at the University of Nebraska some years earlier. Mott was a member of a prominent eastern family that included the founder of Mott's apple company, the reason one of his sons was named Jonathan. Mott later joined the faculty at the University of Texas at Austin, where he remained for the rest of a distinguished career. Robert Hassler (1989) provides a history of anthropology at the University of Nebraska in which the early years are well treated, but his discussion of the latter ones is marred by a bitter assessment of cultural resource management (see Bleed 1989).

Lincoln was not only the capital of Nebraska but without question the intellectual center of the state. The museum of the Nebraska State Historical Society, directed by archaeologist Marvin F. (Gus) Kivett, was only a few blocks away; he became superintendent of the society itself in 1963. The society's superintendent while I was there was James C. Olson, a distinguished historian who later became president of the University of

Missouri system, where I met him again in the 1980s. As editor of the journal *Nebraska History*, he politely rejected the first paper I tried to publish, when I was a senior in 1954. It concerned the movements of the Arikara Indians in the years following Colonel Henry Leavenworth's bombardment of their village above the Grand River in South Dakota, focusing on their subsequent residence in Nebraska between 1833 and 1835. During this time they aroused the animosity of the Cheyennes, the Delawares, and the Skiri and Republican Pawnees. I'd become interested in their movements when I researched the origins of some putative Arikara pottery rim sherds at the Ponca Fort site in northeastern Nebraska. Franklin Fenenga kindly ran the piece the following year in the fourth number of the *Plains Anthropologist* (Wood 1955a).

John M. Roberts joined the anthropology staff sometime later while he was completing his Ph.D. at Yale. Jack was a World War II infantry captain and a veteran of the Battle of the Bulge in December 1944. He was an outstanding cultural anthropologist whose courses were both incisive and stimulating. He brimmed with projects, and he daily dropped fascinating ideas for student papers and theses that, unfortunately, were rarely archaeologically oriented. He didn't remain long at Nebraska, for he soon went to the University of Pittsburgh, where he succeeded his former teacher, George Peter Murdock, as the Andrew W. Mellon Professor. In a biography of Roberts, Ward Goodenough quoted a colleague who described Jack as "one of the most brilliant and creative anthropologists of the second half of the twentieth century." It was an assessment with which I'd heartily agree, and it was a great loss to the department when he left. For me as an archaeologist, Jack's most important work was his 1951 *Three Navaho Households*, in which he perceptively compared the inventories of three interrelated Navajo households. It has numerous implications for an approach to archaeological fieldwork and analytical studies of hamlet- or village-dwelling peoples that I recommend to archaeologists. We corresponded regularly until 1973, when both of us became swamped in our respective careers.

The department and the MRBS were housed in the east end of the basement of Burnett Hall. There were offices for Champe and for Paul L. Cooper, director of the MRBS office in Lincoln. Two classrooms separated their offices from a large room that contained desks occupied by MRBS staff: John E. Mills (then acting as a historical archaeologist and often ribbed as being a "tin can archaeologist"), Donald J. Lehmer, Franklin Fenenga, Robert B. Cumming, Richard Page Wheeler, George Metcalf, and others. A large adjoining open space, grandly called the Laboratory of Anthropology, was filled with tables and was used as a laboratory for Department of Anthropology and MRBS projects. The tables were cleared and the room filled with chairs every fall when the Plains Conference, then called the Plains Archaeological (or Archeological) Conference, convened in Lincoln.

By the hall door at the end of the large room was a table used by the coffee klatch that met during twice-daily breaks, attended by resident staff and whoever happened to be passing through town. I silently joined this august group and learned a great deal about the administrative and practical side of the national problem arising from the construction of federal reservoirs, for the MRBS in Lincoln was one of several regional offices dedicated to what was then called salvage archaeology in those reservoirs. Burnett Hall was small space indeed for a group responsible for salvaging prehistory from the postwar flooding that was to affect streams across the entire Missouri River Basin.

The coffee klatch was joined by the many visiting archaeologists who passed through Lincoln, and anyone who was present could meet such nationally known figures as Frank H. H. Roberts Jr., director of the River Basin Surveys and associate director of the Smithsonian's Bureau of American Ethnology in 1952. Roberts, a renowned southwestern archaeologist, was a frequent visitor. He was one of the most gracious and unpretentious individuals in American archaeology, courteous to the most junior field hand. I recall him best at social gatherings, at which his favorite pose while seated was to lean into a conversation, one elbow resting on his knee. He was never arrogant, unlike some prominent individuals who scarcely deign to speak to graduate students. His conversations with Paul Cooper, an old hand in Plains archaeology, provided many useful insights into the practical and political aspects of their work. I was also deeply impressed by Irving Rouse, for on my first solo meeting with him as a graduate student he treated me as a colleague, asked about my master's thesis, and appeared to be quite interested. Many years later, though, when I had lunch with him and his former student, Richard A. Krause, I was somewhat put out after a conversation on the Plains, about which he said, "I've always been interested in marginal areas."

There were other important visitors, including Smithsonian archaeologist Waldo R. Wedel, as well as John Otis (J.O.) Brew of Harvard, Frederick Johnson of the Robert S. Peabody Foundation, Henry W. (Ham)

Hamilton, and other members of the Committee for the Recovery of Archaeological Remains. John M. Corbett, chief archaeologist in the Washington office of the National Park Service, was a frequent visitor. Six-foot-five-inch John towered above everyone around him and was a brilliant and innovative individual who did a masterful job with the limited resources available to him. The three-martini lunch I had with him on the occasion of one of my visits to Washington made me wonder, however, how anyone could function in the afternoon in that environment.

The Committee for the Recovery of Archaeological Remains was established in 1945, when Frank H. H. Roberts and Julian Steward alerted members of the Society for American Archaeology of the impending loss of archaeological resources behind the growing number of reservoirs that were being proposed for construction. Some of them, especially along the Missouri River, were of colossal size. Oahe Reservoir, for example, flooded the Missouri Valley between the state capitals of North and South Dakota. The committee was composed of representatives from three nongovernmental organizations: the Society for American Archaeology, the American Council of Learned Societies, and the American Anthropological Association. It gave explicit guidance to the salvage effort, and free of political control or pressure, it was able to lobby for federal support of the program. Two of the primary participants in that committee later published a review of its significance for the development of the River Basin Surveys and its importance in American archaeology (Wendorf and Thompson 2002).

When World War II ended in the spring of 1945, the U.S. Army Corps of Engineers and the Bureau of Reclamation had ready an ambitious program to create dozens of reservoirs throughout the United States. I have no doubt that the planning department for the corps had prepared specifications for a dam on every major stream in the United States under its jurisdiction. All a congressman had to do if he wished some "pork" for his district was to check with the corps and it could provide him with one or more plans for a dam to assure his constituents that he was working for them. The coordinated plan that was put together by the two government agencies became known as the Pick-Sloan Plan, after the two men of their respective agencies who finalized it, Colonel Lewis Pick and Glenn Sloan.

The dams, of course, had noble objectives, principally flood control on the Missouri River and the production of hydroelectric power, with added benefits from irrigation and recreational potential. Had the land that was to be flooded been obtained more ethically, there would have been less objection to these environmentally monstrous projects, but some residents of the Oahe Reservoir, at least, were forced to sell their land at sometimes ruinous prices. Furthermore, reservation land that American Indians had been assured would be theirs "as long as the sun shall shine" was similarly appropriated, and their finest agricultural bottomland was flooded. In addition to the monumental environmental damage caused by these reservoirs, they brought about the wholesale destruction of our natural and cultural heritage for shortsighted goals, for the dams will fill with sediment in about a hundred years. What then will be the fate of the billions of dollars' worth of floodplain development downstream of these structures? Only time will tell, but there will come a point (for many of us, it's long been here) when the work of the Corps of Engineers on the Missouri and other rivers will be regarded as drastically detrimental to our nation. Even today, some reservoirs, some of them quite large, are being "decommissioned" and removed to restore lost habitats. In 2010, in what could be the largest dam removal project ever completed in California, a Monterey water company agreed to tear down the 106-foot-tall San Clemente Dam. Built in 1921, the dam once stored drinking water, irrigated golf courses, and helped run factories. Today, however, it is 90 percent silted up, choked with sand and mud, and no longer provides electricity or flood protection—the ultimate fate of every such reservoir.

The waters to be impounded by the dozens of reservoirs proposed for the Missouri Basin would flood thousands of square miles of the most fertile farmland in the river bottoms, inundate uncountable numbers of prehistoric archaeological sites, and destroy innumerable historic ones. The Smithsonian Institution, the National Park Service, and numerous cooperating agencies such as the State Historical Society of North Dakota and universities in many of the Plains states worked together in this undertaking. Eventually, sixteen such institutions cooperated to salvage what they could in the face of these impending losses. The National Park Service provided the funds, and the Smithsonian Institution provided general oversight for salvage projects throughout the United States. Field offices were established in different regions to conduct and coordinate these efforts. In July 1946 Waldo R. Wedel set up a field office in Lincoln to conduct work in the Missouri River Basin. Wedel accepted John Champe's offer to put the office in the space occupied by the Department of Anthropology. As mentioned, when I arrived in the fall of 1949, the department and MRBS were commingled in the basement of Burnett Hall.

The National Park Service contracted with various cooperating state agencies to conduct work in reservoirs either in their own states or in states where the cooperating archaeologist wished to work. My own labors over the years included efforts for the State Historical Society of North Dakota, the University of Arkansas, and the University of Missouri. The first regional archaeologist with the National Park Service in the Omaha regional office was Jesse D. Jennings, who moved into that position from one on the Natchez Trace. He was followed by Gordon C. Baldwin, later an author of popular books on archaeology, and Baldwin was succeeded by Paul L. Beaubien. These individuals acted as liaisons between the National Park Service and the Smithsonian Institution as they carried out their mandate to survey, excavate, and interpret the archaeological resources that were to be lost in the various reservoirs planned for the Missouri River Basin. Jennings especially made it a point to learn the prehistory of his region, so much so that in 1948 he authored a brief mimeographed overview of the Plains titled "Plainsmen of the Past," followed in 1954 by another unpublished synopsis, "The Archeology of the Plains: An Assessment." Waldo Wedel was so upset by this newcomer's synthesis that he undertook to write and publish his own Plains-wide overview, *Prehistoric Man on the Great Plains* (Wedel 1961). Wedel's book stood as the standard for nearly forty years, until the publication of *Archaeology on the Great Plains* (Wood 1998).

Paul Beaubien was a gentle, helpful, and intelligent man who had once worked with Etienne B. Renaud. Born in France, Renaud taught anthropology at Denver University for many years and conducted numerous investigations and surveys in eastern Colorado and adjoining areas. Paul had been on one of Renaud's crews around 1930. Renaud was proud of the fact that he was able to feed his crew on one dollar a day—a diet that I was told consisted largely of beans. As the season progressed, Paul told me, the crew began experiencing health problems. Their skin became blotched and their teeth became loose and it was painful to eat. A visit to the doctor revealed they had scurvy, a consequence of the lack of vitamin C in their diet. With a change in eating habits they slowly recovered. One can do fieldwork too cheaply!

I didn't meet Jennings until much later, for he left the National Park Service the September before I arrived in Lincoln; he took a position with the newly established Department of Anthropology at the University of Utah, where he was destined to become an icon of Great Basin prehistory. However, his contributions to Plains anthropology should not be overlooked. In addition to his "Plainsmen of the Past" and "The Archeology of the Plains," Jesse organized the sixth Plains Conference and established the *Plains Archeological Conference Newsletter* in 1947. He edited it until 1950, when Franklin Fenenga took over, and Frank edited it until it closed down in 1953, later to be resuscitated as the *Plains Anthropologist*. Jesse was also largely responsible for the first use of power equipment to remove the overburden from Great Plains sites, beginning with Upper Republican sites in the Medicine Creek Reservoir that were deeply buried in loess, something that both Waldo Wedel the administrator and Marvin Kivett the archaeologist at first strenuously opposed (Jennings 1994:136–138).

I registered at the university in my required courses, including German, but I also was able to take introductory anthropology because, after a meeting with Champe, he decided that my readings (Andrews, Black, Hooton, and Weidenreich) were adequate prerequisites. I also volunteered to do laboratory work, and one of my first tasks was to catalog pottery and other artifacts that had been recovered from a recent dig at Leary (25RH1), an Oneota village site in Richardson County, Nebraska. John was balding and addicted to wearing a checked Pendleton wool shirt and a western string tie, his trousers supported by a Navajo sand-cast silver belt buckle in the form of a spider. I was later delighted to find an identical one at Thunderbird Jewelry, an Indian supply house in Gallup, New Mexico, which I wear in memory of his influence on my career.

It was at this time that I first met J. Mett Shippee. He was a field technician for the MRBS and a longtime member of the Missouri Archaeological Society. Discovering my Missouri roots, he signed me up as a member of the Missouri Archaeological Society in 1950; we were to be lifelong friends, and I became a permanent member of that society (and by 2010, its oldest living member) and finally editor in 1990 of its journal, the *Missouri Archaeologist*. Mett was, I believe, a carpenter but a talented avocational archaeologist as well, and a skilled fieldworker who published several useful papers during his career. He was the first to describe Nebo Hill points from a site just east of Kansas City, believing them to be Paleoindian in age because of their lanceolate shape. It was an understandable error, for their form mimicked that of true Paleoindian forms, and it would not be until the late 1950s that their Late Archaic age would be demonstrated, assisted in part by my 1958 excavations in Blackwell Cave, Missouri.

I entered the University of Nebraska intending to become a physical anthropologist specializing in fossil humans, the logical outcome of my fascination with *Pithecanthropus* and related primates and the readings I'd

Figure 7. John Champe's Laboratory of Anthropology, University of Nebraska, 1950. *Left to right*: Bob Cumming, Alan Woolworth, James Gunnerson, Mott Davis, Raymond Wood, and Dolores Gunnerson. *Author's collection.*

done in following up my brother's anthropology class notes. One summer in Missouri I'd even fashioned a life-sized Neanderthal skull that I modeled from illustrations in my readings, using clay carefully collected from exposures on the farm. Today I grimace when I contemplate what Champe must have thought when I proudly showed it to him, but my recollection is that he handled it with due concern for my feelings. John was not a great classroom teacher, though I learned much from him, especially in ethnohistory and scientific method, but he was an excellent role model, and I treasure the experience I had with him, although his perfectionism prevented him from sharing in print much of what he had learned. John's one-on-one instruction out of class was inspirational, and I'm deeply grateful for his tutelage. John had talked either the administration or the faculty in photojournalism into providing a darkroom for his use in the west end of Burnett Hall. It was available to his students, and I soon obtained practical darkroom experience in developing and printing. All of John's students and colleagues were fond of his gracious wife, Flavia, who was known

Figure 8. John L. Champe at an early Plains Conference, about 1955. *Courtesy University of Nebraska State Museum.*

throughout Lincoln as a talented dancer and teacher of dance, for she had once been a professional ballet dancer. After John's death she became an accomplished writer.

John had accumulated a vast collection of photostats of early maps of the American West and Southwest that he used in his investigation of tribal movements. They had been an integral part of his 1949 study of Apacheans that he used in his *American Antiquity* essay "White Cat Village." He'd also prepared the photostat copies of the maps that Waldo Wedel used in his classic 1936 book, *An Introduction to Pawnee Archeology*. My long-standing interest in maps certainly was reinforced by John's infatuation with these fascinating historical documents and how they can augment the narrative record. (Today this valuable collection is in the Nebraska State Historical Society.) John and Waldo Wedel had once been good colleagues, but somewhere along the way they had such a serious falling-out that when Champe died in 1978, Wedel abruptly refused to write his obituary, responding to the request by the *American Anthropologist* obituary editor by saying, "Never!"

So I was asked to take up the task, and I was pleased to honor the memory of my old professor and friend. Flavia opened their home and John's archives for me to do so (Wood 1979d).

Graduate and undergraduate students in the department formed a genial cadre that participated in informal weekend digs and helped with chores around Burnett Hall as members of what Champe called the "Beaver Patrol." Somewhere we actually obtained a small but scruffy (the word was carefully chosen!) stuffed beaver as a mascot. One weekend we accompanied Champe to Manhattan, Kansas, where we helped Lynn Hogden of Kansas State University salvage what he could of a Central Plains tradition house site. It was tough going, for the earth had been greatly compacted by heavy equipment near the site of the Tuttle Creek Dam. As a favor, Lynn obtained tickets for us to a local football game (my second and last such attendance). We could hardly turn down his generosity since some of his friends had given up their seats for us.

The Beaver Patrol also helped around the lab at odd hours. One weekend I was helping Champe move some desks from one room to another when a tall, thin gentleman in khakis, like those worn by the janitor, came down the steps, and I asked him if he'd grab the other end of a desk I was moving single-handedly. He cheerfully obliged, then spent some time talking to Champe and left. On his departure Champe turned to me and dryly said, "In the future, please don't ask Dean Oldfather to help with our housekeeping!" A building on the campus now honors his tenure at the university.

There was no academic competition among members of the Beaver Patrol, but rather, mutual helpfulness. When one of us decided to make a presentation at the Plains Conference, we'd circulate a draft of it among ourselves, take the advice of our peers, and revise it. Next we'd submit the new draft to any member of the MRBS office we could con into reading it, and then we'd prepare a second revision. Only then did we take it to our professors for a final review. By that time, our papers bore sufficient resemblance to a professional offering that we were never embarrassed in presenting them. It was wonderful training, teaching us to accept criticism and to write for the reader, and I've never hesitated to have someone else review what I've written—and I believe my writings have benefited accordingly. I've always written in straight, direct English in the belief that (unless one is dealing with theory or very technical subjects) there's nothing so esoteric about our profession that everyday English is not capable of expressing what we need to say, so we should avoid jargon. In addition, Carlyle S. Smith, of the University of Kansas, introduced me to a rule that should be pounded into the head of every writer: "Eschew obfuscation." He also reminded me that one should "stamp out and eliminate redundancy." Writing simply and in everyday language also puts your writing within the reach of specialists in other fields, whereas if you write in jargon they are likely to ignore it.

At the time I entered the university, it was mandatory for freshman and sophomore men to take classes in the Reserve Officer Training Corps (ROTC). Some aspects of these courses were helpful to me, such as the unit on reading maps; others were less so, such as the exercise in which we learned to dissemble and reassemble the Browning Automatic Rifle (BAR). Military uniforms were provided for attending classes and for such activities as parades, and given my nonexistent clothing budget, I wore the uniform almost daily. Hard as it might be to believe today, many students (including me) routinely mailed their laundry home to be done by their mothers. I had a small aluminum case that was bound with straps for the purpose, though I sent clothes home only for my freshman year. The most appropriate nonclassroom use of the ROTC uniform was at the annual Military Ball, which always attracted a major big band; that of Lionel Hampton, which performed at the one Miss Ramey and I attended, is the only name I now recall.

My first fieldwork was memorable. One weekend Champe drove me and other Beaver Patrol members to the Lime Creek site (23FT41) in Frontier County, Nebraska. The site was about two air miles west of the future Medicine Creek dam and today is inundated by the waters of Harry Strunk Lake. This Bureau of Reclamation dam was then under construction nine miles northwest of the town of Cambridge and was being built as a response to a disastrous flood that struck the town some years before. Mott Davis, then an anthropology instructor in the department, was investigating the deeply buried early Archaic period site for the University of Nebraska State Museum, and it was to form an integral part of his doctoral dissertation at Harvard. My weekend was spent troweling in an occupational level at the base of the high cutbank on Lime Creek adjoining the massive bulldozer cut that exposed the deposits. Digging in the thin occupational layer at the base of the forty-five feet of windblown loess that towered above me at the water's edge gave me a deep appreciation for the kinds of climatic events that had shaped human life in the Great Plains.

For how long and under what conditions had so much sediment accumulated over this ephemeral campsite, and in such a short time? The answer was to come some years later.

I recall finding nothing noteworthy that weekend, but the experience of delving deeply into the past was a moving one, though not necessarily one that changed the direction of my life (that experience was to come the following summer). My first lesson in archaeological ethics came when I picked up a chert flake from the backdirt to keep as a souvenir. Davis quickly told me that a professional does not retain such items as personal possessions. I quickly dropped it, and to this day I've never had an archaeological specimen in my home.

In addition to its other merits, the University of Nebraska was home to what we would today call an interdisciplinary mentality. John Champe's study of the stratigraphy in Ash Hollow Cave stressed the importance of geomorphology and other natural sciences in archaeology. Champe's final words in his conclusions to *Ash Hollow Cave* were a call for interdisciplinary research. Pointing out that the archaeologist will not go far without the help of colleagues in related sciences, he wrote, "The present study, for example, has leaned heavily on the work of geologists, botanists, and others, not alone for the solution of specific problems, but for basic concepts as well." He continued, "The Missouri Valley development has become the proving ground for a genuine cooperative effort between archaeology and the other sciences whose field data are endangered. This teamwork has been shown to be wholly practical, and in the area with which this study is primarily concerned, it has become a prime necessity: let it begin at once" (Champe 1946:97, 98). John's monograph, and others by paleontologist Bertrand Schultz and his colleagues in the state museum, emphasized the necessity of exploring the interrelations between natural forces and the sites of human occupation. The Lime Creek experience quickly drove these points home to me.

Indeed, the essay by Rolfe D. Mandel in *Geoarchaeology in the Great Plains* asserts that "for the most part geoarchaeology in the western hemisphere emerged and developed on the Great Plains" (Mandel 2000:3). This came about, as he notes, because "from the 1860s through the 1930s the controversy over the antiquity of humans in the New World dominated North American archaeology, and many sites in the Plains (e.g., Frederick, 12 Mile Creek, Clovis, Lindenmeier, 'Nebraska Loess Man,' Lansing, Scottsbluff) were at the center of this debate" (Mandel 2000:287). The discovery in 1929 of a Paleoindian projectile point by C. Bertrand Schultz at the Cumro fossil bison site in western Nebraska led Schultz to call in William Duncan Strong, then at the University of Nebraska, to help evaluate the site. David W. May remarks, "It was Schultz who initiated the first formal working relationship between a geologist and a professional archaeologist in Nebraska" (May 2000:169). The quest for other "Early Man" sites was of course well under way, paved by the discovery of Folsom points associated with an extinct species of bison at the Folsom site in New Mexico in 1926.

Geology and archaeology thus had an early start and continuing presence at the University of Nebraska, for in 1948 Schultz brought in E. Mott Davis to excavate the deeply buried Red Smoke and Lime Creek Paleoindian/Archaic sites in the Medicine Creek Reservoir to authenticate their early age. Preston (Pres) Holder and his wife, Joyce Wike, also dug nearby at the Allen site. Somewhere along the line, however, a rift developed between Schultz and his archaeological imports and their colleagues. Perhaps it was Holder's propensity to chop through bison skulls so he could maintain a clean vertical soil profile. Schultz must have fainted at the sight, particularly because of his significant contributions to the geologic history of bison in the Great Plains.

Lebsack's Bar at 1126 P Street in Lincoln was a popular and convenient place for lunches, at least as long as the MRBS office remained in Burnett Hall, but in 1953 the office moved to larger quarters in a downtown store building at 1517 O Street, in a space now occupied by the parking garage for the Robert Denney Federal Building. In 1963 the office moved again to a building on 1835 P Street (now demolished), and in 1969 the center moved to quarters on 27th Street (now the location of an overpass). A few years later the center made its final move to the fourth floor of the Federal Center. This was its last location before it was absorbed by the National Park Service and became the Midwest Archeological Center.

Archaeologists serving with the MRBS, and those working at cooperating institutions that submitted manuscripts to the National Park Service, were required to use the spelling of *archaeology* without the middle *a*, at least in their reports. This ruling by the Government Printing Office (GPO) had been in force since the founding of the Bureau of American Ethnology, because the *ae* in the original spelling was properly printed as a digraph (i.e., *æ*), and its elimination was a convenience to the printers. The alternate spelling, which was not begun or even devised by the GPO, finally became widespread, for federal involvement in reservoir construction and salvage was intense not only in the Great Plains but in Texas and the Columbia River Basin as well. Use of "government spelling" was to persist for many years among those indoctrinated with it, and pockets of it still endure, as in the Archeology Office at the Kansas State Historical Society. Today the *ae* spelling is considered the proper one by the Society for American Archaeology and is the preferred form in the sixteenth edition of the *Chicago Manual of Style.*

The Tiber Reservoir

The spring of 1950 arrived: my freshman year at the University of Nebraska was nearly over, and I needed a summer job. When I approached Paul Cooper to ask for employment, he acquiesced and assigned me to work with Walter D. Enger Jr. in the Tiber Reservoir, a Bureau of Reclamation impoundment planned for the Marias River in extreme northwestern Montana (today's Lake Elwell). Enger was a doctoral candidate at the University of Utah in Salt Lake City who previously had excavated some mounds near Warren, Utah, in 1946 that he'd reported in 1947 in *American Antiquity*. Our assignment was to carry out excavations in "Tiberia," as Smithsonian archaeologists called the Tiber Reservoir, alluding to its remoteness from Lincoln, for it was in the uppermost reaches of the Missouri River Basin. We drove out of Lincoln carrying with us some venerable equipment. When the MRBS was organized, it obtained surplus army Wyllis jeeps and a variety of other transportation. Some of its field equipment was left over from Frank Roberts's Smithsonian excavations between 1924 and 1940 at the Folsom Lindenmeier site in Colorado; reportedly, the shovels we used that summer had been employed there.

It was a long drive to Tiberia. The crew rode in the back of a Smithsonian pickup truck the entire distance, alternating in the coveted front seat. About all that I can recall of the journey is the fact that Don Lehmer accompanied us part of the way and we stopped at Richard Wheeler's camp at the Angostura Reservoir south of Hot Springs, South Dakota. There we inspected the Ray Long site, a Paleoindian encampment that Wheeler was excavating, and spent the night in his field camp before continuing the long drive across most of Montana. Frank H. H. Roberts once commented that the makers of the parallel obliquely flaked points found at the Long site must have been knappers who were "showing off," for the points were made of quartzite, a stone that is notoriously difficult to flake. As we neared our destination, we drove through mile after mile of strips of wheat and fallow land in endless linear patterns across the landscape, often extending to the horizon. Two brothers owned much of the land along our destination, the Marias River, and they owned alternating sections, so that the less than desirable land was divided more or less equally between them.

We set up camp on the south bank of the Marias River in a small park just east of an iron-frame bridge that spanned the river. We were south of the town of Galata, which then consisted of little more than a saloon at the crossroads of U.S. Highway 2 and the gravel road (Bootlegger Trail) that led some ten miles south to the river. The town of Shelby, our nearest source of supplies, was twenty miles west of Galata on Highway 2. Shelby's place in history is marked by an event that took place on July 4, 1923, when a highly publicized World Heavyweight Championship boxing match took place there between Jack Dempsey and Tom Gibbons. For a variety of reasons, its backers lost fortunes, a local bank closed, and for a time people used IOUs for money because cash was so scarce. A stadium for the fight had been built that would seat forty thousand spectators (believe it or not!), but too few of the seats were sold. The main street was still graveled when we were there, but eventually the town recovered economically.

We appropriated a picnic table in the park for our camp and set up our tents around it amid a towering grove of cottonwood trees not far from the riverbank. It was here that I was introduced to army cots, not realizing that I was destined to sleep on those back-killers for hundreds of future nights. We remained there from June through the middle of September. Our field crew consisted of about seven workers: Grover S. Krantz, a budding anthropologist like myself; two young biologists, James Mosiman and George B. Rabb; Noel Rasmussen, a fellow undergraduate and a geology major at the University of Nebraska whom I'd met and befriended in introductory geology; a student from India; and one or two others whose names I cannot now recall.

After the summer I saw only two members of the crew again. One was Grover Krantz, who left Montana on a bus at the end of the season with a bison skull in his backpack that he'd salvaged from a cutbank. I saw him only once after that, when I gave a talk at Washington State University in Pullman, where he taught physical anthropology and where he became a world authority on the footprints of Sasquatch, or Bigfoot. He is said to have toured Sasquatch country with a spotlight and rifle, hoping to shoot one of these elusive beasts so he could describe the creature's anatomy. When he died in 2002, he donated his skeleton to the Smithsonian Institution, where his remains and medical record are today curated with those of his three giant Irish wolfhounds (along with a book written about one of them). Grover's remains made a side trip on their way to the Smithsonian. He was skeletonized at the University of Tennessee's Anthropology Research Facility, better known as the Body Farm, where anthropologists observe the processes of postmortem decay. Established by Dr. William M. Bass III, it was the first such facility in the world. Other such installations are now under construction to provide forensic data on human decomposition to aid in criminal investigations.

I briefly associated with Noel Rasmussen at the University of Nebraska in the geology fraternity. I later saw Mosiman and Rabb only as a bibliographic entry, though Rabb went on to become an international authority on amphibians and their conservation. Their evenings in Montana had been spent pursuing, catching, and preparing the skins and carcasses of varying reptiles and mammals. Eventually, they published an article on the herpetology of the reservoir (Mosiman and Rabb 1963). On one occasion they leaped from their test pit when they spotted a rattlesnake swimming across the Marias, ran to the river, and scooped the hapless reptile into a burlap bag as it arrived on shore just below our dig. Our dinner table was often the scene of skinned and partially dissected native fauna. No one seemed to mind.

The camp was isolated, and no one had a radio; indeed, there was no need for one, for there was no electricity. One Saturday night in June, as the assembled crew was having a drink in the bar in Galata (where they were casual about age), the bartender looked up and said, as he wiped a glass, "Well, what do you think about the war?" There were stunned faces as he described the opening of the Korean War on June 25, when the Communist government of North Korea attacked South Korea. Despite much speculation among us, no one in camp was called into the service during the season, though I have no idea what happened after we parted company that fall. Because my older brother had been killed in action in 1943, I had no draft status: following the loss of the five Sullivan brothers when the USS *Juneau* was sunk during World War II, the U.S. military adopted regulations that exempted anyone from the draft or combat duty if he was a sole surviving son. This exemption was given popular exposure with the release of Steven Spielberg's 1998 motion picture *Saving Private Ryan*. I always anticipated entering the service, but I never got around to enlisting, though I never lost the feeling I should have done so when many of my friends disappeared into the military.

An MRBS survey team consisting of Wesley L. Bliss and Jack T. Hughes in 1946 and 1948 had discovered the sites we were to investigate. Intrigued by the hearths they found buried under several feet of sediment in presumably ancient terraces along the river, Bliss and Hughes believed they might be of great antiquity. It was for this reason that we focused most of our attention on the Galata site (24TL26), which was deeply buried in alluvial deposits on the south bank of the Marias River not far west of our field camp. We dug two units along the riverbank, disposing of our back-dirt directly into the river. We exposed two occupational units, one of them almost five feet below the surface and another and richer level at eight feet. It was there that I found the first pottery sherds of the summer—among the earliest, in fact, to be discovered in situ in Montana since the excavations in 1937 and 1938 at Pictograph Cave near Billings and at the Hagen site near Glendive. We were surprised and delighted, but at the same time disappointed to find pottery in a site we'd hoped to be very old.

Enger vanished shortly after our return to Lincoln, presumably to return to graduate school, and never wrote up the site. I wasn't able to locate him in later years, for obviously he dropped out of the field. A descriptive report on our work in Tiberia was published thirteen years later by Smithsonian archaeologist Carl F. Miller (1963), though his conclusions are of necessity superficial, for virtually no comparative data existed at the time. What is worse, the site has never been reinterpreted using the rich new data now available from sites across the state. We tested three other buried hearths and campsites and one stone circle but obtained no significant results.

I did a great deal of reading in the evenings at camp, as much as was possible with our Coleman lanterns. Another recreational option was taking long hikes, and we sometimes visited nearby sites that were above the pool level in the reservoir. Stone circles ("tipi rings") abounded in the uplands, and we inspected at least one bison drive. On a number of occasions Grover and I walked along the riverbank, occasionally leaping on a block of earth that was about to cave into the water, planning to hop off before it plunged into the river. Fortunately for both of us, we were unsuccessful in dislodging a block. We survived the summer, but not through any mental prowess on our part.

Another of our adolescent acts was to walk to the steel-span bridge over the river, climb to its top, walk across the topmost girder, clamber down, and hike a quarter-mile or so up the Marias, then in flood. There we plunged into the river and swam across, and the strong current rapidly carried us to a point near camp. Recall that this was in June, the month that Lewis and Clark halted at the mouth of the Marias in 1805 to determine whether or not it was the Missouri. The Marias, also then in flood, was of a magnitude that made such a decision difficult for the captains. (Eventually, they chose correctly and proceeded to Great Falls.) In a less foolhardy, albeit naive, effort, Rasmussen and I chopped down a giant cottonwood, intending to hollow it out and float back to Nebraska in this makeshift pirogue. Leaving camp in September, we'd have been frozen in somewhere not far from our point of departure; we were also blissfully ignorant of the fact that we'd have to paddle through the length of the 135-mile-long Fort Peck Reservoir in the eastern part of the state in a vessel that hardly bobs like a cork. We quickly abandoned the project when the magnitude of our efforts made it apparent this was a fool's dream. In any case, we had only an ax, and no tools to hollow out the log.

One weekend, to reward a crew that was beginning to suffer cabin fever, Enger bundled all of us into the back of the Smithsonian pickup and we headed west on Highway 2. We stopped in Browning on the Blackfeet Indian Reservation to visit the Museum of the Plains Indian and its director, archaeologist Claude E. Schaeffer. The museum's first director had been the renowned Plains ethnohistorian John C. Ewers. Better known as Jack, Ewers went on to become the premier ethnohistorian of the Plains Indians. Only Clark Wissler, his mentor, had an equal though quite different impact on Plains Indian studies, for Wissler was a generalizing ethnographer whereas Ewers was a topic-specific ethnohistorian. Jack's many insightful contributions were widely acclaimed, such that when a historian was asked for a definition of ethnohistory, he explained, "That's what John Ewers does" (Taylor 2003:10). Despite his astonishing productivity, he managed a remarkable correspondence. On several occasions when I wrote him asking a question, I'd receive a two-page typed letter that not only answered my query but also provided insights into a wide variety of related matters. He was as helpful and unfailingly courteous in person; little wonder he was universally admired personally and respected professionally.

After a brief visit with Schaeffer we drove on to Glacier National Park and set up camp in a National Park Service campground near Many Glacier Hotel. The next morning Noel Rasmussen and I hiked for six miles up Grinnell Valley, past Lake Josephine, climbing ever higher until we reached Grinnell Glacier, nestled at the base of the Garden Wall between Mount Grinnell and Allen Mountain, passing on the way some of the most beautiful mountain scenery in the American West. The Garden Wall is a wondrous panorama of colorful rocks, exposed in a massive glacial cirque. Having taken introductory geology the previous semester, we were intrigued by our firsthand experience with this former classroom subject and clambered around on the glacier and its margins, observing striations on the rocks and crevices in the ice. The glacier, about one square kilometer when we visited it, has melted back by more than 40 percent, and a proglacial lake with miniature icebergs now adorns its former outer edge. Grinnell Glacier and other local features were named after George Bird Grinnell, noted for his conservationist activities as well as for his many ethnographic writings on the Blackfeet, Cheyenne, and Pawnee Indians.

We were so near the continental divide (it was along the crest of the cirque wall) that we decided to climb the short distance to it from the icefield, a matter of only a few yards. The last few feet of the ascent over slippery and crusty snow was so steep that I slid back time and again, but finally we made it to bare rock and climbed to the divide. Exposed on a narrow sandstone ridge there, only a meter or so wide, were ripple marks, perfectly preserved beneath our feet. The experience truly brought our geology lectures to life, standing as we were on the ridgepole of the continent more than 7,000 feet above sea level. We sat for a time on the ripples, watching as the sun began to sink amid colorful clouds in the hazy mountains to the west of us.

At that point we began to think, belatedly, about getting back to camp, for we suddenly realized we'd never make it back while it was still light. As we contemplated the 1,600-foot descent down the steep narrow path we'd taken to the glacier, we spotted a structure across an alpine meadow about a mile to the northwest. We decided to hike to it and let matters come as they would. The building, it turned out, was Granite Park Chalet. Built in 1914 by the Great Northern Railroad, today the chalet is a National Historic Landmark hotel administered by the National Park Service. This small stone structure perches on a promontory on a bare granite outcrop that features stunning panoramic vistas of the surrounding wilderness, including views of Mount Kipp and Ipasha Peak. On arriving, we called the National Park Service campground and left a message for Enger assuring him we'd not been eaten by a grizzly bear (attacks, sometimes fatal, on ignorant tourists are common enough in that country) and that we'd return in the morning. Luckily, we were able to afford a room for the night (today the rate is $70), and we spent a pleasant evening around a giant campfire with a girls' group that had booked most of the chalet that weekend. It was a welcome interlude after staring at some seven other males for most of the summer.

The next morning we hiked back to camp on the path down Swiftcurrent Pass (just north of the one we'd taken to the glacier) and arrived in camp without mishap save for the chewing-out we got from Enger for our thoughtlessness. That afternoon we drove into Canada and visited Waterton Lakes National Park, where Enger and I rented a motorboat at Lake Marie and harassed the rest of the crew, who'd been rash enough to rent only a rowboat. The student from India had insisted on having his passport stamped as he'd entered Canada (to augment his "collection"), but for reasons I no longer remember he was almost denied reentry into the United States. By the time we finally persuaded the border guard to let him pass, he was nearly hysterical.

Back in the United States, we drove up the Going to the Sun Highway that evening to a nightclub that featured an entertainer named "Rocky Mountain Kate." Enger recognized her as "Southwestern Kate," whom he'd seen the previous winter in Albuquerque. Most of us consumed more than we needed that evening, and at closing time I was deemed the one most fit to drive back down the mountain. Somewhere on the return trip we stopped for a call of nature, and when we stepped out of the pickup we saw an unworldly aurora borealis swirling above us. Tall colored curtains of light were moving along the horizon, seemingly meeting above our heads, placing us under a moving bowl of multicolored light. I've never seen a display even remotely similar or dramatic since, though it's possible that the number of beers in us added to its spectacular appearance. We continued on our drive and returned safely to camp on the Marias. It had been a glorious weekend.

The crew was paid one dollar an hour, the standard rate at the time, and by early September I'd earned almost six hundred dollars over the course of the year. Because my father had requested that I not exceed that figure, else he'd lose me as a dependent on his income tax, I asked Enger to be taken off the payroll. However, I remained on as a volunteer for several more weeks, for two quite logical reasons: it was cheaper than taking a bus or other transportation back to Lincoln, and I was enjoying myself there at little cost. These perfectly selfish reasons nevertheless impressed Paul Cooper at the MRBS, convincing him of my newly found dedication to archaeology, and helped ensure that I'd be hired the following summer. Despite paying for food during the summer, I was able to save enough of my wages to pay my tuition in Lincoln that fall, though of course I had to find jobs to tide me through the school year. Given today's astronomical cost of a college education, it's hard to believe that I left college without becoming burdened by debt or borrowing from my parents, though they occasionally sent me a few dollars. I suspect my brother had preconditioned them for such donations.

The summer had been exhilarating. I had learned the fundamentals of excavation, patience in exposing buried material, effective use of the trowel, and related skills in "reading the soil." I'd also learned to recognize the kind of detritus that archaeologists are used to finding, augmenting my limited experience with the Leary site materials and those at Lime Creek. It had been my basic training session, though it was hardly a "boot camp," for I enjoyed the summer immensely. My growing enthusiasm for archaeology meant that Enger had more in common with me than others in camp, so we spent many hours talking about archaeology and its promise as a profession—discussions that were decisive in my transition to a life in archaeology. The season indeed marked the beginning of my career, and on my return to Lincoln all thought of fossil humans were gone, for I was to become an archaeologist. On the drive back to Lincoln we made a brief stop in Cody so I could say hello to my parents, and I told them as much, and Enger gave them a probably overenthusiastic appraisal of my abilities. I'd found a profession that meshed ever so neatly with my interest in ancient history and in the past in general.

My father retired in March 1953, and my parents moved to Citrus Heights, California, to be near my sisters, both of whom were then living in San Francisco. Because Mother was thirteen years younger than Dad, she was still of employable age, so she worked in the security office at McClellan Air Force Base until 1963. When I went to register for my university classes in the fall of 1954, I automatically put their California address on my registration forms. But when I reached the table where I was to pay my tuition, I was stunned to discover that the new address rendered me an out-of-state student despite Dad's long Nebraska residence, and the cost for me was not only astronomical but impossible. I mumbled something about having left my money at home, returned to a desk and filled out the forms again, this time using my Cody address. I came back the following day and paid my tuition to another clerk at a different counter. I felt like a criminal, but it meant the difference between attending school and dropping out.

I'd been magna cum laude in high school (what a coup, for there were only four of us!) and had been awarded a prestigious Regents Scholarship to the University of Nebraska for my freshman year. But my newfound freedom of lifestyle inevitably led to diminished grades, including flunking my first language course (German did not come easily) and sleeping through the final examination in introductory sociology, having studied for it all night. Consequently, at the end of my sophomore year I was dismissed from the university. I spent the following year taking night classes to elevate my grades to the point that I was allowed to re-enroll. I never admitted that humiliating episode to my parents, but I'd learned my lesson, and I did famously in my junior and senior years once I'd cleared the hurdle of German. I did especially well in English composition classes taught by the legendary professors Orin Stepanic and Wilbur Gaffney. Stepanic took great interest in his students (at least in those who attracted his attention), for when he found that I was thinking about graduate school, he wrote away for some literature from other universities. I never dreamed he'd do such a thing, but one evening he asked me to stay after class and after presenting the information to me he urged me to continue my college career. Gaffney was a lifelong member of and a well-published author in the English department. The establishment of the Wilbur Gaffney Expository Writing Award was a well-deserved honor. Both men were inspiring teachers.

I attribute much of my success in those classes to the many novels I was reading, for I read as voraciously then as I had in high school, and in Lincoln I had real bookstores in which to browse and a wonderful selection from which to choose. Furthermore, most paperback Pocketbooks were only twenty-five cents at the time, affordable even for someone who'd often read a book a day. W. Somerset Maugham was a favorite. I especially remember *The Razor's Edge*, Ernest Hemingway's *The Old Man and the Sea*, and the racy fantasies of Thorne Smith, especially *The Passionate Witch* and *The Bishop's Jaegers*. Smith provided popular escapist literature for readers during the dreary days of the Great Depression; I later found a kindred admirer of them in Jesse Jennings. I rediscovered them to my delight about the time I retired. The trivial plots of these novels were redeemed by the vivid imagery of Smith's language and his lack of reverence for convention.

I've enjoyed reading all my life and have returned time and again to several dog-eared favorites: *Beowulf* (Burton Raffel's 1963 translation, for the beauty of its language, though Seamus Heaney's new translation is easier to understand); Edmond Rostrand's *Cyrano de Bergerac* (oh, yes, in translation); T. H. White's *The Once and Future King* (what delightful imagery!), and James Hilton's *Lost Horizon*, also a depression-era fantasy published as the world edged toward World War II.

Employment in Lincoln

My college days were supported by a variety of menial jobs. As a sophomore I took turns as a busboy and a soda jerk at the YMCA when it was on the corner of 13th and Q Streets in Lincoln (later the site of a movie complex). My favorite concoction was a butterscotch/pineapple malted milk rich enough to draw the fillings out of your teeth. I had a small apartment on the fourth floor of the YMCA that I shared with a redheaded roommate whose name I've forgotten, who played the French horn in the Lincoln Symphony; the following year I shared a room with an Iranian graduate student. My stint as the storekeeper for the eating establishments in the university's Student Union lasted rather longer than many other jobs. It also provided meals (I probably never ate better for a longer time during my college years). I was also a short-term member of a small housecleaning company that washed windows at private homes and mopped down the floors of businesses after hours. My only professional job came as a graduate student in 1955 and 1956 when I was hired part-time to draft maps for the MRBS office, producing original maps and tracing others that had been made in the field by archaeologists to illustrate their final reports. My high school avoidance of shop and the drafting experience I obtained then had paid off.

Over the years I lived at many addresses around Lincoln; those that were near the downtown area are today either parking lots or the sites of office buildings. When I returned in the fall of 1952 from work at the Buffalo Pasture site and lived at the YMCA, I drove a 1936 Ford convertible I'd purchased that summer for fifty dollars from one of the crew. It needed no ignition key, and to start it one simply pushed a button on the dashboard. Unfortunately, my friends discovered this fact; on occasion when they saw my parked car they'd move it around the corner or down the street, and

I'd spend no little time looking for it. Fortunately, it died a natural death shortly after my return to Lincoln, and these hunts ended. I didn't buy another car (a DeSoto) until I was a senior.

One short-term job that netted little or no pay, but very good food, was as a busboy for the Gamma Phi Beta sorority near the Student Union. One of my friends, Robert Spale, and I somehow managed to get this plush job. Essentially, it involved carrying meals from the kitchen to the girls in the dining room and cleaning the tables and dishes afterward. Since we were independents and therefore scum in the eyes of the sorority, we were not allowed to fraternize with our "clients." One of the girls, though, was forever putting her hair up in curlers. In this condition she was deemed unfit to eat with the rest of her gaggle, so she came to the kitchen and ate with us. All was well until we became better acquainted, and she would sit on our laps and we'd spoon-feed her. It was all in good fun until the evening the housemother unexpectedly entered the kitchen and found me spooning mashed potatoes into her mouth. The housemother was not amused: Bob and I were called to her office after dinner and summarily dismissed. Her dismissal was so subtle, however, that it didn't dawn on us until we were leaving the house that we were not to return. It was the only time in my life I was ever fired.

The job I had the longest was with the Lincoln Health Department. Its laboratory was housed in a small brick building west of the university, on or near 10th Street (it was razed years ago). I was a laboratory flunky and gofer who carried out whatever task needed to be done, including sterilizing the needles used to take blood samples for marriage licenses and the equipment used in testing for bacteria in the milk products from local dairy companies. Every week I drove to the several dairies in Lincoln and picked up one sample each of whole milk, skimmed milk, whipping cream, and the like, as well as raw samples from each of their suppliers from the arriving milk cans. The director would take perhaps half a cubic centimeter from each container in a pipette and smear it on a petri dish and, after incubation, inspect it for colonies of bacteria. As my salary was modest, I consumed the remaining milk as part of my regular diet for well over two years, mixing the cream products with the skimmed milk for a more nutritious and better-tasting drink. Curiously enough, I still enjoy fresh milk. I suspect my bones are in good condition.

My meager financial resources meant that food was always near or at the top of my list of needs, and on occasion I truly went hungry. The father of one of my friends, Peter Miller, ran a restaurant at 27th and Cornhusker Highway, and on occasion he'd take me there to have a T-bone steak. If I was truly desperate, I could always call Pete and dine in style, but it was an option I was careful never to abuse. There was a Safeway Store only one block off campus where I did most of my shopping. In rare but desperate times I'd drop in to buy a box of soda crackers and then palm a tin of sardines on the way out. It was a not very nutritious dinner for which my conscience still haunts me.

I took time off from my job with the Health Department in the summer of 1953 to accompany John Champe to Carlyle Smith's University of Kansas dig in the Fort Randall Reservoir (today's Lake Francis Case) near the mouth of the White River. I no longer remember why I didn't work as a shovel hand on an MRBS crew that summer, but the several-day outing with Champe and Smith was a welcome relief from the routine of my laboratory duties. Champe was a superb tour guide on the trip: en route we stopped at and discussed Ton-won-tonga, the historic Omaha Indian village near Homer, Nebraska, where Champe told me the town marshal was one of Al Capone's brothers (Richard "Two Gun" Hart)! We also visited Nánza, the Ponca Fort near Verdel, for I was working on the artifacts from it at the time. Carl had set up his field camp in a dilapidated but usable abandoned farm home while he dug the Spain site (39LM301), a river-bottom earthlodge site that he interpreted, surely correctly, as a winter village. He adorned his field camp with a sign over the gate to its frontyard: "It costs no more to go first class." Carl spent his entire career at the University of Kansas, where he founded the anthropology department. He was proud of his doctoral diploma from Columbia University, for it was signed by Dwight D. Eisenhower during his tenure as its president. I greatly enjoyed spending time with Carl and his lovely Hungarian-born wife, Judy. Carl always saw the humorous side of life. He often went hunting with his departmental colleague Felix Moos, said to be a nephew of Baron von Richthofen, of World War I aerial fame, and had told him, "For a German, you don't shoot very well." I visited Carl in the hospital in Kansas City the night before his second heart bypass surgery, when he told me, "Tomorrow I'm having a pig valve installed. This summer I'm going to France and look for truffles." His humor and courage lasted to the end, for he did not survive the operation.

A popular late-night hangout in downtown Lincoln was the Tepee, a restaurant in the Cornhusker Hotel (later it was imploded and a new one built). After movies and dates it was a favorite place to buy a ten-cent cup of coffee that came with endless refills. For a time, there was an art shop across the street that also sold jewelry. When I was a graduate student, my roommate Ray Price and I made a little money on occasion by selling the owner pieces of silver jewelry we made in our apartment.

With one brief exception I remained an independent on campus, for I joined only one fraternity (I've forgotten its name), as an upperclassman. Its house (later razed) was directly across the street from the girls' dormitory on 17th Street. For reasons I no longer remember, my membership was short-lived, and my only other social fraternal association was the brief period when I dated a sorority president at Nebraska Wesleyan University. In 1956 I joined Sigma Gamma Epsilon, the honorary professional fraternity of the earth sciences that met in Morrill Hall; it gave me my only claim to be a card-carrying geologist. I enjoyed my geology classes in the building and often wandered through its halls, for it contained the University of Nebraska State Museum and was amply endowed with all manner of mounted Tertiary mammal skeletons. One of my favorites was the Eocene-age Titanothere, a horned vegetarian about the size of a rhinoceros, whose fossils were perhaps the inspiration for the "thunder horse" of Lakota Indian legend. However, the display on the evolution of American bison, beginning with the giant Pleistocene *Bison latifrons* and ending with the diminutive modern form, was equally intriguing, as were the Miocene-age diminutive ancestral beavers (*Palaeocastor fossor)* that dug spiral burrows into the ground. A few dinosaurs were featured on the second floor. The main hall across from the entrance was the drawing card for most people: the Hall of Elephants, which gave the building its informal name, Elephant Hall. This huge room contains the mounted skeleton of the largest known Imperial mammoth, plus the remains of mastodons, gompotheriums (Miocene-age four-tusked mastodons), and still-living proboscidians. The Mueller Planetarium was added to the back of the building in 1958.

The Oldham Site and Franklin Fenenga

By the end of my summer in the Tiber Reservoir my interest in physical anthropology had been abandoned—a loss supported by the fact there was no physical anthropologist in the department to encourage me. So when the summer of 1951 arrived, I was ready for a second field season, and again I signed on as a shovel hand with the MRBS. I was chosen to accompany Robert B. Cumming Jr. to the Oldham site (39CH7), a prehistoric to protohistoric earthlodge village of uncertain affiliation in the lower reaches of what was to become the Fort Randall Reservoir (now Lake Francis Case). We established our field headquarters in an abandoned farmhouse not far from the banks of the Missouri River near the mouth of Platte Creek, some twenty miles southwest of the town of Platte, South Dakota. One of the crew members was George O'Neill, who lived near us in a tent with his wife, Nena, and their young child. In 1972 they gained notoriety as the authors of the best-selling book *Open Marriage*. Royalties from at least seven printings surely brought more income than his summer salary! It was also translated into German (but, curiously, not into French).

Cumming brought with him Walter W. Taylor's recently published *Study of Archaeology* (1948), a memoir of the American Anthropological Association. Taylor was a student of Clyde Kluckhohn at Harvard, who himself was a critic of Mesoamericanists and other prehistorians, especially southwestern archaeologist Alfred V. Kidder, who worked, Taylor wrote, essentially without theory. Taylor's book was the subject of many heated discussions within the profession, for it lacerated leading archaeologists of the day as being little more than dilettantes, including Kidder, Frank H. H. Roberts Jr., and James B. Griffin. Taylor's criticism of their culture-historical approach as essentially chronicle that ignored culture process was well taken, though as a prospective sophomore I was scarcely in a position to evaluate the volume. I later noted that Taylor never published any study that incorporated the very principles he advocated in that monograph for the proper interpretation of archaeological materials. He was properly accused of saying, "Do as I say, not as I do." Cumming also brought with him a copy of one of Gilbert L. Wilson's insightful monographs, *The Hidatsa Earthlodge*, which introduced me to the congruence between what we were digging and ethnographic observations. It was another prescient peek into my future.

The abandoned farmhouse at Oldham provided a comfortable setting not far from the site. I claimed a small room on the second floor, where I set up my folding cot and gear. The time I spent with Cumming increased my experience in reading the soil as we excavated earthlodge floors, cache pits, and associated features. Postholes, rodent burrows, and other such phenomena became familiar as my field experience grew. But my time with him was short, for within a month I was transferred to the crew of Richard Page Wheeler, another MRBS archaeologist, who was digging in the Keyhole Reservoir along the Belle Fourche River in northeastern Wyoming. Because he couldn't obtain enough local help, several of us were siphoned away from Cumming's crew and transported to Dick's camp by Lawrence (Larry) L. Tomsyck.

My first real contact with Larry was his arrival at our field camp. He was the fiscal officer for the MRBS office in Lincoln and, later, for the Midwest Archeological Center before becoming a long-time treasurer for the Plains Anthropological Society. In retirement, he and his wife, Janice, were the publishers of J&L Reprint Company ("Janice & Larry"), devoted to reprinting out-of-print classics in Plains archaeology and, on occasion, new material (the printer was one of Larry's golf partners and his good friend). He and Janice deserved a medal of commendation for their selfless service to the community of Plains scholars, and they were indeed joint recipients of the Distinguished Service Award at the Plains Conference in 1997.

Larry drove us to Wheeler's camp in one of the Smithsonian's Chevrolet carryalls, unpretentious precursors of today's SUVs, for certainly they were neither stylish nor luxurious. It was a long drive across South Dakota, the monotony broken by our stop at what was then a modestly sized Wall Drug Store. It was enlarged to unrecognizable proportions when I saw it again a quarter century later (though the mechanical cowboy band remained). There must have been five thousand people in town the next time I saw it, and I remarked to my wife, Carolee, that surely there must be someone in town whom we knew. Sure enough, a few minutes later, as we waited to get a hamburger, I saw a fellow professor from Columbia, Osmund Overby, standing in line at the same counter.

The terrain near the Keyhole Dam is typified by near-desert conditions characteristic of the Western Plains, whereas its upper reaches begin to blend into the adjoining and forested Black Hills. I spent the next month with Wheeler in his tent camp a few miles northeast of the town of Moorcroft, a fictional version of which later figured as the town being evacuated in Steven Spielberg's motion picture *Close Encounters of the Third Kind.* Our camp was not far from that of William T. Mulloy, of the University of Wyoming. Mulloy had just begun work on the McKean site, the type site for the Hypsithermal-age projectile points and culture complex that today bear that name. Much about camp life is informal, but Wheeler (an easterner and Harvard graduate) insisted that we dress "formally" by requiring shirts at dinner! In contrast, I recall Mulloy's camp as consisting of scattered shelter halves for the crew and a firepit with two immense logs serving as chairs on either side and surrounded by a ring of discarded bean cans. Perhaps a member of his former crew can correct this startlingly austere impression.

Wheeler, assisted by J. Mett Shippee, was digging rockshelters, an experience that was entirely new to me. Digging in the reflected heat from the sun bearing down on light-colored sandstone was hot work, but at least the humidity was less than it had been on the Missouri. This work in the shallow deposits in the Belle Shelter (Wheeler 1996) gave me no preparation for the rock overhangs in Missouri, especially Rodgers Shelter, where I was to dig in later years. My experience here was short-lived in any case. A few weeks after I arrived, another MRBS archaeologist unexpectedly showed up in camp, Franklin Fenenga. Descended from Dutch Fresians, Frank was a solidly built blond with a ruddy complexion and an outgoing personality. He'd gained a reputation working in California and came to Lincoln in about 1950, and he was to spend the next several years with the MRBS.

Frank's assignment that summer was to conduct surveys in various proposed reservoir areas. He remained in camp for about a week, participating in field activities and camp life. One evening as I was resting in my tent, I heard a scream and rushed out to see Fenenga hanging by his arms from a tree branch with his feet doubled up beneath him: he was terrified by rattlesnakes, and he'd heard a rustle that he mistook for one. After we threshed around without finding any reptile, he dropped back to the ground rather sheepishly. Then one evening he abruptly asked me if I'd like to accompany him as his survey partner for the rest of the summer. His time spent in camp had been to appraise the crew for a compatible partner, and he'd chosen me because he felt we'd get along. We certainly did, for we became good friends and remained close until he left the MRBS and returned to California.

We spent the next month or so like gypsies. We lived in a carryall, sleeping outside on cots when the weather was good and cramped inside when it rained, and cooked most of our meals on a Coleman gas stove. We spent the beginning of August surveying the Alzada Reservoir, a small impoundment planned for the upper reaches of the Little Missouri River in Crook County, in the far northeastern corner of Wyoming (it was never built). We discovered only twelve prehistoric campsites. One of them, 48CK221, contained a few sherds of pottery, a rarity in Wyoming. We took the opportunity to visit the nearby Devil's Tower before we moved to eastern North Dakota, stopping at Donald D. Hartle's dig at Rock Village (32ME15) in the future Garrison Reservoir, and On-a-Slant Mandan village in Fort Abraham Lincoln State Park near Mandan, North Dakota, as we crossed the state. We next settled in to conduct a survey in the Jamestown Reservoir on the James River north of Jamestown. The weather, however, was so

Figure 9. Excavating at a hearth exposed by wind erosion at site 48CK231, Alzada Reservoir, Wyoming, August 1951. *Author's collection.*

consistently rainy that many roads flooded and survey became impossible, so we abandoned the project and drove to central Kansas, where we spent some time in the Glen Elder Reservoir. In September we also did limited survey in the area to be flooded behind the Gavins Point Dam, on the Missouri River between Nebraska and South Dakota a few miles west of the town of Yankton.

It was a stimulating period. Fenenga was an excellent teacher and mentor with a vast range of knowledge, and we had unending opportunities to discuss anthropology and archaeology, not to mention practical aspects of site survey, excavation, and interpretation, often during meal preparations over our Coleman stove in the Great Plains outback. We spent the evenings reading and went to sleep early, rising at the crack of dawn. In an obituary Francis Riddell said that students were always welcome at Frank's office and his home, where his wife, Barbara, served coffee and beer. I couldn't agree more. I spent many evenings visiting with him in his home in Lincoln, though we eschewed the latter drinks for good bourbon. He was ever helpful and considerate of my inexperience. Frank also enjoyed a night out with the boys. On one occasion, when Barbara was not in town, Frank somehow became involved in a fracas at a local nightclub and was soundly berated by Champe the following day for having lost his (Champe's) borrowed university library card. It had been discovered after the disturbance by the police and traced to its innocent, and indignant, owner.

3

The Plains Conference and More

Archaeology is the imaginative recapture of the past within the hard boundaries of the evidence.

— Gordon R. Willey, *An Introduction to American Archaeology*, Vol. 1: *North and Middle America*, 1966

Plains Conferences

In the early days of the MRBS there were so few archaeologists working in the Plains that everyone knew everyone else. Indeed, most professional archaeologists in North America knew almost everyone in the field. Every session of the Plains Conference was a plenary one, most of them meeting in the large open room in John Champe's Laboratory of Anthropology. The meetings drew some 50 to 60 individuals, including students. The conference grew slowly: the 20th Plains Conference, in 1962, for example, drew a grand total of 131 participants; in 2009 the attendance was 268 (down about 40 percent from the previous two years). The conference had begun quite informally in Vermillion, South Dakota, in 1931 and was held erratically before World War II; meetings were discontinued during the war. They resumed with the fifth conference in Lincoln in 1947 and have been held without interruption ever since.

The 7th Plains Conference for Archeology was held in 1949 in the Laboratory of Anthropology over the Thanksgiving holiday, as it would be for some years to come. Because it convened during my first semester on campus, I knew nothing of its future significance for me, so I went home to spend the holiday with my parents. However, in the fall of 1950, after my summer with an archaeological field crew in Montana, I decided to attend it. Late November was not, however, necessarily a good time to aggregate in Lincoln, and on at least one occasion Burnett Hall was emptied of participants like rats abandoning a ship as the news of an approaching blizzard sent people fleeing for home to avoid being snowed in. It was at one of these early meetings that Alfred E. Johnson and I became friends, he being at the time an undergraduate at the University of Kansas and a protégé of Carlyle Smith, whom I'd first met at Carl's Talking Crow site in South Dakota. Al sometimes stayed with me when he attended the conference, throwing his sleeping bag on the floor of my Lincoln apartment. After obtaining a doctorate at the University of Arizona, he returned to the University of Kansas and spent much of his early career there investigating Middle Woodland sites along the Missouri River in both Kansas and Missouri. He devoted his later career at Kansas to developing the Museum of Anthropology and its wonderful collections.

The 1950 conference was the first time I'd missed being with my family on Thanksgiving for the traditional cranberries and turkey. Attendance nevertheless was strong despite its timing and family objections, and devoted archaeologists faithfully attended, professional and avocational alike. The conference was marked by intense discussions of a new dating technique that was beginning to make its results known. Radiocarbon dating had been introduced in 1948, and it was confirming some former estimates of the antiquity of certain remains while proving more than disconcerting to the pronouncements of others. For the first time, the dating of sites did not depend on estimates of the rates of geological change and personal evaluations of the rate of culture change. Little did we guess how many geophysical dating techniques lay on the horizon and would soon lend ever-greater precision to our timing of prehistoric events.

Only later did family pressure force a change in the date of the conference, and it was thereafter held at the convenience of the hosting institution, normally in a university city and on a weekend when no football game was scheduled so rooms would be available and less expensive. Because of Lincoln's central location on the Plains, the meetings continued to be hosted by various groups there until 1959, when it was decided to alternate between Lincoln and other cities. This was done, though not consistently, until 1968, after which time meetings were held randomly across the Plains, wherever the volunteer hosts dictated. For example, in 1979 Al Johnson, F. A. Calabrese, and I hosted the thirty-seventh conference in Kansas City, a locality intermediate between our homes.

Early Plains Conferences were intimate groups of a few dozen individuals. Even the most novice student archaeologist rubbed elbows with such luminaries as J. O. Brew of Harvard, the organizer (with Frederick Johnson) and a perennial member of the Committee for the Recovery of Archaeological Remains (CRAR), and John M. Corbett, chief of the Division of Archeology of the National Park Service. Having dinner with such men was easy: simply remain underfoot. The ensuing conversations one overheard were highly educational from many points of view. Well, the ploy didn't always work. At the 1956 Plains Conference I'd managed to maneuver myself into sitting at a banquet dinner table with a culture hero—William Duncan Strong, my major professor's major professor, and my academic grandfather, so to speak. I slunk away when he turned to me and said, "Beat it, kid. I'm having dinner with my friends." Even though he'd been drinking, it was a violation of the democratic spirit that prevailed at these conferences.

Years later (1982) I attended a meeting of the Western History Association in Phoenix with Gary R. Moulton and James P. Ronda, and the three of us presented a mini-symposium called "New Directions in Lewis and Clark Scholarship." When it ended, the audience broke up for lunch; simultaneously, an eager young student came up to me and began pelting me with questions that I couldn't answer quickly. As I watched Gary and Jim vanish down the hall, I was almost overcome by the urge to say, "Beat it, kid. I'm having lunch with my friends." But I couldn't bring myself to do anything of the sort, remembering Strong's devastating comment, so I invited him to join me for lunch, where he continued his questions. I enjoyed the experience, perhaps to spite Strong.

The folks I met at these meetings were to become my oldest friends and acquaintances, at least those with whom I have remained in contact over the years. I first met Dale R. Henning and R. Bruce McMillan at the meeting in about 1956. They became major figures in my later career and remain among my closest friends. I also met David A. Breternitz about that time or a little earlier. Dave was a dedicated southwestern archaeologist, but his rare excursions onto the Plains, and his more frequent sponsorship of studies east of the Colorado Front Range, brought him and his lovely wife, Barbara, to Plains Conferences for many years. He and Wilfred Logan and I were especially close and spent much time together, sometimes all night and usually to our physical detriment. Dave reminds me of the University of Missouri and University of Colorado's "exchange program," whereby Missouri students Bruce McMillan and Marvin Kay went to Boulder for their doctoral degrees and Steve Sigstad came to Missouri.

The conferences were far less formal than those we attend today, where many speakers sit down with no questions from the audience. Back then, papers were often given extemporaneously. Questions, sometimes rude, were likely to interrupt the presentation, and lively arguments and rebuttals were commonplace. It was Harold Huscher who once told a speaker, "I want to take exception to practically everything you just said." John Champe ran the early meetings in Lincoln and was merciless in keeping speakers to their allotted time. He would set a darkroom clock and warned the speaker when time was about up. If you ran overtime, the timer emitted a shrill alarm until the speaker gave up and sat down. It was hardly subtle, but this very effective device worked.

Students, both beginning and advanced, regularly attended the meetings. One evening at a post-session party in Franklin Fenenga's home, a young and not very knowledgeable student approached Marie Wormington, who always wrote using her initials, H. M. (Hannah Marie), and earnestly told her, "Mrs. Wormington, I've read all of your husband's books." Marie graciously accepted the compliment (on behalf of Pete, her geologist husband in the oil business) but did not disabuse the student of his notion. Marie was a charming and gracious woman, strikingly beautiful, who had captured the hearts of many male archaeologists (and surely many others!) in her younger days. Like many others, I often stopped to visit her when I passed through Denver. She was a charming hostess whose eggs Benedict were outstanding. I attended several parties and other social functions at her home.

Marie did not always share my sense of humor. At one of the Plains Conferences I was having a conversation with her, unaware of her love of cats. Somehow the subject of zooarchaeology came up, and I told her a story I'd heard about Paul W. Parmalee, one of the founding fathers of that discipline. He had done his doctoral dissertation on the food habits of feral cats, and to obtain data he'd cruise back roads after dark and shoot the strays he found. He was always sorry, he said, when he found one full of milk. My amusement as I told the story did not sit well with her, nor with another cat lover sitting nearby. Parmalee obtained his Ph.D. in wildlife management from Texas A&M. From his first position at the Illinois State Museum he moved on to the University of Tennessee, where his research on freshwater mussels and his wide-ranging interests helped establish the new field of zooarchaeology, together with paleontologists Theodore E. White and John Guilday and zoologist Stanley Olsen. His long and productive career in the Midwest helped develop behaviorally and ecologically focused approaches to archaeological faunal collections.

By 1952 there were substantial numbers of MRBS and cooperating archaeologists working every summer in the reservoirs in North and South Dakota, and they found that there was a growing need to visit with one another and discuss mutual problems of every conceivable nature. The major summary of archaeology in the state of North Dakota was the primitive but insightful work by George F. Will and Thad. C. Hecker (1944), awkwardly titled "The Upper Missouri River Valley Aboriginal Culture in North Dakota." William Duncan Strong's (1935) pioneering *Introduction to Nebraska Archeology* and Waldo Wedel's (1940) "Culture Sequence in the Central Great Plains" were the most comprehensive works available for the Central Plains, though numerous papers, including a series edited by Earl H. Bell (1936) in *Chapters in Nebraska Archaeology*, provided site-specific data. Little of significance existed for South Dakota beyond Strong's 1940 essay "From History to Prehistory in the Northern Great Plains" and the reports being produced annually by the South Dakota Archaeological Commission, especially those written by Wesley R. Hurt Jr., of the University of South Dakota. Scattered archaeological and ethnohistorical papers by Waldo Wedel and Mildred Mott Wedel and a few others did not provide a coherent frame of reference for the masses of data that were rapidly accumulating from the accelerating excavation program in the Missouri Basin.

By this time the idea that the Plains had been essentially uninhabited before the arrival of horses had been thoroughly demolished by William Duncan Strong (1933, 1935, 1940). Knowledge of Paleoindians, however, was as yet little more than rudimentary, though a good beginning had been made on some of the later Woodland cultures and, of course, on the late prehistoric Upper Republican and Nebraska cultures and the protohistoric and historic Pawnees. A preliminary cultural chronology for the Central Plains was available based on the stratigraphic sequence that John Champe described from the deposits in Ash Hollow Cave (Champe 1946), and Ernst Antevs's 1948 three-episode postglacial climatic model was gaining a wider audience following its presentation in *American Antiquity* (Antevs 1955). Antevs showed that after the Pleistocene the cool but warming Anathermal was succeeded by a mid-Holocene temperature maximum, the Altithermal, followed by a cooling or Medithermal period (now the Boreal, Hypsithermal, and Neoglacial geologic-climate units, respectively). This climatic sequence, originally based on the chronology of varves in Swedish lake sediments, predated the development of radiocarbon dating by the team led by Willard Libby at the University of Chicago, and it would be solidly confirmed and refined by later scholars. The apparent lack of mid-Holocene archaeological sites in the Plains (the so-called Altithermal hiatus) still dominated thinking, as it would until Brian O. K. Reeves (1973) published his explanation for the hiatus: sampling bias and poor preservation. As we were to learn, the Plains were never abandoned, though life there during the Hypsithermal, or the mid-post-glacial warming period, would have placed great constraints on its residents.

Plains archaeology was still in its infancy, and the need for discussion was acute. In 1953 Gordon C. Baldwin (then the regional archaeologist for the National Park Service in Omaha), John L. Champe, Carlyle S. Smith, Wesley R. Hurt, and Robert L. Stephenson made a field trip to visit sites being dug in reservoirs along the Missouri River in South Dakota. On their return to Lincoln a spontaneous "Accidental (or 10½) Plains Conference" took place that developed a taxonomy for cultures in the Central and Northern Plains, a scheme that was a focus for discussion at the 11th Plains Conference that November. The results of these deliberations were published in the first issue of the *Plains Anthropologist* the following May (Stephenson 1954). In later years the "½ Plains Conference" was held in the field, usually at the airport in Pierre, South Dakota, where the MRBS had storage facilities and which provided a central location for archaeologists working in the reservoirs along the mainstem of the Missouri River in the Dakotas. These meetings facilitated useful field discussions of mutual concern, though they resulted in no further publications.

The annual meeting of the Society for American Archaeology was held only once in Lincoln, but in May 1956 the membership was small enough that it could be accommodated in settings that would astonish the approximately 4,000 members who attended it in 2010. There were 130 registered participants and no concurrent sessions: only twenty-three formal papers were on the printed program—three of which were canceled! Two of the sessions were held in a classroom on the first floor of Burnett Hall in a space that I find amazingly small today. Attendees were able to obtain single rooms at the Cornhusker Hotel for $5.50 to $9.00 and doubles for $8.00 to $12.00. Even so, people stayed with friends in town when they could, especially students. A number of Plains Conferences were later held at the Cornhusker, but some of them were so spirited in the evenings that on more than one occasion the hotel declined to host the event. The conference sometimes shared the hotel with celebrities. At one of them I was exiting an elevator with a young lady when someone excitedly said, "Do you know who that was? Grace Slick!" My response: "So, who is she?" Obviously, I was not familiar with Jefferson Airplane, as the group was then known. That evening some of the band came around to one of our parties, in the course of which one of them asked, "Just what's the status of Neanderthals these days?"

Early Plains Conferences were in effect small symposia, with lively discussions on matters of mutual concern, including the MRBS program. There was, however, no research design or grand strategy underlying the MRBS fieldwork. General goals were set by consensus of the individuals involved in the investigation of different time periods and regions of the Plains. This consensus was reached with the assistance of archaeologists brought into the MRBS from many separate universities in different parts of the United States, men who were hired by the MRBS to act as archaeologists for greater or lesser periods of time. Donald J. Lehmer, for instance, brought with him his experience and knowledge of southwestern taxonomy, and he thereby revolutionized that of the Central and Northern Plains. Different perspectives were offered by such administrative personnel as Frank H. H. Roberts and by members of CRAR, which included J.O. Brew and Henry Hamilton, an influential avocational archaeologist and farmer in mid-Missouri and the president of the Missouri Archaeological Society for decades. (His farm produced a special corn that was used for corncob pipes, one of which, he claimed, was smoked by General Douglas MacArthur.) The participation of CRAR meant that the overall goals of the program were at least consistent with national perspectives in the field.

It has been a popular pastime among some present-day archaeologists to criticize the salvage archaeology program and its results, but any reasonable assessment of that program finds that it was a successful application of what was known in our field at the time. Working with limited resources, the MRBS archaeologists did a remarkable job of bringing Plains archaeology from infancy to adolescence, providing a sound (if limited) database that we continue to augment today. The demise and replacement of most of the approaches and techniques of that day was inevitable, necessary, and desirable, for much of the work done then is of course inadequate for many purposes today, just as contemporary work is scheduled for certain obsolescence in the future. Nevertheless, denigrating the MRBS for being a product of its time illustrates the ignorance and arrogance of some recent archaeological practitioners.

In 1976 Margot Liberty and I organized a two-day symposium for the 34th Plains Conference in Minneapolis, "Anthropology on the Great Plains: The State of the Art," which was published five years later in revised and reduced form by the University of Nebraska Press: the subtitle was dropped as being too pretentious (Wood and Liberty 1980). A complete set of audiocassettes of the symposium was deposited in the archives of the Plains Anthropological Society, in the Archives and Special Collections, I. D. Weeks Library, University of South Dakota, Vermillion. The volume was an attempt to provide topical material that would complement the coverage being planned for the Plains volume of the Smithsonian Institution's work-in-progress, the *Handbook of North American Indians* (DeMallie 2001). Little did we know that the latter volume would not appear in print for another twenty-one years! Nor did the planners of the Smithsonian volumes realize the Herculean labor necessary to produce such an encyclopedic inventory. Indeed, the project was so gargantuan and time-consuming that only fifteen of the twenty volumes projected had been published as of 2010.

I was chair of the 45th Plains Conference when it was held in Columbia, Missouri, in 1987. I'd thought of asking several people to be banquet speakers, among them Louis L'Amour, the famous western novelist (he was born in Jamestown, North Dakota), but for some reason this never materialized, and I talked Jesse Jennings into agreeing to relate his experiences with the early MRBS on the Plains; unfortunately, a health problem led him to cancel his participation. I then happily recruited E. Adamson Hoebel, a distinguished Plains scholar who'd written widely, including books on nonliterate legal systems and on the Cheyenne Indians. I was deeply impressed when his wife turned to me at the head table at the banquet and said, "You know, all of his books are still in print." It was something I had to share with the audience in my introduction to his talk, imploring them to emulate his example. A show of hands also revealed that an amazing number of audience members had used his general textbook when they took introductory anthropology.

The 50th Plains Conference was held in Lincoln, Nebraska, in November 1992, at which time many of my former students put on a symposium on my behalf, "From Prehistory to Ethnohistory." Fortunately, it wasn't a meeting of the American Anthropological Association, or else it might have been what is called a "dead person session." In any case, the event was better appreciated as an entry on my vita than as one in my obituary, and I expressed my profound gratitude to the perpetrators. I suspect that there might be another paradigm extant in the Plains than the one expressed by this session. In 1983, at the 41st Plains Conference in Rapid City, South Dakota, one of my friends told me he'd had a hard time going to sleep in his hotel because of a loud party in the adjoining room. Just as he was dozing off, he heard someone say in a loud voice, "God *damn* that Ray Wood!" So keep in mind T. C. Chamberlain and his theory of multiple working hypotheses; there's always an alternative paradigm. Somewhere on the Plains there must be someone to whom *Wood* is a four-letter word.

Presentations at the symposium also illustrated a truth expressed almost two decades before, that after a season in the field "the crew has as much on each other as they will ever need" (Sellers 1973:144). Driving into a small town in eastern Montana one fall, I saw a delivery truck with the name and address of a laundry on its side, and on its back was painted a truism: "Drive Carefully: Blood Spots Are Very Difficult to Remove." None of the spots left that day by the presenters were hard to remove. I thanked Richard Krause, whose anecdote about us preempted the one I was going to tell on him. Cal Calabrese is the only individual I know who managed to get the airplane's shadow directly in the center of the house pit he was photographing from the air. Stephen A. Chomko is the only student who has tried to murder me, but he wasn't decisive enough to settle on drowning me or using a deadfall. David B. Madsen is the only person who was able to lift my 250-pound, solid rock-maple chopping block from the floor of my kitchen single-handedly. Greg Fox was gracious enough not to explain the details surrounding the "theft" of my Fiat X1-9 after our carefree night on the town in Lincoln. Teresita (Terry) Majewski was equally gracious in not alluding to the X-rated movie, "A Dirty Cowboy Movie," she was induced to go see under the impression it was a comedy. Finally, for our mutual protection, Bruce McMillan and I had an unspoken agreement to forgo personal anecdotes.

Theodore E. White and Zooarchaeology

Theodore (Ted) E. White was a vertebrate paleontologist from Harvard University who joined the MRBS in April 1947 to survey prospective reservoirs for their fossil potential. He did so in a number of cases, and though

I'm not sure just what work he actually carried out, it seems the surveys were not especially demanding of his time. In any case, Ted's efforts in the world of fossils weren't major topics of conversation among archaeologists, and we heard little of his traditional professional accomplishments, which themselves were considerable. In about 1949 he began the identification of the animal bones recovered from two archaeological sites in the Angostura Reservoir in South Dakota, and then he started analyzing those being dug from earthlodge village sites along the Missouri River. His first paper on the interpretation of animal bones, initially presented at the 8th Plains Conference in 1950, soon appeared in *American Antiquity*. Certainly it attracted more of our attention than his papers on bats and the new species of alligator he described from Miocene deposits in Florida.

Ted rapidly became the preeminent pioneer in the then-embryonic discipline of zooarchaeology. His work on the percentage of usable meat in varying animals and his studies of the bones from a series of archaeological sites, published in a set of papers in *American Antiquity*, have inspired continuing research and ensured his lasting reputation. He certainly was an inspiration for Paul W. Parmalee, of the Illinois State Museum (and later the University of Tennessee), who became a beacon for zooarchaeological studies in the Midwest. In 1953 Ted transferred to the National Park Service and eventually became the superintendent of Dinosaur National Monument in northwestern Colorado. He was in charge of exposing specimens in the dinosaur quarry wall under a protective structure. When I visited him there in 1964, he seemed to have little enthusiasm for administering the monument, for most of the work had been done; certainly it didn't challenge his intellect. I believe that was his last position before his death.

Ted was unmarried when he was in Lincoln, and because he lived a rather solitary life, on occasion I'd have dinner with him. When I ordered a well-done steak in a local steakhouse one evening, he peremptorily ordered me to eat at another table "if you're going to treat good steak that way." Offended, I asked why, as that's the way my mother always cooked them. He responded that the only way to have steak was rare, so I reluctantly changed my order and discovered that my mother had indeed been in error! I spent what time I could with him in the basement of the MRBS office at 1517 O Street learning the fundamentals of bone identification, and I found his patient instruction to be highly educational. I've always been grateful to him for his friendship and guidance, though I've used those skills productively only once, in my publication of the bison bone from Vista Shelter in Missouri, which I discuss later.

Buffalo Pasture

My survey experience with Fenenga in 1951 led him to select me as one of his crew members for the following summer in South Dakota. I was delighted to have the opportunity to dig along the Missouri again. I began my duties by driving a Smithsonian jeep to Fort Pierre overnight to what would become our field headquarters, the abandoned buildings of Scotty Philip's ranch. James "Scotty" Philip was born in Scotland but eventually became a cattleman, holding lands near the present town of Philip as well as property a few miles west of the town of Fort Pierre. His ranch buildings there lay directly in the path of the future spillway of the Oahe Dam. Philip is famed as the eccentric who tried his best to put bison to practical use, sometimes hitching them to wagons (before, I suspect, the wagon was torn to pieces), and he pastured his herd along the Missouri River just north of the future site of the dam. He is properly revered as one of the individuals responsible for saving bison from extinction, even providing them to Custer State Park in the Black Hills. In 1907 Philip made a substantial wager with some Mexican owners of fighting bulls that his bison would mop up the ring in a confrontation with any of their bulls. The results of that encounter in Juárez, Mexico (Dickson 1996), should be required reading for all Plains scholars (sorry, no punch line here: you'll have to read it for yourself—it's available in the *Plains Anthropologist*).

The principal site we were to dig was a protohistoric Arikara village called Buffalo Pasture (39ST6), and it lay on the river's edge on a high terrace in the field where Scotty once pastured his bison. The original site today is deeply submerged in the lake west of the dam's spillway. We were continuing the work in the vicinity begun by Donald Lehmer, who used his 1950 and 1951 excavations at the Dodd site (39ST30, soon obliterated by dam construction) and the nearby Phillips Ranch site (39ST14, misspelled after Scotty Philip) for his dissertation at Harvard, which led to his grand synthesis of the village cultures of the Great Plains (Lehmer 1954). In that overview Don perceived two major cultural traditions, the Central Plains tradition in the Central Plains, and the Middle Missouri tradition in the middle reaches of the Missouri River in the Dakotas. In late prehistoric times, he believed, these two traditions fused to become what he called the Coalescent tradition, one that embraced the historic horticultural village cultures of the Central and Northern Plains: the Plains Village tradition. No such grand concept could escape deficiencies, and Don attempted to repair them over the years, notably in his *Introduction to Middle Missouri Archeology* (1971), which served as a regional vade mecum for well over a decade. Details have changed, but its overall structure survives.

Here I interrupt this narrative to insert commentary on Don's concept of the Coalescent tradition, based on an article I published in the *Review of Archaeology* (Wood 1993b). It's not generally acknowledged that the Coalescent tradition was first presaged by Robert H. Lowie, of the American Museum of Natural History, based on "several summers' work among the Crow and the Village Indians of the upper Missouri." This fieldwork resulted in a brief but insightful paper, "Some Problems in the Ethnology of the Crow and Village Indians" (Lowie 1912), a contribution that, surprisingly, is rarely consulted (or at least cited) by Plains specialists.

The first two pages of the article merit close attention by archaeologists, for Lowie comments on the influence and importance of the Caddoan Arikaras in the history of the Northern Plains through their impact on the cultures of the Omahas, Mandans, Hidatsas, and Crows. He not only called attention to the adoption by the Omahas of the Arikara-style earthlodge, and their probable adoption of the Arikara Medicine Pipe ceremony, but also noted the adoption of that ceremony by the Hidatsas and Crows. "In addition we have Maximilian's statement that the Hot dance of the Ruhptare Mandan and of the Hidatsa had been purchased of the Arikara." Likewise, he found it reasonable to suppose (as archaeologists now know) that the Mandans and Hidatsas adopted their historic circular-style earthlodge from ancestral Arikaras. Lastly, Lowie hinted at the influence of the Arikaras on Mandan and Hidatsa military organizations and on their secret medicine-bundle ("shrine") fraternities (Lowie 1912:60–61).

Although Lowie's article contains many useful observations, the most interesting aspect for archaeologists is its bearing on the concept of the Coalescent tradition. Lehmer (1952) first formalized this tradition, in the broader context of the Plains Village pattern, in his doctoral dissertation at Harvard. The dissertation was published in slightly revised form two years later, forty-two years after the appearance of Lowie's paper (Lehmer 1954). Lehmer's grand scheme included at least four of the historic Plains village farming tribes: the Caddoan-speaking Pawnees and Arikaras and the Siouan-speaking Mandans and Hidatsas. The Omahas and Poncas probably also belong in this tradition, as well as the Algonquian-speaking Cheyennes. "The late village sites are characterized by some traits which appear to be new in the Plains," he wrote, "and by a majority derived from either the Middle Missouri or the Central Plains Tradition" (Lehmer 1954:150).

Lehmer never offered an explanation for the factors that led to the Coalescent tradition, stating only that it resulted from culture contact and interchange between the Central Plains and the Middle Missouri traditions. He believed the impetus for the Coalescent tradition was an influx of proto-Arikara Central Plains tradition populations into the Northern Plains from the south. This hypothesis is no longer tenable as stated, although it is known that the Arikaras moved north along the Missouri valley trench in late prehistoric times after separating from their Pawnee relatives. Lehmer's work nevertheless demonstrated that many of the conspicuous differences in domestic architecture and material culture between the Central Plains and Middle Missouri village farmers were muted by their adoption of elements from one another.

Lehmer's remarkable archaeological synthesis stood nearly intact for more than twenty years, but the cumulative effect of continued research in the Northern Plains began to reveal significant flaws, especially with respect to the Coalescent. That tradition has been undergoing major revision, and parts of his original formulation have been discarded, especially the genesis of the Coalescent. Nevertheless, Lehmer detected in the archaeological record what Lowie had seen ethnographically, and he was correct not only that the historic Plains village Indians were remarkably uniform in architecture and material culture but that the proto-Arikaras were in large part responsible for that homogeneity.

But why did these late prehistoric village cultures engage in this exchange of tools and ideas? What economic, technological, or other reasons led them to do so? And what was the role of the Arikaras in the genesis of the Coalescent? Architecture and ceramics are the most conspicuous elements in the archaeological record and in the Coalescent tradition. Building homes and making pottery traditionally were women's roles in the Plains, and coincidentally, the results of these activities have been major foci of Plains archaeological research. How did they spread? We can eliminate village exogamy as a force for trait exchange if the social rules in the historic period are applicable to the past (a plausible if arguable assumption). Plains villages were strongly but not necessarily exclusively endogamous. Perhaps 10 percent of the males in a Pawnee community might have married outside the village at any given time. None of the women in a village, however, was likely to so marry. For men, the village was dominantly endogamous; for women, it was totally so (Gene Weltfish, personal communication, February 1976). Out-marriage therefore cannot be invoked as a cause for the spread of traits, though the presence of Arikara women (as either wives or war captives) at Ponca Fort, a historic Ponca village in northeastern Nebraska (Jantz 1974), is documented by skeletal data.

There was, however, much ceremonial exchange between villages, a topic that I discussed at length with Gene Weltfish at a meeting of the New York Academy of Sciences that I attended in 1976. A major feature of such exchanges was the Hako, the Pawnee version of the Calumet ceremony (Fletcher 1904). In this ritual many of the residents of a Pawnee village would go to another Pawnee village or, say, to an Omaha one, bringing numerous possessions to be used as gifts. The Calumet was sponsored by prominent men in a village who had established trading contacts with men of equivalent status in other villages. By "adopting" the men of the other villages, they established a fictive kinship bond with them. In the ceremony a visiting group of Pawnees called the Fathers visited a Son in the village of another band or tribe, carrying with them large numbers of gifts for the Son. The visiting group consisted of many people of both sexes, who might remain with their hosts for several weeks.

The participants thereby established a kinship structure so that communication between the two bands or tribes could take place on a peaceful level, because "people with whom one dealt as equals had to be placed in some kin category." At the conclusion of the Calumet ceremony the gifts taken by the Fathers established peace and security by means of a tie as strong as that of kinship (Weltfish 1965:260). Each village might send a calumet party to another group annually and be treated to several return visits, so a fictive kinship network united many Plains tribes, especially those involved in the Plains-wide trade system.

Alice C. Fletcher was aware of the broader, diffusionist importance of the Hako and wrote, "Apart from the social and religious significance of the ceremony, it became a means of exchange of commodities between tribes. The latter took the garments, regalia, and other presents brought by the Fathers...to some other tribe, when they in turn became the Fathers. Thus manufactures peculiar to one tribe were often spread over a wide territory, and the handicraft of one region became known to different sections of the country" (Fletcher 1904:281). That is, the Calumet contributed to cultural uniformity between distinctive groups and provided a means of leveling cultural differences over wide areas, and for this reason I believe it was a major factor in Clark Wissler's recognition of the Great Plains as a distinctive culture area, one that he refined and popularized in his *The American Indian* (Wissler 1917).

The Hako, as described by Fletcher and by Weltfish, was a five-day ritual. The traditions of neighboring tribes support the claim of the Pawnees that they originated this ceremony. Two different groups were essential to the rite: they could not belong to the same clan of a tribe, and they were often of different tribes (Fletcher 1904:18). The Hako was a mechanism for interband and intertribal trade, the calumet pipe being a "safe-conduct pass" through alien territory (Weltfish 1965:31). The long procession of the calumet party traveling overland to the other village was an impressive sight, and since it was easily recognized, it was avoided by war parties (Fletcher 1904:301–302).

It often took the Fathers more than a year to gather gifts for the ceremony, including embroidered shirts, leggings, moccasins, robes, and ornaments. The Father presented these gifts to the Son, who in turn distributed them to younger men and others (the "Children") of the host village. The Father also gave the Son the food bowls, sitting mats, and other implements used in the ceremony (Fletcher 1904:50, 259). The Children, in turn, gave their visitors gifts of horses and horse gear and dried bison meat. Other gifts carried by the Fathers included dried vegetables, bowls, cooking utensils (presumably pottery vessels), blankets, "jewelry," and ornamental objects. Furthermore, when the Fathers returned to their village after the ceremony, they left behind not only their gifts but all their other belongings as well (Weltfish 1965:176). In short, the Fathers carried with them a large proportion of their material culture and returned home without it, but they returned with the many gifts provided by their hosts. The ceremony was a perfect means for exchanging everything in a group's cultural inventory.

It is possible that the proto-Arikara offshoot of the Pawnees intensified the use of the Calumet as this group moved up the Missouri River into the Northern Plains, if it in fact did not introduce the ceremony there. In this way the Arikaras could have introduced the cultural changes that Lowie and Lehmer observed, which acted as models or paragons for change by direct diffusion. I once said to Lehmer, "You know, you could have cited Lowie and saved yourself the trouble of so much writing." He was not amused.

Surely the Calumet ceremony explains some of the "trade sherds" and vessels that occur in so many Plains village sites. The vessels themselves were not necessarily exchanged, but their contents changed hands in the ceremony. Pottery sherds of ostensibly Arikara origin (Stanley Ware rims) are found in the historically documented Big Village of the Omaha Indians and at Ponca Fort in northeastern Nebraska. In addition, sherds originating in the Lower Loup Phase of central Nebraska are found in historic Osage Indian sites in west-central Missouri. In an even earlier context the late prehistoric Huff site contains a four-post subcircular lodge of a kind known in the fourteenth century farther down the Missouri River. There also are Steed-Kisker and Oneota trade sherds in Nebraska phase sites in eastern Nebraska. The list could be greatly expanded. In short, not just vessels were exchanged—entire inventories changed hands.

The origin of the Calumet ceremony has been the subject of several studies. Donald Blakeslee (1975), for example, suggests it originated on the eastern margin of the Plains, perhaps about AD 1250, among Nebraska phase populations living along the Missouri River. Calumet-style pipes appear for the first time in their sites. He too feels that the Calumet ceremony was in large part responsible for cultural exchange that led to the Coalescent, an argument consistent with the requisite factors of time and space. However, the acceptance of new elements and the displacement of existing elements in a culture involve more than simple exposure to them; merely carrying home new implements does not mean the recipients will adopt the new styles in place of their own. What in Caddoan culture led to the acceptance of novel elements by others? Why would the Caddoans have been models for change? Why should the Mandans, for example, have adopted so many alien elements when their own were so well adapted to their existing social and physical environment? Yet the Mandans and Hidatsas adopted Caddoan elements on a massive scale and very quickly, perhaps in a generation or so. It is not difficult to explain the advantages of circular earthlodges over the long-rectangular dwellings the Mandans and Hidatsas used before about 1500; circular lodges are far more heat-efficient structures. Other changes, however, especially in ceramics, were not functional, merely stylistic.

Ceremonial exchange exemplified by the Hako is a plausible hypothesis for the development of the Coalescent tradition. However, the social background for the acceptance of the goods being transferred, and their replacement of indigenous goods, needs further explanation. Why, for example, did the Caddoan Wichitas, close relatives of the Pawnees, not participate in this exchange more than the archaeological record suggests? Closer collaboration between archaeologists and cultural anthropologists may yet shed more light on this question. Here I end this digression, though I'm reminded of A. L. Kroeber's (I believe) definition of culture, which I memorized sometime during my undergraduate years: "Culture is an epiphenomenon elusively protean in the changeability of its manifestations."

No MRBS field crew, to my knowledge, ever routinely stayed in a motel except while traveling. The usual accommodation was a tent camp or an abandoned house near the site being investigated. In 1952 Fenenga's crew lived in the grain bins at Scotty Philip's abandoned ranch, less than a mile from the midline of the Oahe damsite. We had to drive through an area where construction equipment was parked; near one building was a water tank with the sign "Bone diggers keep out," a holdover from Lehmer's stint in the area. We set up a processing lab in one of the outbuildings, and our kitchen and dining area was in Scotty's barn. Our cook, as I recall, was one Mrs. Colombe, after whom Don Lehmer named one of his pottery types. A flag featuring the Smithsonian torch and the lettering "For the Increase and Diffusion of Knowledge Among Men," which I hand-painted on a discarded bedsheet, provided a formal touch. Every night we could hear the roar of earthmovers as they worked around the clock to complete the dam under floodlights that made it unnecessary to illuminate the ranch grounds. It was an otherworldly setting.

The Hopscotch Bar in Fort Pierre was the favorite watering hole for our crew and for those who came to visit. It remains a local favorite. We also patronized the more spacious Silver Spur Bar, its competitor for visiting archaeologists on a Saturday night; it too serves patrons to this day. The latter bar was renowned at the time as a hangout for Casey Tibbs, a nationally famous champion rodeo rider. Once featured on the cover of *Life* magazine, he was described therein as a fast-living, hard-drinking, gambling brawler. For a time, I patronized his restaurant in Pierre when I passed through town at dinnertime. Tourists driving through downtown Fort Pierre today on U.S. Highway 83 will see a roadside life-sized bronze statue of Tibbs astride a bucking bronco.

When Carlyle Smith visited us from his downriver dig and other visitors were in town, they and their crews assembled in one or the other of these bars, as we did when Smithsonian Institution/National Park Service inspection teams arrived to review our work. On one such occasion, when Wesley R. Hurt from the University of South Dakota joined us, he noticed a number of obviously underage boys and girls drinking in the bar. Wes was wearing his customary khakis, and on a whim he went to the entrance and began asking other underage would-be entrants for identification. The ploy worked, since the local police wore virtually identical clothes, and soon a

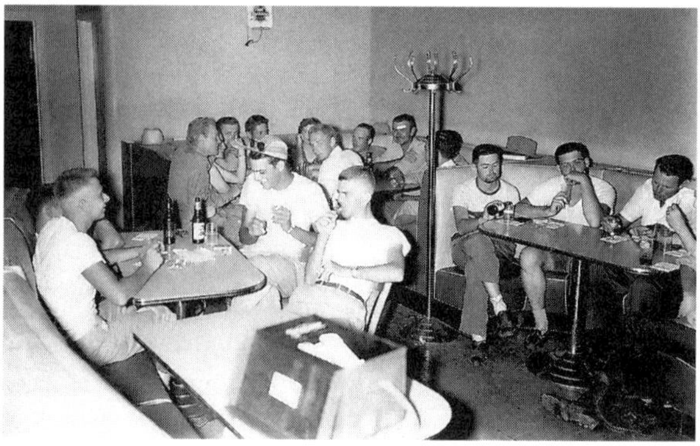

Figure 10. Gathering of archaeologists at the Silver Spur Bar in Fort Pierre, South Dakota, summer 1952. *Left to right, front left table*: unknown person, Thomas Newman, Raymond Wood, and Thomas Cummings. *In background, left to right*: Franklin and Barbara Fenenga, Karl Heider, Alfred Johnson, Judy Smith, Richard Keslin, Roger Grange, Carlyle Smith, unknown, Donald Lehmer (*hidden*), Benjamin K. Schwartz, and two unknowns. *Author's collection.*

knot of teenagers accumulated outside the door wondering about this new admissions policy. Eventually, he tired of the game or became thirsty and rejoined our table. A visit to Fort Pierre in 1993 revealed that the sights (and the pungent aroma) of the Hopscotch have changed little over the past forty years except for the addition of topless dancers.

Fenenga and I drove down to visit Carlyle Smith, who was digging the Talking Crow site, a few miles downstream from the Big Bend damsite, near Fort Thompson, South Dakota. Our visit happened to coincide with his completion of a small model earthlodge about a yard in diameter. Carl burned it that afternoon and filmed its destruction. However, the dynamics of fire and airflow in the model were unlike that in a full-scale lodge, and he could not get it to burn. To complete the filming, we had to douse its interior with gasoline, deposited by the cupful as crew members and I raced by and dashed the fluid into the entry, then sped away from the resulting fireball. Carl parlayed this reconstruction and destruction into an article that Robert F. Heizer later published in a collection of essays, *The Archaeologist at Work* (Smith 1959).

One afternoon, as we slaved away at Buffalo Pasture, it was blistering hot, and the sun radiating from the light-colored loess lodge floors added to our discomfort. I walked down to the river several times to soak a handkerchief in the water and wrap it around my head; it was dry by the time I was back on the site. Fenenga was in camp that day filling out monthly MRBS forms, but suddenly he drove up and slid to a stop in a cloud of dust, called us all to the carryall, and told us we were quitting work for the day. He'd just heard on the radio that the temperature was 120 degrees, so we sped into Fort Pierre and entered the blissful coolness of the Silver Spur. We spent the rest of the day there, and that night we experienced the most awesome thunder and lightning I've ever witnessed in my life. The bar literally shook to its foundations.

Pierre is the capital of South Dakota and was named after Fort Pierre Chouteau, itself named after one of the giants of the Upper Missouri River fur trade. But do not pronounce Pierre as the French would do: it is pronounced "Peer." One afternoon, as I was paying for fuel at a gas station in downtown Pierre, a tourist entered carrying a road map and innocently asked the manager, "How do I get to Fort Pierre?" (Wrong pronunciation!) The manager looked him straight in the eye and said, without a smile, "Never heard of it." The man returned to his car and sat staring at his map, and when he looked back at the station we could see his mouth moving. I could guess what he was saying.

We spent most of the season at Buffalo Pasture, excavating five earthlodges, several of which we stripped of overburden using a borrowed Fresno slip scraper that we pulled with our jeep. It was effective and saved us a lot of labor, but it created many bruises before we mastered its use. We also did limited testing in a few nearby sites, including excavating two earthlodges at the fortified Indian Creek site, also a protohistoric Arikara village (39ST15). Though the site lay about two miles below the dam, the overflow spillway would destroy it. Both houses had an earthen altar opposite the entry; the smaller one surely was a family lodge, and the larger one was likely a ceremonial lodge. We worked hard that summer. Fenenga was demanding but easy to deal with, and the work was enjoyable, for Buffalo Pasture had been built on a loess-capped terrace, which made it simple to distinguish between native sediment and cultural disturbance. Postholes and the openings to cache pits and other features were readily visible.

One of the houses at Buffalo Pasture (No. 5), presumably a ceremonial lodge, had been destroyed by fire, and its floor was clearly defined by the hard-baked sediment created by the heat. I discovered what was believed to be the charred remains of a bow on one wall of the structure. Another of the houses had a three-tiered cache pit, the only such feature that I'm aware of on the Plains, though two-tiered ones have been found at the Talking Crow site and at an Upper Republican site (25HN11) in Harlan County, Nebraska. The second level in the Upper Republican example contained fragments of feathers and may have had some ceremonial function (Gunnerson 2006:620). When I finished removing the earth from the lowermost floor, I stood nearly twelve feet below the adjoining ground surface. There was little in the pit except the usual detritus, leaving us to wonder the about the function of this curious feature. My 1950 experience at the Oldham earthlodge site had been short-lived, but here I was exposed to all the features (and more!) normally found in a Great Plains earthlodge. And it was here that I learned how to heave a shovelful of dirt over a considerable distance onto a given spot outside the excavation, a skill we crew members honed as we competed with one another: it made the work more like a game. Placing the earth where we wanted it meant we didn't have to clean back the rims of our excavation to keep it from spilling onto the floor.

This was the first time I'd had the opportunity to visit earthlodge sites since working at Oldham, and many pristine examples of them were not far away. We often spent weekends visiting the Sully Village site, Arzberger, Thomas Riggs, and others, including the remains of the military Fort Sully II. This could only be done on Saturdays when it had not rained the day before, for the local and abundant Pierre shale weathers into a most durable gumbo, whose adhesive qualities will turn a pair of boots into twenty-pound lumps.

Sometime during the summer I purchased a 1936 Ford convertible from one of the crew for fifty dollars. It gave me mobility for the first time in my life. One weekend several of us drove to Bismarck and visited the museum of the State Historical Society of North Dakota and Russell Reid, its superintendent (and a future employer), and some of the village sites in its vicinity, including the Double Ditch and Huff sites. Both sites greatly intrigued me, but I could hardly anticipate that eight years later I'd return to excavate Huff and that exactly half a century later I'd participate in testing Double Ditch.

One of the sites I visited somehow struck my fancy: the McClure site (39HU7) is an Extended Coalescent village on a terrace below the upland Arzberger site about five miles east of Pierre. Fenenga gave me permission to use the Smithsonian jeep and field equipment, and one weekend I took some volunteers to test the site. Our work had to be on Sunday, for the landowner was a Seventh Day Adventist and prohibited work on his property on Saturday. We worked hard all morning and into the afternoon and exposed part of an earthlodge floor. By mid-afternoon we'd exhausted our drinking water, and I drove into Pierre for a fresh supply. As I drove down Main Street I was struck by the noble idea of rewarding my hardworking volunteers, and I filled a gallon thermos with cold draft beer from a tavern on Pierre Street. It was eagerly accepted on my return and as eagerly dispatched. A few minutes later we were all lying bleary-eyed on the backdirt piles: our workday was ended and a lesson learned. Still, I had an artifact sample that Fenenga encouraged me to write up on our return to Lincoln, though Bob Cumming was amused by the presumptiveness of this neophyte. Well, I finished my report, and he never did, because he vanished from professional sight a short time later.

The writing experience was invaluable, for Frank patiently helped me prepare the report (my very first), editing and critiquing my efforts as though I'd been a colleague. We'd opened a quadrant of one of the lodges in the southeastern part of the site and recovered a modest sample of artifacts that I carefully described under Frank's tutelage to provide comparative material for work then being done in the Oahe Reservoir above Pierre. No publication resulted from my efforts, nor (fortunately) was the report preserved, except in summary form as a presentation I gave at the 63rd annual meeting of the Nebraska Academy of Sciences. An MRBS field team under Richard B. Johnston later conducted formal testing in this protohistoric Arikara village. My excavations are thought to be the first excavation by an MRBS crew in the future Big Bend Reservoir (Johnston 1982:2).

Fenenga's field assistant that summer was a classical archaeologist, in Near Eastern studies I believe, but after a few weeks he left us. I cannot recall his name or the reason for his departure. Fenenga then chose two of his crew to replace him: Richard O. Keslin (a graduate student at the University of Wisconsin) and me (a flunked-out sophomore at the University of Nebraska). When I'd gone to work for Frank that summer I was determined to repay his confidence, and I worked that season as hard as I believe I ever have. Without being obtrusive about it, I made myself available for any task, filling the role of an unbidden assistant, as it were. Certainly this was instrumental in my promotion. I've given similar advice to many students as they've left for summer jobs over the years.

I became the project cartographer and mapped each of the houses we dug. I don't recall that we had a transit or level, but the task was easily performed by a technique that Fenenga taught me. We set a plane table over the center of the central fire pit using a plumb bob. A common straight pin was stuck in the center of the paper on the board, and sighting along the top of a triangular ruler set against the pin, we drew a line to the center of the posthole or other feature, sighting on a rod held by a helper. He then measured the distance to the subject using a tape measure attached to a chaining pin stuck in the ground in the center of the hearth and called out the diameter of the feature. It was simple but efficient.

One afternoon a small, low-wing aircraft flew low over the site and dropped a glass bottle. We ran to pick it up and found it contained a message: "Come to the Hopscotch Bar. Ralph." The Smithsonian had authorized an aerial reconnaissance to photograph selected sites in eight reservoirs that summer, and pilot Ralph Solecki had dropped the note. Fenenga went to the Pierre airport and picked up Ralph and his companion, an accomplished photographer, Nathaniel Dewell. They were engaged in the first coordinated attempt to take aerial photos in the United States. Ralph and Nathaniel went on to take photographs of other sites in Nebraska, North Dakota, and Wyoming (Wood et al. 1984:28–29). Dewell took several fine aerial photos of the site the following day, and that fall I used these images and on-the-ground measurements to prepare the site map. During the summer James Deetz, on leave from the army, passed though Pierre to visit his fiancée and later wife, Jody Kelly. He'd met her in 1950 when he made field drawings as one of Don Lehmer's crew at the Dodd site. Jim came to see us (in uniform) when he heard there was an MRBS field party in the area and spent most of the day helping us dig.

I recall the names of only two of our field crew: Mark Heddon, who I believe became an archaeologist in Maine, and Benjamin K. Schwartz. I especially remember Ben, for he was prone to borrow my Ford convertible for dates with local girls that ended dismally (at least for me). One evening, as I waited for him to return from a date, he walked in into the Hopscotch Bar to tell me that my car had broken down. Actually, as it turned out, it was high-centered on a glacial erratic overlooking the Missouri River on the slope of Snake Butte, the highest butte in the neighborhood west of Pierre, one that provided a vast panorama of the Missouri River. It was a magnificent place to park and, coincidentally, provided the name for one of Don Lehmer's early (and later discarded) taxonomic units. My car had lodged on its slope (narrowly avoiding a plunge over a cliff into the Missouri River) after a vain attempt to start it by jumping the clutch. Despite this lesson, I loaned him the car a second time, and again he walked in to tell me it had broken down. The next morning we went out to tow it to town and found it filled with stolen watermelons. This time it had indeed broken down, and we had to tow it to a garage in Pierre. Ben went on to a career in archaeology, at least for a time, but eventually I lost touch with him.

For whatever reason, Fenenga did not write up his fieldwork for that season, and Don Lehmer and David Jones later published the Buffalo Pasture and Indian Creek sites, both of which were mid-eighteenth-century Arikara communities (Lehmer and Jones 1968). The villages are in the right place and were occupied at about the right time to have been visited by the La Vérendrye brothers in March 1743. After their father's visit to the Mandans in 1738, the brothers went back to their villages near Bismarck and made a long circuit of western North and South Dakota (and perhaps eastern Montana) before returning to Canada. A lead plate commemorating their visit to the vicinity of the Bad River was found in 1913 on a hill overlooking downtown Fort Pierre, some five miles south of our sites. The find is consistent with Vérendrye's son's statement that "on an eminence near the fort [an Arikara village] I deposited a lead tablet bearing the arms and inscription of the king" (Smith 1980:113 (quotation), 123–125). A monument atop the hill today commemorates that visit, overlooking another of the town's memorials, the bronze statue of Casey Tibbs.

On our return to Lincoln that fall, Fenenga became in effect a second adviser to me, and I often visited his home, where he and his wife, Barbara, treated me much as they would a son. Frank was one of the most knowledgeable men I've ever met, having an encyclopedic grasp of archaeology, anthropology, and antiques. I continued learning from him for as long as I knew him. One semester he taught a night course in North American Indians at the university. I took it and did well, though it led to one of my most embarrassing anthropological moments. In an examination question asking us to list the language affiliations of a number of Native American groups, I was stumped by one entry. Leaving it blank, I asked him as I left the room, "What language do the Eskimo speak?" His condescending look and one-word response sent me flying from the room.

Frank was the first editor of *The Plains Anthropologist*, the first issue of which appeared in an 8½-by-11-inch format in May 1954 and ran through Number 8 in 1960. The "*The*" in its title was dropped when the journal was reduced in size, and continuous publication resumed in May 1960 under the editorship of James B. Schaeffer. It has since become one of the most respected regional journals in the United States. Between 1972 and 1974 I was privileged to be its fifth editor, for volumes 17 to 19, or Numbers 55 to 60. My duties included far more than its present editors would believe. I read and accepted or rejected submissions and edited their contents, then sent the manuscripts to the printer, who returned long sheets of galley proofs. These I cut up and glued on boards that mimicked the journal format, attaching squares of red construction paper to fill in for the illustrations, and mailed the boards back to the publisher. I felt I did most of the work for the journal, aside from cranking the handle on the printing press. Initially, I had too few articles from which to choose, so I published the second reprint issue in the journal's history, Number 57, consisting of Waldo Wedel's 1940 "Cultural Sequence in the Central Great Plains" and Duncan Strong's "From History to Prehistory in the Northern Great Plains." It gave me the opportunity not to have to publish everything that arrived on my desk simply to fill the journal. About this time I also initiated peer review, which meant that I could blame someone else for not publishing a submission. We continued to move toward a professional journal whose content was not published solely at the editor's discretion.

In my junior year Champe excused me from taking a field school, normally required for a major in anthropology for those specializing in archaeology. By that time I'd had four full seasons of fieldwork, including both survey and excavation, and had served as a field assistant for Frank Fenenga's Smithsonian field party at Buffalo Pasture for two months—a total of twelve months of survey and fieldwork under people (especially Enger and Fenenga) I admired and respected. I was pleased to have this reprieve, for I'd heard stories about Champe's field schools and I wasn't looking forward to the experience, especially in view of the financial cost. Furthermore, I don't know where I'd have found the money to attend, for I had to work that summer to afford tuition for my senior year.

By the beginning of my senior year I'd completed most of my required courses and had planned to major in anthropology, with minors in geology and zoology. However, my next classes in those two fields were high-risk courses in stratigraphy and comparative anatomy. When I discovered that many students would first audit these courses so they'd have a reasonable chance of passing them when they did register, I decided two majors would be preferable, and I chose English to accompany anthropology. During my senior year I took fifteen hours of each to complete my requirements: I was truly tired of Shakespeare by the time I graduated! I obtained my bachelor's degree in June 1954, together with Carolee Ramey. She and I had dated for the past two years and were engaged when we graduated, but circumstances intervened, and it was to be thirty-nine years before we married, in February 1992, after both of us had married others and raised families. (At that time I acquired three stepchildren and three grandchildren, and eventually also great-grandchildren.) Our parents came to graduation, an event that once had been clouded by my dismissal from the university in 1951. Carolee and my parents and I visited Aunt Edith on the farm in Missouri, and then we returned to Lincoln. I left town a few days later to do historical archaeology with Alan Woolworth in North Dakota: I was headed for a new set of experiences.

Alan R. Woolworth

There were several graduate students in the anthropology department while I was an undergraduate. Prominent among them were James H. and Dolores (Jim and Dee) Gunnerson, James H. Howard, and Alvin W. Wolfe. Jim Gunnerson wrote his master's thesis on the Dismal River aspect (later published by the Bureau of American Ethnology) and obtained his Ph.D. at Harvard; Dee later obtained her Ph.D. at the University of Utah. They both specialized in the Apacheans of the Southern Plains and southwestern United States, Jim with their prehistory and Dee with their history. Jim Howard's thesis was on the Ponca Indians (also published by the Bureau of American Ethnology). He became a prominent ethnographer of Plains Indians after completing his doctorate at the University of Michigan. Alvin Wolfe proceeded to obtain his Ph.D. at Northwestern University and became a noted cultural anthropologist. He was director of the Center for Applied Anthropology at University of South Florida from 1978 to 2002 and retired as Distinguished University Professor Emeritus. These students were in time augmented by Mary Kiehl Rusco, who later became affiliated with the Center for Archeological Survey, Nevada State Museum, and by Raymond S. Price Jr., who was to become my close friend and roommate. We became known as Ray and as Ray-square. After obtaining his M.A. from Champe in 1956, Ray took a job at the Nebraska State Historical Society, where he worked with Iris Nunley Daugherty in preparing exhibits. Iris also produced the stunning backgrounds for the University Museum's wildlife dioramas in the basement of Morrill Hall. Ray then moved on to a permanent museum career with the National Park

Service, ending as the chief of wayside exhibits at Harpers Ferry Center, West Virginia.

Among my undergraduate peers were Thomas M. Newman, David M. Gradwohl, Frederick McEvoy, and John Henry Russell; there were others I don't remember and with whom I socialized little. Newman obtained his Ph.D. from the University of Oregon in 1960 and became a founding member of Portland State University's anthropology department. He was a dedicated teacher, and the Thomas M. Newman Scholarship Fund was established in his honor in 1985. Gradwohl made his way to Harvard for his doctorate and ultimately taught at and retired from Iowa State University. McEvoy went on to become an Africanist, and Russell became a farmer along Nebraska's Loup River.

Among the upperclassmen was Alan R. Woolworth, who graduated with a dual major in anthropology and history soon after my arrival. Alan was born in Clear Lake, near Watertown in extreme eastern South Dakota, in 1924; he was at the university from 1948 to 1950. After obtaining his bachelor's degree, he left for the University of Minnesota, where he received his M.A., writing his thesis on the ethnohistory of the Oto Indians. He went on to devote his career to the history and ethnohistory of the Prairie-Plains region, drawing on both his undergraduate training in history and what amounted to a mentorship in ethnohistory with Smithsonian historical archaeologist G. Hubert Smith. By 1954 he was the chief archaeologist with the State Historical Society of North Dakota in Bismarck. He was now seeking an assistant for an archaeological field project, and when I graduated with my B.A. in the spring of 1954, he chose me for that position because of our past acquaintance and his knowledge of my field experience. I was of course in need of employment and eagerly accepted his offer (Woolworth 2006). We were slated to become close friends.

I took the longest bus ride of my life up to that time to get to Bismarck, riding the Jack Rabbit Stage Line through the Dakotas (it's no longer operational as a competitor for Greyhound). It was a fascinating trip. On the way I visited the Corn Palace in Mitchell, South Dakota, a major tourist attraction and a whimsical bit of Americana to this very day. Accompanying me on the trip was another of the field crew, art student Bruce Conner, also recruited in Lincoln, whose revulsion at the Corn Palace was a topic of his conversation for the rest of the trip. (He later became an artist of some note.) We arrived in the little town of Garrison, in McLean County, North Dakota, and hitchhiked out to the site, first to a hamlet named Emmett, then some twenty miles south over the prairies by dirt roads to the field camp, set on the north bank of the Missouri River. The camp was pitched on the edge of a high terrace overlooking an abandoned river channel, the terrace extending far to the east and north to the distant river bluffs. Across the river to the south the bluffs were bisected by L'Ours qui Dance (Dancing Bear) Creek.

Alan and Hubert Smith welcomed us to camp. Alan had contracted with the National Park Service, through the State Historical Society of North Dakota, to excavate the ruins of Fort Berthold, an American Fur Company trading post. Fort Berthold had been built on the north side of Like-a-Fishhook Village, an earthlodge village founded in 1845 by Hidatsa Indians who had moved upriver from the mouth of Knife River, near Stanton. There they were joined by remnants of the Mandans, who had nearly been destroyed by the great smallpox epidemic of 1837. By 1850, continuing attacks by Lakota Sioux raiders made it necessary for the residents to build a post palisade around the village; indeed, dozens of attacks by the Lakotas took place over the years the village was occupied. Frost, Todd and Company built a second and competing trading post, Fort Atkinson, on the south side of the village's palisade in 1858.

The population of Like-a-Fishhook Village swelled in the summer of 1862, when the Arikaras arrived. Fort Berthold had been destroyed earlier by a Sioux war party, and its ruins quickly vanished from view as the Arikaras built their lodges over its burned remains. Like-a-Fishhook was the last earthlodge village occupied by the Mandans, Hidatsas, and Arikaras on the Upper Missouri, and it continued to be the home of the three tribes until 1885, when they moved onto the reservation named after Fort Berthold. The earthlodge village and Fort Atkinson slowly deteriorated until their grassy sites were marked principally by shallow pits created by collapsed cache pits and the circular depressions left by earthlodges. The bustling life of the village and traders was gone, replaced by grazing horses and cattle. Now even those reminders of the past were scheduled to lie at the bottom of a lake to be created by the Garrison Dam.

James H. Howard had dug at Like-a-Fishhook Village in 1952 for the State Historical Society of North Dakota, at which time Alan served as his field assistant. They excavated a number of earthlodges, and the season was nearly over when they began digging their last lodge (House 20), in the Arikara sector of the village. When they found two straight-sided trenches on its exposed floor, Alan decided they were traces of Fort Berthold. This is one of the rare instances in North American archaeology in which an Indian site was stratigraphically superimposed over a Euroamerican one. Needless to say, this led to a confusing array of archaeological features.

The same season this discovery was made, Smithsonian archaeologist Hubert Smith, assisted by George Metcalf, excavated the site of Fort Berthold II (Fort Atkinson was so renamed after the destruction of the first Fort Berthold). Hubert had been hired in 1951 by the MRBS expressly to research and excavate historic fur trade and military sites that would be flooded by federal reservoirs built in the Missouri Basin under the Pick-Sloan plan. Historic-sites archaeology was in its infancy and was widely denigrated by professional prehistoric archaeologists as "tin can archaeology." Curiously enough, some professionals today have much the same attitude toward the archaeology of World War II. It was through the efforts of individuals such as Hubert that "tin can archaeology" attained prominence and respectability. Most of Hubert's work was done in what became the Oahe and Garrison Reservoirs, where many of the larger trading and military posts in the Dakotas had been built. At that time, the excavation of such lesser sites as, say, farmsteads was unheard-of.

Fur trade archaeology in the Plains began in North Dakota with the work done by Hubert. The early history of historical archaeology on the Upper Missouri River and the upper Mississippi Basin in fact cannot be told without repeated references to him. Hubert was a native South Dakotan, from the little town of Miller, some seventy miles east of Pierre. He trained at the University of Minnesota under Albert E. Jenks, perhaps best known for his studies of wild rice and his discovery of Brown's Valley Man (now identified as a woman). Hubert later worked for the Minnesota Historical Society and other agencies, including the National Park Service, before moving to the Smithsonian Institution's MRBS office in Lincoln.

Hubert was a consummate scholar, and virtually all his fieldwork eventually was published on Forts Berthold I and II and Fort Stevenson in North Dakota, and on Fort Manuel, Fort George, Fort Bennett Agency, and Red Cloud Agency III in South Dakota. Some of his research was published after his death, including his years-long study of the La Vérendrye family and their explorations in the Northern Plains, which I edited for the University of Nebraska Press, and his Fort Manuel excavations, edited and published by John Ludwickson for the South Dakota Archaeological Society (Smith 1980; Smith and Ludwickson 1981). Hubert was one of the most kindly individuals I've ever met, one who'd go out of his way to help you with a problem.

Conversations and correspondence between Alan and Hubert in 1952 and 1953 led to their decision to excavate Fort Berthold in the summer of 1954. It would be a race to do so, for in early 1954 they learned that the rising water in Garrison Reservoir would flood the site before the fieldwork could be carried out. The Corps of Engineers, however, generously agreed to hold more water for a time in Fort Peck Reservoir and release more water in the Garrison Reservoir. This, with luck, would give them until about July 1 to complete their fieldwork. Consequently, the State Historical Society of North Dakota collaborated in the project with the MRBS. Hubert arrived in the middle of May with his crew, including Lee G. Madison and Raymond S. Price. A little later, the Corps of Engineers provided a road grader, permitting the entire fort to be stripped of its overburden. While Alan and Hubert had use of the machine, they had its operator also expose the trench in which the posts of the village palisade were set (Woolworth 2006: 661–662).

Our camp was north of the ruins of Fort Berthold, adjoining a small gully that flooded to create a small, deep bay. From the terrace above it we could watch the slowly rising water of what was to become Lake Sakakawea. Our living quarters and kitchen consisted of four surplus U.S. Army pyramidal squad tents and a smaller white one that housed field equipment. Ray Price systematically mapped the hundreds of features of the fort and its overlying Arikara occupation. In 1852 Swiss artist Rudolph Friedrich Kurz had prepared a few sketches of the fort that were helpful for understanding the post and its architecture, but we wished he'd been as generous with his views of Fort Berthold as he had with Fort Union. The rising water in the lake was only yards from our excavations, and we often took mid-afternoon breaks by plunging into its cooling bliss and longer, more leisurely swims after work. We floated two immense logs to the bay beside the camp and nailed a platform on them, creating a gigantic raft that Ray Price christened "The City of Memphis."

In the evenings we sat around a fire pit we had dug in front of the tents and socialized until bedtime, discussing the site, its history, and its ethnohistory. The mosquitoes were especially fierce when I arrived in early June, and before retiring nightly I'd take a shovelful of glowing embers from the dying fire, place them in a cast-iron Dutch oven we'd found on the village site, sprinkle sage leaves over them, and set the oven inside my tent. When enough smoke had accumulated to drive out the mosquitoes, my tentmate and I crawled into our sleeping bags and went to sleep. I suppose this didn't damage my lungs any more than the cigarettes I smoked at the time.

Figure 11. Tent camp at Fort Berthold I and Like-a-Fishhook Village, North Dakota, summer 1954. *Author's collection.*

Before I arrived, the site had been stripped to the level of the fort's foundations by the road grader. Our job was to excavate and map the 780 features that had been exposed. I was to direct and oversee the excavators, choose the features to be dug, and record them. Accompanying Hubert Smith was Lee Madison, an MRBS professional field hand and a man with years of fieldwork dating back to the 1930s, when he dug with the Nebraska State Historical Society on prehistoric sites throughout eastern Nebraska. Given his long professional seniority, I felt uncomfortable giving him orders, but Lee assured me, "That's your job. Don't worry about it."

The camp was isolated, and we welcomed visitors. One regular weekend guest was Bernard (Bernie) Weinreich, a well-known figure in Bismarck because of his acting, music, and photographic talents. Visitors usually brought a watermelon or some other treat (preferably a case of cold beer) to brighten our monotonous camp fare. Bernie and I became great friends and shared many pleasant hours during the time I later spent in Bismarck; he also took photographs of artifacts for our reports. The season was a great success; we completed the excavation of the fort just before the water rose to cover it. The following June (1955) I completed writing up "Native Pits and Artifacts on the Site of Fort Berthold I (32ML2)" for our report on the dig for the National Park Service. Some years later, Hubert condensed each of the six prior reports on the fieldwork by different individuals into a single monograph, enhanced by his insightful summary of its history. The National Park Service published the monograph almost two decades later (Smith 1972).

The features of the fort were easily seen in the loess-mantled terrace on which it was built. The soil conditions were identical to those at Buffalo Pasture and Indian Creek, where the features were also readily visible. All that was new were the post-lined palisade trenches, the small rectangular pits that had contained foundation posts for the fort's buildings, and unfamiliar pit outlines. It was my first experience in "tin can" archaeology, and our work provided historians with data on the fort and its architecture, and archaeologists with important information on its content.

We broke camp at Fort Berthold in July. Hubert Smith, Lee Madison, and Ray Price returned to their Lincoln office, and Alan and I moved our camp and crew upriver to a new location and a new project. We spent the remaining part of July and into August excavating the site of what we called Kipp's Post (32MN1). This Columbia Fur Company trading post was near the mouth of the White Earth River, about fifteen miles northwest of the town of New Town (formerly Sanish), North Dakota. The post, established by James Kipp in November 1826 for the Assiniboine Indian trade, had been burned and abandoned in 1829 or 1830. In 1951 Hubert Smith had verified its identity and location by exposing three of its four corners in test pits. Excited about the new project, we packed our equipment and personal gear into an ancient wood-paneled station wagon and a 1935 Chevrolet truck and moved upriver to the mouth of the White Earth, a few miles above New Town. It took a bit of coaxing to get the truck to move properly—it was the only vehicle I ever drove that necessitated adjusting the "spark"—but it performed admirably if grudgingly, at least in retrospect.

We had a genial crew at our new location, and everyone got along famously. Only one of them (Frederick D. McEvoy, who'd been a fellow undergraduate at Nebraska) went on to pursue a career in anthropology. Since there were no facilities for bathing, we swam in the Missouri at the mouth of the White Earth, where the sun warmed its slow-moving water. One afternoon as we were preparing for a swim a rainstorm of biblical proportions struck camp, and on a whim I stripped bare and soaped down in the downpour, but the rain ended as abruptly as it had appeared and the sun came out before I could rinse. The crew gleefully pumped water from a deep well and poured ice-cold buckets of it over my head to purge me of the remaining soap. Surely I'd lived in the Plains long enough to realize the short happy life of a summer storm!

We established our field camp in and around a log cabin that formed the nucleus of an abandoned farmstead a few hundred yards west of the fort. We pitched two army squad tents in the adjoining yard, using the cabin as a kitchen and dining room. Kipp's Post had been stripped in its entirety by a road grader. The fort, as usual, had been built on a loess-mantled terrace, and as always, features showed up beautifully in this sediment, so our work quickly revealed a very clear picture of the post. Given the fact that the fort was occupied for only about four years, its floor plan and interpretation were not complicated. The palisade, bastion, and entry were all clearly demarcated, including the range of three log buildings on the north side of the enclosure, some of which retained their charred plank flooring.

The ground plan thus exposed was mapped in enough detail to permit me to draw a reasonably accurate interpretation of its appearance. I used images in George Catlin's work to illustrate in his style the bluffs on the horizon (Woolworth and Wood 1960:Figure 21). It was a good representation, though I erred in not placing a beam along the top of the palisade, leaving it with an irregular profile like those wrongly portrayed in Hollywood epics. We recovered eleven fragments of a one-pound cannon, one piece of which was found in front of one of the structures as though it had been used as a doorstop. A small pit in one corner of the enclosure yielded the boxed remains of an infant about six months old, smothered in thousands of blue seed beads, clearly demonstrating that at least one of the traders had an Indian wife.

The Indian wife may also have had a hand in meal preparation. The reason? A long trench that might best be characterized as a kitchen midden was behind the buildings and yielded many animal bones and broken dishes, providing detailed evidence of the traders' table settings and diet. We found the bones of bison, deer, and other game in the midden trench, together with those of skunk, muskrat, bobcat, prairie dog, and domestic dog. A recipe for skunk is unlikely to be found in any white housewife's kitchen (then or now!), but in the fall many Plains Indians esteemed its fatty flesh. Striped skunks do not hibernate, but they become torpid or dormant in very cold weather, and the fat serves the same purpose as it does for hibernating bears. Other clues to the presence of Indian wives were the presence of Indian artifacts commonly used by women: chipped-stone end scrapers, a serrated metapodial fleshing tool, grooved-stone mauls, and large stone chopping tools. These finds came as no surprise, given the propensity of traders at the time to marry Indian women.

Because the post was occupied so briefly, its contents gave us a snapshot of the lives of its traders, and the trade goods we found provided a sample of what was being traded during a narrow slice of time. The site has now been destroyed by wave action from Lake Sakakawea, but its movable effects and ground plan are on record for the use of historians of the American fur trade in the Far West.

There's a great deal yet to learn about many aspects of that trade. Nothing is more illustrative of this than the recent identification of the mysterious Fort Floyd, the predecessor of Fort Union. William J. Hunt Jr., the National Park Service archaeologist who worked for many years at Fort Union Trading Post National Historic Site, has convincingly identified Fort Floyd as the post we called Kipp's Post (Hunt 1994)—ironically, from documents that have long been in our possession. To date, we've only scratched the surface of the fur trade records, and our efforts so far may well be called a cream-skimming operation. The moral: the more we dig in the archives, the more we learn, the more exciting our work becomes, and the closer we come to the men and women who participated in the trade. Beginning students of the fur trade need not worry that all the "good stuff" has been done. We've merely provided a basis for that generation to build on, elaborate, and improve.

After we finished digging the post, Alan had one final project before the season ended. The rest of the crew was dismissed, and we went downriver to the mouth of the Little Missouri River, where an MRBS field crew led by Donald D. Hartle and George Metcalf had begun the excavation of Grandmother's Lodge (32ME59), a feature venerated in Hidatsa folklore. Grandmother was a supernatural figure in Mandan-Hidatsa lore who ensured the fertility of crops, especially corn. As recently as 1952, Crow Indians had visited the site and left offerings, including cigarettes and coins bearing dates as late as 1948. The depression for this lodge was created by a long-rectangular house whose form was characteristic of those of the prehistoric Middle Missouri tradition. The lodge was the northernmost such site known on the Missouri River, and it, too, was soon to be permanently inundated by Lake Sakakawea. We enjoyed our relations with a nearby neighbor, the Rev. James Holding Eagle, grandson of the last Mandan Corn Priest, Moves Slowly, and son of Scattered Corn (or Scattercorn). After we completed excavating the lodge and mapped its remains, we headed back

Figure 12. Alan Woolworth (*left*) and the author in the State Historical Society of North Dakota's museum workroom, fall 1955. *Author's collection.*

to Bismarck. Alan's brief report on the lodge (Woolworth 1956) became the first published site report on a Missouri Valley village people in North Dakota to appear in the half century since George F. Will and Herbert J. Spinden (1906) reported the Double Ditch Mandan village site.

At this time the State Historical Society of North Dakota was housed in the Liberty Memorial Building, a stone structure just southeast of the state capital that we shared with the State Library. Alan and I had a spacious laboratory on the second floor, and though it was somewhat claustrophobic, we usually kept the door closed to prevent visitors from wandering in. The heavily Scandinavian population of the state became very much in evidence, for a surprising number of them wanted to ask about or tell us about evidence for Viking visitors to the state. Museum aide Norman Paulson was a constant source of help in finding specimens and assisting us with any needed task, and we became good friends. That fall I prepared my first museum display, one that replaced an entire case of hundreds of projectile points with a single panel illustrating their development, drawing on examples I'd seen that were prepared by my artistic friend, Ray Price. On one occasion I accompanied Alan on a trip to the western part of the state to attend to various projects, and we were taken by a local rancher to a locality where he had told Alan that Theodore Roosevelt had inscribed his name on a rock. We were intrigued to discover that it was before Roosevelt had learned to spell his own name, for it was written "T. Rosevelt." It would not be my only wild-goose chase following up on a supposed lead to an important find.

In Bismarck I first met Paul Ewald, a prominent local businessman with many friends and contacts and a staunch ally of the State Historical Society. But he had a dark side, and later Don Lehmer and I called him our "fat friend." When Lehmer and I were testing sites in the vicinity of Stanton in 1968, we tested the Clark's Creek site, just downstream from Fort Clark State Historic Site. Paul drove out from Bismarck in his Cadillac to see me there, and we had an amiable visit, but on leaving us he sped into town and called the state land commissioner, asserting that I was digging on state land (a school section) without permission and claiming trespass. Ray H. Mattison, then superintendent of the State Historical Society, called the commissioner to tell him that yes, we indeed had permission to work there. I never found out what problem he had with our working in North Dakota, but we'd have appreciated an honest confrontation instead of sneak attacks. In 1960 he even accused me of stealing state property when I purchased matt boards to take back to Oregon with me to prepare the plates for my report to the National Park Service on my work at Huff, work that the society itself had sponsored.

Today the Liberty Memorial Building houses only the State Library, for the State Historical Society has moved into the modern and more spacious North Dakota Heritage Center, built immediately to its east under the superintendency of James E. Sperry. The Heritage Center is a wonderful building with great exhibits, and the state is likewise fortunate in having attracted a marvelously competent and loyal staff. When I first arrived in Bismarck, Theodore Roosevelt's North Dakota ranch cabin had stood on the site of the Heritage Center, having been moved to Bismarck from its original site on Roosevelt's Maltese Cross Ranch in western North Dakota. It must be one of the most widely traveled log cabins in the Great Plains, for during his presidency it had made a trip to Portland, Oregon, and to the St. Louis World's Fair. It has since been returned to his ranch in Theodore Roosevelt National Park.

That fall (1954) I discovered the artifacts from the Biesterfeldt site in storage in the museum's sub-basement. Biesterfeldt (32RM1) is an earthlodge village on the Sheyenne River in eastern North Dakota that apparently was occupied by the Cheyenne Indians in the mid-1700s. An

Figure 13. Restoring a pottery vessel from the Demery site at the State Historical Society of North Dakota, fall 1956. The finished product is illustrated in Woolworth and Wood 1964. *Author's collection.*

archaeological party from Columbia University under the direction of William Duncan Strong had investigated it in 1938. Strong summarized his findings in his seminal paper, "From History to Prehistory in the Northern Plains," but he never formally reported this important site, the only known Cheyenne earthlodge village (Strong 1940). I decided to describe the ceramics from it because the pottery had much in common with that currently being described from village sites along the Missouri River (Wood 1955b). Because the Cheyennes had lived along the Missouri in the middle to late eighteenth century after leaving Biesterfeldt, I hoped the description would help us identify any Cheyenne village that might be found along the Missouri. It was not until 1967, however, that I found time to undertake a formal description of the site itself and its contents in monograph form. This necessitated obtaining copies of Strong's field notes and photographs, data that were graciously provided by Ralph Solecki, then at Columbia University. My report appeared as one of the Smithsonian's *Contributions to Anthropology* (Wood 1971a). It is not well known that Solecki had worked for a time in the Plains. Among other things, he'd dug at Ash Hollow Cave, though he is best known for the Neanderthals he exhumed in Iran at Shanidar Cave—a remarkable shift in time and space.

About half of Biesterfeldt had been disturbed by plowing even before Strong investigated it in 1938, but after he left, the landowner continued to protect the remainder of it from further disturbance. In 1980 the State Historical Society of North Dakota nominated the site for listing on the National Register of Historic Places Inventory, but it remained endangered by its potential sale to parties that might not be sympathetic to its preservation. When its owner and protector died in 2003, the land was liable to be sold at auction and the remainder of the site surely would have been placed under cultivation. Fortunately, the Archaeological Conservancy purchased a forty-acre plot enclosing the site as a part of its national system of archaeological preserves, thereby preventing its further degradation. The purchase was direly needed, for Biesterfeldt remains unique on the Northern Plains. Though the site is traditionally identified as Cheyenne, and is historically recorded as such, the village and its contents most closely resemble protohistoric Arikara towns along the Missouri River. In 2006 I was asked by the National Park Service to assist in preparing a nomination for Biesterfeldt to be registered as a National Historic Landmark, recognition the site richly deserves. Michael G. Michlovic, of Minnesota State University–Moorhead, was contracted to prepare a new map and supply further data on the site, for no map had been drawn there since one was prepared by personnel from the State Historical Society ninety-nine years earlier.

The photographs of the site that Strong took in 1938 reveal a landscape almost barren of trees; today one cannot even see the horizon because of them. Following the great drought of the 1930s, farmers began planting trees by the thousands along roads, around their farms, and along section lines; they were designed to break the everlasting wind. Many years ago I drove through the town of Devil's Lake, North Dakota, and stopped for lunch at a picnic table in the city park. An elderly Indian man strolled by and asked if he could sit at the other end of the table. "Sure," I said, and offered him a sandwich and a soda, which he quietly accepted, and we silently sat eating as we looked out across the tree-studded prairie. I was wondering just how many trees there had originally been on the horizon when he suddenly said, "Trees! There weren't any trees when I was a boy." I felt akin to the old man and his memories, and it led to an interesting conversation on how things had been in his youth.

While I was writing the Biesterfeldt report, I was in frequent contact with Elden Johnson at the University of Minnesota, who assured me that the Biesterfeldt material resembled nothing in that state, the region from which the Cheyennes traditionally moved. That remains true to this day, though further archaeological and ethnohistorical work may eventually prove differently. When I started working on the site, I began to consult the journals of Lewis and Clark ever more seriously. Their journals mention an old Cheyenne village at the mouth of Porcupine Creek, just north of Fort Yates, but I was unable to find any trace of such a site when I visited the locality during fieldwork in the area for the State Historical Society in 1955 and 1956. My quest for other Cheyenne village sites along the Missouri River that were mentioned in George Bird Grinnell's studies proved equally fruitless. In his book *The Cheyenne Indians*, Grinnell had brought together Cheyenne and Dakota traditions concerning these villages and had visited the locations of two of these presumed sites, which had been identified by local Dakota informants not far from the town of Fort Yates (Grinnell 1923:1:23–25). I visited both sites and recovered pottery and other debris. Such finds had previously supported Grinnell's supposition that they were Cheyenne, but our recent archaeological work in the vicinity indicated that all these materials came from prehistoric Middle Missouri tradition components. I suspect that most if not all of the historically documented Cheyenne villages on the Missouri were tipi encampments, not earthlodge villages. In any event, we have yet to find Biesterfeldt-like pottery anywhere along the Missouri.

I stayed on in Bismarck that autumn to work on the material that Alan and I recovered from Kipp's Post, delaying my return to graduate school until the second semester. Alan and I shared an apartment that winter about a mile from our office. Spending the winter in Bismarck gave me added appreciation for the hardiness of the Indians in the Northern Plains. One morning we awoke to find that the temperature was 40 degrees below zero. My car wouldn't start: the starter motor made a single click and then remained silent. Fortunately, I had the proper winter gear to walk to the museum for the next three days, wearing double layers of every conceivable article of clothing. Today it is hard to imagine how Native Americans lived in tipis through such temperatures, even in sheltered areas, but it must have been exhilarating, to say the least. Even the diminutive winter earth-lodges the villagers built to conserve heat would have been a challenge to keep warm.

I'd taken the bus to North Dakota that summer, but I was driven back to Lincoln by a family from Texas I'd met at Like-a-Fishhook. I'd expected the husband to accompany us, but that was not to be. The ride was with the wife, the family cat, and their two teenage daughters. I did most of the driving, with the cat perched on the seat behind me with its whiskers in my ear; the two daughters alternated sitting beside me in the front seat. The reason for the invitation became immediately clear: I was pummeled by subtle hints that they were of marriageable age. I knew they married that young in Texas, but not where I came from! I was ecstatic when they dropped me off in Lincoln.

That winter I had a tiny second-story room in Lincoln in an apartment building a few blocks from campus, and I soon became friends with its various occupants. Since I lived on a slim income, beer was a luxury, and I decided to make a batch of home brew. Several of the neighbors along the hall bought into my project, and before long we were in production. I scrubbed the bathtub clean in my apartment, and one afternoon we filled it with fifty gallons of brew. (For the time being, I bathed in the apartment next door.) When I returned late that evening after work and opened the door, I was nearly suffocated by the gases the brew was emitting, and it took several hours with the windows open to air out the place before I could go to bed. We obtained several cases of empty bottles from a nearby bar and had a bottle-washing and bottle-filling party about a week later. It was a successful batch, for not one bottle exploded. Later batches were made in more modest quantities with a twenty-gallon crock.

4

Graduate Years at Nebraska

How do you know when the prairie is in you?
When you see a tree as an eyesore.

— William Least Heat-Moon, *PrairyErth*, 1991

My Master's Degree

I left Bismarck and returned to the University of Nebraska in January 1955 to begin classes for my master's degree. I also worked as a part-time draftsman for the MRBS. My roommate during that time was Raymond S. Price, who, as an MRBS employee, had mapped Like-a-Fishhook Village and Fort Berthold in 1954. Our next-door apartment neighbor was MRBS employee George Metcalf and his daughter Margaret. George had long experience with archaeology in Nebraska, but despite his lack of formal training, he was a superb field man, surveyor, and archaeologist, and he wrote many technical reports on his work. When the MRBS was transferred to the National Park Service, he went to work for Waldo Wedel at the Smithsonian in Washington. We became friends for two reasons: our association at the MRBS and the fact that Margaret and I had become acquainted when we took the same introductory anthropology class when I was a freshman. They often came to the parties Ray and I had, for George was a genial partygoer. Some of his fingers on one hand had been lost years before in a gunshot accident. Someone once asked George how he'd lost one of his eyes. He responded, "By peeking though a keyhole at something that was none of my damned business!"

I didn't look forward to Christmas in 1955 because I was broke and had nowhere to go, but I was spared a lonely holiday when Ray invited me to go with him to visit his sister in Las Cruces, New Mexico. It was my first trip to the Southwest, and while we were there, we used the occasion to go sightseeing. We drove over the San Andreas Mountains to roam White Sands National Monument, visited the ruins of a local adobe fort, and explored back roads near the mountains. When we stopped to admire one scenic vista, I looked down and saw a Clovis point beside the road, the only one I've ever found. Sometime later I gave it to Marie Wormington, and today it resides in the Denver Museum of Natural History (now the Denver Museum of Nature and Science).

As an undergraduate I spent a great deal of time looking over the collections housed in Champe's Laboratory of Anthropology. One wall of the lab was lined with drawers containing fascinating artifacts from a range of sites that the university had investigated over the years. One of the sites was Ponca Fort (25KX1), a historic Ponca fortified earthlodge village set on a high hill near the mouth of Ponca Creek, in Knox County a few miles west of the town of Niobrara. In 1932 the University of Nebraska initiated the first formal archaeological work in northeastern Nebraska, and between 1933 and 1940 the Nebraska State Archaeological Survey subjected the area to intensive survey and excavation. In 1936 and 1937 field parties under the direction of Perry Newell carried out excavations at Ponca Fort with fieldworkers supplied by the Works Project Administration. The material still lay undescribed in drawers, and though I knew next to nothing about the Poncas (aside from having met and visited with Jim Howard's Ponca informant, Peter Le Claire), here was an opportunity to study something that begged for analysis. In 1953 Champe gave me permission to begin a study of the site that I essentially completed in 1955. *Nánza, the Ponca Fort* eventually was published by the Society for American Archaeology as the third number in its experimental microcard series, but because that technology was obsolete by the 1990s, I updated its text and J&L Reprint Company reissued it in hard copy (Wood 1960a, 1993a).

The archaeological remains at the fort and the historical documents relating to it demonstrate that the Poncas lived in this fortified village between about 1790 and 1800 and were participating fully in the Plains village way of life. Ponca Fort is unique in being the only known village the Poncas occupied in historic times that is identifiable today. It was unfortunately occupied too late to yield more than a few native-made artifacts, for by this time most of the Poncas' material culture had been displaced by European-made alternatives, making it impracticable to trace its antecedents into

Figure 14. Giving a talk at the 11th Plains Conference, 1962. *Author's collection.*

prehistory. My first foray into ethnohistory did not succeed in tracing the Poncas into the past, but perhaps someday the search will be continued with more positive results.

No identifiable Ponca pottery was recovered, though two occupations clearly were present, a Central Plains tradition one represented by prehistoric Nebraska phase pottery, and the historic Ponca component. Curiously enough, however, sherds identified as Stanley ware (a historic Arikara pottery type) were recovered. The sherds imply intimate contacts with that tribe, perhaps intermarriage, a circumstance that earlier led me to compile the story of Arikara visits to Nebraska (Wood 1955). Interestingly enough, a similar sherd was found at Ton-won-tonga, the historic Omaha Indian village near Sioux City (O'Shea and Ludwickson 1992:214).

This research was the stimulus that led me firmly into ethnohistory, a field I found so congenial that its attraction has never dimmed. I perused early explorers' accounts of travel on the Missouri River for clues to the age and affiliation of Ponca Fort, and inevitably I was led to *Before Lewis and Clark*, the seminal history of the early Missouri River by Abraham P. Nasatir (1952). This primary source is so valuable that it has been twice reprinted in past decades. I compiled a calendar and chronology of travelers' accounts of the fort and chalked them on a blackboard in one of the classrooms. Champe came in, sat down and crossed his arms, leaned back in a chair against the wall, and critiqued my presentation as I wove the accounts into a narrative that I later published in an early issue of the journal *Ethno-*

history (Wood 1959). John was fond of telling graduate students—I was certainly no exception—to proceed cautiously: "Tiny steps for little feet," he'd say. It was an expression that led many of us to grit our teeth, as we of course thought of ourselves as budding professionals.

John taught me the essentials of the ethnohistorical approach, an approach that Raymond DeMallie (in Lowie 1982:ix) reminds us can be traced to the works of Oscar Lewis, Joseph Jablow, and Frank Secoy, each of whom used historical sources for cultural data and insights. Sarah Jones Tucker was among the first to elaborate on its merits as a formal approach, in an article that John Champe reproduced in ditto (a now long-obsolete form of reproduction) and that all of us students had to read, though I've lost the paper and its citation, if any: perhaps it was an unpublished conference paper. Tucker was a student of Fay-Cooper Cole and Robert Redfield, early advocates of the approach. Tucker participated in a statewide ethnohistorical survey of the tribes of Illinois in which she annotated the cartographic data (Tucker 1942; see also Temple 1975), though the narrative account to accompany the atlas was not published for another thirty-five years (Temple 1977).

It was David A. Baerreis, in his essay "The Ethnohistoric Approach and Archaeology" (Baerreis 1961:49), who pointed out that Clark Wissler may have been the first to use the term "ethno historical" in his 1909 work "The Indians of Greater New York and the Lower Hudson" (Wissler 1909:xiii). Wissler urged the combined use of archaeological and documentary evidence to reconstruct prehistoric cultures. (Baerreis's article appeared in a symposium devoted to the use of ethnohistory in anthropology.) In the 1950s the U.S. Indian Claims Commission was established by the Justice Department to deal with a flood of Indian land claims against the federal government. Anthropologists were retained by both Indian tribes and the Justice Department to present and defend Indian claims for lands lost in treaty negotiations. This stimulated the first real consciousness of ethnohistory as an approach, for early documents relating to Indian territories were essential in this legal process. The approach gained maturity when the Ohio Valley Historic Indian Conference, under the leadership of Erminie Wheeler-Voegelin, founded the conference bulletin *Ethnohistory* in 1954. The bulletin rapidly grew into a journal, later to be sponsored by the American Society for Ethnohistory. The conference and journal were designed to bring together historians, ethnographers, archaeologists, and linguists to cooperate in the study of historic Indians. In the first issue of the journal

Erminie Voegelin (1954:2) commented, "If there are few ethnologically minded historians, there are also equally few historically minded ethnologists." Fortunately, this is no longer true of either ethnologists or anthropologists of other persuasions, and it is increasingly untrue of historians as well. Initially dedicated to essays on culture-historical and other themes traditional at the time, the journal and its conference have morphed into offerings more akin to sociology and social issues. Paradigms happen.

Two of the explorers whose accounts I consulted about Ponca Fort and related sites were James Mackay and John Thomas Evans, who arrived at the Omaha Indian village of Ton-won-tonga (Big Village) near the present town of Homer, Nebraska, in the early winter of 1795. Sponsored by a St. Louis Spanish trading company, they built a trading post, Fort Charles, a few miles south of the Omaha village. In 1954 Champe sponsored a trip for me to visit the locale of that fort. Though I made a detailed inspection of early and contemporary maps and U.S. Department of Agriculture aerial photographs beforehand, the quest came to nothing, as, indeed, every similar quest by others has ended. The fort perhaps has eroded into the Missouri River, for its channel has swung from one side of the seventeen-mile-wide valley to the other in the years after Lewis and Clark. Fort Charles and Ponca Fort later would figure in my more extensive study of the Spanish expedition led by Mackay and Evans between 1795 and 1797 (Wood 1995b, 2003a).

I can no longer remember why I didn't use my research on Ponca Fort for a master's thesis, for eventually I settled on reporting four earthlodge villages near the mouth of Ponca Creek. In 1937 and 1938 the Nebraska State Archaeological Survey had excavated the Redbird I and Redbird II sites (25HT2 and 25HT3), the Wirth site (25KX4), and the Minarik site (25KX9). Like those from Ponca Fort, the materials from these sites resided in the artifact drawers in Champe's Laboratory of Anthropology. I christened these sites the Redbird Focus and arranged them in a sequence based on the presence of Euroamerican trade goods, Oneota pottery, and pottery-type frequencies, and estimated they dated to between about AD 1600 and 1700. I argued that the most parsimonious identification of their occupants would be the Ponca Indians, for they lived in this vicinity in the early historic period (Wood 1965). The identification admittedly remains questionable, though more plausible occupants have yet to be proposed.

My only teaching experience before I actually began to teach at the University of Missouri many years later was with Champe. I was his laboratory assistant for his course in physical anthropology, my duties being to teach the parts of the human skeleton. To avoid embarrassment and keep up with the students, I had to cram mightily every night to memorize the names of the landmarks on the skull from which we were to measure it and the nomenclature for the rest of the points on the skeleton. I still have facility in skeletal identification, though I recall most of the names of the lesser postcranial landmarks only when I see them.

Only one of my graduate courses at Nebraska stands out in my mind: a seminar in geography and anthropology that stressed the interrelatedness of environment and archaeology. This stimulating class was taught by an interesting combination of scholars, anthropologist E. Mott Davis and geographer Jonathan Sauer. Mott was the grandson of William Morris Davis, and Jonathan was the son of Carl O. Sauer, both of whom had been influential figures in the field of physical geography in the early twentieth century. The course introduced me to a wide range of topics in geography and further enhanced my interest in both the environment and ecological principles.

As I went through the artifact drawers in John's Laboratory of Anthropology collection, I chanced on a small tray that held a number of potsherds that obviously were of southwestern origin. I became so intrigued by them that I asked Champe's permission to visit the location recorded for them and see what could be found. Checking the legal description of their finding in western Nebraska, I left Lincoln with the anticipation of discovering something of real interest. Fred McEvoy, an undergraduate in the department, accompanied me, for his home was in or near the town of North Platte. The only unpleasant part of the trip was our arrival at the proper legal description, for it was barren grassland near a road in the middle of nowhere that contained absolutely nothing of archaeological interest. We returned to Lincoln to report our results to John; he seemed remarkably unconcerned about our failure. I believe he knew we'd find nothing, but he wanted to reward my curiosity.

The Redbird Focus Field Trip

Champe sponsored a far more exciting and productive field trip for me to northeastern Nebraska while I was writing my master's thesis. He provided funds for me to drive my aging DeSoto to check out what I would call the Redbird Focus sites near the mouth of Ponca Creek. It was a spartan voyage: I was alone, with a set of kitchen utensils borrowed from my apartment and the backseat of my car as a motel room. I visited the Redbird sites near the mouth of Ponca Creek in Holt County and then drove up the Niobrara to visit others. I made what surface collections I could and committed to notes and memory details of the sites. The trip was productive if uneventful until I headed south, to the Elkhorn River Valley. I was aware of sites in the valley near the town of Neligh that contained pottery reminiscent of Redbird pottery, and I visited a number of them (I ultimately decided they were not closely related). In doing so, I spent one of the most exhausting days of my life.

One afternoon I drove across an isolated part of a lowland pasture and over a wooden bridge, pursuing an elusive pottery lead that had been given me by a resident of Neligh. A few yards beyond the bridge my car wheels unexpectedly sank into the soft mud beneath the deceptively dry-looking grass. I got out and surveyed my car, sunk to both axles, miles from any possible help. I spent some time swearing in despair, then walked back to the bridge, removed two of the giant planks that formed its surface, and dragged them to the car. Using one of them as a support, I jacked up the car and placed the other board under one of the rear wheels. Repeating the process, I placed another board under the other rear wheel. Two more trips to the bridge yielded more boards. Again repeating the process, I set them under the front wheels. I then managed to back up perhaps six feet before a wheel slipped off one of the boards. I jacked up the car again and replaced the board. After more than six hours of hard labor I got the car back on solid ground, but it was then necessary to replace the boards on the bridge before I could back over it to safety. What the farmer must have thought when he saw the ruts in his pasture can only be imagined. But I slept soundly that night. Perhaps I dreamed of breaking rocks in a penitentiary.

I wrote my thesis, "The Redbird Focus," during the 1955–1956 academic year. Most of it was written late at night, after midnight, in the basement of Burnett Hall. It was eerily quiet save for occasional unidentified sounds, and one night I was nearly scared out of my wits when the night watchman silently approached the door and said loudly, "Hi there!" I asked him to please whistle as he approached next time. Scheduling made it necessary for me to defend my thesis that summer. I was in the field with Alan Woolworth in North Dakota at the time, but I took leave from work at the Demery site and drove to Lincoln, where I defended on July 20, 1956, with committee members John L. Champe, John M. Roberts, Franklin

Fenenga, and A. C. Land (geology). My friend Pete Miller supplied a brief R & R after the examination and took me motorboating and waterskiing on Lincoln's Oak Lake. I drove directly back to North Dakota to rejoin Alan in the field and was unable to return for the commencement the following month, though I went back to Lincoln for classes after the field season ended. I spent three semesters in residence in Lincoln completing the degree, and I eventually revised and published my thesis as Memoir 2 of the *Plains Anthropologist* (Wood 1965a).

Back to North Dakota

I returned to North Dakota in June 1955 to assist Alan Woolworth in another project. I drove out of Lincoln one noon, accompanied by an anthropology student from the East, Oriol Pi-Sunyer, who was to work with us that summer. Afternoon found us in east-central South Dakota, where the temperature was blistering and a hot dry wind was behind us. Periodically, I had to stop and let the car's radiator cool down, for it rapidly overheated and I could not drive west often enough to do much good. It was a tiring trip; thereafter I left Lincoln in the evening and drove through the cool of the night, arriving in Bismarck in the early morning. I never again met my passenger and co-worker after that summer. Oriol later taught at the University of Massachusetts–Amherst.

A few days after I arrived in Bismarck, Alan and I visited the Ward site (32BL3), a prehistoric village perched atop a high bluff within Bismarck's Pioneer Park, overlooking the Missouri River on the north side of the city. In about 1936 the city built three full-scale circular earthlodges on its site, but one after the other, they were consumed by fires set by careless picnickers. The last one was gutted by fire and collapsed in early June just before my arrival. I photographed its still-smoking ruins and noted a number of features that I thought might be useful to archaeologists excavating such structures. Principal among them was a crevice one to two feet wide that encircled the outer rim above the base of the leaner posts that rested against the wall posts. This feature undoubtedly accounts for the stratum of water-laid deposits sometimes seen near the walls in excavated lodges. It became the topic of a two-page note in the *Plains Anthropologist* that illustrated the forensic characteristics of a collapsed earthlodge (Wood 1957a).

It was probably Thad. C. Hecker who carried out excavations at Ward sometime before 1936, after which the city of Bismarck built the three lodges. The city engineers erected the circular form of lodge used by the historic Mandans, but they had some difficulty doing so on "the sub-rectangular type lodge floor" that had been excavated. "Up to that time it was assumed that all earth lodges in the area were of the [historic] circular type" (Will and Hecker 1944:81). This was the first recognition of the presence of the long-rectangular houses that typify the Middle Missouri tradition, a form that Hecker was to demonstrate fully when he excavated another of them in 1938 at the Huff site.

Our current concepts of the cultural developments in the Missouri Valley of North Dakota do not depart radically from the skeletal framework proposed in 1944 by George F. Will and Thad. C. Hecker in their *Upper Missouri River Valley Aboriginal Culture in North Dakota* (1944). There is good evidence that this framework was in large part devised by Hecker. At this date we will never know how much each of the two men contributed to this synthesis, but it is worth noting that the original manuscript, at the State Historical Society of North Dakota, is written in the purple ink that was the hallmark of most of Hecker's notes and manuscripts. For this reason, I feel we are more deeply indebted to this self-taught collector turned fieldworker than most of us in the past wanted to admit. Using little more than surface collections and historical documentation, Will and Hecker conceived a scheme that survives today under more precise terminology and definition.

Our project in 1955 was to investigate the Paul Brave site (32SI4), which was earlier known as the Fort Yates site but which we renamed to honor its former Lakota Sioux landowner. Gordon W. Hewes, of the University of North Dakota, had tested the site in 1947, and we proceeded to conduct formal excavations in three of the dwellings at this Middle Missouri tradition community. It was six miles south of the town of Fort Yates, lying on a high terrace between the riverbank and the abandoned Burlington Northern railroad grade that had become the "river road." The railroad had been completed from Mandan to the town of Cannon Ball, where the tracks ended, but the finished, unused rail bed provided an excellent road from Cannon Ball downriver to the former small (very small) town of Kenel, just south of the North Dakota–South Dakota boundary, where construction ended. The town of Fort Yates was then a small and isolated town served by gravel roads, though it was the headquarters for the Standing Rock Indian Reservation. The town had an aura of oldness about it. One Saturday, as I was checking a collection of postcards in the drugstore, I discovered a number of them bearing photographs of steamboats taken by local photographer Frank Fiske around the turn of the century. I bought their remaining stock and later donated them to the State Historical Society of North Dakota.

During my time in Bismarck I became acquainted with a collector of Indian artifacts named Martin Mossbrucker, who had done extensive digging at the historic Mandan Boley site north of Mandan. He'd found a rectangular chipped-stone celt during some construction in the city of Mandan, different from any found locally in archaeological sites, and asked me about it, for archaeologists are (usually) expected to know about such things. In this case I did, for I'd seen just such artifacts illustrated recently in the literature on the European Neolithic, and I told him as much. When he sent it to the Smithsonian for identification, he was informed it was chert of Scandinavian origin, and given the Viking lore that permeates North Dakota—based on discoveries of "mooring holes" and axes—this naturally ignited his imagination. My efforts to suggest that it had been lost by a recent Scandinavian migrant to the state went unheeded.

The river road north of Fort Yates crossed the Cannonball River, though there was no bridge over the stream at that time. During low water I normally crossed at a much-used ford and continued to Bismarck rather than detour several miles to the west. When William G. Buckles drove his Volkswagen "Bug" on this route, his wheels didn't reach the river's gravel bottom, but he simply drove into the stream and floated across the narrow channel to the other side. Bill worked with Wesley R. Hurt in the summer of 1959 at the Four Bear site (39DW2) in Dewey County, South Dakota. He later became an icon among the archaeologists in the Colorado Rocky Mountains.

Our field quarters were in town in the girls' dorm (it was vacant during the summer) of the Standing Rock Reservation Indian school. This location placed us in daily touch with resident Hunkpapa Lakotas and Yanktonai Nakotas, and we hired some of them as members of our crew. We sometimes attended local powwows with them. One special event stands out: I attended a reenactment of the December 1890 death of Sitting Bull at the site of his home on the Grand River in South Dakota. Indian police had gone to arrest this great Lakota leader, for James McLaughlin, the agent at Standing Rock Reservation, feared he would join the Ghost Dance that was disrupting other Sioux reservations. However, when Sitting Bull was taken from his home, he had been shot and killed by the Indian police, whereupon a fight broke out in which both police and Sitting Bull supporters were killed. Insofar as practical, the reenactors at this event were descendants of the original participants. When the Indian "police" swung the bodies of their "victims" into a horse-drawn wagon to haul their bodies away, they did so with such enthusiasm that we heard grunts and muttered oaths as the victims landed in the wagon bed atop one another: there was still animosity between the two groups of descendants.

Our quarters in the dormitory allowed us, for the first time in our field lives, to enjoy a truly comfortable camp with real beds. We took our breakfast and dinner in the Employees Club next door. The cook even packed lunches for us, but after several days of consuming the cold egg sandwiches he made from breakfast leftovers, we decided to drive back to town for lunch, and the quality of our meals improved dramatically. The summer was hot and humid, and we often ate our lunches in one of the immense bell-shaped pits in one of the houses. There was room on the shady side for us to place our backs against the cool wall, though our feet were in the sun. This was one of the most climatically miserable seasons I'd ever endured, and our custom after work was to stop at a bar on the south side of town for a cold beer (or two) before proceeding home. The bartender was told that when he saw us drive up, he was to open the proper number of beers and set them on the bar, ready for us when we walked in. He did so, and we consumed them with gusto.

The site was deeply buried in loess, and we used a bulldozer to strip the overburden down to within about a foot of the floor levels of the houses we excavated. Surface indications suggested there were at least nine other structures set on a terrace overlooking the Missouri River. The artifacts in them were virtually identical to those from the Thomas Riggs site (39HU1), which Wesley R. Hurt had excavated in 1952 near Pierre, South Dakota. There was no hint of fortification at our site, though air photographs later revealed a ditch at Thomas Riggs. One afternoon we were visited by George F. Will, North Dakota's renowned botanist-anthropologist; this was the only time I met him, for he died the following October. He was pleased to see the artifacts that he and Hecker had called "Archaic Mandan" and our fully exposed houses, for he'd never seen one fully exposed before, since the one Hecker had dug at Huff had been done piecemeal. Alan and I assigned the site to Hurt's Thomas Riggs focus (Hurt 1953; Wood and Woolworth 1964), but in 1966 Donald J. Lehmer, using the new classification of Gordon Willey and Philip Phillips (1958), more realistically reassigned it to the

Figure 15. The Paul Brave site, summer 1955. *Author's collection.*

Fort Yates phase of the Extended Middle Missouri tradition. Archaeologists agree that this tradition provides at least part of the foundation for the prehistoric Huff phase and, in turn, for the historic Mandan Indians.

The site yielded two polished elk canine teeth that had been perforated for suspension. I became curious about the use of such teeth, for I'd seen them on many women's costumes when I was a child watching Indian dances in Gordon. They were commonly placed in rows on their dresses, sometimes in the hundreds. A survey of the literature revealed that there was a functionally integrated cluster of traits in the use of these teeth that was valued by numerous village and nomadic groups in the Northern Plains. Such decorative elements likely first appeared in fourteenth-century sites believed to be ancestral to the historic Mandans and spread to other groups in the Northern Plains after about 1800. Their display on women's dresses in great numbers denoted wealth and prestige, their role being somewhat analogous to that of mink coats in past American culture. My paper reporting these conclusions was accepted for publication in *American Antiquity*, my first appearance in that journal (Wood 1957b).

I was responsible for describing the pottery from Paul Brave for our report. The material corresponded so closely to that from the Thomas Riggs site that I described it much as Glenn Kleinsasser had done in Wesley Hurt's (1953) report on that site. I did so, however, with reservations, and modified his classification by separating the recurved or S-shaped rims (which I called Fort Yates ware) from those with straight to flaring rims (which I called Riggs ware), using Don Lehmer's model for ceramic typology. Based on his experience in the American Southwest, Don had defined pottery types from the Dodd and Phillips Ranch sites in terms of wares, or as "groups of types which share a majority of basic characteristics including the fabric of the pottery itself, the general vessel form, the surface finish, and the basic rim form. The types which are included in the wares are primarily groups of similar rim sherds, all of which are decorated in more or less the same way" (Lehmer 1954:41). Following Don's lead, I redefined the pottery using rim form rather than decoration as a primary sorting device. I made the right choice, for Lehmer's typology remained the preferred one until the advent of attribute analysis, though many of the old types are still useful for some purposes.

In May 1812 the Spanish fur trader Manuel Lisa ascended the Missouri River from St. Louis with a party of traders and established a post, known today as Fort Manuel, just south of the present North Dakota–South Dakota boundary, a short distance from what would become the town of Kenel. In the 1930s the Works Project Administration erected an open stockade around the former location of the post, the decaying remnants of which were still visible in 1955. Not knowing that Hubert Smith would fully excavate the site a decade later (Smith and Ludwickson 1981), Alan and I took a small party to the locale one afternoon and dug small cross trenches across the trenches that had supported the post palisade that enclosed the fort. We discovered that the trenches were identical in dimensions to those we'd found at Kipp's Post, and we prepared a map of our work but did nothing further. Fort Manuel is perhaps best known for the fact that Toussaint Charbonneau and Sacagawea had accompanied Lisa's party, and that Charbonneau's wife (a "Snake" or Shoshone Indian) died there "of a putrid fever" in December 1812 (Luttig 1920:106). The fort was short-lived, however, and it was abandoned in the spring of 1813, having been in use for less than a year. Luttig's journal demolished the notion advanced by Grace R. Hebard in 1932 that Sacagawea lived to old age and died in Wyoming.

The following summer I joined Alan for a third season, this time with Frederick Hadleigh-West, who later worked in Alaska and still later edited the *Review of Archaeology*. He will remember the day I ran over a piglet in the society's station wagon, so injuring the animal that we had to shoot it. Fred shot it in the head twice, but the bullets ricocheted from hard parts on the skull with ominous whirring sounds; when I shot it between the eyes, the poor beast at last expired. It was the only animal I ever executed, for I've never been a hunter.

That summer we investigated the forty-acre Demery site (39CO1), which lay a few hundred yards south of the North Dakota–South Dakota boundary. Our inspection of a pottery surface sample before excavation intimated that the site contained a mixture of pottery typical of two separate and culturally distinct groups, one represented by horizontally incised ceramics and the other resembling that from local long-rectangular house villages such as Huff. We chose Demery to investigate because the horizontally incised pottery was far more common farther south on the Missouri River, and we hoped that our work would shed light on the northernmost reaches of the complex it represented. Thinking that Demery had two different components that might be stratified, we believed the site would aid in placing the groups in chronological order. When I later plotted the distribution of the pottery we excavated, it became clear that the two ceramics were evenly distributed in features across the site. We concluded that the village had a single component (Woolworth and Wood 1964).

The four houses we excavated were circular structures having four center posts, but they differed significantly from historic earthlodges in having no vertical outer wall posts. Apparently, the leaners or rafters rested on the ground surface outside a shallow house pit, with their upper ends supported on beams that connected the center posts. This kind of architecture meant that the houses would have been distinctly conical in profile, not dome shaped. Such steep-walled structures would have been far less roomy than historic Mandan or Arikara lodges. David Baerreis was especially intrigued by these distinctive lodges, and on one of his visits he carefully checked their floors to see if we'd missed the wall posts. Alan and I were perplexed as to how to interpret the position of the site in the taxonomic framework for the Missouri Valley, and recent scholarship by Craig Johnson (2007:180) reveals that the site's position in the regional culture-historical scheme remains problematical.

In my off-hours I investigated a group of four mounds which straddled the North and South Dakota boundary and which I named the Boundary Mounds (32SI1). Originally, the locality was believed to have been part of an Arikara village because of the presence of pottery and other debris on the surface (Will and Hecker 1944:88), though George Bird Grinnell reported that the Sioux had said it was of Mandan origin (Grinnell 1923:1:25). I chose to test one of the mounds that had been partially removed by a Burlington Northern Railroad cut, digging a cross trench that bisected it at right angles to the railroad cut. It yielded secondary human remains and artifacts in a subfloor pit that clearly were related to those of the Baldhill Mounds, found along the Sheyenne River in eastern North Dakota.

This 1956 work was one of the earliest systematic examinations of a mound on the Missouri River in the Dakotas. The first few mounds were dug in 1947 and 1948 in the lower reaches of the Fort Randall Reservoir (Lake Francis Case) in Charles Mix County, South Dakota, but they were never reported. In 1960 MRBS archaeologist Robert W. Neuman excavated the other three Boundary Mounds and described the group as part of the Woodland Sonota complex, which dates to between about AD 1 and 600. These mounds are now believed to be mortuary sites of the Besant phase, though the mode of burial and a few of the artifacts have distinctly Hopewellian or Middle Woodland overtones. Neuman's work revealed that whole or nearly entire bison carcasses had been placed around the central burial pit, something we'd not seen in our more limited work in the first mound. His discovery demonstrated the importance of bison for these Woodland people, a dependence that was strikingly reinforced by the large amount of bison bone he recovered from the Stelzer occupational site (39DW242) (Neuman 1975; Wood 1960b).

A nearby field party from the University of Wisconsin, led by David Baerreis, was digging the postcontact Spiry-Eklo Arikara site in the Missouri River bottom immediately south of the town of Mobridge. His crew was often the subject of jokes because one of their nearest neighbors was the "Mobridge Riding Academy," one of the rare open brothels in the state of South Dakota. We visited each other's field camps and had congenial wiener roasts on the banks of the Missouri.

I remained in Bismarck that fall to help Alan write up the report on Demery, and we shared an apartment about a mile from our office. That winter was a stark reminder of the region's continental climate. For several days running, my old Ford simply would not start, and I walked to work at temperatures of 40 degrees below zero, giving me firsthand experience with what the original residents of the region had to endure in their tipis and earth-covered lodges. I was led to believe that a temperature of 30 degrees below zero and a wind of 30 miles an hour was sufficient to freeze exposed flesh in 30 seconds. That's not hard to believe in a state where the average annual temperature ranges from 37 degrees in the northeast to 43 degrees along its southern border—not that far above freezing! A few years earlier I'd experienced a day of 120-degree heat while I was with Fenenga at Buffalo Pasture, a temperature range of 160 degrees.

One day, I have no idea what year it was, Russell Reid called me to his office and introduced me to a Mr. White. "Mr. White" was interested in some of our museum materials, and Reid told me, "Please help him find what he needs." Because Alan was elsewhere, I dutifully did so, but I was mightily miffed later to discover that "Mr. White" had been none other than Dr. Leslie A. White. This renowned anthropologist, noted for his contributions to cultural and social evolution, was at the time following the travels of Lewis Henry Morgan as part of his preparation for editing *Lewis Henry Morgan: The Indian Journals, 1859–62*, published in 1959. White did not explain his goals or reveal his identity, and he left without my recognizing this icon of cultural anthropology.

Despite having been born in Nebraska, I sometimes think of myself as having multiple home states, including Missouri and North Dakota. Except for summer and temporary jobs with the MRBS, my first professional position after getting my bachelor's degree was as Alan Woolworth's assistant between 1954 and 1956. I've returned to North Dakota many times since, each time with a sense of homecoming. I've always been grateful to Alan for his kindness and generosity. I was his assistant, not a co-principal investigator, yet he granted me coauthorship on the Kipp's Post, Paul Brave, and Demery reports, going so far as to give me senior authorship on the Paul Brave report. Each of these studies became River Basin Surveys Papers published by the Smithsonian Institution's Bureau of American Ethnology. The field and laboratory experience I gained, and the further education I received from Alan in the methods of ethnohistory, were to be foundations for much of my future work. Alan gave me my first real job, initiated me into historic-sites archaeology, and treated me as an equal partner in everything we did at North Dakota. I'll never forget his helpfulness to me as a fledgling archaeologist.

5

The University of Missouri, Round One

The Great Plains are in many respects the perfect place. They're so big that you could never know all there is to know about them—your fantasies could never wear them out.

— Ian Frazier, *Great Plains*, 1989

I Leave North Dakota

Work at the State Historical Society of North Dakota was interesting, instructive, and professionally rewarding, though at the time I didn't realize how valuable it had been. But correctly or not, I felt the position was essentially a dead end, and one that also paid very poorly, and I was set on saving money so I could go on for my doctorate. Russell Reid, the immensely popular superintendent of the society, had been deeply affected by the Great Depression, and he handled the finances of the society accordingly, on occasion turning back money he'd not spent by the end of the fiscal year. Had either Alan or I stayed with the society, it's likely that one of us would have become its future superintendent, for our archaeological successor was James E. Sperry, who became superintendent after Ray Mattison, who had replaced Russell after his death in 1967. Jim remained in that position until he retired in about 2000. Jim was also a product of John Champe and obtained his M.A. from him shortly after I left Nebraska. Jim's tenure at the society was marked by its move into the new North Dakota Heritage Center.

In 1956 both Alan and I began searching for new positions. In April, Alan obtained a position at the Dearborn Historical Museum in Dearborn, Michigan, though in 1960 he moved to the Minnesota Historical Society in St. Paul, where he remained until (and after) he retired. My first nibble came when Preston Holder called and offered me a job as his assistant in the salvage excavation of a mound in or near Cahokia Mounds State Park, Illinois. I didn't accept the offer, for I was well aware of his eccentric nature and I also had reservations about the move, especially since it was a temporary position. Holder was once characterized by James Howard as "brilliant, irascible, and non-productive," and his nickname was "the penis [a euphemism] of the Plains," a sobriquet more commonly applied to the Nebraska state capitol building. Among many stories that could be told of him, I witnessed one episode: while hotel staff members were preparing to set up a cash bar at a Plains Conference in Oklahoma, Preston casually nudged an entire basket of glasses onto the floor. As the staff was cleaning up the shattered mess, Preston slipped a bottle of Chivas Regal into his pocket and invited several of us to his room.

Soon after declining Holder's offer, I was contacted by Carl H. Chapman, director of the American Archaeology Division at the University of Missouri in Columbia. We had met in 1953 when I stopped briefly in Columbia to visit the university on my drive back to Lincoln from the annual meeting of the Society for American Archaeology in Bloomington, Indiana. We had lunch at the Heidelberg Restaurant, which was to become a familiar haunt in later years. Carl was now seeking someone to conduct a survey of the Pomme de Terre Reservoir in southwestern Missouri. Almost no archaeological work had been done in the area, and the region had acquired a lackluster reputation because of its hilly terrain and its location, so remote from the more exciting complexes to be found along the Mississippi River and in the vicinity of Kansas City. Once I was asked what I expected to learn from those "prehistoric hillbillies"—snobbery was afoot. In any event, Reid was gracious about our departure and took Alan and me out to dinner the evening before I left North Dakota. My years there had been a pleasant and invigorating period that provided an immense professional boost I could hardly have imagined at the time.

Columbia, Missouri

The dam on the Pomme de Terre River, then under construction by the Army Corps of Engineers, was about two miles south of the town of Hermitage, the county seat of Hickory County, on the northwestern rim of the Ozark Highland. Chapman had done limited survey and excavation in the reservoir in 1952, but a resurvey of the reservoir and the excavation of any significant sites that might be found were to be supported through a cooperative agreement with the National Park Service. The dam was being built just downstream from the junction of Lindley Creek with the Pomme de Terre, so the reservoir was shaped like a giant, lopsided Y. I accepted the assignment, and the reservoir survey and its write-up were to consume the next two years of my life.

I arrived in Columbia and was at the university, ready for work, on April 1, 1957. It is a beautiful campus, the older red-brick buildings surrounding an expansive quadrangle graced by the standing columns of Academic Hall, all that remains after fire destroyed the building in January 1892. The original tombstone of President Thomas Jefferson at Monticello was then on the lawn in front of the administration building, Jesse Hall. After his reburial Jefferson's heirs had presented the stone to the university to honor the first state university to be founded in Jefferson's Louisiana Purchase. It was later moved to a more visible position on the quadrangle. Columbia is also noted for a prominent women's educational institution, Stephens College, though actor George C. Scott also attended there years ago. Columbia was in addition the "home" of Miss Mizzou, a seductive character in Milton Caniff's 1950s comic strip, "Steve Canyon."

The office of the American Archaeology Division was then, as it would be for many years, in the basement (of course!) of Switzler Hall, Room 15. My yearly salary as a research associate was a munificent $3,900. Richard A. Marshall, who would obtain his M.A. from Chapman the following year, also was a research associate in the division, though we rarely interacted outside the office, for he did most of his work in the bootheel of southeastern Missouri. Richard O. Keslin, my old friend from Buffalo Pasture days, was teaching in Columbia and working on his dissertation on the role of salt as an element of cultural diffusion. I met the legendary Jesse Wrench, founder of the Missouri Archaeological Society and a living symbol of the university, just once before leaving Columbia for my duty station the following day.

Arriving in Hermitage, I checked into the Lightfoot Hotel (now Lightfoot Hardware) and rented a room from kindly old Mr. Lightfoot. Armed with topographic maps and site forms, I began surveying the river bottomlands near the dam site the next day, slowly working my way south and up the reservoir. I had no idea what to expect. The archaeology of Missouri was as yet a mystery to me, though I had no trouble fitting into the local and very rural scene. My summers as a farm boy in Montgomery

County were a great help in my relations in this small farming community. I gained the friendship of a number of townsfolk and even accompanied some of them to the Missouri State Fair in Sedalia, where we met and talked with Sally Rand after one of her celebrated fan dances. She'd been born in the nearby small town of Elkton and was a local celebrity. Many of the roads in the area were still graveled, and I've never before had such a row of flat tires. The gravel was crushed local limestone that contained nodules of chert, and the resulting razor-sharp flakes made driving those roads after they'd been freshly graveled hazardous indeed.

The small town of Hermitage was graced with a brick county courthouse built in 1896 and an equally ancient stone jail boasting a strap-steel door, windows, and cells—accommodations that are illegal today. I soon became friends with the county sheriff, a man known to friend and foe alike as "Scab" Taylor (a term derived, I was told, from earlier horse-trading days). We often had coffee together, and he told me about the seamier side of Hickory County. Friend or not, I couldn't at first bring myself to call him "Scab" to his face as others did. After a stint at the Lightfoot Hotel I rented a farmhouse about a mile south of town that provided room for my crew that summer, though we ate in restaurants in town for very reasonable prices. I recall that breakfasts generally were only forty-five cents for coffee, toast, and an egg. I don't remember what we left as a tip, but it would have been equally modest.

This was my first experience in dealing directly with landowners, for I had to obtain permission to enter those lands that were still in private hands. One of the first landowners I approached asked me, "Why are you doing this?" I expected a refusal, but to my relief, at the end of my impassioned delivery on the merits of archaeology he said, "Huh. Well, you never know until you ask. Go ahead." Perhaps the most contrary statement was one I heard on the streets of Shelby, Montana, seven years earlier when I worked in the Tiber Reservoir. A passerby noticed the government license plates on our pickup and asked me what we were doing. Following my explanation, he snarled, "Well, I've been a Democrat all my life [Harry S Truman was president then], but I've never heard of anything so goddamned stupid in all my life!" I stared at his back as he stalked off, happily spared the necessity of a response.

As I trudged the fields and hills that spring, I soon gained a field assistant: Rolland E. Pangborn, who lived in a small town nearby with the unlikely name of Humansville. Rolland was picking a guitar in a Springfield,

Missouri, nightclub at the time, but the opportunity to be paid for what he'd done in his spare time for years (look for artifacts) was too great a temptation. He was an eager and fast-learning field technician and soon became a valued member of the American Archaeology Division. Chapman later hired him as a research associate, which he remained until his death in June 1981. A meticulous field man and recorder, he directed a number of digs, especially of rock-and-earth mounds in southwestern Missouri, and we coauthored several conference papers and publications on our fieldwork. I always had Rolland seek a landowner's permission for me to dig, for as a local who often knew the owner's friends or relatives, Rolland could speak their dialect, was privy to local events, and was able to talk the most recalcitrant landowner into letting us work on his property.

By June we'd surveyed as much of the reservoir as was practical, and after my crew assembled later that month to begin digging, we worked until September. Much of our work involved burial tumuli—the Mount India Cairn, the Holbert Bridge Mound, and the Murelle Mound, for example—and we tested miscellaneous surface sites with a mechanical ditch digger to detect stratigraphy, though these investigations yielded little in the way of useful information. My first visit to the Murelle Mound introduced me to a midwestern delicacy, morel mushrooms. The mound was blanketed with them, and I gathered nearly a grocery shopping bag full of them, more than I've ever seen since. The next morning it was raining, and we sautéed them in a giant iron skillet smothered in butter and ate our fill (they taste like beefsteak).

I moved to Columbia that fall and began writing up the results of my summer's work. My laboratory was in a World War II surplus Quonset hut set next to the Student Health building, a few steps west of Switzler Hall. It was a quiet and secluded niche, for aside from my ample workspace, the other end of the building was used for storage. But it could also be lonely and claustrophobic, so I welcomed the occasional visitor. It was a bit chilly in the winter, but fortunately I didn't have to endure working there during truly hot weather, though there was a fan to bring in fresh air to cool the metal building. I had more than enough room to spread out the hundreds of projectile points from my survey that spring and the artifact yield from the summer's excavations. I now embarked on a crash course in the modest literature on the prehistory of Missouri.

One of the major problems I faced that fall was the lack of a frame of reference for the sites I'd investigated. No archaeological work of significance had been carried out locally, and I'd found no caves or rockshelters within the reservoir that could offer me a stratigraphic sequence. When I mentioned my dilemma to Rolland, he solved my problem, telling me about Blackwell Cave (23HI172), on the Pomme de Terre about a mile north of Hermitage. A visit to the site led me to believe it was likely to have deep deposits. It fulfilled its promise during excavations the following season, for its five-foot deposits were nicely stratified, both physically and culturally, and provided a solid temporal framework for the region.

I was of course still thinking in terms of the Midwestern Taxonomic Method's components and foci; it took some time for Willey and Phillips's (1958) scheme to take hold in American archaeology, and Missouri certainly was not leading the pack in adopting it. I augmented these units in a synthesis of my work by using the idea of an *aggregate* (borrowed from Robert J. Braidwood) and *complex* (for sites that might conceivably become foci with the accumulation of more data). I tried to follow the lead of Irving Rouse in correlating my finds, though he later expressed reservations in a letter to me about how I'd merged his ideas with other elements. My synthesis nonetheless represented, as Michael O'Brien generously said, "a historical point of introduction of a formal methodological approach to Missouri archaeology" that "has withstood the test of time" (O'Brien 1996: 243, 245, Figure 5.20).

Indeed, the cave's stratigraphy illuminated the chronology for two important projectile point types, Afton and Sedalia (or Nebo Hill). Lanceolate points were found with Afton points in the same pre-pottery stratum. The lanceolate specimens were much thinner than Nebo Hill and Sedalia points, but they nonetheless lent early support to the fact that Nebo Hill and Sedalia points were Late Archaic in age and not Paleoindian forms, as their lanceolate form initially suggested. Furthermore, I also found Afton points in the Holbert Bridge Mound, a discovery that provided the first clue to the burial complex of their makers (Wood 1961:101–102). This mound and the Hatten Mound (23MN275), excavated by Dale R. Henning in 1961 in the Salt River drainage in northeastern Missouri (Klepinger and Henning 1976), were among the earliest regional indications that mound interment began in the Late Archaic and was not solely a marker for the Woodland period. These findings were to help shape a new paradigm for midwestern archaeology.

Another important site we investigated in 1958 was Vista Rockshelter (23SR20). It contained sherds of shell-tempered pottery that I initially hoped would document an Osage Indian occupation. But a close inspection of the pottery quickly disproved that assumption, dashing the hope of finding a prehistoric Osage site, not one of which has ever been discovered. Instead, the pottery was not distinguishable from that found in late prehistoric Steed-Kisker villages near Kansas City. An analysis of the animal bone in the shelter, following the techniques advocated by Theodore White (1956), and an understanding of the remains in the Kansas City area villages, led to the hypothesis that the shelter was a hunting camp of the Steed-Kisker focus and that Vista was a site-unit intrusion of that complex in the Osage River Basin (Wood 1968). The speculation that the hunters at Vista returned smoked or dried meat to their villages in the Kansas City area—sites that are notable for their lack of bone—seems agreeable to those who have more recently studied the Steed-Kisker sites and the aboriginal exploitation of bison in Missouri. Long-range bison hunts apparently characterized this prehistoric complex, as they did many historic Plains and Prairie-Plains groups. Though the 1968 paper accurately anticipated much of the taphonomic research of the 1980s and early 1990s, it had little impact on the literature at the time, likely because American archaeologists were then more interested in diet than in behavior. The analytic techniques first developed by White, and which I applied at Vista, became commonplace only in the 1970s and early 1980s with the development of similar methods in Africa to address questions of hominid origins.

In the fall of 1957 I took a brief vacation and drove to Colorado, where Bonnie L. Humphrey and I were married in her home in Montrose on September 7. We'd met about a year earlier at the wedding of mutual friends in Lincoln. We returned to Hermitage and took up residence in the abandoned but partially furnished farm home I'd rented just south of town, for I was still involved in fieldwork. The house was more than rustic: most new brides hardly anticipate having field mice jump out of the silver drawer.

During this general period I sometimes engaged in fruitless investigations. An unspecified group of Shawnee Indians is documented on an 1819 General Land Office map in Benton County as living in "Old Shawney Town" on the south bank of the Osage River directly opposite the mouth of the South Grand River. Today the locality is beneath the waters of the Harry S. Truman Reservoir about a mile upstream from the dam near Warsaw, Missouri. When I visited the locality with a metal detector, I found no trace of metal, so perhaps the site had been buried beneath overbank deposits left by the Osage River. On another occasion I investigated some remains along the Osage River in Vernon County that were, I hoped, the ruins of Fort Carondelet, a trading post built for trade with the Osage Indians in 1794 by Pierre Chouteau, but they turned out to be the remains of a long-abandoned farm home. About this time I also visited a farmer in the St. Louis suburb of Chesterfield who had reported mastodon bones to the Missouri Archaeological Society. When I asked to be taken to the site, however, he demurred because the bones were not on his property, and he would not reveal the landowner's name because he'd been trespassing, so I returned to Columbia empty-handed and with no data to compensate for the trip. Such wasted endeavors are well known to any field archaeologist.

Ozark Highland Mound and Cairn Sites

Many of the sites my crews excavated in the Pomme de Terre, Stockton, and Kaysinger Bluff (later renamed Harry S. Truman) Reservoirs were mound or cairn sites that were dug over the course of nearly two decades, but it's parsimonious to deal with them collectively here. Thousands of these burial sites are scattered on hills throughout the Ozark Highland. Most of them are on bluff tops or ridges or on gently sloping ground not far from the crests of ridges, invariably with a commanding view of the adjoining river bottoms. I spent most of the summers of 1964 and 1965 excavating them in the Stockton Reservoir. Rolland Pangborn assumed most of the responsibility for their excavation after 1966, when my grant from the National Science Foundation led to a greatly expanded excavation program at Rodgers Shelter.

These burial sites either consist of cairns, composed principally of stones gathered from the surrounding hilltop, or contain rock and earth that was scraped from the nearby ground surface, with every intermediate combination of materials. Many of them are low and inconspicuous, but others, especially large cairns, may be spotted from a distance. We excavated many of these tumuli, not because they would be inundated but because they would be subject to disturbance from construction and from shoreline activities after the lakes filled. Virtually every one of them contained a pothole in its center, some of them quite ambitious: looters had dug two feet into the fractured limestone bedrock at the base of Mound 3, a very large cairn at the Fairfield Mound Group. During our excavation of its four structures in 1958, we loaded the spoil into wheelbarrows and made new circular heaps of the stone nearby. Later visits to the hilltop revealed potholes in the centers of these new "cairns."

Cairns especially were havens for small wildlife, some harmless and some not. I lifted one stone at the Mount India Cairn to find a copperhead as thick as my arm awaiting me, but I moved significantly faster than it did and it paid with its life for trespassing on my site. I was less alarmed to find a five-foot-long blacksnake in another mound, but I was stung by other denizens of the structures. Scorpions are common in southwestern Missouri, and I was stung twice on the hand, once at the cairn containing the blacksnake and again at the Holbert Bridge Mound. In both instances the sting was only moderately painful (wasps hurt more), but a little later my arm became numb to my shoulder: I could move it, but there was absolutely no feeling in it. Happily, the numbness vanished in about an hour. Chiggers were common nuisances, and ticks left us scratching for days after removing them by whatever means. One morning at breakfast during our survey of the Harry S. Truman Reservoir in 1976 or 1977, a crewman who'd been complaining of an earache canceled a trip to the doctor after a fat tick smothered in wax crawled out of his ear (some of the women on the crew left the table). But he was saved the expense of an office call.

I was also startled to find tarantulas in two mounds in the Stockton Reservoir that were either living among the rocks or going into hibernation. Though these spiders may attain the diameter of a dinner plate, they are not the things of science fiction, for they are harmless. I took one of them home one weekend in a wire cage to show my children. It attracted dozens of small fry from all over the neighborhood, and after appropriate admiration they hurried away to tell their friends. Word spread quickly, and within minutes I had an equally large and appreciative audience of gaping parents. I took my specimen back to the woods and released it where I'd abducted it, though most residents of the area took care to drive over them when they saw them on the road.

We spent considerable time seeking village sites in the lowlands that might be associated with these Late Woodland to Mississippian cemeteries, but to no avail. Eventually, I defined two closely related Late Woodland burial complexes, the Fristoe and Bolivar complexes, though today I'm more than dubious that they have any taxonomic validity. The burials within them were extraordinarily diverse, including primary extended and flexed inhumations, bundle burials, cremations, and extremely fragmentary burned and unburned remains that were scattered throughout the mound fill. The latter remains I called "broadcast burials." The artifacts buried with them were likewise highly variable in type and number (Wood 1967a; Wood and Brock 1984, 2000).

The Eureka Mound (23DA250) contained a Caddoan water bottle of the type Spiro Engraved, dated to about AD 1000–1450. This perfectly proportioned, delicately engraved vessel is superior in form and decoration to any other such vessel I've seen in collections in Oklahoma. What was it doing in a modest Late Woodland mound in Missouri? In the course of our work we discovered that this rock-and-earth burial tradition in the western Missouri Ozarks began in the Late Archaic and remained remarkably stable through the Woodland and Mississippian periods and into the historic era despite the widespread changes that were taking place in other spheres of life. The Holbert Bridge Mound was a Late Archaic mound, yet the Comstock Mound (23DA221) was clearly historic, for it contained Euroamerican trade goods that dated to about AD 1800. Nothing in the content of the latter mound was definitive, though the date and its location suggest it might be of Osage Indian origin.

My two sons, Stanley and Eric, later helped me in the field during a number of field seasons. Eric's major contribution was as a crew member during the excavation of Phillips Spring. In 1974 this important site yielded seeds and rinds of squash seeds in a sealed Late Archaic horizon, augmenting other evidence from east of the Mississippi River that the Eastern Agricultural complex had begun by 4,300 years ago (Chomko and Crawford 1978). Indeed, today these remains constitute the earliest evidence of domesticated squash (*Cucurbita pepo*) in eastern North America (Smith 2006:12225–12226). Son Stanley helped excavate a number of mounds and cairns and was a useful member of the flotation crew at Rodgers Shelter. Both boys also contributed labor when we excavated circular earthlodges in the summer of 1969 at the Extended Coalescent Lower Grand site in South Dakota and long-rectangular houses at the Extended Middle Missouri Cross Ranch site in North Dakota. Because of their small size, they could work in cache pits that were uncomfortably cramped for grown-ups. By the time Stanley took introductory archaeology at the University of Missouri, he had more and broader field experience than most doctoral candidates. He took a major in geography at the university in Columbia, becoming a computer-cartographer with the Center for Agriculture, Resource, and Environmental Systems (CARES). He prepared the many

Figure 16. Elbert Stanley Wood as a sergeant on National Guard maneuvers, 1983. *Author's collection.*

Figure 17. Eric Wood in imitation of Abraham Lincoln, 1990. *Author's collection.*

Figure 18. After my daughter Marigene's wedding, August 1992. *Left to right*: Rudi Holtkamp, Marigene Holtkamp, the author, and Carolee Wood. *Author's collection.*

fine maps that illustrate the chapters in my edited volume *Archaeology on the Great Plains* (1998); later he moved to a private computer-based firm. My daughter, Marigene, became the accountant for a Columbia paint firm and married Rudi Holtkamp, a native of the Netherlands. All of them live not far from me in Columbia.

The Jaguar Gorget

I'd found no historic Indian sites in the Pomme de Terre Reservoir during my early survey, and discussions with Rolland Pangborn in 1957 led him to tell me about a group of mounds and cairns near the little town of Fairfield. They were set on a high, juniper-mantled hill at the confluence of the Pomme de Terre and Little Pomme de Terre Rivers a few miles south of the town of Warsaw. On a visit to the site we retrieved two brooches of white metal, some thin shell-tempered sherds, and a large Rice side-notched projectile point/knife from Mound 2. The trade goods and pottery finds suggested an Osage Indian (or perhaps Steed-Kisker) component, so we planned excavations for the following summer at what I named the Fairfield Mound Group (23BE6).

Rolland and I lived in a stripped-out school bus while we dug there. We parked it at the base of the hill and cooked our meals beside it, but we spent part of the evening on the porch of the grocery store in Fairfield. Driving the bus to and from Columbia on weekends was a challenge; buses don't weave easily in and out of traffic, and since Interstate 70 was still under construction, it was necessary to drive across the old steel bridge at Boonville. The bridge had a steel mesh floor through which we could see the river below, and although it was an illusion, it felt as though the vehicle was weaving from side to side as we crossed the bridge. This was especially distressing when we met the ever-present eighteen-wheelers on the span. Because our vehicles at that time were purchased from state surplus, I also drove a World War II army repair truck and an army ambulance for a while. We nicknamed the ambulance the "Big Black Borheygi" in honor of a memorable, Hungarian-born archaeologist who taught at the University of Missouri in 1952 and who later became the director of the Milwaukee Public Museum.

One beautiful fall day Rolland and I were slowly clearing away the sediment that separated the closely spaced stones in Mound 2. As we knelt on sun-toasted bedrock in the hot afternoon sun, digging near the center of the feature, we exposed several Scallorn and Rice side-notched points, then a ground-stone "mammiform object" that resembled a large and bloated golf tee. Next I exposed a curved white surface, the convex side up. Brushing away the dirt, I noticed it was in two pieces, and I carefully removed half of it and handed it to Rolland. He brushed the concave side clean with the proverbial camel's-hair brush and then exclaimed as I removed the other half, "It has writing on it!" When we delicately cleaned and fitted both halves, we saw the engraved image of a jaguar. It was the most exotic thing I'd found in my then-brief career as an archaeologist (indeed, it still is), and it created a minor sensation when I took it to Columbia.

The autumn after its discovery I began a literature search for comparable specimens. But the imagery on the gorget is unique in American Indian art. The only comparable artwork I could find was in Warren K. Moorehead's illustrations of figures engraved on bone from the Hopewell mound group in Ohio. One of them, said to represent an ocelot, was somewhat reminiscent of the jaguar's style but nonetheless different (Moorehead 1922: Figure 64). He also illustrated a polished mammiform object said to be of slate, and though it was broader and perhaps larger than the one from the Fairfield mound, the forms were undeniably similar.

To seek further information, I forwarded a drawing made by Eleanor Chapman of the specimen to James (Jimmy) B. Griffin at the University of Michigan's Museum of Anthropology. He responded that he believed it represented a general Hopewell to Late Hopewell specimen. I found it parsimonious, on the basis of that information, to identify the gorget as of Hopewell inspiration, particularly in view of the gray siltstone mammiform object that was found near it, an identification reinforced by Waldo Wedel's recovery of similar artifacts at the Renner site, north of Kansas City, the type site of "Kansas City Hopewell." Wedel also found a number of points at Renner that are classifiable as Rice side-notched, almost matching those found with the gorget. Eventually, I concluded that the principal component at Mound 2 was part of a Late Woodland complex that contained "specifically Hopewell traits," including shaped wolf maxillae, the gorget, and the shale mammiform.

The image of the jaguar has adorned Missouri Archaeological Society flyers and other publications for years and has been a favorite logo for the University of Missouri's anthropology department. It inspired the acronym PUMA for the department's 1995 one-time student publication, *Publica-*

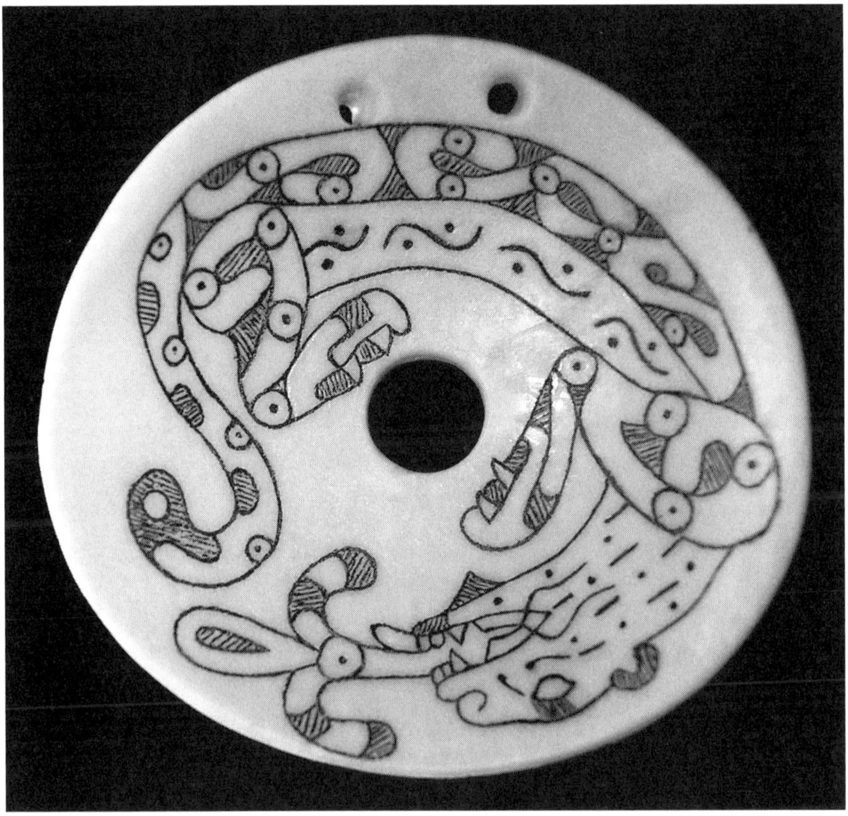

Figure 19. Cast of the jaguar gorget from the Fairfield Mound 2, Missouri, 1958 (9.8 by 10.4 centimeters). *Author's collection.*

tions of the University of Missouri Anthropologists. One of our former graduate students even has it tattooed on his arm, and it provides the logo for the Northern Jaguar Project, a foundation dedicated to conserving this magnificent feline. The discovery of this artifact was an exciting event, but its subsequent history provides instructive lessons in the interpretation of prehistory.

When I was in graduate school at the University of Oregon (1958–1961), I decided to pursue the identity of this feline image further when I took a course in primitive art from Theodore E. Stern. I sent a copy of its image to a number of authorities in the southeastern United States and asked their opinion of the specimen. Their letters generally agreed that the figure was reminiscent of eastern culture, but William Haag, of Louisiana

State University, responded that "it is the first object I have seen that looks really 'Mexican' or Middle American to me that has come from central United States" (letter of April 25, 1960).

However, the response from Alfonso Caso, of the Instituto Nacional Indigenista in Mexico City, was negative. He wrote that the "speech symbol" on the jaguar resembled nothing in the art of Mesoamerica, and he found no parallels in Mesoamerican art to the marks on the jaguar's body (letter of April 21, 1960). Caso's response, while of course accurate, ignored the importance of the jaguar in Mesoamerican art. Nonetheless, on the basis of these conflicting comments, I discarded the idea of a term paper on the gorget and instead prepared an analysis of the patterns that were incised on the shoulders of Plains village pottery vessels. It was a far more satisfying project that I later published in *American Antiquity* (Wood 1962). My analysis of those patterns reaffirmed Franz Boas's assertion on the essential unity of Plains art, for I found that a static, geometric, rectilinear pattern of embellishment characterized the pottery vessels of the late prehistoric and historic periods. This conclusion also was in line with the fundamental sexual dichotomy in Plains art, in which women created geometric forms and men created life forms.

Carl Chapman never accepted the Hopewell affiliation of my jaguar. Indeed, he assigned the specimen to the Mississippian tradition in the popular book he coauthored with his wife, Eleanor, *Indians and Archaeology of Missouri*. The conflict in attribution boils down to an identification based on the age of the artifact versus the age of its context. Judging by its distinctive art style, we have no reason to question that both the gorget and the mammiform are of Middle Woodland inspiration, if not manufacture. Regardless of the age of the gorget, it reveals important parallels with a significant religious motif in Mesoamerica. In countless Mayan glyphs the jaguar figures as a symbol of the underworld. Nevertheless, Richard A. Diehl has told me that every Mesoamerican archaeologist to whom he showed the design agreed that the jaguar resembles no known Mesoamerican art style.

Philip Phillips and James A. Brown treated the gorget in detail in their study of the shell engravings from the Craig Mound at Spiro, Oklahoma, reinforcing the Middle Woodland derivation of the specimen. They note that engraving on shell may be traced back at least to Hopewellian times, if not before, though Hopewellians preferred to engrave on bone, especially on human bone. Hopewell art was elaborate and often realistic, and

Phillips and Brown named one of their styles the "Fairfield style," using the Fairfield jaguar as the type specimen. They also compared it with the "ocelot" engraved on bone from the Ohio Hopewell site (Phillips and Brown 1978:157–158). In short, the Middle Woodland derivation of the style seems assured.

For decades, the complex Mississippian earthworks and associated materials in the southeastern United States were believed to derive, in some fashion, from prototypes in central Mexico. This idea led archaeologists to "see" relations between the two areas when in fact there are none, for it seemed obvious to them that the elaborate developments in the Southeast had been influenced by the high cultures of Mexico. Today, rather than view the complex of Mississippian features as deriving from Mesoamerica, we see that developments in the eastern United States have a long and independent history that does not require an outside source for their genesis. If there is any relation between the Mesoamerican concept of the jaguar and the animal depicted on the Fairfield gorget, it represents some form of stimulus diffusion from Central America. Like many of my colleagues, I prefer to think of our southwestern Missouri artifact as an independent use of the jaguar motif (Wood 1999).

A footnote: when I published the conclusions reached in Wood 1999, I titled it "The Jaguar Gorget: 'The Missouri State Artifact'" to acknowledge its forty-year popularity as an icon of Missouri archaeology. Later, as I was visiting with a fellow archaeologist, he asked me when the state legislature approved the bill authorizing its status. I was surprised by the question and said it had never done so, to which he responded, "You can't do that!" However, the state has never prosecuted me for my indiscretion.

The Loftin Site

At the conclusion of my summer's work in the Pomme de Terre, other projects demanded attention. Carl Chapman and Richard Marshall had begun investigations in 1956 at the Loftin site (23SN42) in the Table Rock Reservoir. They used a mechanical ditch digger to cut nearly a mile of trenches in this village and mound site on the immense terrace at the junction of the James and White Rivers in southern Stone County. The trenches exposed what were believed to be house floors, but premature flooding of the reservoir in June 1957 placed these remains under seventy-five feet of water. The Corps of Engineers had underestimated the potential rainfall of the area, and rising waters overtook dam construction, so water poured through the unfinished central part of the dam in a miniature Niagara Falls. Our site was not exposed again until September, when a thick layer of silt blanketed everything. For a time, we had to reach the site by boat from the south side of the river. One day, as we were pulling into shore, we were momentarily startled when something began flopping about on the floor of the boat. It turned out to be an eighteen-inch-long carp that served as dinner (for some of us) that evening. It had become caught between the boat and the shore, and to escape, it literally jumped from the river into the frying pan.

Rolland Pangborn and I were delegated to examine the suspected house features at the Loftin site and verify their identity. They were indeed houses, and we excavated Houses 1 and 2 in October and November and did some preliminary work on the mound. I was intrigued to find that both houses were square structures supported by four center posts, remarkably similar to the Central Plains tradition houses with which I was familiar in Nebraska (except there were no posts in the corners of our Loftin houses). House 1 had burned and left charred timbers on its floor in such a fashion that they yielded architectural details rarely recovered in such structures in the Ozarks. We left Loftin with the onset of cold weather, going directly to the Plains Conference in Lincoln. However, Rolland and I returned to the site in July 1958 and excavated House 3. One afternoon, as we shovel-skimmed the house floor and carried out routine recording, two hunters approached and sat on a backdirt pile for nearly an hour, watching us and engaging in idle conversation. Finally, one of them became exasperated and blurted out, "Just what the *hell* are you people doing?" We gave them credit for their patience: they'd tried to figure it out for themselves.

Chapman and Dale Henning later returned to excavate Houses 4 and 5 and to investigate the complex structure of the mound at this prehistoric civic-ceremonial center. The mound and houses were identified as components of Caddoan culture, better known from sites in eastern Oklahoma (Wood, ed. 1983). The houses had either two or four center posts, an architectural form common in Caddoan settlements farther to the south and west. Though occasional Caddoan pottery and other trade artifacts are found in southwestern Missouri sites (witness the Eureka Mound, 23DA250 and its Spiro Engraved water bottle), the Loftin component remains unique as a Caddoan site-unit intrusion in the White River drainage. It probably dates to about AD 1000–1180.

6

Graduate School in Oregon

While I've not lost my pleasure in wooded hollows,
I've come to cherish absolute treelessness.

— William Least Heat-Moon, *PrairyErth*, 1991

Eugene, Oregon

The work in Missouri was valuable experience, but I was anxious to return to school, for without a doctorate one's choices were, and still are, limited in the archaeological job market. Luther S. Cressman, preeminent among the archaeologists in the Great Basin (and known as the first husband of Margaret Mead), was head of the department at the University of Oregon in Eugene. He had founded the department in 1935 and remained its head until his retirement in 1963. He was, incidentally, one of Mead's staunchest supporters when critics began debasing the results of her first fieldwork as published in her vastly influential work, *Growing Up in Samoa*. Cressman and Mead, of course, had been among Franz Boas's students at Columbia University. My adviser for the master's degree, John Champe, had been a student of William Duncan Strong, who was in turn one of Alfred L. Kroeber's students, and Kroeber was Boas's first graduate student. I've often encouraged students to trace out their "academic genealogy" because it's an exercise in the history of our discipline, and it helps them discover their academic roots.

A close undergraduate friend at the University of Nebraska, Thomas Newman, had earlier chosen to pursue a doctorate in Eugene, and Cressman had been so impressed with him that he'd told Champe, "If you have any more students like that, send them out." Champe passed the word on to me one afternoon when I was in Lincoln, and in December 1957 Bonnie and I drove to the West Coast, where we visited my parents and then went on to Eugene to see Cressman. I decided to pursue my studies there, particularly since he offered me a $1,600 assistantship that paid for my schooling and housing (the stipend was increased $100 the following year, all of which was absorbed by an equal increase in the cost of student housing). I was delighted when Cressman agreed that my manuscript study of the prehistory of the Pomme de Terre Reservoir could serve as a dissertation. Arriving with a dissertation already written? What a bonus: I was afloat!

In the fall of 1958 I resigned my position as a research associate at the University of Missouri and moved to Eugene, pulling a small trailer I'd just purchased for the trip behind my 1949 Mercury. Because Bonnie was expecting our first child at the time of the move, she went to Montrose, Colorado, to be with her mother. Our first son, Elbert Stanley Wood, was born there on October 12, 1958. A few weeks later Bonnie, her mother, and Stanley joined me in Eugene. I'd obtained an apartment in student housing not far from campus near a number of other graduate students in the department, including Frank C. Leonhardy and Lionel A. Brown, with whom I'd continue to interact in the future. Brown was later with the MRBS in Lincoln for several years and wrote on Central Plains tradition sites in the Missouri River Valley in Iowa and on lithic sites in the Bighorn Canyon in Montana. Before Leonhardy took a position in the Pacific Northwest, he worked for the Museum of the Great Plains in Lawton, Oklahoma, and excavated the Domebo mammoth site. Undergraduates included James A. Goss, later with Texas Tech University and a participant in the continuing debate concerning the Numic expansion in the Great Basin.

The weather in Eugene was far removed from my experience. The winter (a monsoon season) led me to believe that the sidewalks in town were designed for one of two purposes, to be high enough to elevate your feet above the surrounding ponds of water or low enough to act as canals to drain the accumulating pools. I bought my very first umbrella and raincoat there. I also found that winter temperatures were warm enough that for the first time I didn't need antifreeze in my car. Indeed, it was never especially cold because the incessant clouds held in the heat, though temperatures fell when the sun came out and dissipated the overcast. We kept our two-room student housing warm using only a portable electric heater that I bought at a secondhand shop, though in our second year it had to be replaced with another from the same inexpensive source.

One reason I chose Oregon for further graduate studies was its distinctiveness and distance from the Great Plains, for I felt I needed broader

Figure 20. Bonnie H. Wood with three-month-old son Stanley in Eugene, Oregon, December 1959. *Author's collection.*

experience. My curriculum included Theodore E. Stern's courses in linguistics, in which we worked with a Samoan Islander (said to be a prince) and created a simple vocabulary and grammar of his language. Another, more useful class was Homer G. Barnett's cultural dynamics course, in which we used his text, *Innovation: The Basis for Culture Change.* I recommend that students in archaeology become familiar with this book despite its age, for innovations are the transformations in technology and social institutions that correspond to genetic mutations in biology. I also took area courses in India and South Asia from Stern, Africa from Vernon R. Dorjahn, and the Pacific Islands from Barnett. I felt these courses were indispensable, for anthropologists should have a rich background in the variety of human culture to distance themselves from egocentric leanings. I became attracted to African studies as a consequence of my association with Dorjahn, eventually accumulating enough related hours that it would have counted as a minor had it existed. My childhood reading of a ragged copy of my grandfather's book, James W. Buel's *Heroes of the Dark Continent*, had consciously fueled my interest in Africa. Grandfather had read widely and had named my father (as I also named my first son) after African explorer Henry M. Stanley.

Oregon was then on the quarter system—instead of two semesters, there were three smaller ones—which meant that I ended up writing three more term papers each school year. I can recall the topic of only two such papers that I wrote there, one for Barnett's course on the cultures of the Pacific Islands, "The Function of the Menehune in Hawaiian Mythology," and the other on Plains Indian pottery, in lieu of the jaguar gorget I discovered in Fairfield Mound 2, for Stern's course in primitive art, as mentioned in Chapter 5. The Menehune were believed to be little people who lived in the forests and deep valleys of the islands, far from the eyes of the other islanders. Needless to say, that paper ultimately ended up in a round file, though, as I recall, both received good grades; the one on Plains pottery I published (Wood 1962).

One of my best "archaeology moments" took place when I accompanied Tom Newman to the Oregon coast near the town of Tillamook to work on a prehistoric village he was using in his dissertation. We spent a miserable rainy weekend digging in one of the houses, but our spirits were enlivened considerably when we found a few sherds of Ming dynasty (AD 1368–1644) pottery on the house floor (Newman 1959). Speculate as you wish, for such sherds are generally ignored in regional studies because they and similar finds are believed to come from prehistoric shipwrecks (Woodward 1986). Such incidents apparently had little if any effect on coastal cultures.

After my first year in Eugene I spent the summer of 1959 on one of Cressman's digs in the John Day Reservoir on the Columbia River, on an excavation sponsored by the Columbia Basin Project, the regional equivalent of the MRBS. We set up camp on the south shore of the Columbia River near the hamlet of Blalock, Oregon, east of the Cascade Range. Thus we were out of Oregon's western moist region and over the boundary into its eastern desert, and here I learned the real meaning of aridity. For this reason, I'm further grateful I chose to attend Oregon. Luther Cressman usually worked there, in one of the most desolate parts of North America, and he naturally had come to embrace the growing use of ecology in anthropology; in many ways his interdisciplinary approach mirrored that of John Champe. I was fortunate indeed to have had two such outstanding mentors. During the mid-twentieth century anthropologists of every stripe who concentrated on cultures that lived in harsh environments around the world had developed the pragmatic ecological outlook that typified Cressman and many others. I was impressed, for example, by Daryll Forde's stimulating 1934 book on African societies, *Habitat, Economy and Society,* and my frequent conversations with Cressman (we called him "Chief") furthered my developing interest in ecology.

The John Day Reservoir now floods the sites we investigated along the Columbia River, and the nearby town of Blalock likewise has vanished underwater. The excavations for which I was responsible (Area 3, the cemetery at Wildcat Canyon, 35GM9) posed new and challenging problems, for the site was a prehistoric cemetery in which the dead had been placed in pits dug into pure sand and then covered with blocks of basalt. The weight of the basalt had crushed the bone, and excavation progressed slowly, for we faced numerous problems in exposing and preserving them. Rodents had also had a heyday churning the material. Needless to say, there were many frustrating moments but it was an instructional summer, and the deep, basalt-lined Columbia gorge was a distinct change from the Missouri valley trench. I enjoyed the scenery and desolation, and in midsummer I did not leave camp for one solid month.

My block excavation for the cemetery was dug into the right-of-way for U.S. Highway 30 (today it is Interstate 84), so every passing motorist gaped at us while speeding by, though not one of them stopped to see what we were doing. Across the highway to the north, near the bank of the Columbia, fellow graduate student Tom Newman directed excavations at a three-component living area designated Area 2. Most of the remains from the cemetery, and some of those from Area 2, ultimately were assigned to the Wildcat phase (about 500 BC to AD 1000). How it relates, if at all, to the Tenino Indians who historically inhabited the locality is not clear (Dumond and Minor 1983).

We set up a tent camp on the shore of the Columbia River a short distance upstream from the sites. We also established bathing facilities: a pump by the river carried water in a small hose to a shower stall. It was a simple matter to tell when the first bather entered the stall, for the warm water in the hose was soon exhausted, and when the ice-cold river water came through, everyone in camp could hear the scream. Because most of the camp was pitched on a sand dune, the floor of at least one of the U.S. Army squad tents used for a dormitory was covered with straw, becoming known as the "elephant tent." The terrible daytime heat soon led us to abandon a normal work schedule; we rose before dawn, ate a hearty breakfast, left for the site about sunrise, and quit work early in the afternoon. This meant we had more of the remaining daylight left. What to do during those hours? Well, adjoining us was a commercial peach orchard, and when it was time to pick, a number of us went to work for the owner. The peaches were magnificent: they were about the size of softballs, and the temptation to take a bite out of the overripe and unsalable ones we were told to discard was overpowering. It compensated somewhat for the fact that the owner stiffed us on our wages.

One day at work was especially memorable. The year 1959 was the centennial of the state of Oregon, and a grandmother in (I believe) Kansas City decided to walk to Portland to celebrate the occasion. Her progress was duly noted in newspapers along her route, so we knew she was fast approaching our digs. One morning we saw her coming far down the road and watched her pass in silence, for she stared directly ahead and stonily continued down the highway until she passed out of sight. A little later I looked up to see the head of a giraffe protruding from the back of a passing truck. I shouted to my crew, "Look! A giraffe!" but by the time they looked, the truck was out of sight, and they claimed the heat had gotten to me. Only when we read a newspaper the next day was I vindicated, for the Portland Zoo had obtained a new long-necked resident, lately of Africa. Late that afternoon came the day's capstone. A horse-drawn wagon train, also celebrating the centennial, pulled into sight and turned off the highway onto the level grassy ground between Newman's excavations and my own and set up camp for the night. We spent some time talking with the reenactors and admiring their wagons and costumes. They left early the next morning. Other days could only be described as humdrum. There was utterly nothing to do in Blalock, and a drive back to Eugene would have consumed an entire weekend and, in any case, my only car was in Eugene with Bonnie. I did a lot of reading that summer, though Lionel Brown and I had a memorable rubber raft trip through some (minor) rapids on the Columbia River.

The summer was an informative one, though in some respects the season was disagreeable, in large part because of a personality conflict I had with David L. Cole, Cressman's field supervisor for the project, and I didn't look forward to another such summer. One of my best friends on the dig, as well as in Eugene, was Neil Kirschner, who reappears later in this narrative. My departmental assistantship continued through the coming school year, and most of it was spent redrawing the summer's field maps for the final report. However, I was saved the fate of returning to the Columbia the following season because I maneuvered an alternative scheme, and I was privileged to dig at a renowned village site in North Dakota that had long incited my interest.

Excavations at Huff

In my second year at Oregon, Paul L. Beaubien, regional archaeologist at the National Park Service office in Omaha, Nebraska, wrote to ask if I'd be interested in conducting salvage work at the Huff village site in the upper Oahe Reservoir. Sometime earlier I'd written Paul asking if there was some work along the Missouri he could offer me, and he'd promptly obliged, for at the time there was no archaeologist at the State Historical Society of North Dakota to undertake work in the state. Huff Indian Village State Historic Site was owned and managed by the society, and Paul quickly made the necessary funds available to the society for me to work there. I was a known quantity to Paul because of our frequent contacts in Champe's Laboratory of Anthropology and at the Plains Conference, and of course he was aware of the three reports to the National Park Service that Alan Woolworth and I had authored on Kipp's Post and the Paul Brave and Demery sites. I was delighted with the opportunity, for this distinctive fortified village was and remains one of the most intriguing sites on the Missouri River. I'd been fascinated by it ever since I first visited it in the summer of 1952 when I dug with Fenenga at Buffalo Pasture. I was to spend June to September 1960 digging at this remarkable village.

After I told Cressman that I'd been "summoned" by the National Park Service, he released me from my summer obligation on the Columbia River and permitted me to go to North Dakota: he never realized my subterfuge in the affair. But his permission carried a proviso, that I use Huff for my dissertation instead of the Pomme de Terre material. I wasn't happy about this turn of events, though in the end it was one of the best conditions ever imposed on me, for the resulting dissertation was published as a solo bulletin of the Bureau of American Ethnology (Wood 1967b). The Pomme de Terre "dissertation" was instead submitted to the *Missouri Archaeologist* and appeared in print while I was writing my "second" dissertation (Wood 1961). My old professor at Nebraska, John M. (Jack) Roberts, and I often exchanged reprints, and after he'd read my dissertation in 1962, he mentioned that he and Richard Wheeler had planned to do a joint paper on what he called the "village revolution on the Upper Missouri." Jack was to provide the cross-cultural data and make ethnological inferences, and Wheeler was to assemble the best-known sites and their relevant materials. Jack suggested that if Dick didn't want to complete the enterprise, he would ask if I'd join him in doing so. But Wheeler never came though—he was such a perfectionist he found it difficult to finish anything—and I'm sad that our collaboration never came to pass. His approval of my dissertation, though, meant a great deal to me. I was able to meet with him only once after he left Nebraska: I got him to Missouri in March 1966, when he gave a talk titled "Expressive Models in Culture."

Huff was a wonderful opportunity. James H. Howard, of the University of North Dakota, had dug there the previous year, but he largely ignored his obligation to salvage remains along the riverbank, where house depressions were scheduled to be destroyed when the U.S. Army Corps of Engineers constructed a rock emplacement to prevent erosion by the rising waters of the Oahe Reservoir. Instead, Jim dug one house near the bank edge as instructed but then dug a bastion and a very large structure, surely the village ceremonial lodge, well away from the area slated for destruction. Russell Reid, the society's superintendent, directed me to "do things right this time." I did, but in the end the Corps of Engineers did not bevel away the bluff edge as it planned; it simply placed a rock embankment along the river's edge because we were so near the upper end of the reservoir. The panic had been for nothing, for the site was not touched by the construction.

When the arrangements for excavation were complete, I looked about for an assistant. My choice was Neil Kirschner, a fellow graduate student with whom I'd worked on the Columbia River the previous year and who needed a job for the summer. Neil and I had become close friends despite the disparity in our backgrounds, for he was from New York City and had never lived in a small town. After graduate school Neil became a faculty member at Wenatchee Valley Junior College in Washington State and conducted archaeological work in the Wanapum Reservoir. We traveled together to North Dakota in June 1960 by Greyhound bus, stopping briefly in Moscow, Idaho, to visit Alfred W. Bowers, whose ethnography of the Mandans was mandatory reading for me. We arrived in Bismarck early one morning.

The Huff site was on the rim of a broad, high terrace nineteen miles south of the town of Mandan on what was then a gravel road, on the west bank of the Missouri River half a mile south of the hamlet of Huff. The bluffs facing east along this reach of the river are very steep and high, and for this reason they are often referred to as the "Huff Hills." Indeed, one of the few ski resorts in North Dakota today occupies rugged terrain about three miles from the site. Not far away some prehistoric group had run bison over the rim of the bluffs.

The crew was a genial one, consisting of John Berg, Walter H. Birkby, Lawrence W. Hanson, Jon Muller, and brothers Gordon F. and Stephen W. Robinson, sons of the noted historian at the University of North Dakota, Elwyn B. Robinson. Walter Birkby went on to become a prominent forensic anthropologist at the Arizona State Museum. He was from my home town of Gordon, Nebraska, which coincidentally was also the birthplace of Melvin L. Fowler of Cahokia fame (who retired from the University of Wisconsin–Milwaukee). Jon Muller became a noted southeastern specialist at Southern Illinois University–Carbondale and, in retirement, was presented the distinguished service award at the 2006 Midwest Archaeological Conference. Steve Robinson had worked with Alan and me at the Paul Brave and Demery sites and had also dug with me in the Pomme de Terre Reservoir in 1957. His subsequent career led to a doctorate in physics at the University of Indiana, and later he designed and oversaw the construction of the radiocarbon dating laboratory for the U.S. Geological Survey at Menlo Park, California.

Robert (Bob) P. White, the caretaker of Fort Abraham Lincoln State Park, helped us establish our camp at Huff. Because the land around the site was privately owned, we set up camp just inside the barbed-wire fence that surrounds it but outside the bastioned fortification ditch that encloses the village itself. Bob pulled in a small white trailer that the State Historical Society used for fieldwork, and behind it we erected three surplus army squad tents, our living and sleeping quarters. The trailer had a gas stove and a mess table that served a dual purpose. We prepared our meals and ate in this wonderfully snug and dry environment, and every evening the crew gathered around the table to read and write letters, using the light from our two Coleman lanterns. It was a convivial setting, but it was far too crowded and noisy for my comfort. Trying to collate and check the day's excavation notes and photographic log amid the bustle was distracting, so I changed my daily routine. I went to bed at about nine in the evening and set my alarm for four in the morning. Rising early, I worked on my notes until sunrise, at which time I went to the river bluff a few yards distant, dangled my legs over the bank, and had a cigarette as the sun rose over the bluffs, bathing the valley in the soft golden alpenglow of morning. Then I made breakfast for the crew. When the weather turned oppressively hot, we adjusted our schedule to work from five in the morning until two in the afternoon.

We began working immediately north of camp, planning to excavate in turn the row of houses adjoining the river bluff, the ones that supposedly were endangered. Thad. Hecker had excavated the third house in the row in 1938 for the State Historical Society, and James Howard had dug the seventh the year before we arrived. We first cleared the floors of the ceremonial lodge (neither of them had been backfilled) to get an idea of soil conditions and house architecture. Because I was not satisfied with the map Howard had prepared, I created a new one of the lodge; later we also cleared and remapped the floor of the house that Hecker had dug for the same reason. They were all long-rectangular structures with a central ridgepole and an entry facing directly southwest. This orientation typifies all the houses in every site of the Middle Missouri tradition, and it holds true whether the entrance faces the river or away from it. The reason for this orientation is surely embedded somewhere in Mandan folklore, though its meaning has yet to be understood. We went on to investigate seven additional structures along the riverbank, and we also cleared and remapped the bastion that Howard had excavated.

I had a good and experienced crew, and the work went smoothly throughout a very hot and dry summer. The terrace on which the village had been built was of course capped by loess, and when it is freshly exposed, loess is a delight to excavate, but after a few days in the sun it becomes almost rock hard. To make digging more manageable, I rented a water pump, but the forty-three-foot pull up from the river level was too great to allow more than a trickle of water to reach the house floors, and the experiment was abandoned. Because of the heat the crew was dragging by quitting time, but somehow everyone managed to find the energy to run a few laps around the fortification ditch before supper.

One Saturday I neglected to buy meat on my weekly grocery run to Bismarck (I did most of the cooking), and on Sunday we were at a loss as to what to have for supper. The solution was simple: buy some chickens. I climbed into the state station wagon and headed for the farm at Schmidt, a few miles north of Huff, and bought two plump hens from the farm wife. Returning to camp, where water had been set to boil as we left, I asked Walter Birkby to prepare them for plucking. Walt picked up the two chickens by their heads, swirled them in each hand like propellers, and the two birds were decapitated—one flying in front of him, the other behind. He was left with a chicken head in each hand, an image far removed from the sanitary view one has of chickens in a delicatessen. Neil witnessed their flopping death throes in horror, but though the technique was new to me, I was familiar with the results, for when I'd been my mother's chicken executioner when I was young, I'd simply chopped off their heads with an ax. It may have been the smell of the birds being scalded in the boiling water before being plucked that clinched Neil's decision not to eat chicken that evening. The aroma of a bird being scalded, after all, makes the smell of a wet dog seem like cologne, and plucking them is scarcely better.

Our site had been named after the small, unincorporated town of Huff and lay on the west side of what is today State Highway 1806 (Highway 1804 parallels the river on the east bank, both roads honoring the passage of Lewis and Clark). There was a small bar there, the only business in town: John's Bar. It was housed in a low and disreputable-looking shack set next to the highway and had neither decor nor atmosphere, at least in the usual sense of the words. Its main attraction was that it was near our camp. John could open beers, but he was no bartender. One afternoon I asked for a screwdriver, and he opened a drawer and handed me one; I settled for a beer. Ordering a martini was out of the question. On another afternoon a carload of Indians from the Standing Rock Reservation walked in, sat down at the counter, and ordered "Indian Killers." John poured each of them a water glass of red wine. Some years later a new bar with normal amenities was built on the north side of town.

During the field season MRBS archaeologist Robert W. Neuman was excavating mound sites in the valley nearby. Because we had an established camp, I invited him to stay with us, an invitation he readily accepted, for we were old friends, having known each other in Lincoln, and I was grateful to him for introducing me to chicory coffee, a Cajun delicacy. He had a largely Indian crew, and they spent a pleasant week or so with us until it was time for them to move on. They had their own camping gear, but they ate with us in the trailer. I enjoyed Russian rye bread and had also bought some dark-colored smoky salt, so his crew asked Bob if they should pitch in more money for food—they were sure we were on poverty rations since we couldn't afford white bread or salt. Part of Bob's schedule that summer was to excavate the remaining three mounds at the Boundary Mound Group, which I'd reported in the *Plains Anthropologist* the previous year.

Sometime in midsummer I drove my crew downriver to the Leavenworth site, which was being dug by a field party from the University of Nebraska under Preston Holder, who had replaced John Champe as chair of anthropology at the University of Nebraska. (Pres was abruptly removed from that position by Warren W. Caldwell when the MRBS was turned over to the National Park Service in 1968, though he remained on the teaching staff.) The Leavenworth site was a historic Arikara village on the west bank of the Missouri a few miles north of the town of Mobridge. It had been destroyed when Colonel Henry Leavenworth and his Sioux allies attacked it in 1823 in retaliation for an Arikara assault on the fur-trading party of William H. Ashley. Here I first met Richard Krause, with whom I'd interact and collaborate far into the future. After Dick completed his doctorate at Yale University under Irving Rouse, he returned to the study of Plains cultures. He was later employed by the University of Missouri, where he was my friend and supervisor and an inestimable help in my research, but eventually he went to the University of Alabama, from which he retired, but we've remained close friends and have kept in contact ever since. No one else on the Plains controls archaeological method and theory as he does.

Huff was an exhilarating experience. It was the first major excavation I'd directed entirely on my own, and the responsibilities kept me busy. Neil was a fine assistant, but he'd never been on the Plains before and had no administrative experience. Happily, I had no need to field-train my crew. Neil had dug with me the summer before when I supervised work at the Wildcat Canyon cemetery on the Columbia River. Walter Birkby and Jon Muller had come with the recommendation of William M. Bass III, then at the University of Kansas. Steve Robinson, by now a veteran digger, also was there. I'd not budgeted for aerial photography, but that oversight was remedied one day when a North Dakota National Guard helicopter landed on the site. The pilot, himself a collector, was interested in what we were doing, and he generously (and perhaps illegally) took me for a short aerial hop during which I was able to snap several good views of the site. My pleasure at digging this remarkable site was tempered by the fact I was sorely neglecting family responsibilities, for our second son, David Eric Wood, was born in Eugene on September 10, 1960, as I was preparing to close down the dig and return to Eugene: another example of poor planning!

The materials we excavated during our ten-week season were shipped back to the University of Oregon, where I studied them during the winter

Figure 21. Field camp and excavations at the Huff site, summer 1960. *Author's collection.*

of 1960–1961. Cressman provided me with a hall-like office in the anthropology building for use as a laboratory, though it also housed an impromptu office mate. Fay-Cooper Cole, retired from the University of Chicago, had been hired to teach the course in North American prehistory. Cole was a pleasant office companion, and in some of our many illuminating conversations he discussed his role as an expert witness for Clarence Darrow in the 1925 Scopes "Monkey trial" in Tennessee. I remember only one of his anecdotes. Since their team couldn't obtain living quarters in town, they'd rented a farm home in the country. One evening during a bad storm a bolt of lightning struck near the house as Darrow and his team of defendants sat discussing courtroom strategy. Darrow looked at his companions and said, "Gentlemen, if that bolt had struck this house we'd be sure to lose this case!" When word of Cole's presence on campus became known, a constant parade of students began visiting him, because an English professor was using the transcript of that trial in the classroom. To eliminate this distraction, which affected both of us, Cole accepted an invitation to deliver a general university lecture, at which there was standing room only.

I signed up to take Cole's course in North American prehistory, pleased to have the insights of this icon of midwestern archaeology. One day after class I tactfully pointed out to him some minor error in what he'd just told us about the Plains. I was promptly invited to give the next lecture (I never corrected him again). During one of his lectures he mentioned a number of his illustrious classmates at Columbia University who had studied with him under Franz Boas; then he stopped and almost whispered to himself, "But they're all dead now." He was silent for a moment, shook his head, and then went on. He, too, was dead within the year.

Cole was but one of the three famous visitors the department hosted while I was there. Another was Margaret Mead, who attracted great attention, in part because Cressman had been her first husband. A short, dynamic person, she carried a stout walking stick in the style of—and probably consciously so—a biblical prophet. However, Louis S. B. Leakey commanded the department's greatest attention. He came to talk about the latest discovery made by his wife, Mary, in Olduvai Gorge, *Zinjanthropus boisei* (now *Australopithecus boisei*). Entertaining Leakey while he was there was delegated to one of the faculty who specialized in Africa, Vernon R. Dorjahn. Because my old friend and fellow graduate student Tom Newman and I were both interested in Africa, we and our wives were invited to have dinner with Leakey at Dorjahn's home one evening. How Leakey managed to gum down his steak when he barely possessed two teeth that meshed simply amazed me. After dinner he entertained us with anecdotes and made a series of complex cat's cradles, explaining their value in his dealings with native Africans. If he were having trouble socializing with either a group or an individual, he'd sit down and begin making one of his many patterns. Soon he'd have a friendly audience and tensions would disappear; he often entertained guests and hosts with these string figures. Dorjahn and his wife were gracious hosts, Leakey was enthralling, and it was a remarkable evening.

During my graduate career at Oregon I'd come under the spell of this enthusiastic young Africanist, a member of my doctoral committee who'd done ethnographic fieldwork in the high country of Sierra Leone. Both Tom Newman and I registered for his classes in African archaeology and ethnohistory, in which I focused on West African forts and slaving posts, and Tom on Sierra Leone, where he did fieldwork in 1961. One afternoon, on his way to visit some fellow Africanists at Northwestern University, Dorjahn stopped by my office and asked if he could help in any way with my research. It was a perfect opening, and I told him I'd really appreciate any help he could give me in locating the site of Lord Greystoke's cabin. "To the best of my knowledge," I said, "it has to be somewhere on the coast of Sierra Leone." He agreed to help. A few weeks later he returned to my office, pelted me with expletives, and otherwise verbally abused me, for his Northwestern University colleagues were more widely read than he in

Edgar Rice Burroughs's Tarzan books. Since he was on my committee, I'm grateful to have graduated, but fortunately he had a sense of humor sufficient to forgive me.

The following year a National Science Foundation grant to Cressman provided funding for me to prepare an interpretation of Mandan culture history based on my work at Huff. The goal of my research was to isolate some of the factors that had shaped Mandan culture and to propose a general hypothesis to comprehend the trends in their history. The Mandans' nomadic neighbors, I believed, probably were responsible for the coalition of the Mandan into compact, fortified villages during a period of climatic desiccation and for more elaborate expressions of Mandan solidarity, including their famous Okipa ceremony. That ceremony was a great renewal ritual in which the Mandans celebrated their existence as a people. I also found that contacts with downriver Arikara village groups provided new alternatives for a number of Mandan traits. Historic Mandan culture, I concluded, emerged about AD 1500 under the stimulus of two separate but contemporaneous factors: cultural cohesion stemming from pedestrian nomadic aggression, and acculturation fostered by trade and contact with sedentary village peoples deriving from the Central Plains, ancestors of the historic Arikara Indians. I documented this acculturation at Huff with the discovery of a four-post house which was structurally similar to those of the late prehistoric Arikaras farther downriver and which marked the transition from the Mandans' existing long-rectangular, gable-roofed houses to the fully circular, four-center-post houses of the historic period. Further, the village-margin plaza on which the ceremonial lodge faced had moved to a position at or near the village center, emphasizing its centrality to the Mandan belief system. I believe this is still a defensible hypothesis, though today I'd omit or downplay the role of a "period of climatic desiccation." Today the site has been more accurately dated to AD 1443–1465.

I'd gone to North Dakota with a very different point of view. One of the reasons I'd been so interested in Huff was its distinctive village plan. There had been much speculation that the plan for its fortification had been directly or indirectly derived from such Middle Mississippian sources as Aztalan, in southeastern Wisconsin. This remarkable twenty-acre site lies on the bank of the Rock River some thirty miles west of Milwaukee (Barrett 1933). The general plan of its fortification is patently similar to that at Huff, but there are many differences in the details of its construction. Aztalan is twice the size of Huff; the palisade was composed of large, closely spaced posts whereas those at Huff were small and spaced about a foot and a half apart; Aztalan bastions are square, and the gorges are lined solidly with posts, quite different from those at Huff; and Aztalan lacks Huff's fortification ditch, though its palisade was mounted in a bank of earth like that at Huff. On the other hand, the nonceramic artifacts at both sites have wide spatial and temporal distributions that hold little promise of revealing a relation between them. There are no distinctive parallels in pottery, though at both sites the horizontally applied cord impressions on vessel rims are sometimes interrupted by cord-impressed triangles (Barrett 1933:Figures 84–85, 108, 110). The surface of Aztalan pottery, however, was roughened by a cord-wrapped paddle, not by a grooved paddle and then smoothed.

Even considering these differences, I suspect some connection between the sites. Aztalan demonstrates a Middle Mississippian intrusion in about AD 1100 into an area dominated by Woodland peoples and reveals that there were close ties between the intruders and the locals. The community may have persisted until about AD 1300. No fortified sites with bastions similar to Huff are known outside the Missouri Valley in the Dakotas; indeed, one has to go to Aztalan itself to find the nearest similar plan. This fact supports the idea that this village form may have diffused north along the Missouri River from northwestern Iowa, for some early villages in the Big Bend Reservoir below Pierre (for example, Black Partizan, 39LM218) superficially resemble Huff. For these reasons, there is no compelling reason to derive the village plan overland from such Middle Mississippian sources in the east as Aztalan. I therefore abandoned my quest for such ties during my research when I found nothing at Huff to demonstrate an eastern Woodland association. While there surely are some connections between the cultures of the Mississippi Valley and those of the Middle Missouri Valley, the details remain to be demonstrated. Fifty years of excavation after my dig at Huff have yielded no resolution to this enigma, though speculations abound.

My third year at Eugene was a busy one, for coursework was winding down and I was frantically working up the Huff material. Except for my problems in passing the German language exam (it took five nerve-wrenching tries), coming up with topics for my term papers that I felt worthwhile was my sorest trial during my stay in Eugene. Ted Stern monitored my sequence of German exams, and when I complained after the fourth try that the tests were becoming increasingly difficult, he responded,

"You've been studying, haven't you?" My heated response might have terminated my graduate career there and then, but the next exam was a reasonable one and I ended that grueling contest.

After the trauma of my German exams, I was delighted to finish my French on my first try after three weeks of truly intensive study. Among other strategies, I'd carried a box of French/English flash cards to and from class daily and successfully memorized them. I was proud of the fact I'd been able to read and quote French ethnographies for my term papers, but I was distressed when I picked up a French novel and couldn't get through the first sentence, much less paragraph. Nevertheless, I was almost home: I defended my dissertation in June 1961 with anthropologists Cressman, Barnett, Dorjahn, Raymond D. Gastil, and Stern; they were joined by J. Arnold Shotwell, a paleontologist in the Museum of Natural History, and Kenneth W. Porter, a preeminent scholar of western American history. I'm sorry I did not have more contact with Porter, but I came to know Shotwell rather well. Over the previous winter I had spent much of my time drafting maps for the past summer's work at Wildcat Canyon in part of his work space, and we had an opportunity to discuss his interests and the ecological views of Luther Cressman. Shotwell was a specialist in the paleoecology of mammals, and one of his articles on taphonomy was influential in the developing field of zooarchaeology; I'd be remiss if I did not thank him for his contribution to my growing interest in paleoecology (Shotwell 1955).

Originally, Cressman had told me I'd have to have a Plains specialist on my committee, for he'd had an experience with a student who'd submitted a dissertation in an area that he and his committee didn't control and had pulled a fast one on them. However, after he returned from the annual meeting of the Society for American Archaeology in New Haven, Connecticut, in 1960, he never again mentioned a Plains reader. Later I learned he'd talked with Robert L. Stephenson and other MRBS archaeologists and had concluded that I was trustworthy. Fortunately, I had in my own library most of the archaeological sources necessary for writing the dissertation, but I found it intriguing to check out other needed references in the university library. In those days one signed one's name in a slip in the book when it was checked out. I often consulted books bearing the names of such luminaries as Alex D. Krieger, Robert L. Stephenson, and Fred W. Voget. I experienced no difficulty passing my written and oral exams, though I understood that I was the first person in the department to do my written exams on a typewriter (admittedly, with many strikeouts).

Cressman had told me he'd not read a dissertation of more than one hundred pages, so I wrote up the Huff site as a separate report and sent it off to Russell Reid at the State Historical Society of North Dakota for submission to the National Park Service to fulfill our contract with them. Four months later I submitted to Cressman an introduction, the environmental and cultural setting, the Mandan sequence, and my interpretation of the nature of Mandan culture change in "An Interpretation of Mandan Culture History." I wrapped these sections around the National Park Service report when it was published as a bulletin of the Bureau of American Ethnology (Wood 1967b).

My three years in Eugene ended with my graduation on June 11, 1961. I was the last one to leave the commencement stage during a ceremony in which diplomas were individually handed out to everyone from bachelors to doctors. The last words I heard as I descended the platform steps were "Thank God, that's over!" from one of the officials who shook the hands of recipients. I couldn't have agreed more, as did the now-aging Cressman, who sat beside me throughout the ordeal. I was delighted that my mother was able to attend the ceremony, though I was saddened that the stroke that had recently crippled my father prevented his being there. When I went to pick up my diploma, the woman behind the desk could not find mine. I began sweating, for after I'd passed my comprehensive examinations all the requirements for my degree had been satisfied, and I stopped going to classes with Ted Stern. Did I actually have a degree after all? My relief when she found that it had been misfiled can well be imagined. After long minutes of tension our three years at Oregon were over, and we prepared to move.

7

A Detour to Arkansas

To describe… this beautiful and romantic country, to picture with the pen those boundless solitudes—so silent that their silence alone increases their grandeur—to gather inspiration from nature and to attempt to paint the scene as my eye beheld it, is a task before which a much readier pen than mine might well hesitate.

— George Armstrong Custer, *My Life on the Plains*, 1874

Fayetteville, Arkansas

My next job was at the University of Arkansas in Fayetteville, where I arrived in the middle of June 1961 with my wife, Bonnie, and our two young sons. We drove out of Eugene with our aging Mercury loaded to the level of the back windows with our few goods and the two boys, pulling my little trailer covered by its now-ragged tarp. At a fuel stop in Nevada the question of our destination came up with the station attendant as he gassed up our car, and I replied, "We're on our way to Arkansas." The attendant smiled widely, whereupon I said, "It looks like we're coming instead of going, doesn't it?" He laughed. I'd struck the nail on the head.

Thinking I might be hired at the MRBS in Lincoln, I'd taken an examination for federal employment, but I preferred a university position where I might teach. I no longer remember how I was recruited for or applied for the position at Arkansas, but I was appointed curator of anthropology in the University Museum, housed in Old Main, one of the landmark buildings on campus, and commenced my duties on July 1. My office was on the fourth floor in the southeastern turret of the building; the view would have been superb had the windowsills not been eight feet above the floor. The director of the museum was Charles R. McGimsey III, ably assisted by Hester A. Davis (the sister of my former instructor, Mott Davis). I did no teaching, and indeed very little as a formal curator while I was there, though I did develop a few creditable (I thought) archaeological displays, drawing on lessons I'd learned from Ray Price, who'd created some of those at the Nebraska State Historical Society while we were in graduate school in Lincoln. Rather, my time was devoted to writing up existing archaeological collections in the museum, conducting salvage excavations at rockshelters in the Beaver Reservoir, and carrying out emergency salvage digs at the Denham and Crenshaw Mounds. My "laboratory" was a table in one corner of the "Pottery Room," an immense room filled with shelves of hundreds of pottery vessels of Mississippian and Caddoan origin from sites throughout the state.

Home in Fayetteville was at first in a miniscule brick apartment building a few blocks north of the old Student Union (now Memorial Hall) and a short walk from my office in Old Main. When time permitted a more leisurely search, we moved into an old white frame house at 333 Rollston Street, about four blocks east of the campus and some six blocks from Old Main. Today the home is said to have been "gentrified." I'm not sure how far Fayetteville is from the buckle of the Bible Belt, but on telling a clerk in a local store that I was new in town, I was asked, "Have you found your church home yet?" I don't recall my answer. The last of our three children, daughter Marigene, was born in Fayetteville on October 8, 1962. At long last I managed to be home for this happy event.

James A. Scholtz, another archaeologist in the museum, became a close friend. I found this serious young man the most compatible of the museum's employees, and many weekend evenings we played a game of Scrabble from late evening to sunup (he took the game very seriously). I also haunted a bookstore on West Dickson Street, about a block distant, and there I purchased a book that was to change forever my recreational reading from novels to recent history, for it was a paperback copy of William L. Shirer's *The Rise and Fall of the Third Reich.* I was fascinated by Shirer's explanation of the political background for World War II (a topic I'd first learned about in my geography seminar in high school at Chadron) and the horrors it had wreaked on Europe. Initially, I read it so late at night that I had to ration the time I spent on it so I could get up early enough in the morning to go work.

My first fieldwork for the museum was to dig the Bushwhack and Breckenridge Rockshelters, both of which were set in the bluffs of the

Figure 22. Eric, Stanley, and Marigene Wood, Columbia, Missouri, 1964. *Author's collection.*

deeply incised White River Valley near the town of Eureka Springs, sometimes known as the Switzerland of the Ozarks, and for very good reason, given the rugged hills in this part of the state. The shelters bordered the reservoir to be created by the Beaver Dam on the White River, an impoundment being built by the Army Corps of Engineers, named not for the animal but for the town of Beaver, not far from the dam site. We again worked under an agreement with the National Park Service to salvage sites that were endangered by the construction. One beautiful summer afternoon Jim Scholtz escorted me to Bushwhack Shelter (3BE2). We clambered down the valley slope to a delightful rock overhang and sat in its shade as we discussed what was to be done there in the following weeks. After I'd hired my field crew and left for our first day of fieldwork, I drove optimistically to our parking area on the hill above the shelter. We unloaded our standard shaker screens and hand tools, augmented by the crowbars and sledgehammers we'd need to move and break up the rockfall that littered the shelter floor. Somewhere I took a wrong turn, and we spent hours wandering up and down steep ravines before finding the overhang, by which time the crew was in a mood I was afraid might cost my life. We spent only a few hours at work that day. Ronald A. Thomas, a graduate student at the university who later became Delaware's state archaeologist, ably assisted me at both shelters.

We decided to commute to the shelter daily from Fayetteville instead of establishing a field camp. This meant a daily round trip of more than seventy miles, the latter part of it over some of the most scenic, winding roads in the Ozarks (including one curve of fifteen miles per hour). The long commute resulted in less than a six-hour work day. The crew rode in the back of a pickup truck equipped with benches and a canvas-covered roof. For the first time in my career, we had shade throughout the day from either the shelter itself or the canopy of trees that fronted it. Our hope that the overhang would be stratified was not realized, for the shelter's deposits were a shallow mixture of rock and earth. The deposits yielded a modest inventory of artifacts, but there was no way to distinguish specimens from the different occupations that began in the Archaic period and ended with a group or groups that made pottery and used the bow and arrow (Wood 1965b). Having found nothing of significance, we abandoned the site.

We resumed investigations in Breckenridge Shelter (3CR2), where we indeed found deep and stratified deposits. One of our tests exposed a six-inch-thick slab of limestone rockfall that we had to remove piecemeal with sledgehammers. We finally reached the underlying deposits, which bottomed out on shale bedrock. Breckenridge provided a ten-foot-deep record that spanned the period from 9400 B.P. to late prehistoric times, beginning with a point reminiscent of Agate Basin but ending before the arrival of Europeans (Wood 1963a). Many of the rockshelters in this part of the Ozarks contain dry deposits that preserve a wide array of perishable items: cordage, basketry, and the like. Our investigations at Bushwhack recovered a few such items, though they added little to our knowledge, and the deposits at Breckenridge were too damp for such preservation, but they yielded useful information on the local prehistory.

That winter I lost most of my immunity to poison ivy when Jack Scholtz and I went to test what we believed to be a rock-and-earth mound. It was covered with brush and vines, most of which we removed by hand. The bark on the vines often tore away and was slippery with sap, which we wiped on our clothes. The mound turned out not to be aboriginal; rather, it was a historic rock feature. Not surprisingly, the next day we had poison ivy rash on our hands and other, unnamed parts of our bodies, though Jack was far more afflicted than I was.

The Denham and Crenshaw Mounds

My next duty was to salvage what I could from a small earthen mound scheduled to be leveled to increase a farmer's acreage. The structure was on the Ouachita River on the boundary between the Ouachita Mountains and the Gulf Coastal Plain, near the town of Malvern in Hot Spring County. Landowner Wallace Denham had contacted museum personnel to invite them to excavate the mound before it was bulldozed. I arrived at the site in October 1961 with an assistant, Jack E. Porter, and a few members of the University Museum staff. After they helped us get settled and departed, Jack and I were left alone to excavate what we could of the structure. We lived on the site for the several days we had available, cooking at a mound-side campfire and sleeping on the ground during the beautiful Indian-summer weather.

We began a cross trench we hoped to dig to the mound base, but the hot, dry summer had drawn most of the moisture from the earth, leaving it with an almost cement-like consistency, so the final trench hardly measured up to our expectations. We nevertheless detected three separate stages of construction in our probe of this rectangular, pyramidal mound. A startling event marked the day I was cutting the trench walls smooth in preparation for drawing profiles. When I peered into a small hole I'd exposed in the wall, I faced an irate and hissing opossum, disturbed in its underground quest for warmth. I enlarged the hole to let it escape lest it be bulldozed into oblivion. We later watched as the mound was leveled and managed to salvage a few additional specimens, including the first and only freshwater pearls I've ever found.

This three-stage, truncated-pyramidal substructure Caddoan mound was a sharp contrast to other components of the local Fulton aspect, in which substructure mounds generally are lacking. The mound showed a clear pattern: each structure on its surface was burned before the addition of another, higher earthen stage. We collected charcoal from each stage, though it has yet to be dated. My final report was published in the first issue of the anthropology series issued by the University Museum (Wood 1963b).

Less than a year later I was involved in another mound salvage. The Crenshaw site (3MI6) is a large mound and cemetery complex on the banks of the "Great Bend" of the Red River in extreme southwestern Arkansas. It was due east of Texarkana on what was then a long, dusty road lined with the miserable tar-papered shacks of black sharecroppers who lived in abject poverty. Consisting of a large truncated-pyramidal mound and five dome-shaped mounds, the complex had been investigated by Clarence B. Moore in 1911 and had been explored by collectors ever since. In 1961 some collectors from Texarkana leased the very large Mound C and began exposing numerous burials as they systematically removed the structure. They were unable to dig the central part of the mound, however, because of an electric power pole set on its crest. When their lease expired, the University Museum moved in, and I began salvage work supported by the National Science Foundation. More than half the mound had been removed by the time we arrived in April 1962. We spent the remainder of the month working there.

The regional director of the Southwest Arkansas Electric Cooperative (locally known as the REA) cooperated with us in moving the power pole on the mound apex. An avid Arkansas Razorback football fan, he also made it possible for members of the University of Arkansas football team to aid us in testing the site, as did numerous local members of the Arkansas Archeological Society. All of them proved to be hardy, enthusiastic, and competent field technicians. Because we lived on the site for the duration of the work, we set up our tents (in a driving rain) in a grove of pecan trees just north of the mound. My home and "office" was in a pyramidal squad tent beside which the REA erected a photoluminescent streetlight for us, together with outlets for our electric frying pan and, the ultimate luxury, a telephone, for which they strung a wire to my tent from a nearby line, the only time in my life I've had such service in a tent camp. We soon began excavating and mapping the site. Some of the mounds were in wooded areas, and when I made the site map, it was necessary to sight in some of the points at night, using a lantern to see through the underbrush.

Because the site was on a low terrace of the Red River, its soils had developed in reddish-colored sand, which likewise composed most of the fill of Mound C. It made for easy digging, but it posed risks for the ignorant. I had my first near-death experience when someone noticed a crack in the profile exposed in a deep pit where I was working near the mound center. I leaped out just before tons of sand cascaded into the pit. However, the sandy nature of the mound made it easy to brush clean the several burials we recovered, some of them moderately endowed with artifacts. I made one of the most spectacular finds in my life as I was shovel-chopping a profile on a control block in the mound center when I heard a loud "clink." I had nearly bisected an exquisite, bifacially flaked, side-notched Gahegan-style biface made of almost black Talahina chert nearly 25 centimeters long.

Associated with Burial 1, it was less than a meter from the base of the REA pole on the mound crest, which had preserved much of the mound's content from the looters. We later exhibited the object at one of the annual meetings of the Arkansas Archeological Society in a display of artifacts titled "Real or Fake?" The attendees unanimously declared it to be a fraud. Had I not found it in place myself I'd have agreed with them.

We determined that the structure was a three-stage Coles Creek mound that, contrary to its truncated pyramidal form, revealed no evidence that it was ever used as the base for any structure, for it contained only burials. The Coles Creek burials at its base and within the mound date to between about AD 700 and 1000, but it also contained later and intrusive Caddoan graves. I concluded that the earlier occupation represented the tip of Coles Creek expansion up the Red River from its heartland along the Mississippi River. Later investigations revealed the probability that there was a Fourche Maline, or Woodland, component at the site.

My final report on the site incorporated previous excavations in several cemetery areas around the mound that contained either Coles Creek or Caddoan Haley focus burials. They had been carefully and professionally exposed and mapped in past years by local collector M. P. (Pete) Miroir and other residents of Texarkana. After the project ended, I spent a few days at the Gilcrease Institute in Tulsa, where I studied the Crenshaw material in its collections and stayed as a guest in the home of Thomas Gilcrease. I completed my report on the work in June 1963, and though it was never published, a twelve-page summary appeared in a synopsis of the year's activities by the museum (Wood 1963c). I was fortunate that Clarence H. Webb was able to visit the site and offer advice. Webb was a pediatrician and also one of the most knowledgeable amateur archaeologists in the region—indeed, in the United States. He was a past president of the American Pediatric Association and had even been nominated for the presidency of the Society for American Archaeology. My consultations with him on the site and in his home in Shreveport, Louisiana, greatly aided my understanding of this complex site.

The University Museum contained a number of old collections made under the auspices of the Works Project Administration in the latter years of the Great Depression. Excavations at the Poole site (3GA3) in 1939 and 1940 by Glenn Martin had yielded one such collection that had never been written up, a job that fell to me. Since all the site features were exposed immediately below a shallow plow zone, there was no stratigraphy, but from its artifact content I related the early, pre-Caddoan component there to the newly defined Fourche Maline "focus" of eastern Oklahoma. The mortuary and artifact associations of a later Caddoan occupation remain unique in the upper Ouachita River Valley.

The Woodland-period Fourche Maline phase is a pottery-making culture that predates the Caddoan occupation in the region, and the phase persisted throughout most of the first millennium AD. The most remarkable aspect of the site was the exposed floor plan of a structure, among the few found for the phase and still unique among those in the region. This long-rectangular structure, 30 meters long and 8.5 meters wide, had closely spaced wall posts and a roof supported by a central row of seven large posts. Debate continues whether the structure was of Fourche Maline or Caddoan construction. Though it had ample room to house a large group, it contained a single hearth, so most interpretations lean toward a religious or ceremonial function. Nineteen years later Ann M. Early published the descriptive portion of my manuscript report with her updated conclusions (Wood 1981a). She concluded that there was an ephemeral Late Archaic occupation at the site, followed by Fourche Maline and ending with burials she ascribed to the newly defined Buckville phase of the Caddoan tradition.

The Gambia River Project

In 1962 I submitted a proposal to the National Science Foundation for a research grant to initiate an archaeological and ethnohistorical survey and interpretive program in the former British crown colony of The Gambia, West Africa. This miniscule nation of only 4,003 square miles consists of a strip of land twenty miles wide and almost two hundred miles long on either side of the lower reaches of the Gambia River. The smallest nation in Africa, the country had the merit of appearing to be politically stable (and indeed it has remained so) and had the additional attraction of being English-speaking, though entirely surrounded by French-speaking Senegal. The region had not been studied archaeologically since 1906, yet the land adjoining the river and the region in general contain hundreds of circles of upright laterite stones that even today have not been properly investigated. These circles of standing stones, properly *megaliths*, may contain pillars weighing as much as ten tons. Today we know they contain pre-Islamic, pre-European burials of uncertain age, perhaps dating to between

300 BC and AD 1500. Some of these sites are now on UNESCO's World Heritage List.

African nationalism was fueling a growing interest by native Africans in their own history, and since the history of The Gambia before colonial times was all but unknown, I felt that I could make a contribution to the history of West Africa, a field that I'd developed in my doctoral program. I hoped to integrate my archaeological findings with the rich ethnographic setting of the area and with the documentation that existed from early visits by Portuguese, French, and English explorers and slavers. I also planned to make test excavations at James Fort, on an island near the mouth of the river, to obtain trade goods that I hoped would aid in the dating of occupational sites. Originally built by Baltic Germans (Courlanders) in the mid-1600s and occupied by all subsequent European colonists, James Fort today is also listed as a UNESCO World Heritage Site and is currently being investigated by archaeologist Flordeliz T. Bugarin of Howard University, Washington, D.C.

My proposal was not funded, however, and Albert C. Spaulding, anthropology director for the National Science Foundation, provided the boilerplate explanation that although it had merit, the number of meritorious submissions meant that not all of them could be funded. I was disappointed, and any prospects and enthusiasm I had for becoming active in African prehistory and ethnohistory slowly evaporated as I became increasingly involved in midcontinent American archaeology. The $30,952 budget that I submitted for my year's fieldwork in Africa seems incredibly small by today's standards, but it included such necessary amenities as a domestic staff: a "cook-steward and small boy" for nine months for $243. Ultimately, I recovered what I could of my background research for the project for an article that appeared in the *Journal of African History* (Wood 1967c). The article traced the development of European settlements, forts, and slave "factories" in The Gambia and Senegal from their earliest foundation to 1870.

I soon became restless with my position at Arkansas, for I was at the beck and call of others and, with the rejection of my African proposal, had no real choice in the direction of my research. What's more, there was no assurance that my position at the museum would be funded after July 1, 1963 (the date I'd hoped to begin my African program), and my former colleagues at the University of Missouri were urging me to return.

8

The University of Missouri, Round Two

But the patterns made by the historian are never complete. There is always something lacking, a residue, fragments suggestive of other patterns which might be formed if one only knew how to put them together or where to find the missing parts.

— Walter Prescott Webb, *The Great Plains*, 1931

Life in Columbia

It took little persuasion for me to leave Arkansas. The opportunity came in July 1963, when Carl Chapman invited me to return to Missouri and rejoin the American Archaeology Division as a research associate and director of River Basin Archaeology. I did so happily, at a nine-month salary of $6,500, almost twice what I was paid there in 1957. At that time the division was a subdivision of the Department of Sociology and Anthropology, for we did not gain departmental autonomy until September 1966. Our family arrived safely in Columbia and moved into faculty housing, a series of temporary barracks in what is today a gigantic open parking lot for the University of Missouri Hospital. I settled into my duties of investigating, with the assistance of agreements with the National Park Service, archaeological resources that would be flooded within the state by the numerous reservoirs that were being planned or under construction by the Army Corps of Engineers.

I've remained at Missouri ever since, though from time to time I interviewed for other positions. In March 1968 I was contacted by the Bernice P. Bishop Museum in Honolulu, which was seeking an archaeologist to conduct a full year's survey of the Makaha Valley on the west coast of the island of Oahu, not far from the Makaha surfing beach. Because by then

I had become immersed in the investigation of Rodgers Shelter and the nearby spring bogs, not to mention a variety of projects in other reservoirs, I regretfully declined the offer. It probably would have been a life-altering experience, for the work at Makaha became a major event in Hawaiian archaeology and is credited with being the first contract archaeology conducted there. I've often wondered what the consequences might have been for me.

In early 1966 J. Charles Kelley, at Southern Illinois University–Carbondale, asked me if I'd be interested in the position of curator of anthropology at the University Museum. I interviewed and was accepted for the position, but when I reflected that I'd be supervising the wife of a major figure there, it seemed best to decline the position—and my university countered the offer with a $1,000 raise in my salary. Robert L. Hall was also interviewed and likewise declined; much later he told me that Kelley had said he became tired of raising the salaries of archaeologists throughout the Midwest. A few years later I applied for a position at the University of Kansas in Lawrence. I had a pleasant interview, unaware that two of my close friends were simultaneously being interviewed, for the hiring committee cleverly managed to keep us apart the entire time. They were Thomas M. Newman, with whom I'd gone to school in Nebraska and Oregon, and Alfred E. Johnson, a native Kansan who used to camp out in my basement apartment when he attended the Plains Conference in Lincoln. Fortunately for Kansas, Al was chosen for the job, and he devoted his entire career to the prehistory of Kansas and to establishing the Museum of Anthropology on the KU campus, something I'd never have done. In February 1973 I also interviewed at the University of Illinois–Champaign, but the selection committee chose not to hire an individual who would require tenure. And in 1976 I was interviewed for the chair of anthropology at Southern Methodist University. Whatever the interviewers thought of me, they eventually decided to elevate one of their existing faculty to the position. But I've never regretted having remained at Missouri.

My new title was Director of River Basin Archaeology, and I was to coordinate and direct salvage excavations in reservoirs within the state, but later I was able to direct some of those activities through a growing cadre of exceptionally high-quality graduate students. Later still I also contracted with the National Park Service to continue work along the Missouri River at the Lower Grand and Walth Bay sites in north-central South Dakota, and I initiated independently funded work in the Stanton-Sanger area above Bismarck in collaboration with Don Lehmer, then of Dana College in Blair, Nebraska.

At first my office was in a second-floor room in Switzler Hall, one of the oldest buildings on the Columbia campus, built in 1872. Aside from being rustic, it had its hazards. One year a section of its second story fell to the ground, exposing one side of the chairperson's office to the elements. Fortunately, no one was walking below at the time or they'd have been buried beneath a pile of bricks. My office immediately adjoined the anthropology department office, conveniently in the same building as the office of the American Archaeology Division, which was, not surprisingly, in the basement. I soon found that anyone passing by who had a spare moment to kill would stop to talk, sometimes interminably. Often I'd shut my door and turn off the lights so I could work undisturbed. When the opportunity arose, I moved across the quadrangle to an office on the second floor of Swallow Hall. This gave me an opportunity to walk to Switzler twice daily and get some exercise when I went to pick up my mail. The geology and geography departments had recently vacated Swallow Hall for new quarters, and its last occupant, the University of Missouri Press, also was preparing to move in preparation for occupancy by the anthropology department. Since the rooms adjoining the immense one that I chose to occupy were standing empty, I moved my lab into one of the (at that time) ivy-covered towers of the building, and my graduate students into the two small offices adjoining it. I was able to obtain a large table for the room in the tower, and when the class was small enough, I used the room for seminars. I could walk to the next room and get whatever book or item I might have forgotten which I wanted to use to illustrate a point in class, and it was impossible to forget that I had class. In addition, when someone came to my office, I knew it was expressly to see me, not to pass the time in conversation.

When I moved into my office complex, there were hookups for a sink in the tower room, though the sink itself was gone. Since the second story of the building was now vacant, some of my graduate students confiscated a sink from a room down the hall and installed it in the tower room they were using as office and laboratory space. Sometime later, before the University of Missouri Press moved its offices from the floor directly below, two university plumbers burst into my office and asked to see the sink. It had developed a leak overnight, and water was dripping onto book manuscripts lying on the desk in the office of the director. I showed them the offending basin, and they immediately set to work on it. Suddenly, one of the men uttered a heartfelt oath and choked out, "*Masking tape*?" I feigned ignorance of any knowledge of this ill-conceived installation, and the plumbers eventually went away, their repair completed, still muttering to themselves. Little wonder the press was delighted to move to newer and safer quarters.

Over the years the adjoining rooms were used by a host of graduate students, a group that came to be known (through the medium of F. A. "Cal" Calabrese) to other archaeologists at the Plains Conference as the "Missouri Mafia." This cadre included many who were to become influential in Great Plains studies: Calabrese, Stanley A. Ahler, William Butler, James A. Donohue, Carl R. Falk, Ann Mary Johnson, Kerry A. Lippincott, Paul R. Picha, Donna C. Roper, Fred Schneider, Rain and Susan C. Vehik, among others. Some students became prominent in Missouri archaeology, including Larry Grantham and Jack H. Ray. Others achieved distinction in more distant areas, including William T. Billeck as the director of NAGPRA at the Smithsonian Institution, R. Eric Hollinger in Oneota studies, Walter E. Klippel in the Southeast, David E. Madsen in the Great Basin, George P. Nicholas in the Pacific Northwest, Robert E. Warren in the prehistory of the Prairie-Plains at the Illinois State Museum, and Daniel J. Provo as a museum director, most recently at the Oklahoma History Center. Those who did not have laboratory or office space adjoining my office were housed in the decidedly inferior basement of Swallow Hall, which was musty and would flood during heavy rains. One afternoon as I waded barefoot through its halls, I found a sign tacked to the wall that read "Beware the Alligators." More luxurious were the quarters we obtained when the division acquired the use of an old brick residence at 703 Missouri Avenue, a few blocks south of Swallow Hall. It became the headquarters of the Missouri Mafia until we lost it when the buildings along the street were demolished, and its site now lies in the grassy mall between the new law building and the Reynolds Alumni Center. It was here that Calabrese lost a mustache and his eyebrows while relighting its gas furnace.

For many years, the Missouri Mafia got together almost every summer to celebrate their profession, socialize, and exchange data in a manner reminiscent of the old "½ Plains Conferences" held by the MRBS and its cooperating archaeologists in the Dakotas. There was an outstanding spirit of cooperation and sharing among them and a tradition of helping others. The project, indeed the profession of archaeology, was more important to them than individual egos. This isn't universal. Not everyone in the Plains is equally eager to share information. In fact, in rare cases data are withheld until milked dry by their holder, a tactic this group would regard as beneath contempt.

Fridays after five o'clock our group often congregated for beer. For a time we met at an institution called "The Shack," consisting of a set of interconnecting sheds on Conley Avenue south of Swallow Hall. It had a low ceiling that demanded you stoop as you walked to a table, and its wooden tabletops were heavily carved with generations of initials and names. It had been established in 1920 by a man from California who parked a truck there and began selling hamburgers on the spot, adding shacks, literally, as he expanded. At one time (well before our time) it had been the hangout of Mort Walker, later the creator of the comic strip "Beetle Bailey." The Shack was destroyed by fire in 1988, and its site became a grassy mall east of the luxurious Reynolds Alumni Center. A "life-size" bronze statue of "Beetle" seated before a beer now adorns the front lawn of that center. A later and more permanent watering hole for us was the Heidelberg, on 9th Street across the street from the Museum of Art and Archaeology. It too was destroyed by fire in 2003, but its owner, sensitive to tradition, rebuilt it to the same floor plan, and this landmark continues to be a campus favorite.

By the mid-1960s I had enough responsible graduate students that I was able to take time out to accompany Wilfred D. Logan, Zorro A. Bradley, and other personnel from the National Park Service and the Committee for the Recovery of Archaeological Remains on their summer inspection tours of sites in the Central and Northern Plains that were being dug by other institutions. Sometimes I took the tour alone with Wilfred Logan. These tours were always educational. On one trip to Montana to visit Lawrence L. Loendorf's work in the Pryor Mountains, we saw a herd of wild horses. When we inspected the piles of dung the stallions deposited to mark their territory, we found small piles of gastroliths from dinosaur gizzards—stones that prehistoric peoples used as raw materials for making chipped-stone tools. Returning from our tour on a very hot afternoon, we stopped for a Moscow Mule in a tavern outside Billings. When we returned to the government car, we discovered that the motor was still running with the keys in the ignition, and the vehicle was locked. I don't recall who had the responsibility of smashing out a window to gain access to the keys and save the motor.

For a time there was a riding stable a few miles west of Columbia at the Rocheport exit on Interstate 70. One afternoon Ann Johnson, William Butler, and I drove out to have a ride in the country. We all saddled up and left the corral, following a trail that led toward the bluffs and past a very large burial mound (with a large hole in its center, of course). All went well until we'd gone about a mile. Suddenly my horse decided it was time to return to the stable, turned around, and tore off toward home at break-neck speed along the narrow path. It was exhilarating until the beast left the path and darted between two closely spaced trees. My left hip struck one of the trees and I was brushed from the saddle; for a few yards, I held on to the saddle horn with one hand as my right foot dragged on the ground while the left was caught in the stirrup. When it came loose, I released my death grip on the saddle horn, tumbled backward, and landed in a heap. As I began walking back to the stable, one of the owners rode up in a panic to find out why one of the horses had returned without a rider. My left hip soon sported a nauseous circular rainbow bruise in shades of black, blue, green, and yellow. I was terribly sore for a time but delighted that my pelvis wasn't shattered, though I lost a pair of glasses that I never found.

One of my students became interested in the 1837 smallpox epidemic at the Fort Clark site, the one that nearly exterminated the Mandans. Michael (Sonny) K. Trimble wrote both his master's thesis and dissertation on that subject. After graduating he began working for the Army Corps of Engineers in St. Louis. His first major project was to persuade the corps to invest in curation facilities for the many archaeological projects that had been conducted in the various reservoirs. After a long fight he accomplished this purpose. In 1994, in a major change in his life course, he went to Iraq to head the Iraq Mass Graves Investigation Team, which was dedicated to unearthing some of the mass graves of the victims of Saddam Hussein. The team unearthed many such graves, some of them two-tiered and as much as eleven feet below the surface. He and his team lived in a heavily guarded special-purpose compound not far from where they dug. At Saddam Hussein's trial, Trimble's testimony and that of Douglas D. Scott helped convict the dictator of crimes against humanity.

In the fall of 1963 members of the American Archaeology Division were called on to help expose the skeleton of the Grundel mastodon. The remains of this beast had been found during scraping activity adjoining a deposit of gravel deep within one of the loess hills overlooking the Missouri River Valley near the town of Craig, in extreme northwestern Missouri. The landowner, Russell Grundel, brought it to the attention of geologist Maurice G. Mehl, who, to my knowledge, was the only vertebrate paleontologist ever to teach at the University of Missouri. We exposed parts of the skeleton of an old female in a Farmdalian loess deposit (25,000 years of age) but were disappointed to find no evidence of human association, especially after we found a large, basin-shaped pit filled to the rim with charcoal about 250 feet from the bones. Our excitement ended abruptly when we received the results of a radiocarbon date on the charcoal of about AD 680 (Mehl 1966). Nevertheless, this was my initiation into the excavation of the kind of large mammal bones we'd later find in several swampy spring bogs in southwestern Missouri near Rodgers Shelter.

Rodgers Shelter and the Spring Bogs

My first major project at the University of Missouri—little did I know it would occupy a significant part of the next fourteen years—was to investigate Rodgers Shelter, located on the Pomme de Terre River in northern Benton County. The shelter was at the base of a steep hill overlooking what was to become the floodpool of the Kaysinger Bluff Reservoir (later renamed the Harry S. Truman Reservoir). The locality was to assume great significance in Missouri archaeology, for an ancient abandoned meander of the Pomme de Terre River, locally known as Breshears Bottom, was one mile south of the shelter; it was found to contain an astonishing variety of archaeological, paleontological, and ecological treasures in a series of spring bogs. Most of these resources would be flooded by 1978, when construction of the dam was complete. The summers spent in the reservoir were research intensive and never served as field schools, for the pace of work and the range of activities involved left no time for either formal or informal academic lectures or teaching. It was nonetheless a time of learning for everyone involved: long before the project ended, I felt it was superior to any postdoctoral training in natural history I could have had anywhere.

Rodgers Shelter and Breshears Bottom were in an enviable ecological setting. To the north and west are the prairies of western Missouri, and to the south and east lie the oak-hickory forests of the Ozark Highland. This lowland setting also contained a mosaic of bottomland forest and patches of prairie. Nearby were large areas of prairie that occupied much of the dissected upland surrounding the Pomme de Terre, providing a mosaic boundary between the western prairies and the forested Ozarks that could be called ecotonal positioning for the shelter. That is, the setting was on the northwestern margin of the Prairie Peninsula, that great triangle of grassland that extends eastward from the Great Plains as a wedge between coniferous forests to the north and the oak-hickory forests to the southeast. Set in the midst of this ecological diversity, Rodgers Shelter was just a few hours' walk from either upland or bottomland habitats and resources. We found bison and other prairie species commingled with woodland species throughout the shelter deposits, though there were notable increases in bison and other prairie species in its middle deposits, reflecting the spread of prairies during the Hypsithermal, the warm period that characterized the middle postglacial period.

The overhang, named after the genial former landowner, Jack C. Rodgers, was ten air miles south of the town of Warsaw, which itself was near the mouth of the Pomme de Terre River. Rolland Pangborn discovered the shelter during a routine survey in the spring of 1962, and in the summer of 1963 it was investigated by two graduate students at the university, William E. Sudderth and Sidney Denny. They discovered about a meter of significant Late Archaic and Woodland deposits above an almost sterile gravelly layer. They stopped digging on finding that the gravels lacked cultural remains. Because of the richness of the overlying deposits, however, it was decided that the shelter should be further investigated the following summer.

The American Archaeology Division's research associate, R. Bruce McMillan, took charge of the excavations in 1964, and the following year, when I assumed control of the project, I retained him as the field director. A native Missourian, Bruce had worked on varying projects for Carl Chapman beginning in 1955 and was an astute excavator, observer, and convivial companion. He remained a research associate and the archaeologist-in-charge at the shelter for the duration of my participation in the project, and we codirected it as amiable colleagues. Eventually, he used the results of his work, supported by a National Science Foundation Fellowship, for his doctoral dissertation at the University of Colorado–Boulder in 1971. Marvin Kay, of the Illinois State Museum, conducted later work at the shelter.

Bruce decided it was necessary to punch a hole until we reached either bedrock or incontestably sterile deposits. A five-foot square was begun near the terrace edge and quickly penetrated the nearly sterile gravels that led Sudderth and Denny to stop digging. McMillan then exposed a clay-rich layer that contained abundant Middle to Late Archaic materials. We continued deeper in 1965 until we reached, almost simultaneously, the water table and a chert scraper and other chipped-stone tools in a charcoal-flecked occupational level at a depth of seven meters. The hole was so deep and cool that I could see my breath at its base, but it was more startling when one of the crew discovered that it was possible to see stars, albeit faintly, from its floor during full daylight. This "elevator shaft" became known as the "Mid-Mo Mohole" after the deep Pacific Ocean probe that recently had investigated the Mohovoric Discontinuity. That winter Allen Eichenberger cast the flake scraper in acrylic, for the depth at which it was found hinted that it was of great antiquity.

The decision to dig deeper was the key to the entire project. Certainly it was not common to do so, for as James A. Brown has pointed out, "The beginning of the new perspective toward Midwestern archaeology began in 1964 when buried archaeological strata were discovered at Rodgers Shelter in southwestern Missouri. Up to that time, it was routine to regard sterile sediments underlying surface sites as the bottom of the excavation. After this discovery, however, one could no longer be content that this was so, especially with regard to sediments in shelters and on floodplains that have been subject to aggradation since the Pleistocene. What had once been treated as a safe assumption had now to be treated very differently" (Brown 1983:5). The decision to reach the base of the deposits was reinforced by my contacts with geologists years earlier at the University of Nebraska.

We investigated Rodgers Shelter for three years under contracts with the National Park Service, working on the basis of agreements negotiated with Wilfred D. Logan, the archaeologist at the regional NPS office in Omaha. But it rapidly became clear that what needed to be done vastly exceeded the level of funding the National Park Service could provide. As work progressed, we realized the site had the potential to contribute greatly to our knowledge of the archaeology and paleoecology of the western Ozark Highland. Consequently, in January 1966 I applied for a National Science Foundation research grant for four years for the sum of $189,574 to continue the excavation and analysis of the unexpected bonanza at Rodgers. Bruce and I planned an interdisciplinary approach to the site and the several nearby artesian spring bogs. The shelter would provide an archaeological calendar of its prehistoric inhabitants, and coordinated field studies in the springs were expected to furnish paleoecological data to augment the interpretation of the shelter deposits and outline the paleoecology of the western Ozark Highland during the terminal phases of the Pleistocene.

We had reason to be optimistic: in 1840 an entrepreneurial German immigrant, Albrecht C. Koch, had found a mastodon skeleton and other fossil bones in one of the nearby spring bogs in Benton County. These deposits intrigued us, for in 1839 Koch had excavated mastodon remains in Gasconade County, Missouri, and suspected that they were associated with humans. Albert (he anglicized his German name) Koch put together what he called the "Missourium," or the "Missouri Leviathan," from a combination of bones, principally of mastodons (*Mammut americanum*) and giant ground sloths that he recovered at what we now call the Koch Hole in Benton County. This unlikely collage was exhibited in Koch's museum in St. Louis and even toured Europe between 1841 and 1844, when the skeleton was purchased by the British Museum (Natural History), disassembled, and correctly remounted by Sir Richard Owen. It is still on display in London. Bruce McMillan positively identified Koch's spring in Benton County because of a conspicuous "table rock" formation on a nearby hillside that Koch mentioned as being near his spring. Furthermore, a pollen profile made from small sediment samples that remained on the skeleton in London matched those we unearthed in the spring. During our own excavations we found evidence of Koch's work, including a platform of walnut logs he'd installed in the muck to provide footings for his excavations (Wood and McMillan 1976:81–96).

The Pomme de Terre was once known as "Big-bone River" and the locale for a "Glaise a l'Elephant" (elephant lick) because mastodon bones had been found on its lower reaches as early as the 1790s. Koch's 1840 dig in Benton County began a rush by bone diggers in the locality, some of whom may have carried out the old excavations I found at the nearby Kirby Spring. Kirby was the first bog I visited, for it was shown on old land plats of the county near the west end of Breshears Bottom. It was surrounded by backdirt bearing small fragments of large bones and flakes of ivory, so obviously it had been dug sometime in the past. Later tests revealed that all or most of its deposits were disturbed or gone, so we expended no further effort there. McMillan (2010) has related the intriguing story of the discovery of these fossil vertebrates on Missouri's western frontier, a story involving President Thomas Jefferson, Auguste Chouteau (founder of St. Louis), and the early naturalists Georges Cuvier and Benjamin Smith Barton.

To achieve a truly interdisciplinary program, in 1965 I began calling on scholars in a variety of disciplines to ask them to collaborate with us and carry out specialized studies. C. Vance Haynes, at the University of Arizona, agreed to conduct geological investigations at the shelter and in the surrounding Pomme de Terre alluvial deposits. He later became nationally prominent in geomorphological and Paleoindian studies. Peter

J. Mehringer Jr. signed on as the project palynologist, though in 1968 he turned his responsibilities over to James E. King, who remained with the project to its conclusion. Paul W. Parmalee, at the Illinois State Museum, Springfield, became the modern faunal specialist, and William M. Bass was to study any human remains we discovered. Bass was then at the University of Kansas, though he soon moved to the University of Tennessee, where he spent the remainder of his career, mentoring an astonishing array of notable forensic anthropologists.

When my National Science Foundation proposal was funded in May 1966, the project had to be scaled back, for we were awarded only $18,000 (GS-1185), only about a tenth of what we'd asked for (and the university absorbed almost $6,000 of that sum in overhead). It was nonetheless a magnificent sum in those days, but wholly insufficient to do what we'd planned. I reapplied the following year with a more modest proposal, for only $38,264, and this time we received almost all of it, $35,900 (GS-1604). A third grant of $37,000 (GS-2112) was allocated in 1967, and we were well under way. Further support was provided by a grant to the Illinois State Museum, with R. Bruce McMillan and Everett H. Lindsay as co-principal investigators, in 1974.

Rodgers Shelter was important because of its uniqueness. The Pomme de Terre once flowed along the base of a steep hill and had undercut the bedrock to form a long, narrow overhang. After the river channel moved to the south, a terrace built up under the overhang, which in turn was buried by colluvium and rockfall from the hillside and the shelter roof. Because humans occupied the shelter for the entire time these deposits were being laid down, and because of the relative rapidity with which the deposits formed, cultural materials were far better stratified here than in other Ozark rockshelters, where thinner deposits have been churned and the natural and cultural stratigraphy has been significantly blurred. We expanded and continued the work at Rodgers until appreciable deposits had been excavated to depths that exposed a number of Early Archaic Dalton occupational lenses, the oldest components we found at the site. (The scraper of hoped-for "great antiquity" came from one of these levels.) Though the site yielded a probable Clovis point, it was not found in a meaningful context. Overall, the excavations provided the finest cultural sequence yet found in the state, its significance enhanced by the fine-grained deposits in which the artifacts were embedded. The depths to which we dug without safety precautions are quite illegal today, but we believed the clay walls would

Figure 23. The deep trench at Rodgers Shelter, Missouri, 1966. Earl Neller and Marvin Kay (*far right*) graphically illustrate its depth. *Author's collection.*

stand—until we arrived at the site one morning to find that an immense slump had occurred overnight. Views of the imposing stratigraphic profile make me shudder even at this late date when I contemplate what could have happened had the slump taken place during work hours.

Just south of the shelter is Breshears Bottom, an ancient cut-off meander of the Pomme de Terre River that, happily but coincidentally, contained three artesian spring bogs, Kirby, Trolinger, and Jones; the Koch Hole lay a short distance upstream. These springs became a focus of our investigation when we realized that the deposits in Rodgers Shelter were deficient in a major dimension: the poor preservation of pollen did not permit a meaningful investigation of the shelter's floral history, so its environmental history would be incomplete. We hoped the springs would provide a floral record that we could correlate with the cultural record in the shelter. Fortunately, animal bone in the shelter was relatively well preserved.

In our effort to locate deposits that might yield a postglacial pollen record, we soon found another spring bog not far from Breshears Bottom: Boney Spring, so called by local residents because large bone fragments sometimes boiled to the surface during times of high rainfall (there also were tales of a giant snake that lived there). The spring originated in a bedrock feeder deep below the terrace surface and had created a funnel-shaped conduit overlain by a heavy mat of vegetation. The conduit was choked with tree limbs and lengths of lumber that locals had thrust into it to determine its depth. In 1966 Peter J. Mehringer and I sank a five-centimeter piston corer in the spring which yielded fragments of proboscidean tusk at a depth of about four meters. In his lab at the University of Arizona, Mehringer determined that the matrix in which they were embedded yielded pollen grains of spruce and larch, and spruce needles, but little pine pollen. We hoped or believed the fragments of proboscidean tusk were from mastodons. Collectively, these elements were suggestive of a late glacial age for the deposits (Mehringer et al. 1968). Mehringer feared that the sample might have been contaminated, so I returned to take another core to confirm his results. Because it replicated the results of our first sample, we began major work there.

One of the other springs we investigated was Trolinger Spring, named for landowners Ivan and Goldina Trolinger. When Ivan first took us to it, the spring was marked by only a small wooden stake driven into the ground in a dry pasture. The stake marked the spot where Ivan had once mired his tractor when the spring was active. However, he told us that the spring had dried up following the great Alaskan earthquake and tsunami of 1964. We found the story hard to believe until friends with the Missouri Geological Survey assured us that some springs in parts of Missouri had indeed dried up, increased their flow, or flowed dirty water during that event. Our skepticism vanished. I sent a crew to the site to cross-section the feature and obtain a pollen sample.

I was at Boney Spring when one of our crew members raced up in a pickup, slid to a stop in a cloud of dust, and said, "We've got big trouble at Trolinger." The bulldozer that was cross-sectioning the spring almost immediately exposed the tusks and mandibles of several mastodons embedded in a complex stratigraphy. Our plans changed abruptly, and we spent a great deal of time there. The bones of five mastodons were in a soupy matrix until we dug a deep sump pit to one side of the spring and succeeded in draining the deposit. This allowed us to expose and remove the bones in plaster of paris jackets in traditional paleontological fashion. The deposits contained abundant pollen of Northern White Pine, mixed with that of some spruce and a few deciduous elements, clearly denoting, together with the radiocarbon dates, a late Pleistocene date.

Figure 24. The author carrying a plaster-jacketed mastodon tusk at Trolinger Spring, summer 1968. *Author's collection.*

We were intrigued to find a diminutive lanceolate point of local chert (the weight of an arrowpoint) about six inches above the proximal end of a mastodon tusk. It is twenty-six millimeters long and generally resembles a Plano point, though it lacks the parallel flaking so characteristic of those specimens (see Wood and McMillan 1976:Figure 6.1). No comparable specimens are known in contexts suggesting contemporaneity with extinct species. The small Clovis point from Blackwater Draw and the tiny point recovered with the mammoth at the Clovis site, however, make the association of our point with the mastodon remains somewhat more probable. In any case, the point cannot be duplicated among local complexes of any date, and because there was no other evidence of contemporaneity with humans, we made no claim of antiquity for the specimen.

Scholars in other fields eventually joined Vance Haynes and James King. Everett H. Lindsay, an accomplished vertebrate paleontologist at the University of Arizona, participated in the study of the megafaunal remains we recovered from the springs, a project that he turned over to Jeffrey J. Saunders in 1971. Jeff systematically excavated Boney Spring and remained with the project to the end, and he wrote his doctoral dissertation on the fauna from the several springs we investigated. He went on to a distinguished career at the Illinois State Museum, at times working with Russian scientists on Siberian mammoths. Donald Lee Johnson, of the University of Illinois, investigated the soils in our study area and related them to the terrace sequence that Vance established in the valley; he likewise attained national prominence in soil science. The team that assembled for this work was a remarkable one. Each member was dedicated to the project, and each participated in refining the research design as the work progressed; all were more concerned with the results of the work than with their egos. Not only did their combined work contribute to the overall project, but the individual participants also made substantial contributions to knowledge in their respective fields. Everyone worked together in harmony, and unlike the case with some similar projects that have fallen apart, we all remain the best of friends to this day. We've held three reunions near Warsaw at intervals of about a decade to reminisce and socialize.

Other members of the field crew went on to distinction in various disciplines. Marvin Kay became a renowned archaeologist and professor at the University of Arkansas; Stanley A. Ahler likewise continued in prehistory (and he is prominent in later chapters of this book). Lewis L. Jacobs became a professor of geology at Southern Methodist University, the director of the Shuler Museum of Paleontology, and a major figure in work on the dinosaurs of Africa.

Our first season at Boney Spring, however, was a disaster. We tried to dig a sump pit to the east of the bog so we could drain it as we'd done at Trolinger Spring. It didn't work, and the conduit continued to hold water high above the bone bed. What was worse, the sides of the conduit began to slump, destroying the overlying deposits. Therefore, we closed down the dig and, during the winter, contemplated ways to continue work. I contacted Waldo Wedel, who'd excavated Lamb Spring in eastern Colorado, and asked him to visit and offer advice, but he told me he'd had such a miserable time at Lamb Spring that he wasn't much inclined to even visit the site! Many alternative means were considered to excavate the spring (the most extreme was to freeze the deposits and chip out the icy remains), but a simple solution was soon in hand. Vance directed a local well driller to place several holes around the spring, and one of them, on the south side, struck the bedrock feeder. A wellpipe was driven into the feeder, and a small gasoline pump was sufficient to keep the spring clear of water to the requisite depth. In the summer of 1971 Jeffrey Saunders directed the removal of the mastodon and other remains at the bottom of the bonebed. To keep the spring dry, we posted a guard during the night to make sure there was gasoline in the pump and also to deter looters who might want to appropriate bones or teeth in our absence. A nocturnal marauder seeking souvenir teeth had earlier broken one of the exposed mastodon skulls.

We were visited at Boney by Paul (Pollen) S. Martin, of the University of Arizona, best known for his advocacy of the Pleistocene overkill hypothesis. After inspecting our work, he had an unusual request: to cut down a nearby large honey locust tree. The branches of such trees are so heavily laden with thorns that no animal can browse on them. However, he discovered that the thorns reached a height of only five meters above the ground. Giant Pleistocene ground sloths could not browse above that height, suggesting that the tree was still adapted to a fauna that was long extinct and further demonstrating that not all aspects of evolution are in phase. This height, he pointed out, was the same as in Africa, where giraffes browse on another variety of thorn tree. On another occasion, the crew was startled to look up and see a hundred horses and riders bearing down on them: the Fristoe Saddle Club Trail Ride had come visiting.

Perhaps the most famous among the parade of luminaries who visited our project was George Gaylord Simpson. Bruce McMillan recalled that when this eminent vertebrate paleontologist and evolutionist visited our excavations in the Koch Hole in 1971, he removed his hat and bowed as a gesture of respect for Albert Koch. While many dismiss Koch as a charlatan, Simpson was well aware of the influence this early nineteenth-century showman had in stimulating interest in New World vertebrate paleontology among the public, as well as among members of the scientific community. Paleontologist Weldon D. Frankforter also visited us at Trolinger Spring. "How many mammoths are you finding?" he asked, and someone replied "None." In one of our more embarrassing moments, he led us away from the spring deposits and pointed to a mammoth tooth partly exposed in the profile several yards from the focus of our work. It was in a more ancient stratum through which the spring had erupted, and we'd been concentrating on the much later late Pleistocene deposits. Ouch!

The little town of Fristoe, a few miles east of our study area, adopted our group and proclaimed itself the "Mastodon Capital of Missouri." Our work was even publicized in a booklet titled *Valley of the Mastodons*, grandly subtitled "A factual story of the most massive and systematic excavation of pre-historic animal fossils of the 20th century" (well, not exactly!). Residents of Fristoe, in an effort spearheaded by Richard and Donna J. Mann (the booklet's author), opened a small museum to which we donated a fiberglass half-cast of one of the mastodon skulls (the museum has long

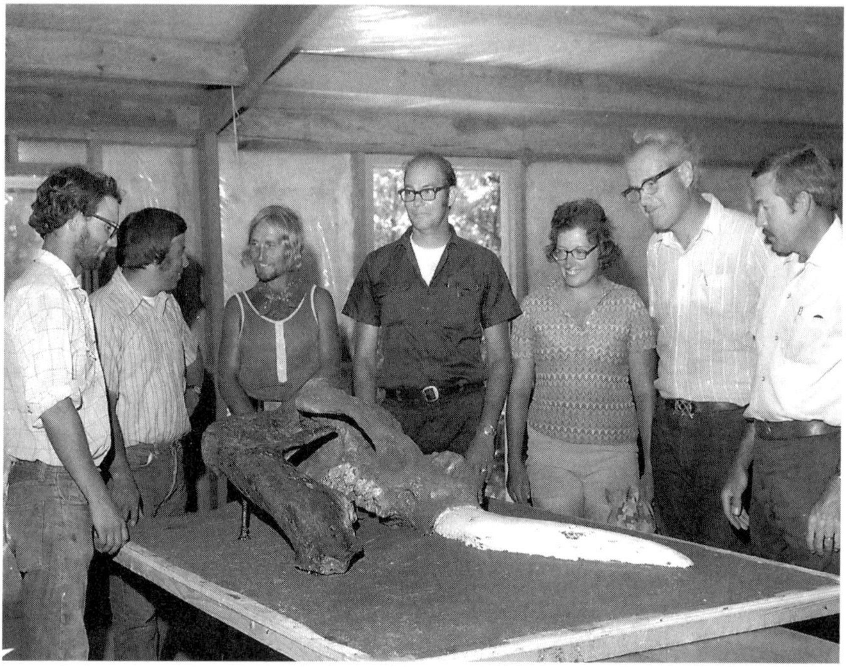

Figure 25. The Western Ozarks Research Consortium at the short-lived Fristoe Museum, 1973. *Left to right*: Louis Jacobs, Bruce McMillan, Jeffrey Saunders, Raymond Wood, Frances and James King, and Vance Haynes. *Author's collection.*

since become extinct). The Manns also had a bumper sticker printed: "Fristoe, Mo.: Mastodon Fossil Capital of Missouri." On one occasion the residents of Fristoe celebrated the town's newfound notoriety during a Jubilee Days parade in Warsaw. Two young people paraded in leopard skins accompanied by a junior-sized papier-mâché mastodon. The events that followed warrant quotation. "Several Saddle Clubs were also participating in the parade. When the horses started arriving they had to pass the mastodon to get in position and when the horses spotted the mastodon, chaos reigned. Horses being transported in pick-up trucks stood on their hind legs, pawing the air, whinnying in terror, trying to escape the monstrous mastodon. Other horses reared, throwing their riders. One horse bolted and ran into a loading dock…but parade officials brought order and maneuvered to keep mastodon and horses strictly apart from then on" (Mann 1971:32).

Fristoe also boasted a bar that we often frequented. One evening, as many of us were cooling down after a blistering hot summer day, the Boney Spring pump-watcher ran in, shouting, "The pump has stopped!" We piled out of the building as if it were on fire and rushed to the spring, where we began bailing water while the pump was being repaired, for the backup pump had also failed. The bones, now dry, would have disintegrated had they been moistened again, but our efforts were successful in stemming the flow of water until the pump was repaired. The crisis evaporated.

Bruce gained some local fame when he saved the lives of three fishermen in 1966 or 1967. One afternoon the crew at Rodgers heard faint cries of "Help, help!" Pinpointing the cries as coming from down the river, Bruce and two of his crew raced to see what was happening. The Pomme de Terre was in flood, and a man and his two sons had been swept out of their boat and were clinging to a tree branch as the water swirled around them. Bruce crawled out on a dangerously slender limb to pull them to safety after his crew members fashioned a lifeline out of their belts and shirts so they wouldn't lose him if the branch broke. It was an exhilarating moment for everyone.

A paleontologist approaching Boney Spring would immediately have felt at home. The bones were carefully exposed, undercut, wrapped in wet plaster-soaked burlap, dried, and removed. We used the same technique at Trolinger Spring, except the bones there were much softer, and before jacketing them in plaster we hardened them, using an early form of epoxy that Vance had discovered. The two springs yielded the partial remains of forty-two mastodons of different ages and a variety of other extinct fauna dating to between 34,000 and 13,600 years ago (middle to late Wisconsin), including giant beaver (*Castoroides ohioensis*), giant ground sloth (*Paramylodon harlani*, but today called *Glossotherium*), and an extinct form of musk ox (*Symbos* sp.). The deposits also included many species that still live in the area today, including deer, raccoons, and cottontail rabbits (Saunders 1977).

The Illinois State Museum later excavated Jones Spring, a short distance east of Trolinger, under the direction of James E. King. The remains there are much older, some of them certainly being of Sangamon age (the last major interglacial), and included the bones of mammoth (*Mammuthus* sp. *jeffersonii*), giant bison (*Bison latifrons*), and American alligator. The giant bison at Jones Spring marks the minimal age of the Rancholabrean fauna, the next-to-last land mammal age in North America. The Rancholabrean is defined by the first appearance of *Bison* in North America south of 55 degrees north latitude and ends with the extinction of the large-bodied mammal species at the end of the Pleistocene (Bell et al. 2004:286). The spring was truly a paleontological bonanza.

Figure 26. The author (*left*) and David Breternitz inspecting the Boney Spring site, Missouri, spring 1967. *Author's collection.*

In many ways our project was a dream come true. It provided scientifically worthwhile problems and friendly and productive working companions, and best of all, it led to significant results in a wide range of interrelated fields. The shelter deposits provided Bruce McMillan with an archaeological record of more than 10,500 years, one that remains a standard against which other sites in the region are still compared. One of the significant finds was a canid burial placed beneath a small stone cairn. The care taken in burying the animal suggests it was a dog, one of the earliest instances of canid domestication in North America (between 6,000 and 8,000 years ago; see McMillan 1970). James King rewrote the biogeography of the late Pleistocene Ozark Highland in his dissertation (King 1973), for he overturned many previous ideas about the history of the vegetational cover in the state. Vance Haynes and Donald Lee Johnson provided the region with an integrated model for alluvial geochronology and the soils that accompany the terraces. Bruce and I edited a summary of the project in the first major monograph on the project, *Prehistoric Man and His Envi-*

ronments (Wood and McMillan 1976). It has been followed by dozens of monographs and articles covering every aspect of the project.

As we continued our work, we referred to our group as the Western Ozark Research Consortium, or WORC. It came about following a day-long meeting with a representative from the Army Corps of Engineers (Richard Leverty) and one from the National Park Service (Lawrence E. "Larry" Aten) at a hotel across from Lambert Field in St. Louis in 1976. In this meeting Bruce and I gained the backing of the corps for projects that supported future Illinois State Museum and University of Missouri projects. We laid out an integrated program explaining how our research at Rodgers Shelter and the spring bogs combined to provide a better understanding of how past cultural processes operated through time and space in the reservoir area. We were a trifle awed and apprehensive when we left the meeting with approximately one million dollars to spend on the work, but we were confident that the project had the value we claimed for it. It did.

When later work in the reservoir shifted sponsorship of the project to the Illinois State Museum, new personnel were added, including the talented botanist Frances B. King (Jim's wife) and zoologist James R. (Rick) Purdue. Between August 8 and 10, 1975, WORC hosted the 23rd Annual Midwest Section of the Friends of the Pleistocene field conference at Rodgers Shelter and the spring bogs. We prepared a detailed field guide and drew a very large crowd from throughout the Midwest (Friends of the Pleistocene 1975). The following day we visited Pleistocene karst features and surficial deposits near the town of Lebanon and in Bennett Springs State Park. A summary and appraisal of the WORC program may be found in Michael J. O'Brien's *Paradigms of the Past: The Story of Missouri Archaeology* (1996:287–309).

Just because we were involved in serious science did not mean we lacked for humor. The University of Missouri's *Alumnus* magazine struck first, with the statement that "in the field, archaeology has many similarities to hard work," an observation the crew in the twenty-five-foot-deep trench through Rodgers Shelter found wholly realistic. While the bones in Boney Spring were being exposed in a tangled mass, a visitor heard someone jokingly refer to some of them as "giant frog bones." Not long afterward Bruce began receiving telephone calls from distant radio talk-show hosts wanting to interview him about this astonishing "discovery." With this stimulation we began to allude to the "Missouri chicken-eating frog" ("*Rana gallovorous*"), but Bruce warned the crew that henceforth they were to be more careful about what they said in the presence of visitors. While we were absent during the project's first winter, the deep trench we had dug to drain Boney Spring filled with water, and one afternoon the following spring one of the well-drilling crew stepped into it, thinking it was shallow: a moment later his straw hat was floating on the surface. He didn't drown, but he was upset!

During this project I initiated a major change in policy in Missouri archaeology, for I hired what were known at the time as "integrated" crews. When I first heard the term, I supposed that it meant a racially diverse crew, but instead it denoted a crew that included women. I hired numerous young women to serve on varying crews, all of them proving equal or superior in their work to many of the men, and the males on the crew at Boney Spring still fondly recall the three bikini-clad and mud-bespattered ladies there as "the Bog Bunnies." One of them went on to a responsible position in a western state's office of archaeology. Near the end of the project the direction of a massive resurvey of the reservoir was delegated to Donna C. Roper, a recent graduate of our department.

Women were beginning to be taken on as members of field schools at the time, but they were not welcomed on most digs because of "problems" in housing and bathroom facilities and the fact that the hot, dusty work was not considered appropriate for women. Yet the Plains and Midwest had long boasted professional women archaeologists who attained national prominence, including Marie Wormington, of the Denver Museum of Natural History. She was the first female Harvard Ph.D. to specialize in archaeology, and in 1967 she became the first woman president of the Society for American Archaeology. One of her protégées, Cynthia Irwin-Williams, initially worked in the Rocky Mountain foothills but later shifted her interests to the American Southwest; in 1975 she also became president of the society.

Throughout most of the WORC program that was under my direction I had such mountains of paperwork and typing projects that it was necessary to hire a full-time secretary. Jean Sparks and Betty Gay Graham filled that position admirably for most of that period, often with the help of Mary Braxton, Michelle Millot, and other competent assistants. Coordinating events, preparing budgets, and other chores associated with administration kept me very busy, and by the time my role as principal investigator was over, I'd had my fill of such duties and had no desire to replicate them.

So far, we'd failed in our attempt to find evidence of the contemporaneity of humans and mastodons in the Pomme de Terre valley. Clues to this effect had been found elsewhere in the eastern United States, but no convincing evidence of such an association had yet become known. This was about to change. Mastodon bones had been found for decades at a site near the little town of Kimmswick, just south of St. Louis. For more than a century, bones had been dug from the sides of a small stream that flowed into the Mississippi River floodplain, beginning with local entrepreneurs Albert C. Koch in 1839 and C. W. Beehler in 1900, William H. Holmes of the Smithsonian Institution in 1901, Robert McCormick Adams of the St. Louis Museum of Science in the 1940s, and still others. Beehler discovered a Clovis point there, but its association with the bones was problematic.

In 1979 and 1980 Russell W. Graham and his colleagues at the Illinois State Museum began investigations at Kimmswick at the invitation of a private group that was petitioning the state to purchase the site and make it a state park. During their investigation Russ and his team discovered the first of two Clovis points embedded in sediments that contained mastodon bones. The point was directly below and in contact with a mastodon bone. It was a monumental find, and to verify and celebrate the discovery Russ invited outside observers to come to Kimmswick and observe the point in situ for themselves. He thereby emulated the invitation that Jesse D. Figgins of the Denver Museum of Natural History had issued on the discovery of Folsom points with the bones of extinct bison in 1926. I came down from Columbia, Vance Haynes flew in from Arizona, Bruce McMillan arrived from Springfield, and yet others came to see the find. We weren't surprised to see a few champagne bottles lying near the small pit containing the point. There was no debate about its context: there were no rodent burrows or other disturbances around it, and I saw that the point was covered with a thick clay cutan, or film, indicative of illuviation, a process in which clay particles that are transported down through a sediment by moisture are slowly deposited on buried solids. Contemporaneity with humans had at last been demonstrated (Graham et al. 1981). Interestingly, dermal ossicles of the giant ground sloth (*Glossotherium harlani*) also were found with the mastodon remains. Because dermal ossicles were attached to the sloth's skin, this discovery probably meant that the Clovis hunters had carried the hides of these animals to Kimmswick. In 1976 the locale became Mastodon State Park, and we were all delighted to attend the dedication of the museum that now graces the hilltop above the find—and we also celebrated Albert Koch's birthday.

The investigation of Rodgers Shelter and the spring bogs had been a resounding success. We'd provided a new yardstick for the prehistory of much of the state and recovered new and reliable data on the paleoecology of the late Pleistocene of the western Ozarks. This record still stands, but it has been immeasurably enriched by excavations at the Big Eddy site by Neal Lopinot and my former student Jack H. Ray, of the Center for Archaeological Research at Missouri State University in Springfield. This site, deeply buried in terrace sediments along the Sac River north of the town of Stockton, has yielded remains that begin with a potential pre-Clovis occupation through Archaic times, filling in and elaborating our record at Rodgers. Together the two sites provide an unsurpassed record of the Holocene human occupation of Missouri. The floor of Rodgers Shelter now lies well below the lake level of the Truman Reservoir and is unlikely ever to be investigated again, certainly not in the foreseeable future. Michael J. O'Brien has said in talks that the WORC project introduced scientific archaeology to Missouri. Certainly what we did was an advance over the descriptive taxonomies and culture histories that characterized prior work in the state, but it was, after all, what our team had been trained to do by a long roster of distinguished mentors who were pioneers in interdisciplinary research.

The combination of archaeological and ecological data embedded in Breshears Bottom and its immediate locality is unique in Missouri and, indeed, in the Midwest. The unusual fact that an alluvial terrace had built up under a rock overhang was a major factor in producing the very deep deposits at Rodgers Shelter. Equally unusual was the presence of no fewer than five springs that contained extinct megafauna within a few miles of the shelter. Nowhere else in the state is such a concentrated prehistoric bonanza to be found. Indeed, the few other springs containing megafauna are widely scattered across the state (see Mehl 1962). The project was a richly educational experience for everyone, and the lessons I learned from the many collaborators led me to design a new course for my department, "Environment and Archaeology." Intended to provide a broad methodological base for the study of Quaternary environments, it focused on the North American record, with an emphasis on the climatological and biological components of regional ecosystems and on environmental reconstruction at the community level. Major topics covered were cultural and natural ecology, soil science, soil mixing, principles of Quaternary stratigraphy, climate as a system, paleoclimatic episodes, modeling past plant and animal communities, fluvial geomorphology, and regional paleoecology. In reality it was nothing more than a course in physical geography that focused on the problems in my own discipline. It was a useful course, one that I hoped to continue to teach after my retirement, as it was agreed at the time. I was permitted to teach it twice; then the agreement terminated when the department could no longer find money for it. Students told me more than once that it was the most valuable course they had taken in graduate school. So much for that agreement!

Today the work we did in the Harry S. Truman Reservoir is featured in a series of displays at the damsite headquarters and overlook northwest of Warsaw. Fiberglass casts of mastodon bones, some of them representing the bones still in the earth, are enclosed by a panorama of images of local history. The central feature of the display is a life-sized enlargement of a photograph of the thirty-foot stratigraphy at Rodgers Shelter, with attached replicas of the projectile points that occurred at different depths, illustrating the changing weapons of Missouri's prehistoric peoples. Visitors view the base of the life-sized profile on the ground floor and its top on the second floor. Designed by staff at the Illinois State Museum, it is an unusual and popular display enjoyed by hundreds of people annually.

In 1969 I had driven with Bruce to Illinois to visit the Illinois State Museum in Springfield, where he interviewed for the position of associate curator of anthropology. He was accepted and within a few years became the museum director. He proceeded to build a Quaternary Studies Program there that employed several of the people who had been involved in WORC, notably James E. King (who later became the director of the Carnegie Museum in Pittsburgh) and his wife Frances, zoologist Rick Purdue, and Jeffrey J. Saunders. Other archaeologist regulars at Rodgers Shelter—Stanley Ahler, Marvin Kay, and Earl Neller—also spent time there. Earl later went to Kalaupupa National Historic Site and was a member of Hawaii's State Historic Preservation Office and the Office of Hawaiian Affairs.

In about 1970 I visited Don Crabtree's flint-knapping school on the banks of the Snake River, near Pocatello, Idaho. There I gained an appreciation for the need to understand flaking technology and was even successful in flaking a few simple bifaces. Using obsidian, of course, made the task far simpler than it would have been with almost any other stone. I was thereafter sympathetic when students wished to explore the technique of knapping and the raw materials that Native Americans used for their tools. Jack H. Ray, for example, wrote his master's thesis in 1981 on the availability, procurement, and use of chert resources in the Truman Reservoir area, a study that culminated in his monograph on the raw material sources and history of chipped-stone tools in the Ozark Highland (Ray 2007). I was also pleased to support Stanley A. Ahler's 1970 master's thesis, "Projectile Point Form and Function at Rodgers Shelter, Missouri," which I quickly published in the Missouri Archaeological Society's research series (Ahler 1971). It became one of the most widely cited master's theses in American archaeology and was greatly influential in the development of flint-knapping studies in North America. Many of these studies and those of my own were illustrated by chipped-stone tools that had been coated by "smoke" from heated ammonium chloride (Holland 1987). Properly photographed with this new technique, the most minute flake scars and other aspects of technology were revealed in a way that drawings could not begin to match.

The MRBS Becomes the NPS and Other Events

In 1965, at the request of the Smithsonian Institution, an ad hoc review committee carried out an evaluation of the Missouri River Basin Surveys program. I did not participate in that meeting, but a second such committee, consisting of Douglas W. Schwartz (chair) of the School of American Research, David A. Baerreis of the University of Wisconsin, Jesse D. Jennings of the University of Utah, and me, was formed in November 1968 to again review the objectives, administrative organization, and procedures of the MRBS. We convened in late January 1969 in Lincoln, Nebraska, with representatives of the MRBS, the Smithsonian Institution, and the National Park Service.

The review was called to consider the changing nature of salvage archaeology in the Missouri Basin. The major reservoirs were now completed and either had filled or were then filling with water. Furthermore, there were by then many more state-affiliated archaeologists available to work in the area. What should be the continuing role of the MRBS in this new environment? There had been ambiguity in the administration of the MRBS from the beginning. Despite outward appearances, it was not an integral part of the Smithsonian Institution but more of an autonomous unit, one that was entirely funded by a second federal agency, the National Park Service. In practice there was no conflict between these two agencies, principally because each of them assumed that responsibility for the operation and its quality control resided with the other.

Smithsonian administrative personnel in Washington seemed to be most concerned about the lack of problem orientation in fieldwork and reports. The committee was asked to consider the publication record of the MRBS, especially its procedures for reviewing manuscripts. Articles and monographs by staff members were routinely and carefully reviewed internally by MRBS directors and relevant staff, but rarely did they undergo outside review except for feedback from papers delivered at the Plains Conference or meetings of the Society for American Archaeology and informal consultations with cooperating archaeologists. Despite this lapse, I believe the bulk of the reports, admittedly emphasizing a culture-historical paradigm, then the reigning one in American archaeology, were consistently of reasonably high quality, certainly in comparison with some of those being prepared by a few of the cooperating state institutions.

The committee contemplated future directions the MRBS might take, but it was obvious to us from conversations with Smithsonian representatives that they were reluctant to maintain any role as a partner in the unit. Our committee debated at length the pros and cons of several options, eventually focusing on four: (1) retention of the status quo but with the addition of research and training, (2) a gradual phase-out of the operation, (3) absorption of the MRBS by the Smithsonian, and (4) absorption of the MRBS by the National Park Service. We agonized over the matter and carefully debated the merits and demerits of each possible course.

To best protect the program and ensure continuity in its activities, the committee eventually endorsed its fourth option, that the MRBS be absorbed into the National Park Service and developed into a regional research center, and we so reported to the director of the Smithsonian (Schwartz et al. 1968; Thiessen 1999:99–103). It was a difficult, unpopular, and controversial decision that engendered no small degree of bitterness in many of the parties involved, but the principals accepted it within the year and the transfer took place smoothly. The result was the formation of the Midwest Archeological Center in Lincoln. After the meeting Jesse and I went out to dinner, the rest of the committee having left for home. We went to an elegant restaurant somewhere on 10th Street (it's no longer there) and ordered a fine meal from a very attractive waitress. Despite my objections Jesse proceeded to proposition her on my behalf, but she remained charming and professional and politely ignored him. I saw to it that we left her a sizable tip. The first chief of the center was Wilfred D. Logan, who assumed its direction in July 1969. For the first few years of its history, the center continued to conduct and support salvage archaeology, but thereafter its concern turned to the management of the archaeological resources within the national parks encompassed by the Omaha regional office. With this transition the MRBS entered history, though its contributions to Great Plains history and prehistory remain a benchmark in Plains anthropology.

During the nearly twenty years of its activity the MRBS and the cooperating state agencies hired hundreds of fieldworkers. Some were students, often but not necessarily archaeology majors, and others were local residents. The experiences of those students who continued their participation in anthropology cannot be measured, for they later spread across the full spectrum of our discipline. James Deetz gained valuable experience with Donald J. Lehmer in South Dakota; Robert L. Hall and Warren L. Wittry with Paul L. Cooper at the Heart Butte Reservoir, North Dakota; David A. Breternitz and William G. Buckles with Wesley R. Hurt in South Dakota; George W. Cowgill with Richard P. Wheeler in North Dakota; R. E. W. Adams, Dena Ferran (later Dincauze), Karl Heider, Roger T. Grange Jr., Paul Tolstoy, and Gary Vescelius with Carlyle S. Smith at the Spain, Talking Crow, or Two Teeth site in South Dakota; and Walter E. Birkby, Frederick H. West, Jon Muller, and Stephen W. Robinson with Alan Woolworth and me at sites in both North and South Dakota. The knowledgeable Plains archaeologist can add other names to this preliminary list, for not all archaeologists are courteous enough in their publications to thank by name the crew members who moved the dirt for them. A substantial number of those listed remained active in Plains research, including Roger Grange, Alfred Johnson, and Richard Krause.

The MRBS program had its faults, but it brought a degree of uniformity to our database. The trinomial site designation system devised by Paul L. Cooper for the Nebraska State Archaeological Survey (NSAS) in the years before World War II was modified for use nationwide when Cooper became the director of the Missouri River Basin Survey. John Champe pointed out (in a neglected little essay) that so many Peterson sites were being found in Nebraska by the NSAS that all sites eventually were named Peterson, then given a county code followed by a site number (Champe 1948:45–46). (The "Peterson" problem came about because of the numerous Scandinavian residents living in the state.) The system was modified

Figure 27. Richard A. Krause on the shore of Lake Oahe, August 1978. *Author's collection.*

to use a numerical designation for the state, based on alphabetical order (before the admission of Alaska and Hawaii), followed by a two-letter designation for the county within the state and then a site number, as in 32MO11 (North Dakota, Morton County, site number 11). The system has been adopted by all but a few of the states, though few archaeologists today know its history. The site designation system and other organizational tools made for easy data recovery. The need for interdisciplinary integration of different sciences began to be realized near the end of the program, though such studies were indeed rare in the profession itself at the time. Certainly, key sites were excavated, and their collections and reports provide insights as well as useful data to this day.

Unfortunately, most of the excavations at the time were undertaken to fill "gaps" in our knowledge of various prehistoric periods and complexes, and there were few studies that attempted any sort of synthesis of the incoming data. Donald J. Lehmer (1954) provided just such a synthesis for the village cultures of the Plains, and William Mulloy (1958) offered a preliminary outline for the Northwestern Plains, but for the most part the fieldwork was designed to obtain data before they were lost forever beneath the reservoirs. It was only toward the end of the program that it began to be realized that one can do "salvage" archaeology and "problem-oriented" archaeology at the same time if the appropriate data are collected. Nonetheless, we continue to use those flawed collections and reports in understanding and interpreting Plains prehistory. Indeed, what database is *not* flawed? There is no doubt that the standards being used today in field archaeology will likewise be disparaged for their weaknesses in the not-too-distant future.

The lessons, both good and bad, that the MRBS experience provided nearly a generation of archaeologists were put to good use in a host of interdisciplinary programs in the following years. The WORC program was one such project that benefited from those lessons (Wood and McMillan 1976). Given the time, funds, and circumstances of the period, we have every reason to be grateful for the contribution to our discipline by those who were dedicated to the MRBS program.

After Wilfred Logan's retirement, Carl R. Falk became chief of the Midwest Archeological Center, and when he joined the anthropology department at the University of Nebraska, he was succeeded by Cal Calabrese, who remained at that post for twenty years (1975–1995), at which time he moved to the regional office in Omaha and Mark J. Lynott took up the reins. Thomas D. Thiessen has admirably summarized the role of the MRBS and the Midwest Archeological Center in the Inter-Agency Archeological Salvage Program between 1946 and 1975 (1999; see also Glenn 1994; Jennings 1985).

In 1966 William C. Sturtevant, at the Smithsonian Institution, conceived the idea of preparing a new edition of the Bureau of American Ethnology's 1907–1910 *Handbook of American Indians North of Mexico*, for by now it was hopelessly out of date, due in large part to the massive research carried out on Native American tribes by participants in the Justice Department's Indian Claims Commission. Drawing on the expertise of a host of regional scholars, the handbook was planned as a twenty-volume series covering the culture areas of North America north of Mexico; its outline was essentially complete by 1971. As of 2010, fifteen of the proposed volumes were in print, including two double-volume surveys of the Southwest and the Plains. I was chosen to contribute all or part of three chapters to the Plains volume: those on the Middle Missouri tradition in 1971 and on the Mandan and Omaha Indians in 1972 and 1973 (Wood 2001; Wood and Irwin 2001; Liberty et al. 2001). Contributors were asked to write articles of about 5,000 to 6,250 words (some twenty-five double-spaced pages, though many of them became far longer), for each of which we were paid $175. Suitable illustrations were chosen that were compatible with the sensitivities of the tribes involved. Each chapter was revised at least three times over the course of the next three decades while the volume was in production.

The first editor of the Plains volume was William W. Bittle, of the University of Oklahoma, but the scope of the work (there was far more to it than anyone anticipated) and the length of time needed to edit the volume led to his replacement in 1983, when Raymond J. DeMallie, of the University of Indiana, assumed its editorship. Final production on the two-part volume began in 1998, and before it went to press I served as the reviewer-editor and coordinator for the chapters on prehistory (DeMallie 2001).

The Lower Grand and Cross Ranch Sites

In 1969 the National Park Service awarded me a contract to conduct investigations at the Lower Grand site (39CO14). This prehistoric Extended Coalescent earthlodge village site lay on the west bank of the Oahe Reservoir opposite the town of Mobridge, South Dakota, and a few miles north of the most recent burial site for Sitting Bull. Alfred W. Bowers, of the University of Idaho, had dug there earlier, but his work had been less than satisfactory. I was assisted by Stanley A. Ahler and Carl Falk: Ahler later used data from the site for his two-volume doctoral dissertation, and Falk eventually prepared the final site report for the National Park Service.

We rented a house on the east side of Mobridge to serve as our field headquarters and spent June and much of August working at the site. Work continued the following season at this distinctive, fortified Extended Coalescent village. In 1969 Ahler and I made a preliminary map of the nearby Helb village site (39CA208), which was fast eroding into the reservoir; excavations were done there in 1972 and 1973 for the National Park Service (Falk and Calabrese 1973). In 1970 and 1971 work in the Mobridge locality continued with excavations at the two-component Walth Bay site (39WW203), also an Extended Coalescent village.

Saturday night in Mobridge was a busy one. Main Street was filled with cars, and saloons were crowded with patrons. People also drank on the sidewalks, and many of them sat on the hoods of cars in front of the overflowing saloons, with their feet on the bumpers or sidewalk. One morning after having parked on the street, I had to lift the hood of my car and bump out the "bun dimples" they'd impressed into the metal. Mobridge also put on an outstanding rodeo that year, but the most exciting event of the summer was watching the landing of the first American spacecraft on the moon. My family was invited next door to witness it on a neighbor's television. After dinner it was pleasant to drive in the country and watch as the lengthening shadows made a kaleidoscope of the rolling hills west of town and squadrons of pelicans floated in the sky above us.

At the conclusion of our 1969 work at Mobridge most of the crew moved to an abandoned house in the ghost town of Sanger, two miles south of Robert Levis's Cross Ranch home in North Dakota. Bob had provided Don Lehmer and me $3,000 for the excavation of the Cross Ranch site, a small Middle Missouri tradition village that lay three-quarters of a mile south of his ranch. The house Bob supplied nevertheless had electricity, so we were able to keep our beer cold in one refrigerator and our food in another, but it had few other amenities except to keep us dry. It became known as the "Sanger Hilton" and was easily identified by visitors because of the saddle-shaped roof on a barn that was slowly collapsing beside the road. Cal Calabrese served as my assistant and later used the material for his doctoral dissertation. Bob Levis subsidized its publication as Memoir 9 of the *Plains Anthropologist* (Calabrese 1972).

As we excavated two long-rectangular houses along the terrace rim, we encountered unforeseen difficulties. I'd expected these houses to be in pits, as my experience elsewhere had led me to believe, but they were not. They were built on a former land surface not far below the present ground level, and their remains lay entirely within the modern A-horizon, so we were unable to detect features on the house floors until we'd stripped them to the base of that horizon, where the black prairie surface soil graded into the light brown B-horizon. This stripping of course truncated the postholes and other features, though the house architecture and its internal features remained clear. I now began to see why archaeologists badly needed at least a rudimentary knowledge of soil science, a realization that was cemented the following summer when I dug at the Old Fort site in Missouri. Many archaeologists at the time, myself included, thought they knew something about soil simply because they'd spent so much time digging in various kinds of "dirt," a term that, by the way, is a dirty word among soil scientists, for "soil" has a very specific and dynamic meaning that I was coming to understand and appreciate.

Because of this increasing dissatisfaction with my comprehension of the natural and physical world, I began to sit in on classes in other academic departments. My first class was "Soils Genesis, Development, and Classification," taught by agronomy graduate student James C. Baker; I attended every class and took each exam. Jim would correct them, but he declined to attach a grade, uneasy I'm sure about the possibility of offending a professor (even one in another department). It was a valuable experience and was followed by two classes in geomorphology, in which I immersed myself in landscape development. The first was a traditional course in geology, but the next one was taught by a recent Ph.D. who passed on to us the newest concepts in landscape evolution. I urged my graduate students to take these classes for credit; many of them did. The classes were admirably reinforced by lessons that were brought home to me in field trips hosted by the American Quaternary Association and the Midwest Friends of the Pleistocene. The unofficial song of the latter group begins, "We are friends of the Pleistocene, but damned little ice we have seen."

As one of our ancillary projects in North Dakota in 1969, we tested a Late Woodland/Besant site (32ME13) atop High Butte, a small but prominent flat-topped butte along the Missouri Bluffs a few miles north of Stanton. Earlier I'd noticed a peculiar anomaly on aerial photographs near the rim of the prominence, and on investigation we found it to be the outline of a turtle, created by grooves carved in the sod, producing what we called a turf-cut effigy. The feature consists of a central rectangular depression twenty-five feet long and seventeen feet wide, surrounded by a shallow trench cut into the sod, with conspicuous extensions on each corner to represent legs and another extension on one end to represent the head. An arc of five depressions surrounded this curious feature. We dug a twenty-foot square test in the center of one of them, expecting to find some form of dwelling, but instead recovered smashed bones, probably the result of the production of bone grease. We also made a total surface collection that I later wrote up with Ann Mary Johnson (Wood and Johnson 1973). When I first reported the site and its effigy at a Plains Conference, Jimmy Griffin looked at me with a smile and asked, "What had you been smoking when you found it?" But the effigy is real and remains unique to this day, and the landowners who manage the nearby Missouri River Lodge bed-and-breakfast carefully preserve the site, now listed on the National Register of Historic Places. I met Griffin, a brilliant but irascible scholar, many times, but one incident stands out in my mind. Following what he regarded as an idiotic remark by a colleague at the Society for American Archaeology's annual meeting in Bloomington, Indiana, he turned from his front-row seat and, facing the crowd, drew his finger across his neck. He usually said what was on his mind.

Don Lehmer was visiting us when we closed down the 1969 field season in North Dakota. When we parted, I gave him my cigarette lighter and discarded my last pack of cigarettes. Over the past few years I'd graduated from a casual smoker to a chain smoker and was consuming three packs

Figure 28. The author (*center left*) and Donald J. Lehmer at the Upper Sanger site, North Dakota, August 1969. *Author's collection.*

a day, and I even awoke from sleep to light a cigarette or two during the night. The next several weeks of withdrawal from such a heavy dose of nicotine were physical torture, but I never again inhaled another cigarette, though it took nearly two years to rid myself of unconscious motor habits related to my addiction.

That fall Don and I obtained a complete photocopied set of the field notes that Gilbert L. Wilson made when he interviewed Mandan and Hidatsa informants on the Fort Berthold Reservation between 1908 and 1918. The notes occupy fifteen binders and fill nearly two feet of shelf space. Their contents had been largely published by Wilson and, after his death, by Bella Weitzner in the papers of the American Museum of Natural History, but the original text provided the verbatim statements we preferred to consult.

In 1970 Don, assisted by Cal Calabrese, returned to North Dakota and worked at the Bagnell site (32OL16), which I'd tested two years earlier; it was a multicomponent village three miles north of the Cross Ranch buildings. Don returned to Bagnell again in 1972 and excavated a long-rectangular house that Wilfred Logan and I had visited on one of our tours of digs being conducted by cooperating institutions. Bagnell was a large site, and Lehmer dug several houses that, unfortunately, were not studied before he suffered a tragic automobile accident near Hamburg, Iowa, that autumn that took the life of his wife and seriously injured Don and his sons. Don and his family had been on their way to Alton, Illinois, to visit Bob Levis when the accident occurred. This important material has never been written up.

Faunal Studies at the University of Missouri

Environmental interests, fueled by the pioneering work of Ted White in zooarchaeological studies, were the impetus for forming a faunal collection at the University of Missouri. Today surely the largest collection of animal skeletal materials in the state of Missouri, it began modestly enough in the 1960s. Carl Falk was responsible for its inception, and my field crews throughout Missouri were recruited to obtain the skeletons of whatever animals came into their hands: the remains of domestic animals, skeletons found in the countryside, carcasses obtained by hunting, and roadkills. In the summers of 1968 and 1969 I secured scientific collector's permits from the North Dakota Game and Fish Department that gave me permission to take nonprotected birds and animals in the state. This allowed us to fill some significant gaps in our collections, including small mammals and out-of-season birds such as pheasants (the permits cost twenty-five cents!). For the first time in my life I went hunting, though my success rate was anything but phenomenal. We also obtained specimens from the Dakota Zoo in Bismarck and the Game and Fish Department. Even my family's Siamese cat was accessioned following its fatal encounter with a car (curiously enough, not one bone was broken).

On a trip to the American Southwest the field crew in one of our American Archaeology Division vehicles saw the nearly intact remains of a coyote on the highway, stopped to pick up this aromatic specimen, and tied it to the rear bumper. At the next fuel stop the station attendant, pumping gas into the tank at the back of the truck, innocently asked, "Say, what happened to your dog?" Some collecting techniques were more imaginative than others. One field supervisor picked up a large live snapping turtle and tried to drown the hapless reptile in a barrel of water (not knowing they can remain submerged for a very long time). After nearly losing a finger testing its vital signs, he eventually tired of the effort and froze it solid in a local locker plant before returning it to our rendering laboratory in Columbia. We maintained a deep freeze unit in our quarters at 703 Missouri Avenue to hold specimens until they were processed. Unfortunately, its electrical supply failed once, and it was not inspected for a considerable period afterward. The resulting stew was astonishingly ripe, and volunteers to clean it out were hard to find.

One unique means to augment our collection was found in an exotic deer farm east of Columbia on the road to Fulton. For many years a private hunt club maintained a small herd of Eurasian fallow deer (*Dama dama*) and other rare species (including peacocks) on its property. Driving past the farm one day in 1965 on my return from the Winston Churchill Memorial in Fulton, I noticed the carcass of one of the deer lying in a gully near the road. I pulled into the club's driveway and sought out the manager. Explaining that I was collecting bones for a faunal collection, I asked if he'd be agreeable to calling me when one of the animals died. He was happy to cooperate, for I'd convinced him it was in the interest of education and an odiferous element was removed from the property. Whenever he alerted me to a death, I'd drive out and pick up the remains, and Walter Klippel and other graduate students would help me skin and deflesh them.

My idea was to macerate the bones of these exotic deer and use them in trade with other institutions for the skeletons of animals we couldn't readily obtain. It worked beautifully. One such skeleton that I sent to a zoologist at the University of Wyoming netted us in return a boxful of prairie dog skeletons and other western species that helped round out our collection. Claude W. Hibbard, the noted paleontologist at the University of Michigan's Museum of Paleontology, also exchanged specimens that were valuable to us but commonplace to him. In turn, we were able to instruct him in the use of papain to deflesh skeletons (papain is an emulsifier that is also used to tenderize meat). The collection grew slowly but steadily by a variety of means. For example, we obtained the skeleton of a dingo from the St. Louis Zoo that we swapped with Hibbard for I forget what. At one point we hired zoology major George Kassler to process the specimens that flowed into Columbia each field season. "Let George do it" became more than an expression. The fume hood in the tower room adjoining my office bubbled with the carcasses of beasts both rare and common; the aroma one afternoon of a dog was surprisingly appealing! On one occasion I caught a whiff of skunk as I crossed the campus and, on returning to my office, confirmed my suspicions, for a fresh example was cooking in the fume hood. One afternoon graduate student Steve Sigstad nearly threw up on a text he was reading when one of the crew passed behind him to deliver a dead turkey vulture to our "rendering room." I met George again many years later when he was an employee of the Missouri Department of Natural Resources.

At first we processed the animals by simply boiling the stripped-down carcasses and extracting the bones from the resulting stew. As time went by, we progressed to dropping their stripped carcasses into papain, which liquefied the flesh. The bones were strained from the resulting soup. For a time we also used dermestid beetles in a steel barrel in the attic of Swallow Hall, but the technique was abandoned when carpenters making repairs near the barrel discovered it. When they opened its cover and found bones crawling with beetles, they refused to work in the area until it was removed. Eventually, we obtained special airtight steel cabinets to house the processed specimens, filling most of a room on the second floor of Swallow Hall. I once considered (after my demise) having my bones mounted in a glass case by the entry and labeled "Our Founder."

The growing comparative collection now permitted us to identify the bones from our excavations with confidence, and we aggressively expanded both the collection and the interpretation of faunal remains from our sites. One summer in the mid-1960s I visited Waldo Wedel's excavations at a prehistoric village site in central Kansas. By this time the backdirt piles at the University of Missouri were no longer sprinkled with skeletal elements, but my suggestion that Waldo send us those that littered his backdirt was politely ignored. He felt that saving the larger identifiable elements was sufficient.

The list of skeletal elements that appeared in the appendixes in most site reports up to that time was all but useless. Only the larger and obviously identifiable bones were saved for the specialist to inspect. The resulting list was predictable, for it could as easily have been compiled by reviewing a roster of locally available animals and including those that modern hunters would have carried home as game (including, of course, some that had been locally extirpated such as bison and elk). Smithsonian paleontologist Theodore White had begun to change that cavalier attitude toward American Indian protein sources more than a decade earlier. Today zooarchaeologist R. Lee Lyman uses the faunal collection we assembled.

The Old Fort

I taught my first archaeological field school in the summer of 1970 after a distinctive site on the Missouri River west of Columbia aroused my curiosity. The Old Fort (23SA104) is an irregular double-ditched enclosure on a high hill overlooking the Missouri just west of the Utz archaeological site (23SA2). Utz is a prehistoric to protohistoric Oneota village that was occupied by the Missouria Indians until about 1794. The Old Fort earthworks had been known for over a century and had attracted the attention of a variety of scholars, but it was not until 1961 that Douglas McKenzie dug some test pits there. Because of the earthworks, and his finds of Middle Woodland pottery, he concluded that the site was not related to the nearby Missouria Indian village but was Hopewellian in origin. The conclusion seemed reasonable at the time, since a cluster of Middle Woodland sites exist along the Missouri River nearby and along the lower reaches of its tributaries. Because both our department and Alfred Johnson at the University of Kansas were interested in Middle Woodland sites at the time, it seemed desirable to investigate this intriguing site to see how it related to them.

Field schools from the University of Kansas (under Al Johnson) and Kansas State University (under Patricia J. O'Brien) joined me that summer in a collaborative effort, sharing both lectures and field experience. Al investigated Fisher-Gabert (23SA128), a nearby Middle Woodland village site, and Pat tested the Utlaut site (23SA162W), an Oneota–historic Missouria Indian burial site a few miles west of Utz. It was an enjoyable summer, and the three of us got along famously. The field school was housed at the Lyman Research Center on the Utz site. Historic-sites archaeologist Robert T. Bray directed the center, and it was maintained by the American Archaeology Division. The unit boasted comfortable living quarters and adequate laboratory space adjoining a well-equipped kitchen. We also had a fine cook. One evening when I went to the laboratory I found the students baking brownies. I noticed they were a little uneasy when I helped myself to some of them, but I thought nothing of it at the time. Not long afterward I felt unexpectedly tired and wound my way back to my room. Whether the students brought their own stash or harvested some of the local and very hardy weed I never learned. There was plenty of marijuana about, for vigorous patches of it remained in isolated areas from the days of World War I, when it had been grown to produce rope. I had a lot to learn.

Though the Old Fort and the land adjoining it are today in heavy timber, our excavations revealed that the earthworks had been dug into a Mollisol (a prairie soil). Seeking an answer to this inconsistency led me to early historic references and to the records of the surveys by the U.S. government's General Land Office. The latter records revealed that the uplands along the river had been entirely free of trees in 1817, but by 1862 they were covered with timber, a condition that persists to this day. The reason? Trees replaced the prairie when the first settlers stopped the fires that maintained the upland grasslands. This was another important lesson in soil science, one that was reinforced by excavations at the site in 1971 by graduate student Gary R. Leaf. He found no aboriginal features when he stripped the A-horizon from two ten-foot-square units, but he exposed numerous small, thin, irregular, and ephemeral patches of light gray soil that changed form when they were even lightly troweled. These patches were identified by Clarence L. Scrivner, soil scientist at the University of Missouri–Columbia, as an incipient E-horizon that was beginning to form because of the acids leaching from the leaves deposited by the tree cover that had mantled the site for the past century. The lessons in soil science I received from this excavation were added to those learned at the Cross Ranch, providing yet another step in my environmental education and leading me into further studies of the importance of pedology in archaeological studies.

After analyzing the artifacts in relation to the stratigraphy in my 1970 excavations at the Old Fort, I concluded that the "fort" was not a Middle Woodland construction but had been built by the Oneota-Missouria Indians as some form of adjunct to their village. This affiliation was demonstrated by the discovery of Oneota pottery resting directly on the floor of one of the trenches, embedded in wash deposits from the earliest erosional events after the ditch was dug. The Middle Woodland pottery in our tests had been cast aside when the ditches were originally dug and had been mantled by Oneota remains (Wood 1973). Carl Chapman disliked my conclusion and felt that further excavation was necessary to support it, for it did not fit his image of Middle Woodland earth management, despite the fact that Oneota earthworks are found scattered across other parts of the Midwest. He nevertheless dropped the Old Fort from his discussion of Middle Woodland in the second volume of his *Archaeology of Missouri*.

The summer was a pleasant professional and social success for Al, Pat, and me, and we cooperated in other ways in the coming years. From time to time in the 1970s, as Al or Anta Montet-White at Kansas University and I taught concurrent seminars, we'd have our students travel to Lawrence or Columbia to present their seminar papers in a mini-conference at the partner university. It was as enjoyable as it was good professional training.

A by-product of that summer was a brief comment I published in *American Antiquity*, "Vegetational Reconstruction and Climatic Episodes" (Wood 1976). Botanists had long used the General Land Office surveys, made between 1815 and 1910, to construct models of pre-Euroamerican vegetation, and archaeologists had just begun to use them to model the vegetation patterns around their sites. The reason: natural vegetation in the East and Midwest has been strikingly modified, if not destroyed, by clearing and plowing. Using General Land Office data, we could make models that provided important baselines for understanding the relations between a site and its occupants. The fly in this ointment is the fact that vegetation mirrors climatic conditions, and climate is remarkably changeable even over short periods of time. The General Land Office surveys were made in the years immediately following what is today called the "Little Ice Age" of about 1550 to 1850. Forest boundaries as well as composition changed as these cold conditions made way for the warmer period that followed. Consequently, data obtained in the closing years of the Little Ice Age are surely more appropriate for late Middle Woodland and Late Woodland times than for any other part of the past millennium. Nevertheless, used properly, General Land Office vegetational constructions can shed light on the setting in which the occupants of a site once lived.

9

Sabbatical in Colorado

The Missouri, whose sources are still unknown, is, however, already classed amongst the largest rivers. It is an object of astonishment to every body. The uninstructed man admires the rapidity of its stream, its extraordinary length, the salubrity of its waters, and their uncommon colour. The experienced traveller is astonished at the riches scattered along its banks, and looking into futurity, beholds this rival of the Nile passing through countries as fruitful, as populous, and more extensive than those of Egypt.

— Antoine Soulard, Surveyor-General of Upper Louisiana, *Descriptive Observations on Certain Parts of the Country in Louisiana*, 1806

Boulder, Colorado

By the fall of 1970 I was ready for a change, and I managed to obtain both a year's sabbatical from my university and a semester's teaching position at the University of Colorado in Boulder. I rented a small apartment in faculty housing on Athens Street, a ten-minute hike north of the campus, and daily walked to my office in Hellems Hall, climbing the high, steep hill that lay between home and my office. I shared my office with archaeologist James J. Hester, who, because of the Walt Disney dwarf–like beard he wore, was nicknamed (at least clandestinely) "Elf." In the fall I taught two classes, a graduate seminar called "Native Trade Systems" and an undergraduate class, "Archaeology of the Plains." More important for my education, I sat in on the seminar "Quaternary Stratigraphy," taught by Peter W. Birkeland in the Department of Geological Sciences. In addition to fundamentals of glacial geology and the Quaternary sequence, the course included a field trip to one of the rock glaciers on Mount Sopris. The glacial geology and related features we observed there provided sharp focus for what we learned in the seminar.

Mount Sopris is a twin-peaked mountain 12,965 feet in elevation in White River National Forest in the Elk Mountains. It rises in west-central Colorado nineteen air miles west of the resort town of Aspen, our last stop before Birkeland led us to the foot of our destination. Glaciation has carved two large cirques into the northeastern flank of Mount Sopris, both of which contain a large and conspicuous feature known as a rock glacier. Such features, which characterize many of the cirques in the Colorado Rocky Mountains, consist of a mass of rocky detritus that has flowed downslope from the cirque face through the action of an ice base or core; superficially, they resemble ice glaciers. We climbed to a proglacial lake at the terminus of the southeastern glacier and clambered up across its surface of boulders, which ranged in size from footballs to Volkswagens. It was an exhausting day spent leaping from rock to rock, and we slept well that night. On a later trip to the mountain on a Friends of the Pleistocene field trip, again led by Birkeland, the venerable soil scientist Heber Lessig was complaining about its difficulty, and I mentioned that this was my second trip up the mountain. Heber's response: "No power on earth could get me up here twice!" Heber was a walking soils laboratory: you could hand him a sample of soil, and he would moisten it, roll it between his fingers, and tell you within a few figures just how much clay it contained. On our first trip we inspected an incipient soil profile that had developed in a small accumulation of sediment high up the glacier, and we examined the patches of the lichen *Rhizocarpon geographicum* that colonizes its rocks. Because patches of this lichen have been shown to grow at a constant rate, it is possible to obtain a relative date for the length of time a given rock has been exposed to the elements. This is an important means of dating high-altitude archaeological sites, where radiocarbon dating is unreliable, for wood will last for centuries above timberline. These alpine geology lessons were reinforced a few months later when I attended the first annual meeting of the American Quaternary Association, in Bozeman, Montana.

Much of my time that fall was spent analyzing the artifacts and stratigraphy from my work at the Old Fort, but I also became interested in a local archaeological problem. Upper Republican sites in south-central Nebraska and north-central Kansas were those of prehistoric horticulturists who lived in scattered hamlets along streams with arable floodplains. Yet there are numerous campsites in the High Plains in Colorado and in adjoining parts of Wyoming and Nebraska that contain distinctively Upper Republican pottery in settings that were incapable of providing garden crops. The material recovered from several such sites was held in the collections at the University of Colorado Museum and at the University of Denver. I began working on an analysis of these sites in the fall and into the spring of 1971. The work also took me to visit Herbert W. Dick at Trinidad State Junior College, Alamosa campus, who had excavated rockshelters near the town of Limon, Colorado.

I was struck by the distribution of the High Plains Upper Republican sites, for all of them were in the grasslands a full day's walk from the Rocky Mountain foothills. Yet every Native American culture from Clovis to its historic Indian occupants had exploited the full range of the landscape from these grasslands to the mountainous setting of Rocky Mountain National Park along the continental divide. What was the reason for this disparity in distribution? And were these High Plains people year-round residents of the area, or were they hunting parties traveling far to the west from their homes in the Central Plains? Radiocarbon dates revealed that the two groups were of comparable age.

The most plausible conclusion I could draw from the available data was that these western sites were hunting stations, not the remains of local hunting and gathering peoples. Though I was not fully satisfied with this conclusion, I reasoned that local peoples would have exploited the full range of the environments available to them, from the grasslands to the adjoining mountains, but the evidence suggested they did not (Wood 1971b:80–81). Upper Republican sites have since been found in the foothills near Boulder, but they have yet to be found in the mountains. Though I later concluded that the local and permanent resident interpretation might be somewhat better supported, I felt that neither alternative could be accepted without further evidence. In 1990 Donna Roper reviewed the problem again and argued that the sites are not the results of penetration by hunting parties from the east (Roper 1990). But the original question remains: why did these people not exploit the mountains? Were groups living there that were hostile to them or their incursions? Alternatively, have we simply not yet found Upper Republican sites in the mountains?

Living in Boulder allowed me to make weekend visits to a variety of important sites, some of them for the first time. One such site was Signal Butte, on the North Platte River near the town of Scottsbluff, and the nearby Scottsbluff Bison Quarry. The view from the top of Signal Butte is indeed impressive, but even more so is the volume of artifacts there and the number of game animals (represented by their bones) that had been carried to its top by its many prehistoric inhabitants, for the only way to its apex was to clamber up a steep rock wall. On the occasion of my visit a small but irate rattlesnake guarded the only route up. Another visit, to the Archaic-age Lime Creek and Red Smoke sites in Harlan County, revived memories from my undergraduate years at Nebraska.

Richard Krause and Alfred Johnson visited me during my residence in Boulder; Al was then editor of the *Plains Anthropologist.* On a drive between Boulder and Denver they asked if I'd consider becoming the next editor of the journal. After some consideration I rashly accepted. Little did I realize what I was agreeing to do. I remained the editor from 1972 to 1974, completing volumes 17 through 19 (Nos. 55 to 66), and I continued to edit the memoirs of the *Plains Anthropologist* until 1979.

When my teaching duties were over at the end of the fall semester, the university housing office sent me a notice to vacate my apartment since I was no longer a university employee. I certainly didn't want to move for the short time remaining and seek other housing, undoubtedly at greater cost, so I approached Joe Ben Wheat, curator of anthropology at the University Museum, with a proposition. He agreed to appoint me a research associate in the museum, legitimately enough, since I was studying the Upper Republican materials in its collections. This permitted me to remain in faculty housing until the end of the spring semester, and I was able to continue my contacts with some of the more remarkable members in the department, including David Breternitz, Alice Brues, and Omer C. Stewart. Dave was a specialist on the American Southwest and a regular attendee at the Plains Conference. Omer, a remarkable scholar of great breadth, was the foremost authority on the Ute Indians and had also written extensively on Native American religions, especially the Peyote Religion (the Native American Church). Joe Ben, though a renowned southwestern archaeologist, was known in the Plains for his outstanding work and interpretation of the Paleoindian Olsen-Chubbuck and Jurgens bison kill sites in Colorado. I first became acquainted with Joe Ben when I visited him at the Jurgens site on my return to Columbia from North Dakota in 1968.

Before leaving Boulder, I went to Bozeman to attend the first meeting of the newly formed American Quaternary Association (AMQUA). Its three-day meeting in August and September 1970 was titled "Climatic Changes from 14,000 to 9,000 Years Ago" and included a postmeeting field trip to Yellowstone National Park. A naive comment by an archaeologist there still sticks in my mind. "I don't believe in the Altithermal. I see no evidence for it in my area." Certainly it was known then, and today it is axiomatic among atmospheric scientists, that climatic change does not express itself similarly in every region: when some areas become warmer, others become cooler, and still others do not change at all.

Harold E. Malde, a mathematician and geologist with the U.S. Geological Survey in Denver, drove me back to Boulder after the meeting. The drive was scenic and the conversation was stimulating, for Hal was not only a fine geologist who explained the history of the landscapes we drove by but a talented photographer who was interested in repeat photography as an aid to the study of landscape change. He would later coauthor a bibliography on the subject, and our dialogue during the trip gave me the germ of an idea that came to fruition on the Upper Missouri River almost a decade later.

Bozeman was my first association with such a wide-ranging group of scientists, for it included specialists in every conceivable natural science, from geology to atmospheric science. I've managed to attend most of the subsequent biennial meetings (through 2010), though my principal contribution to the proceedings was to serve as secretary for six years and give the banquet talk at the meeting in Lawrence, Kansas, in 2004. Sometime after my return to Columbia in 1970, I received a phone call from AMQUA's president, David G. Frey, asking if I'd consider becoming the group's secretary. I readily accepted and subsequently was elected for two terms, serving the group between 1972 and 1978. In the process I became familiar, at least by name, with virtually every significant Quaternary scientist in the United States. I was given help in mailing flyers and ballots by my graduate students, principally Ann Mary Johnson and Margaret (Peggy) Guccione. Margaret later became treasurer of the association. Between 1988 and 1990 I also served on its executive committee as a councilor for anthropology and archaeology. AMQUA meetings provided invaluable and up-to-date information that I incorporated into my seminar on environment and archaeology.

I was exposed to new and exciting topics, as well as meeting some truly great figures in other fields of study. The example that springs to mind is having dinner one evening with a group that included Hans Jenny, then a prominent figure in the study of soil genesis and one of the most humorous conversationalists I've ever met. The meetings were seminars on a wide range of Quaternary topics. Some auxiliary events took a less serious turn. At the AMQUA meeting in Madison, Wisconsin, in 1974 I joined C. Thomas Shay and Charles Schweger on a stroll downtown one evening. We stopped at what should probably be called a speakeasy not far from the capitol building for a beer in a densely packed barroom. Taking the only seats available at the back of the room, we were repelled by the behavior of some drunks seated directly beneath the bar, where a stripper was performing her art, pounding tables with their bottles and shouting "Take it off, take it off!" We ordered our beers and, as the evening proceeded, moved successively nearer the bar as tables vacated. After sufficient beers we found ourselves seated beneath the bar and we too were pounding our bottles and demanding, "Take it off!" I've never seen or experienced such a rapid descent into utter depravity before or since.

Each AMQUA meeting differs in the scholars it attracts, for each addresses a different aspect of the Quaternary. Once the meeting's theme is approved by the executive committee, an organizing committee invites the speakers and arranges the program. Consequently, one speaks by invitation only. Anyone, however, can submit an abstract and display a poster. The most exciting meetings to me were those that bore directly on topics relevant to archaeology, such as the one in Edmonton, Alberta, on the ice-free corridor, and the one in Anchorage, which focused on the peopling of the New World. The field trips are intensely educational seminars in Quaternary science, for there is always someone who can comment on anything, from the clouds drifting above us to the beetles in the rotting logs on the forest floor and the bedrock that controls the landforms we visit. Only meetings of the various cells of the Friends of the Pleistocene, a wholly informal organization without officers, dues, or a journal, can compete in offering such information to their participants.

Plains Villagers vs. Their Nomadic Neighbors

About this time I became increasingly curious about intertribal trade among North American Indians. John C. Ewers, drawing on earlier work by Joseph Jablow, had published a significant article on the subject in 1955, and its reprint (Ewers 1968) had so intrigued me that I began to put together a model for the exchange system between the Northern Plains and the Pacific Northwest. I first became interested in this when I found Pacific Northwest Coast dentalium shells at the Huff site in 1960, and I was further intrigued when I discovered a year later that Robert Lowie had believed that the tobacco grown by the Mandans and Hidatsas, *Nicotiana rustica*, had diffused eastward from sources on the Pacific coast. His conclusion was reinforced by the fact that the Hidatsa and Crow words for tobacco are virtually identical to the terms used by tribes on the West Coast, from southern California to Oregon (Lowie 1982:26).

Slowly I came to conceive of the exchange between the two regions in terms of the newly popular systems theory, with trade between the areas consisting of two interacting regional systems, which I called the Middle Missouri (MM) and the Pacific-Plateau (PP) systems. Both systems I saw as marked by three homologous, interdependent social, economic, and communication subsystems. (1) In the MM system, the presence of the Calumet ceremony created a Plains-wide network of fictive kinsfolk who engaged in trade; in the PP tribes, the children of trading partners had so intermarried that one ethnographer spoke of the historic Plateau as being one great social system. (2) In both systems, trade fairs or rendezvous drew people together from distant and environmentally different zones to exchange the goods they possessed for those they desired. (3) In the MM system, trade was facilitated by the use of Plains Indian sign language, one of the most elaborate means of nonverbal communication in the world; the PP tribes used Chinook Jargon, a pidgin composed of words from a wide variety of West Coast languages. Most students of Chinook Jargon continue to insist that it developed after the advent of European trade, but I persist in my belief that, given the incredible linguistic diversity among the dozens of tribes that participated in that trade throughout the entire plateau, the pidgin is a prehistoric development that was elaborated after contact with Europeans. I first published my conclusions in a collection of essays issued in honor of Luther Cressman, but I later revised them for a wider audience (Wood 1971d, 1980).

In 1974 I expanded these ideas in a paper that considered the effects of trade on the stability and the external relationships of Northern Plains village cultures. I proposed that horticultural groups in the Northern Plains comprised a cultural continuum in stable equilibrium, having undergone only superficial modifications in technology, exploitative activities, and settlement patterning from their first appearance in the area. The positioning of villages along terrace edges overlooking the Missouri River floodplain placed the zoned natural resources within equal reach of all communities. Consequently, these politically autonomous villages also were economically self-sufficient. There was little reason for trade between villages, but there was extensive exchange with nomads from outside the valley. This trade not only diffused elements between nomads and villagers but intensified the village way of life and helped stabilize it, thus reinforcing the division between nomad and villager. There were no village or regional specializations and only a few social mechanisms to stimulate intervillage integration. These factors combined to help maintain the village groups at a tribal level of organization (Wood 1974). This essay led me to take a closer look at the relations between nomads and villagers.

Plains tribes traditionally are neatly divided into villagers and nomads, a distinction that blurs the many similarities that unite them. Much is made of their differences, for the distinction between gardeners and hunters is a very basic one. The horticultural groups, furthermore, are latecomers on the Plains, for villagers were present only for the last millennium of its history, whereas the nomads represent a way of life that endured more than ten times that long and persisted on the western Plains even as the eastern and central horticultural tribes arrived and developed.

I commented on this matter at length in an article in the *Review of Archaeology* (Wood 1991), and because of its importance I summarize it here. A century and a half ago or more, an autumn traveler on the Great Plains would from time to time have seen a procession of Indians, horses, and dogs moving over the landscape in search of bison. Carrying everything they needed on the backs of pack animals or on travois, these groups were under the leadership of military societies that managed every significant aspect of the hunt. The locale of the hunt would have given our observer some clue to their ethnic identity, and there was tribal variation in some aspects of the hunt, the most conspicuous perhaps being in the organization of their circular encampments of tipis. Nevertheless, an observer too far distant to detect their language or subtleties of tribal style would have been hard put to determine whether these travelers were members of a nomadic group or from an earthlodge village along the Missouri or Platte Rivers.

The way of life led by hunters on the Great Plains persisted with remarkably little change from Clovis times until the Old World horse diffused north from Spanish sources in the Southwest. Early Spanish explorers in the Southern Plains saw pedestrian bison nomads living much as their ancestors had lived for millennia. Their descriptions of these tipi-dwelling, dog-using nomads, who followed the "cattle" for their sole livelihood, probably differed only slightly from lifeways established 10,000 years earlier, including, in all probability, the use of dogs as pack animals. Dogs are not presently documented for Clovis or Folsom, though they appear in the archaeological record beginning with the Jones-Miller site, a post-Folsom Hell Gap complex site in Colorado (Stanford 1978). Dog bones occur rarely and irregularly in many later Paleoindian sites, but they are common enough for us to assume that Plains Indians likely had dogs for the last 10,000 years.

A. L. Kroeber and others who tried to interpret the peopling of the Plains in the early years of anthropology imposed their own preconceptions of the area on its occupants, finding it so difficult to believe the Plains were habitable before the arrival of horses that they ignored sound (though still rare at the time) archaeological evidence for the region's long-standing occupation. This is especially curious given the kinds of insight Kroeber accumulated in compiling his monumental *Cultural and Natural Areas of Native North America* (Kroeber 1947).

The hard data of archaeology are best suited to studies of diet, technology, and settlement patterns. Under ideal circumstances, sites can provide abundant and unambiguous data for each of these topics. Even more fortunate, these topics are so intimately interrelated that conclusions based on composite studies permit a level of confidence much higher than individual studies alone could provide. The major change in fact is a reduction in the kinds of animals hunted over the last 11,000 years and in the weaponry and projectile points used to kill them. Neither of these changes seems to indicate any major adaptive shifts, since the change in fauna reflects the loss of extirpated species, "and it is difficult to interpret changes in projectile point style as evidence for substantial changes in other aspects of the Paleoindian way of life" (Bamforth 1988:1–2).

Successful patterns of hunting are likely to persist if the conditions for pursuit do not change. A spectacular illustration of continuity in hunting patterns appears to be illustrated by the remains from a 10,000-year-old bison kill site in northeastern Colorado and by accounts of historic bison pounds, or surrounds, in the Northern Plains. A posthole in the center of the bison skeletal remains at the Hell Gap Jones-Miller bison kill in Colorado is similar to the solitary "medicine poles" erected in the center of historic pounds. Furthermore, a miniature Hell Gap point (little more than two centimeters long) and butchered canid remains were found near the posthole. These offerings may be analogous to the nonfunctional artifacts placed on or near the historic medicine post by Northern Plains hunters seeking a successful kill. Bison pounding was a complex, ritualized, and planned event, and here at least we must postulate 10,000 years of some level of socioreligious continuity on the Northern Plains (Stanford 1978: 95–96).

Despite the many contrasts between the nomads and the villagers, the life of the horticulturists was not profoundly different from that of the nomads. As Wissler (1948:42) pointed out long ago, the villagers lived in their lodges principally "only while planting, tending, or harvesting the crop. At other times, they took to tipis." And when villagers were on their annual bison-hunting excursions away from their lodges, their life scarcely differed from that of their nomadic neighbors. Whether one was nomad or villager, the organization of annual hunts varied only in minor details from tribe to tribe, and in every case was regulated by military societies.

This was true not only of the traditional bison-hunting Indians but of composite groups that developed in the fully historic period. Jeffery R. Hanson has told me that two of the Plains bison-hunting groups that developed in post-European times mirrored the Plains Indian tribes in bison-hunting techniques and organization. The New Mexico villagers known as *ciboleros* (or *comancheros*) and the Northern Plains *Métis* who went out onto the Plains to hunt bison never came into contact with each other, but there are striking parallels in their hunting techniques and organization. Both groups went out en masse, during which time hunt police directed them, and their hunts shared many other details that were borrowed directly from neighboring Plains Indians. The point is that if one is to hunt bison on the Plains, and defend oneself from enemies while doing so, the appropriate organization is not likely to differ significantly from ones developed long ago by Plains Indians, so it is not surprising to find that both the *ciboleros* and the *Métis* borrowed from a common source.

Contrasts between Plains nomads and villagers, then, have been overdrawn. Towns of the horticultural Plains village tribes differed, for example, very little from the bands that characterized the nomadic groups. Townspeople lived in substantial earth-covered lodges in semipermanent villages and relied to varying degrees on the products from their gardens. Save for the specialized architecture of the earthlodge and the presence of pottery and of gardening tools, the artifacts to be found in any given village were only minutely different from those in the encampments of their nomadic neighbors. There is remarkable monotony of pattern in most aspects of material culture on the Plains, whether we are speaking of women's products (such as articles of clothing, parfleches, or even tipis, save for a three- or four-pole foundation) or those presumably made by the men (such as arrowpoints and weaponry). Museum curators have found that without specific tribal allocation it is usually impossible to identify the tribe of origin of any given artifact, for tools and implements, even clothing, used on a daily basis vary only in minor details of style, not of form, and often were traded between tribes. Both formal trade and gift giving were important social events on the Plains, and these popular activities led to massive exchanges of every conceivable element of material culture between villagers and nomads.

Furthermore, each village was politically, socially, and economically autonomous. The political authority of a Mandan chief, for example, was no greater than that of any of those in the nomadic groups, and like the latter, he had no coercive power. Disaffected members of a Mandan town were free to leave one village and join another. Each Mandan village held its own Okipa ceremony (their equivalent of the Sun Dance), each held its own annual trade fair or rendezvous, and each conducted its own annual bison hunt in the autumn. Plains villages, in short, were markedly similar to the bands that characterized the nomadic groups save for the presence of stationary architecture, pottery and a few other artifacts, dependence on garden produce, and, of course, the presence of sodalities that linked and united the villages of a given tribe.

Ethnographic accounts of Plains horticulturists rarely make explicit the kinds and extent of social and political relations between the villages of a given tribe. One reason is that such relations were tenuous; another reason is that ethnographers tended to examine the relations between members of a single village, to the detriment of intervillage relations. The historic Omahas, for example, for the most part lived in a single town, yet they have been interpreted as having organized their communal hunts at the "full tribal level" and of having had a central political organization (Roberts 1964:446, 449–450). Life in a single town of course makes it difficult to interpret leadership as other than centralized. However, we may be assured that the historic expression of the Omahas' political organization differed significantly from that in precontact times, when they lived in an uncertain number of villages.

In any event, the traditional dichotomization of Plains Indians as nomads and as villagers is a legitimate means of describing two differing adaptations to the Plains environment. On the other hand, it masks the many deep-rooted and essential similarities in adaptation they shared. In their activities away from their villages the Plains horticulturists practiced a lifeway as ancient as that of their nomadic neighbors, and one that drew on the same antecedents. There is more unity in the concept of the Plains Indian than is generally conceded. Raymond DeMallie reminds us that Robert Lowie "concluded that the justification for speaking of the plains as a culture area is the antiquity of the distinctive aboriginal cultural complex for ecological exploitation of the buffalo" (DeMallie in Lowie 1982:x; Lowie 1982:204). Were Don Lehmer still with us, he might well have repeated a comment I once made to him: "You know, you could have cited Lowie and saved yourself the trouble of so much writing."

In 1972 I lent my support to a suit brought by the Environmental Defense Fund and the Missouri Wildlife Society to halt the construction of the Harry S. Truman Dam. As matters turned out, it was a losing proposition, for by that time the Corps of Engineers had invested far too much in it; nevertheless, the Truman Dam was to be among the very last of the corps' big dams. The judge in Kansas City who denied our petition did not give the corps free rein to continue the project but enjoined it to abide by conditions that all parties agreed could help protect the environment. One aim of the suit had been to save the paddlefish, or spoonbill catfish, from extinction; thirty-nine years later (2010) it is present but still endangered. Part of the reason the corps had proceeded so far in construction, according to a retired regional director of the Missouri Conservation Department, was that local people there, like so many others, were insensitive to clean water and wildlife and also, surely, were eager for the kind of tourist dollars they saw being spent at the Lake of the Ozarks.

In about 1975 I attended a meeting of AMQUA's executive committee when it was held at the annual meetings of the Geological Society of America in Austin, Texas. While I was having lunch with Donald Lee Johnson and others, the conversation turned to an archaeological site that had undergone some form of soil disturbance. Don and I looked at each other and simultaneously said something to the effect that we should do a paper together on the impact that pedoturbation (soil mixing) has on context in archaeological site formation. As we began writing the paper, we also started giving talks on the subject, and they drew such wide attention that Michael J. Schiffer invited us to submit an article on the topic to the first volume of his new series, *Advances in Archaeological Method and Theory*

(Wood and Johnson 1978). It is one of the most useful studies I've been involved in, for it stimulated others to explore various aspects of the subject and encouraged more archaeologists to study soil science.

I had of course learned about stratigraphy and Steno's law of the superposition of strata in my undergraduate geological coursework at the University of Nebraska, which was reinforced by John Champe in his 1946 study of Ash Hollow Cave. Most archaeologists were familiar with geological strata, but unfortunately they carried this image into their work as they dug through natural soil layers, so soil horizons were often identified as "strata." Even so distinguished a figure as James Deetz referred to soil horizons as strata in one of his publications, when his descriptions clearly identified them as the A-, B-, and C-horizons. Reports today are more fastidious in recording the substrate and overlying soils in sites, and soil scientists are ever more commonly called in to assist the archaeologist in site interpretation, especially when pedoturbation may have disturbed the site deposits.

10

Return to the Dakotas, Part One

By this I mean the Far West;—the country whose fascinations spread a charm over the mind almost dangerous to civilized pursuits. . . . [Who] in the world, I would ask, ever ascended to the pinnacle of one of Missouri's green-carpeted bluffs, a thousand miles severed from his own familiar land, and gazed over the interminable and boundless ocean of grass-covered hills and valleys . . . without feeling a sweet melancholy come over him, which seemed to drown his sense of everything beneath and on a level with him.

— George Catlin, *Letters and Notes on the Manners, Customs, and Condition of the North American Indians*, 1841

Donald J. Lehmer

By 1966, dam construction and reservoir inundation along the Missouri River in North and South Dakota was at an end. That summer Donald J. Lehmer (of Dana College) and I made a trip into the Dakotas to inspect what remained of the archaeological resources along the Missouri in the unflooded remnants of the valley between the reservoirs. Both of us had been involved, in one way or another, with the salvage archaeology program in the Dakotas since 1950 and had developed enduring research interests in the village cultures of the area.

Lehmer and I first met in 1950. He helped drive Douglas Enger's crew to the Tiber Reservoir, then backtracked to central South Dakota and began work at the Dodd site, later to be destroyed as it was engulfed and incorporated into the Oahe Dam. Don and I had close contacts and extensive correspondence before 1966, in part relating to my master's thesis and, later, my dissertation on Huff. But our contacts largely concerned Middle

Missouri prehistory, for in 1964 Don resumed work in the Dakotas at the invitation of the State Historical Society of North Dakota. He wrote me asking for sites I'd recommend he dig that summer, and among those I thought promising was the Fire Heart Creek site (32SI2). Alan Woolworth and I had contemplated digging there in the mid-1950s, but Alan had been unable to obtain permission. Though Will and Hecker had reported the site to be "Archaic Mandan," this two-component village contained early long-rectangular houses as well as the depressions of small, circular houses.

Don assigned the early long-rectangular house component at Fire Heart Creek and the Paul Brave site to the same taxonomic unit, one he named the Fort Yates phase. He identified the later component as a historic Arikara winter camp that may have been the one Lewis and Clark visited when they passed through the area in October 1804. He had a successful season, though his crew roundly cursed me for the fact the later Arikara structures, at least, contained clumps of poison ivy (though I'd pointed this out to Don in my note to him). When I'd dug a five-foot square in one of them in 1955 or 1956, I'd not been affected because at the time I was reasonably immune. Fortunately for my health, I was unable to visit Don that summer due to my obligations in the Stockton Reservoir in Missouri, so his crew couldn't get their hands on me.

The data that Don obtained that summer led him to a new synthesis of the region's archaeology. It had been little more than twelve years since he'd published his first synthesis of the prehistory of the Northern Plains, and he richly supplemented it in his 1966 study of the site (Lehmer 1966). The section he innocently titled "Summary and Discussion" is nothing less than a reinterpretation of the latter part of the culture history of the Missouri River trench in the central Dakotas, phrased in terms of Lehmer and Caldwell's (1966) then-recent article, "Horizon and Tradition in the Northern Plains." Up to this time midwestern archaeologists had used the Midwestern Taxonomic Method to organize and classify their sites. The method was a six-unit, content-based taxonomic hierarchy (ignoring time and space) that began with the content of a site; sites having similar content were placed in a "focus," and foci into aspects, with yet higher units that were seldom used, at least in the Plains. Waldo Wedel introduced the system to the Plains, and then other Plains and midwestern archaeologists began using it (McKern 1939; Wedel 1934). The method was being informally circulated by 1932, but it was formally published only in 1939; Wedel was therefore using it before its publication in a national journal. In the

Central Plains its rationale was published in 1936 in Earl H. Bell's introduction to *Chapters in Nebraska Archaeology*. Lacking pottery and other such time-sensitive diagnostics, the method was ignored in the West, and it became popular only in the eastern United States and in the Plains. Luther Cressman chided me about its use during my years at Oregon; he was right, for it would have been fruitless to apply the method to the kind of remains he was investigating. In 1927 the archaeologists in the Southwest began to devise their own taxonomy in the Pecos Classification.

The Midwestern Taxonomic Method was hierarchical and wholly content-ordered, for when the method was developed there were few ways to determine the age of most sites. Archaeologists were infusing their units with time and space, however, and Lehmer and Warren W. Caldwell felt that a new classification for the village complexes along the Missouri River in the Dakotas was called for. Beginning with Don's 1954 synthesis, they applied to it the concepts proposed by Willey and Phillips in *Method and Theory in American Archaeology* (1958). They divided the Plains area into the Northern and Southern Plains sub-areas, and the Northern Plains into three major regions: the Northwestern Plains, Central Plains, and Middle Missouri. Several *localities* in the Middle Missouri required recognition; these were sections of the Missouri Valley fifty to one hundred miles long. Then they added a second spatial unit, the *district*, to their scheme, a subdivision of a region that includes several localities.

They used Willey and Phillips's basic archaeological units, the *component*, *subphase*, and *phase*, as these were originally defined, and also used Willey and Phillips's integrative units, *horizon* and *tradition*, but in both an inclusive and a restrictive sense. For example, the use of "tradition" comprehended an "earth lodge *cultural* tradition" that was composed of *technological* traditions that are consistently associated through time. There was less agreement with their use of the concept of "horizon" as an integrative unit on the approximate order of a Midwestern Taxonomic Method "aspect." They conceived of the two major cultural traditions as being crosscut by three major horizons. Perhaps they were ill-advised to use horizon in an inclusive sense, but a long-felt weakness of the Willey and Phillips scheme had been the lack of some sort of unit between "phase" and "stage." In any case, their modification of the Willey and Phillips scheme provided a clearer and more systematic visualization of the culture history of the Northern Plains than was offered by adherents to previous taxonomies. No one classification can serve all possible purposes (can this be said too often?), and their scheme was a useful one. It was applied, and inevitably modified, but it would provide the basis for syntheses of the region for years to come.

After leaving the MRBS in 1953, Don spent a short time as a visiting professor at the University of Washington, but by 1961 he'd become established at Dana College, a small private Danish Lutheran school in Blair, Nebraska, some twenty miles north of Omaha. This position provided great freedom of action; moreover, it was near Lincoln with its MRBS office, as well as the library of the University of Nebraska, and Don soon re-immersed himself in the prehistory of the Middle Missouri River. He quickly became a confidant of Wilfred D. Logan, who'd replaced Paul Beaubien as archaeologist in the Omaha regional office of the National Park Service. Following numerous conferences (normally held in Trovato's, a popular Omaha lounge and restaurant), John M. Corbett and Logan contracted with Don to write a review of the work of the MRBS, a manuscript that he completed in 1965. He substantially revised that work when the National Park Service published it in 1971 as *Introduction to Middle Missouri Archeology*, the first number in its short-lived series of anthropological papers (Lehmer 1971). Only one other volume of those papers was issued: Hubert Smith's summation of the work at Like-a-Fishhook Village. A third volume that I had edited had been accepted and was in production when budgetary cuts during the Ronald Reagan administration terminated it. The South Dakota Archaeological Society subsequently published the work as *Ice Glider, 32OL110: Papers in Northern Plains Prehistory and Ethnohistory* (Wood, ed. 1986).

My ties with Don became closer in May 1965 when we attended the annual meeting of the Society for American Archaeology in Urbana, Illinois. We were having drinks with a group of colleagues in a bar one evening after the sessions, and as the others drifted away, Don and I become more and more engaged in conversation. Eventually, we were alone, and it was late that night when, expelled by the bar, we concluded our conversation, during which we laid our initial plans to investigate Plains village cultures in the Missouri Valley trench. We thereafter became close—indeed, inseparable—friends until his untimely death in 1975, from complications related to his 1972 auto accident.

That summer Don and I took a road trip to North Dakota. We spent much of the time discussing the evaluation study that Don was then preparing on the salvage program in the Middle Missouri area for the National

Park Service and visiting digs that were in progress, including James E. Sperry's excavations at the Shermer site. On our return to Dana College, Don's station wagon was filled to the roof with specimens, for we'd borrowed a large collection from the Deapolis site. This was the Mandan village visited by Lewis and Clark in 1804 and 1805 and was the one led by chief Sheheke-shote, or White Coyote (formerly known as Big White). Bismarck residents Ralph S. Thompson and Roger Holkesvik had obtained the collection between 1958 and 1960 when they salvaged a significant sample of artifacts from the site as it was being bulldozed away so its underlying gravels could be extracted (Thompson 1961).

We'd borrowed the Deapolis specimens for a project to summarize what was then known of the archaeology of the historic Mandan and Hidatsa Indians. Working with Chris L. Dill of the State Historical Society of North Dakota, we described the Knife River phase, using data from Rock Village and Nightwalker's Butte, both of which had been excavated by MRBS archaeologists G. Ellis Burcaw and Donald D. Hartle in 1950 and 1951; the Amahami site, dug largely by Chris Dill in 1972; and the Thompson-Holkesvik collection from Deapolis (Lehmer, Wood, and Dill 1978). Later this synthesis was significantly augmented when Stanley A. Ahler began his investigations into Hidatsa prehistory as part of his research associated with the establishment of the Knife River Indian Villages National Historic Site near Stanton.

Don was the only anthropologist at Dana College, and although there were colleagues in Lincoln at the MRBS office some sixty miles distant, he wanted to be able to work at Dana with a fellow archaeologist. In March 1966 he persuaded the college to offer me a contract to join him on the faculty, but the offer was contingent on finding additional funds for my salary from interested federal agencies. However, I'd just obtained a nine-month contract from my university for a half-time teaching and half-time research position, which meant that I no longer had to secure half my salary from outside contracts. Though I visited Dana for an interview, I declined the offer despite the attraction of being able to work with Don. Then, too, the deposits at Rodgers Shelter were beginning to yield exciting results from our deep probe, making it virtually impossible for me to consider leaving and abandoning such a prehistoric bonanza.

During our 1966 trip up the Missouri, Don and I focused our attention on the region between the city of Bismarck and the Garrison Dam. We finally decided to concentrate on the northern or upriver half of this area, since many sites in the southern half were badly disturbed by construc-

Figure 29. Donald J. Lehmer in an aircraft over the Garrison Reservoir, summer 1968. *Author's collection.*

tion in and around the towns of Mandan and Bismarck or were under the protection of the state or the city of Bismarck. Most of the village sites in the area we chose, in contrast, were well preserved, many were pristine, and two of them (Molander, 32OL7; and Fort Clark, 32ME2) were state historic sites. Furthermore, since the area was remote from urban centers, the ecology here more nearly approximated "original" conditions than any other part of the Missouri Valley in the Dakotas. We rented a light plane in Bismarck and flew over the area, taking photos of our projected sites. On our return to Bismarck, Don asked the pilot if he could land the plane (he showed him his pilot's license) and was given the controls, resulting in a very bumpy landing. Don apologized as we left the plane, but the pilot courteously repeated the old saw, "Any landing you can walk away from is a good landing."

We decided to concentrate our work in the area between the town of Stanton and the abandoned town of Sanger, in Mercer and Oliver Counties. This work was confined to the right bank of the river, since the left bank was all but devoid of village sites and existing ones were badly disturbed. We were unable to explain this disparity in site distribution unless the river had carried the older sites away. Still, there was one major village for every mile of this reach of the river on the right bank, so this disparity in distribution made no sense to me, either then or now. Our study area comprised the upper half of what Lehmer had called the Knife-Heart region (Lehmer 1971:29). Near its center we stopped to visit one of the ranches, owned by Robert H. Levis and his wife, Gladys. Bob was an unusual man, highly educated and widely read. (He once bought a station wagon–load of books to read when he spent a winter alone on the ranch.) Though he'd been interested in the archaeological sites on his land, he'd never paid much attention to them, so he readily agreed when we asked if we could dig on his property.

We were a bit taken aback when he asked us, "What kind of flotation techniques do you plan to use?" I was familiar with the technique, having visited Stuart Struever's digs, for Struever was perfecting this new method at his field headquarters in Kampsville, Illinois, but we were surprised to find that Levis also knew of the procedure. As it turned out, Bob had property along the Mississippi River in Illinois near Struever's camp, and he was well acquainted with the technique. Before we left, he gave us permission to dig a site just south of the ranch that we rechristened the Cross Ranch site in view of his promise to support our work (before Bob's purchase the ranch had been known as the Gaines Ranch). As we drove on toward Stanton, Lehmer and I congratulated ourselves on finding an "angel" to support our work. Bob later told us that after we left, he turned to Gladys and expressed his own delight, saying, "Well, we've just bagged two archaeologists."

Cross Ranch was so named because when Levis purchased the property in 1956, he found that the cattle brand that Theodore Roosevelt had used on his Maltese Cross Ranch in western North Dakota was available, and he obtained the right to use it. A giant Maltese cross indeed graced the front of the ranch barn until the structure became unusable and was demolished. Bob and Gladys were hosts to us on many occasions, and they provided living quarters for us for several field seasons. One summer we were accommodated in the bunkhouse, and during our mapping of Fort Clark we occupied an abandoned grain bin. The latter quarters were regal: there were separate sleeping rooms for us, and the center aisle served as a kitchen and mess hall. Our hosts also provided a second building on a more permanent basis, permitting us to store our equipment between seasons instead of transporting it to and from our home bases. One afternoon Bob drove several of us across the river bottomlands to the Missouri, where we observed the succession of timber as the river deposited sediment in its migration across its valley. The trip inspired one of my students, David E. (Curly) Griffin, to write a paper about how the earthlodge peoples along the river chose a locality: it had to be one where the requisite timber was present. A place with old trees would not be desirable, for the earthlodges required timbers of three different thicknesses. The ideal location was in an area where there were young to medium-aged cottonwoods to provide large center posts, medium-sized wall posts, and smaller leaners and rafters; otherwise, timbers would have to be floated or carried in from distant stands. The logic of his paper was inescapable, though some critics deemed it "timber determinism" (Griffin 1977).

As Bob approached retirement, he and Gladys decided to sell their ranch in a way that would preserve this near-pristine segment of the Missouri Valley for future generations. Just before Bob's death in 1982, he sold the ranch to the Nature Conservancy (far below market value), and today the greater part of its lowland holdings are incorporated into Cross Ranch State Park. There is now a visitor center on the floodplain northeast of the ranch buildings, and the gravel road that crossed the park has been paved with asphalt. Originally, the entire road from Mandan to Sanger and on to Stanton was graveled and was principally used by locals. On one of his trips through the area during cold weather Lehmer stopped at a town along the route; while in the post office he detected the aroma of coffee, and hopeful he could obtain a cup, he asked, "Is there anywhere around here where you can get a cup of coffee?" The response was not helpful: "Which direction are you going?"

Leaving Bob and Gladys and heading toward Stanton, we passed over the crest of a hill just north of a prominence on the bluff (known to the Mandans as Buffalo Head Hill), just east of the almost-deserted town of Fort Clark. Lehmer suddenly slammed on the brakes and slid to a stop. A small plane was taxiing up the gravel road immediately in front of and toward us. Instantly, the pilot wheeled the plane around, gunned the engine, and was airborne in a matter of feet. The pilot, Clifford Beeks, a crop-dusting resident of Washburn, later flew me over a number of the sites in our study area. Flying low, of course, was his specialty. On one occasion he landed in a small corral across the road from Levis's ranch home. I boarded the plane nervously and held my breath as Cliff held the brakes and raced the engine until the plane shuddered; then, releasing the brakes, we cleared the corral fence with only feet to spare. Contrary to the expectations of many of his friends, he died quietly in a recliner many years later while he was watching television.

The Stanton-Sanger Project, 1968–1972

I invited Don to visit Columbia in January 1968. He gave a public lecture, "The Other Side of the Fur Trade," which prompted a wag in the department to ask, "Will it be from the beaver's point of view?" Don gave one of the earliest talks on the Indian customers of the fur trade, for practically all studies of the trade up to that time had looked at the trader's point of view—a void that is now the subject of numerous studies. He followed that talk with a departmental colloquium, "Man and Climate in the Middle Missouri," which built on the Bryson and Wendland (1970) model of climatic episodes, which was then gaining currency among archaeologists in the Midwest and Plains. In 1968 two Quaternary specialists at the University of Kansas in Lawrence held a conference that focused on the earth sciences and the past climate, anthropology, botany, and zoology of the Central Great Plains. The published results of the symposium (Dort and Jones 1970) contained the first substantial article presenting the results of our work in the spring bogs in southwestern Missouri (Mehringer et al. 1970). The book also contained a summary of Bryson and Wendland's climatic model and was one of the major stimuli for the continuing use of that model by archaeologists as late as the turn of the twenty-first century. In the same volume, Lehmer (1970) presented his views on how climate change had affected the village cultures in the Middle Missouri region.

Don and I began our investigations in the Stanton-Sanger area that summer in the first stage of what we hoped would be a thorough study of the interrelations of the culture and environment of the Mandan and Hidatsa Indians. Archaeologists working in the Northern Plains had just begun to outline the prehistory of the Mandans, but that of the Hidatsas was virtually unknown. The two tribes were of particular interest, for they lived on the very northwestern margin of effective native maize agriculture in North America. Except for a few historic refugee village groups, there was no significant dependence on maize north of the Hidatsa villages at the mouth of the Knife River near Stanton. Our six-week field season was designed to obtain a representative pottery sample from each of the sites in our study area, as well as information on soil conditions and other data needed to plan further work. We investigated the upper Knife-Heart region until Don's death in 1975, and I published a summary of our results some years later (Wood, ed. 1986).

I spent the summer of 1968 with a small crew testing most of the known village sites in our study area, excluding only those at the mouth of the Knife River, which were to become part of the future Knife River Indian Villages National Historic Site. Five-foot squares were dug in each site in settings we hoped would contain middens so we might have stratigraphic data with which to seriate the sites. One of the sites, Mahhaha (32OL22), yielded a truly unusual feature that I interpreted as a medicine bundle. This object had been placed in a pit dug near the edge of the village and contained several hundred seeds of tobacco (*Nicotiana rustica*), a groundstone pipe of local red siltstone, red and white pigments, European trade beads, three pierced elk canines, a bone whistle, three Pacific Coast *Olivella biplicata* shell beads, a fossil cephalopod (*Baculites*), and a few other items, probably including a mushroom, based on spores in the soil sample. Such elements, usually including a pipe and tobacco, were commonly placed in bundles made by men following a vision quest to symbolize the support they had received from the supernatural world, but in the event the vision did not result in success, they might be buried (Wood 1971c).

These were the years before the bridge over the Missouri River was built at Washburn, and food or beer runs meant driving either to Bismarck or to the small town of Stanton or Center. Fortunately, a recreational center was not far distant, the River Rat Saloon in the hamlet of Hensler, a town so small it proudly boasts on a sign beside the official one, "Hensler / Don't Blink." The bar was in an old schoolhouse and was an after-work haven that also provided evening recreation, including pool. The distinctive odor that drifted upstairs from the restrooms did not deter thirsty workers, though it would have deterred me from converting the building into the private home that now occupies the premises.

We undertook an interesting auxiliary project during a second field season in August 1969. Recalling that Alfred W. Bowers had mentioned a linear earthen mound near the town of Sanger, we found that it was in the uplands in the south pasture of the Cross Ranch. Bob Levis accompanied me and my son Stanley when we visited the 370-foot-long mound, and he surveyed the feature so we could plot it accurately on maps (Bob had a bachelor's degree in engineering). By this time Don and I had purchased 260 large-scale (20-by-24-inch) copies of the 1938 U.S. Department of Agriculture aerial photographs that covered the Missouri Valley from the Garrison Dam in North Dakota to the mouth of the Bad River in South Dakota. When we checked the proper print, we found that the mound was clearly visible as a long white streak.

At that point I became curious to see if we could find more of them on our aerial photographs, and I spent an evening poring over the prints. I indeed detected several other mounds, along with what appeared to be a complex of linear mounds on a high terrace about a mile north of the eventual north boundary of the Knife River Indian Villages National Historic

Site. When Don and I went to the locale, we found seven linear features, one of which is a turf-cut feature 593 feet long with a small dome-shaped mound at the south end. We named them the Stanton Mound Group (32ME104). Another group of three mounds (the Levis Mound Group, 32OL109) lay on the uplands directly above the Cross Ranch buildings. On a flight sometime later my pilot friend, Clifford Beeks, pointed out yet another group in a field north of the town of Washburn. This group has never been investigated, but on a visit to their freshly plowed-over contours one summer I found large numbers of shattered bison bones. Eventually, I was able to plot hundreds of linear feet of these distinctive features along the river between Stanton and Sanger.

These features remain to be adequately investigated, for though Lehmer and Calabrese tested a small dome-shaped mound at the Levis Mound Group in 1970, they found nothing diagnostic accompanying the three burials they discovered in a shallow pit near the mound center. To date, no firm evidence exists to identify their age or origin. Bowers (1948: 131) wrote that his Hidatsa informants identified the Sanger Mound as the course taken by their culture hero Grandson when he left Earth to return to the planet Venus. Given the probable Late Woodland origin for these structures and the traditional late prehistoric arrival of the Hidatsas in the area, I believe that when the Hidatsas discovered these features, they integrated them into their mythology (Chomko and Wood 1973).

A lesson in archaeological observation is appropriate here, for we often see what we're looking for and can be blind to the obvious. My ten-year-old son, Stanley, had accompanied us on our trip to locate and map the Sanger Mound, and he joined us on a later visit to the Woodland-Besant campsite atop High Butte. As we parked on the upland rim adjoining the butte, Stanley looked back and said, "Say, Dad, you just drove over a linear mound." Indeed I had, and I'd repeatedly driven our pickup over it on earlier visits. I'd even done so after mapping the Sanger Mound, so I was properly impressed with his perspicuity. Such experiences prompt us to remain alert observers.

Mapping Fort Clark State Historic Site

When Lehmer and I visited Fort Clark State Historic Site in 1966, we were monumentally impressed with its wonderful degree of preservation, its wide range of archaeological features, and its historical significance. Fort

Clark, one of the principal outposts of the American Fur Company, figured in every significant historical document that related to the Upper Missouri River between 1830 and 1860. In 1968 Don and I dug four small tests in the village to obtain a pottery sample, but plans for further work there ended with Lehmer's death.

Fort Clark State Historic Site contains the premier fur trade post in North Dakota. I say this without detracting in any way from Fort Union Trading Post National Historic Site, for at Fort Clark many additional factors come together to illustrate the early history of the state. It is the location of Mih-tutta-hang-kusch, the village where the Mandans were all but destroyed by smallpox in 1837, and the site of Fort Clark's opposition post, Fort Primeau. After the smallpox epidemic the Arikaras occupied the village until 1861, when they abandoned it after the American Fur Company closed Fort Clark and transferred its operations upriver to Fort Berthold. The Arikaras later moved to Like-a-Fishhook Village, where the remnants of the Hidatsas and Mandans were living.

The history of archaeological research at Fort Clark and the village encapsulates, in a way, the history of archaeology in North Dakota. It was visited and recorded by archaeologists beginning in 1883 with Theodore E. Lewis. Later investigators included Emil Steinbrueck for the State Historical Society of North Dakota (SHSND) in 1904; Alfred W. Bowers for the Logan Museum at Beloit College, Wisconsin, in 1929; Wood and Lehmer for the University of Missouri and Dana College in 1968; Chris L. Dill and Erik Holland for the SHSND in 1973–1974; Wood and others for the University of Missouri in 1985–1986; and most recently, an interdisciplinary team led by Stanley A. Ahler of the PaleoCultural Research Group on behalf of the SHSND in 2000–2001 (Ahler 2003). Dill and Holland had carried out limited testing in the village and in the two forts more than twenty-five years earlier, but this work had been done for appraisal purposes and was never published. Containing as it does two of the remaining unexcavated fur trade posts on the Middle Missouri River, Fort Clark and the adjoining Primeau's Post, the site should not be disturbed simply for curiosity's sake. Archaeological research at a site will tell us a great deal, but it's also destructive: the only difference between a bulldozer and an archaeologist is the quality of the notes and records made by the excavator. In the past we didn't keep some of the specimens or the kinds of records needed by current scholarship, and there's no reason to think that future scholars won't find great gaps in the data from the work we're doing today.

Figure 30. The Mandan/Arikara village at Fort Clark State Historic Site, North Dakota. *Courtesy State Historical Society of North Dakota.*

The pristine Mandan/Arikara earthlodge village, its association with the infamous 1837 smallpox epidemic, the role of Fort Clark as a focal point in the northern fur trade, and the presence of the remains of the two unexcavated fur trade posts were all factors that merited the site's nomination to and listing on the National Register of Historic Places as an archaeological district in 1986. Fort Clark and its competing post were the last of a series of British-Canadian and American trading establishments built on the Missouri River near the mouth of the Knife River for the Mandan and Hidatsa trade. The vast records of the American Fur Company in the Missouri History Museum in St. Louis can be combined with the many other documents produced by a parade of explorers, traders, and other visitors to the site; collectively, they include both ordinary and extraordinary accounts and visual images of the locality and its inhabitants. Because of the richness of its written and graphic documentation, the site permits us to ask many questions not possible for other Plains village sites.

The University of Missouri's major goal at the site in 1985 was to produce an accurate plan of the village and its environs. Numerous sketch maps of the site existed, but they were impressionistic and were useless for detailed investigations. Fieldwork began that summer when I led a party of volunteers to the site and set permanent benchmarks on the property. My Missouri colleague Michael J. O'Brien laid ground controls for low-level aerial photography, and KBM, Inc., an engineering firm in Grand Forks, used these photographs to create a 15-cm contour map of the north half of the state property that encompassed the entirety of the village. We were joined that year by a field party from the Midwest Archeological Center under the direction of Robert Nickel, who carried out magnetometer surveys in the plaza area, Fort Clark, Garreau's earthlodge, and the Indian cemetery west of the fort.

The following summer another University of Missouri party, with the part-time assistance of the archaeological field school of the University of North Dakota, spent a second season there with the goal of preparing an accurate planimetric map of the village and its environs in the metric system, a project that was mandatory before any detailed fieldwork could be done. This map was prepared from black-and-white, color, and color infrared aerial photographs taken by KBM, combined with intensive ground-truth checks and detailed transit mapping. Because even quite modest subsurface features are visible at ground level, our foot-by-foot inspection of the topography exposed many previously undetected features.

Nowhere else on the Plains has an earthlodge village been mapped in such minute detail, though a near-exception to this generalization is the Redbird I site (25HT3), in Holt County, northeastern Nebraska. Steven B. Wimberly dug it in 1938 for the Nebraska State Archaeological Survey. His impressive block excavations of 1,180 ten-foot squares (118,000 square feet, or 2.7 acres) exposed five earthlodges, 118 cache or refuse pits, two pits containing bundle burials, and numerous unpatterned postholes at this Redbird phase village (Wood 1965a). Wimberly had used what was called the "broadcast method," in which the crew began in a trench at one end of the site and dug across it square by square, pitching the backdirt behind them and mapping as they went. For all practical purposes, the entire community was exposed, a feat that will never again be duplicated in the Plains. Donald D. Hartle almost accomplished the same thing in the Garrison Reservoir when he excavated the small butte-top village the Hidatsas called Nightwalker's Butte in the Bull Pasture (32ML39) for the MRBS (Lehmer et al. 1978).

The uncultivated part of Fort Clark Historic Site, as finally mapped, consisted of 92 acres, an area equivalent to about fifty city blocks. More than 2,200 surface features were plotted in the village, including the fortification ditch, earthlodges, and collapsed cache pits. In addition, graves (of both fur traders at Fort Clark and Indians living in the village), borrow areas, and roads and trails were mapped. Each of the 86 earthlodges was verified by the presence of a hearth in its center, the ash and burned earth in them revealed by a soil probe. Some of the smaller depressions within the houses mark the locations of cache pits and, in some cases, even the large center support posts. Entrance passages are visible for most of the lodges, appearing as gaps in the earthen ridges that encircle their depressions. Even the altar in the Arikara ceremonial lodge is visible, covered by a thin veneer of soil and sod. It matches exactly the placement and form of those reported from protohistoric Arikara villages in central South Dakota near the mouth of the Bad River (Lehmer 1954:Figures 11 and 46; Lehmer and Jones 1968:Figures 6, 19).

In 1986 we cross-trenched a lodge on the south side of the village to investigate its microstratigraphy, cross-sectioned the fortification ditch on the west side of the site, and cut five soil profiles along the terrace rim to study the surficial deposits that mantled the site. We discovered that the defensive ditch was only 60 centimeters deep and was surprisingly shallow, considering the depth of many protohistoric ones. We also dug a five-foot square near the south wall of Primeau's Post from which we hoped to get a sample of trade beads. But we unexpectedly came down on a circular pit, near the top of which we exposed some sloping posts. I must have been gathering wool when the discovery was made, for I didn't make the connection between that circumstance and the fact that such elements characterize the Arikara graves at Fort Clark. We certainly did not expect any such find on the site of a trading post, but nevertheless we soon exposed a human skull and immediately stopped work. We took notes and backfilled the pit in accordance with North Dakota state law.

When an Indian member of the North Dakota field school heard of the grave, she broke into a dead run across the site, climbed into her car, and vanished. She returned a little later with an Arikara priest, who approached the grave and performed a brief ceremony in which he offered gifts to the four directions and "purified" the grave we'd violated. Afterward we sat around, had soft drinks, and talked about the site and its history. At one point he asked me, "Do you know Preston Holder?" Knowing Pres's reputation, I cautiously agreed that I did. He then told me that his father had been one of Holder's informants when Pres was collecting data for his dissertation on the Arikaras. Then he smiled and said, "You know, one afternoon Dad and his brother made up a ceremony for him," a clear demonstration of the kind of pranks that informants often play on ethnographers. He had many questions about our work, and he carried a tape recorder that he used to record our comments about the village and the events that had taken place there. I later wondered how much of our information might now find its way into oral tradition. We were honored at a later field season by a visit from Malcolm Wolf, a direct descendant of Mató Tópe (Four Bears), the prominent second chief of Mih-tutta-hang-kusch during the visit of Prince Maximilian in 1833 and 1834.

Two immense ovoid areas surrounded by low earthen embankments west of Fort Clark have been known for most of the twentieth century: they have been called both "gardens" and "corrals." To resolve their function, I used soil chemistry. Had these areas been used as corrals, the animals would have enriched two important substances in the soil, for available phosphorus and total organic carbon build up in such enclosures through the accumulation of animal waste. On the other hand, gardening would not have augmented those elements because local Indian gardeners did not use manure in their plots, for it contained too many viable weed seeds. Laboratory results by agronomist David Hammer of the University of Missouri clearly supported the supposition that the large east enclosure was a corral because of the high concentrations of those elements. The results from the west enclosure were consistent with corrals but were not as convincing.

Some of the more conspicuous linear features visible on aerial photographs are white American roads and Indian trails. The trails we mapped were chosen because of their consistent presence on aerial photographs from the 1930s to the present. Native trails have been indicated on maps of the site since 1883, when Theodore H. Lewis made a sketch map showing four main trails radiating out at right angles from the village. We know that well-established roads connected the Mandan and Hidatsa villages. In 1896 Alexander Henry the Younger said he "proceeded on a most delightful hard dry road" to the Hidatsa village at the mouth of the Knife River (Gough 1992:234). Most of the features we mapped at Fort Clark that radiate out from the village at right angles to the fortification ditch are probably paths, for in at least two cases they originate at gaps in the ditch. Three of them lead to openings in the corrals south of the village. An especially convincing trail, one that begins near the west entry to Fort Clark and leads off to the southwest, appears on Prince Maximilian's 1834 map of the locale.

Much of the activity at any community takes place outside the village itself. Indeed, about two-thirds of the visible surface features on the terrace at Fort Clark are outside the area occupied by houses. Yet virtually every Plains village archaeological study is based on the settlement core, where the dwellings and other buildings stood, and focuses on the architecture and related remains within nucleated village areas. Even the areas between individual dwellings are generally neglected. Consequently, at most sites our knowledge of the activities that took place outside the village is either nonexistent or speculative. Roads, cemeteries, gardens, corrals, shrines, gaming areas, and a host of other features and activities peripheral to the village core have important implications for every nucleated archaeological site, and they deserve equally dedicated research, conservation, and management.

It is curious that historians have never written a general history of Fort Clark and its neighbors, for their importance in the fur trade of the Upper Missouri cannot be ignored. As another step in the interpretation of the site, I prepared an overview in which I integrated the site's ethnohistory and archaeology (Wood 1993d). I had to wait for my editorship of *American Antiquity* to end before submitting it to that journal. My latest major project is a book that encompasses that history, *Fort Clark and Its Indian Neighbors: A Trading Post on the Upper Missouri River*, published by the University of Oklahoma Press (Wood et al. 2011).

Current research is revealing the kind of things we should ask about Fort Clark before we dig—those things that the written documents simply don't tell us. One of our first questions was, just what is at the site? We obtained a better idea of its content after I concluded my mapping program, which extended over two summers. Our final map revealed a great number of things we hadn't known before. For example, the two lines cutting diagonally across the southwest part of the state property are ruts created by the late nineteenth-century Mandan-to-Stanton stage line. The completed map that we presented to the State Historical Society provided a reliable plat for planning and interpretive purposes. It was created after months of work to correlate field observations with aerial photography, a task completed by University of Missouri graduate student William T. Billeck, now chief of the Native American Graves Protection and Repatriation Act (NAGPRA) program at the Smithsonian Institution.

Francis A. Chardon figures prominently in the history of Fort Clark because of his long and detailed account of activities there. When the site map was complete, I felt compelled to name the small and nameless stream that formed the southern boundary of the complex of features at Fort Clark. It had escaped being named because it flowed into Clark's Creek a few hundred feet above its confluence with the Missouri River. "Chardon Creek" was an appropriate choice, and I added it to the map. In October

2000 I gave a talk, "Early Cartography of the Missouri River," in St. Louis to the Council of Geographic Names Authorities. These are the state and provincial representatives who make recommendations to the U.S. Board on Geographic Names on the propriety of new names for geographical features. The meeting prompted me to formally petition the board to legitimize the name I'd given the stream. Because my creek was unnamed and I'd chosen a historical name appropriate to the locale, my application was approved and this fourteen-mile-long stream now commemorates Chardon's contribution to local and western history.

Most of what we know of the Upper Missouri fur trade may be classed as economic history, the rise and fall of fur companies and the biographies of prominent individuals in the trade. Recent changes in the research orientation of historians and anthropologists alike, however, have provided new directions in fur trade studies. Historian William R. Swagerty (University of Idaho) has looked at the social classes in American Fur Company trading posts, and anthropologist Randy H. Williams (University of Missouri–Columbia) provided a social history of Fort Clark in his 1998 dissertation.

Social history, which is nothing more than the story of average people, has become increasingly popular. This field is analogous to archaeology in many ways, for in archaeology we rarely see the products of or glimpse the life of a given person. Rather, we deal with the collective record of many individuals, few of them being the important personalities that historians formerly doted on. Archaeologists study the history of culture—that of ordinary folks—and only rarely do they investigate great personages. The archaeological work at Jamestown, Virginia, for example, revealed the homes and lifeways of nameless individuals, but lifeways that were nevertheless specific to a given period and event in American history. Numerous social history studies now exist, and their numbers are growing. Examples include archaeological and social history studies of gender, examinations of the roles women played in so many situations that both archaeology and history have long ignored.

We have a great deal of demographic data for fur traders on the Upper Missouri. Census records and other documents often tell us where they came from, their nationalities, ages, and occupations, yet we know little of their biological makeup. A recent study of a Caucasoid skull found many years ago at the protohistoric Swan Creek Arikara village in South Dakota provides us with information on the remains of a white trader who'd been buried at that earthlodge village among his customers sometime about AD 1700. Exactly when he died, and the manner of his death, is not known. However, like most men of that period in such settings, he'd led a rough life. His skull revealed three healed depression fractures: he'd been traumatized by severe but not life-threatening blows to the head, testifying to the harshness of life at the time (Jantz and Owsley 1994).

In 1988 I attended a meeting of the Lewis and Clark Trail Heritage Foundation in Bismarck. William T. Billeck joined me there, and after the meetings we rented an airplane from Budd Henderscheid, whose home almost adjoins Fort Clark, and flew numerous loops around the site, taking aerial photographs. We also took soil samples from the earthen enclosures west of the fort, which eventually supported the idea that they are corrals, as already narrated. On the drive back to Columbia I began to pay serious attention to a regional phenomenon known as "prairie dinosaurs," and I append herewith the essence of my findings, musings that I presented at the 53rd Plains Conference in Laramie in 1995 (Wood 2010a).

Prairie Dinosaurs and Other Phenomena

Even the casual visitor passing through North and South Dakota, especially east of the Missouri River, has seen strange, otherworldly creatures along the roadside, on both interstates and less heavily traveled secondary roads. Usually, these beasts are visible atop hills silhouetted against the skyline, posed in settings where they have a clear view of the surrounding prairie. Their heavy bodies, long necks ending in heads so small as to be almost indistinguishable, and long tapering tails immediately identify them as "prairie dinosaurs," specifically *Threshersaurus dakotaensis*, the "Dakota grain-consuming lizard." They're the very image of the giant, lumbering, plant-eating dinosaurs so poorly caricatured in older motion pictures and cartoons. I'm speaking, of course, of the threshing machines that once served farmers in the wheat-growing plains of the Dakotas.

These machines are fine examples of regional folk art, public displays of nostalgia for a time that's long gone. Such visible mementos communicate a message to passers-by. Farmers in North Dakota have told me that these now-useless machines are placed to commemorate an era when their use brought communities together at threshing time. I remember threshing days from my own preteen years: an entire rural community, men and women together, collaborated in bringing in the grain crop of neighborhood farmers. The steam tractors that powered the threshers are more carefully preserved and are rarely exposed to the elements, for they're far too valuable. Many localities today sponsor "Threshing and Steam Tractor Festivals" that attract the elderly through nostalgia and the young through curiosity. All of us have seen books on vernacular architecture—outhouses, for example—and there are innumerable studies of other distinctive features to be found across rural and urban America. It's beyond me why these "prairie dinosaurs" haven't been academically investigated, for such expressions of folk art deserve serious scholarly attention.

Perhaps this is the place to mention the Wood Hypothesis of the Origin of Civilization. It derives from the fact that I love cats (other people's cats), though cat lovers abhor the concept. I offer only the basic outline of my hypothesis, for some details remain to be worked out. I believe the domestication of cats, never before regarded as the first animals to be domesticated, took place in the late Middle Stone Age (a 10,000-year-old cat mummy was indeed discovered in 2007). The process of domestication was a startling success—so successful, indeed, that cats began reproducing exponentially and, in a matter of decades, were so numerous that humans were endangered by the scarcity of food: cats were consuming everything. People were on the verge of starvation until a Neolithic genius invented two critical items: burlap sacks and bricks. These innovations took care of the matter of cats, though the Tigris and Euphrates were polluted for years. Now, however, the populations of the small stone-age hamlets found themselves with a dilemma: what to do with their gigantic warehouses filled to the rafters with sacks and bricks? A second genius kicked off the Neolithic by solving this problem: build cities with the unused bricks, and domesticate grain to fill the sacks. Civilization as we know it was launched.

Other interests of mine include an effort to explain the Loch Ness Monster. The beast poses a distinct problem in natural history, for only once have I ever read or seen on television the inconvenient truth that the loch has been repeatedly scoured by glacial ice over the past several million years. How did "Nessie" manage to survive under such conditions? More practical is my desire to do a forensic analysis of the bones of the dragon that Beowulf slew with his "stabbing knife" sometime in the closing years of the first millennium. After all, one of my colleagues at the University of Missouri, Robert Benfer, studied the sword scars on the bones of Francisco Pizarro and thereby helped verify his remains. Scholars of Anglo-Saxon culture would be forever indebted to me if I could locate the "stone-roofed barrow where he guarded a hoard" in which the beast was slain (Heaney 2000:151, 183).

11

Along the Trail

In short, the historian's aim is verisimilitude with regard to a perished past—a subjective process—rather than experimental certainty with regard to an objective reality. He tries to get as close an approximation to the truth about the past as constant correction of his mental images will allow, at the same time recognizing that that truth has in fact eluded him forever.

— Louis Gottschalk, *Understanding History*, 1958

Summer in Wyoming

In the summer of 1973 I found myself with no obligations and decided it would be interesting to teach summer school somewhere on the Great Plains that was new to me. I called George C. Frison at the University of Wyoming in Laramie, but he had no openings. After a number of other fruitless inquiries, I was delighted when George called back to say that a summer instructor had been unable to honor his commitment to teach because of a family crisis. Was I still interested? "You bet," I said, and I happily accepted: it was to be the only summer I taught indoor classes. When I told a friend of my good luck, his response was, "How on earth did you get stuck with that?" I barely managed a civil reply, for it had, after all, been my first choice!

My temporary home in Laramie was a house on Custer Street that George found for me, only a few blocks from my classrooms. My office was on the second floor of the building that housed the anthropology department and George's archaeological lab. Through my office window I looked out over the roof of a lower story of the building where George laid out skeletons that were being prepared for use in identifying those recovered from sites. I taught two classes during the week, Introductory Anthropol-

Figure 31. The author (*right*) exchanging views with Omer Stewart at the Snake River Rendezvous, Colorado, July 1977. *Author's collection.*

ogy (never my favorite course) and North American Indians, and spent weekends touring archaeological sites and scenic attractions, both in-state and out. I was not used to the altitude (7,200 feet), and although I didn't become ill, as some people do, I sometimes found myself short of breath during lectures. I'd simply stop, take a deep breath, and tell the class, "Sorry, I'm a flatlander." They didn't laugh; they understood. Ruth Heinritze, one of my friends in Laramie, told me it had taken her two years to acclimate to the altitude.

One weekend I visited George in the Bighorn Mountains, and he escorted me to his Medicine Lodge Creek site and to a fantastic mountain-top exposure of steatite. On a later weekend I visited Lawrence D. (Larry) Agenbroad, who was digging the Hudson-Meng site in northeastern Nebraska. The site was north of Crawford and is now open to the public as the Hudson-Meng Bison Bonebed, maintained by the Hot Springs Mammoth Site in South Dakota. All told, the summer was a wonderful introduction to the archaeology and geology of the High Plains. One of the educational capstones was climbing Medicine Bow Peak, a few miles west of Laramie in the Snowy Range. Local residents warned me before doing so about the hazards of eating "pink snow" in the event I ran out of water, for the color is caused by a lichen that can cause diarrhea, clearly undesirable above treeline. The day-long excursion provided textbook cases of mountain and glacial geology (cirques, moraines, protalus ramparts, felsenmer, and patterned ground), not to mention the opportunity to obtain magnificent color slides that I used in my class in environment and archaeology. I've returned to the mountains often, and in July 1977 I attended the Snake

River Rendezvous in northwestern Colorado, where I renewed acquaintances from my sabbatical when I taught at the University of Colorado.

My curiosity about the geological history of Wyoming grew as I drove through parts of the state I'd never visited before. On one drive west of the Snowy Range I thought I was experiencing an optical illusion when I saw the North Platte River, contrary to nature, flowing into the mountains. Consulting a traveler's guide to Wyoming geology, I discovered that in past geologic times local mountain ranges had been partially smothered by deep formations of the sediments that had eroded from them. The land surface between the ranges was therefore once much higher, and as the streams flowing across them cut downward, the Wind, Bighorn, and North Platte Rivers cut deeply into the harder underlying rocks of the buried mountains and formed impressive V-shaped canyons, providing stunning examples of geological change. Driving through the Wind River Canyon, for example, one passes from recent sediments consecutively into older formations (geologists call this going "down section") and finally into pre-Cambrian rocks, then back again to more recent ones.

Back in Columbia, my knowledge of the Quaternary was given a boost by David B. Madsen's research for his dissertation, "Late Quaternary Paleoecology in the Southeastern Great Basin" (Madsen 1973). Dave had obtained a sample of thirteen woodrat (*Neotoma* sp.) middens from several localities. He found that many of them were stratified, and he was able to show how they'd been deposited over long periods of time. By radiocarbon dating the remains in the different layers (some of them as much as 20,000 years old), he revealed a sequence of vegetational changes that he was able to mesh with pollen evidence, thereby helping to interpret major climatic shifts for the region. David distinguished himself in further writing on the prehistory of the Great Basin and was for a time the state archaeologist of Utah. He's not to be confused with his equally prolific father, D. Brigham Madsen, who produced a number of books on Mormonism and other topics.

On one of my later trips to Wyoming I visited B. Miles Gilbert atop the Bighorn Mountains near Lovell. Miles was digging a fantastic Pleistocene faunal site that yielded animals dating from the last interglacial to the beginning of the Holocene. Appropriately named Natural Trap, the feature formed when a limestone cavern roof collapsed perhaps 110,000 years ago and formed a bell-shaped sinkhole with an opening at the top only 10 feet in diameter. Over the course of centuries many careless animals slipped or leaped into the opening after cresting a low rise, falling 85 feet to their death. A cone-shaped pile of debris and fossils slowly accumulated near the center of the 100-foot-diameter floor. Excavations revealed that the unfortunate beasts began accumulating from the time the opening developed, though most of their remains date between 20,000 and 12,000 years ago. Discovered in 1971, it was excavated principally by personnel from the University of Kansas, led by Miles Gilbert and Larry Martin, though later work was conducted by Miles as a member of the American Archaeology Division at the University of Missouri.

Beginning in the last interglacial, the cave ensnared a wide variety of now-extinct Pleistocene forest and open-country animals, including mammoth, bison, muskox, camel, horse, and an extinct bighorn sheep, along with their predators: the giant short-faced bear (*Arctodus simus* or bulldog bear, twice the size of a grizzly), American lion (*Panthera atrox*), a cheetah-like cat, dire wolf, and wolverines, not to mention game animals that still inhabit the area, pronghorn antelope and deer. The trap is on federal land managed by the Bureau of Land Management, which placed an iron grate over the opening to protect the cave from looters. Originally, it had been necessary to rappel into the cavity, but I was pleased to help Miles obtain metal scaffolding so one could climb in and out; otherwise I'd never have ventured into it on my visit. The crew slid down the railings of the steps on the shaky, 85-foot tower like acrobats; they smiled at visitors like me who edged their way down far more gingerly.

Editing *American Antiquity* and an Introduction to Karl May

In October 1984 George Frison, then president of the Society for American Archaeology, approached me at the Plains Conference in Lincoln with a proposal. Would I stand for election as the editor of the society's journal, *American Antiquity*? I provisionally agreed to do so if I could obtain institutional support, for it was a far more demanding assignment than my former one with the *Plains Anthropologist*. That support was indeed forthcoming from the dean of the College of Arts and Science, who granted me a $6,000 subsidy for the journal. Subsequently, I was elected editor for the years 1987 to 1990 and was responsible for volumes 52 (No. 3) through 55 (No. 2). Teresita Majewski, who'd just obtained her Ph.D. in our department, became the managing editor, and Christopher B. Pulliam acted as editorial assistant. It was a smooth-running operation housed in a building not far from my academic office. During my tenure I was pleased to be part of the process that led to the establishment of our sister journal, *Latin American Antiquity*, for there had been a long-standing need for a journal that focused on the southern reaches of our continent and on South America.

Such an editorship certainly helps one comprehend the global nature of our profession and its constantly expanding use of new techniques from every conceivable field of science. Nevertheless, I discovered that my greatest challenge was to find suitable referees, for the range of the journal's contents far exceeds the competence of the most broadly read scholar. Consequently, much of my time was spent seeking appropriate readers. However, the most depressing aspect of the business was rejecting papers, for we could publish only about one-third of those submitted. Toward the end of my three-year term I'd walk every day past a four-drawer filing cabinet that was filled with the dozens of papers that had been rejected. I grew to hate it, thinking of the hundreds of hours that had gone into writing its contents, so I was pleased whenever I saw one of the papers in print in another journal. Rejecting a paper, for whatever reason, was not a enjoyable experience, though the fortunate author has the benefit of constructive advice from the referees for a revised version. I leave it for others to decide what kind of job I did on the journal, but I published only one article in my three years that I bitterly regret letting slip by. Nevertheless, like my experience with the *Plains Anthropologist*, it was challenging, immensely educational, and rewarding, though in my final editor's report to the society I likened my tenure to the labors of Sisyphus, for I was forever doomed to begin a new issue of the journal even before the last one went to press.

In April 1988 I contemplated one last attempt to leave Missouri, though I was in the last phase of my editorship. The Center for Great Plains Studies at the University of Nebraska–Lincoln was seeking a new director. I was one of three finalists, and I believe I had a favorable chance after a pleasant interview. But my uneasiness about the move grew steadily after I returned home. Directing the activities of the center was a challenging and stimulating prospect, but its administrative and financial management was a matter of concern. I'd had quite enough of those burdens when I'd managed the million or so dollars that were involved in the complex operations of the Harry S. Truman Reservoir program as my part of the WORC projects. The longer I contemplated the move the more nervous I became, and ultimately I decided I did not want to leave a position in which I'd invested nearly three decades; I reluctantly wrote the center and asked that they please remove me from consideration. Western and legal historian John R. Wunder was chosen for the position.

Beginning with my purchase of William Shirer's *The Rise and Fall of the Third Reich* in Fayetteville in 1961, I became an avid reader of the literature of World War II and, over time, accumulated a respectable library on the subject. As I read, I became increasingly curious about Karl May, a prolific nineteenth-century German novelist who wrote numerous books about the American frontier (which he never once visited). His novels sold by the millions in Germany, and among his fans were Albert Schweitzer, Hermann Hesse, and Adolf Hitler. The hero in May's western novels was a German named Old Shatterhand, who was accompanied in his escapades by an Apache Indian named Winnetou. Together they roamed the West in scenarios reminiscent of the Lone Ranger and Tonto, in settings that depict the Old West as accurately as Africa is portrayed in Edgar Rice Burroughs's Tarzan series. A publishing house in Germany is devoted solely to publishing May's works, which have been issued in more than twenty languages, though only two of the novels of this "German Louis L'Amour" are available in English.

I was intrigued by an observation that Albert Speer made in *Spandau: The Secret Diaries*: "Hitler would lean on Karl May as proof for everything imaginable, in particular for the idea that in order to direct troops in the African theater of war" it was unnecessary to have gone there. Speer also said that "any account of Hitler as a commander of troops should not omit reference to Karl May. Hitler was wont to say that he had always been deeply impressed by the tactical finesse and circumspection that Karl May conferred upon his character Winnetou" (Speer 1976:384–385). Hitler is reputed to have ordered May's western novels to be sent to the Russian front because he felt German soldiers would find them useful for combating Russian partisans, whom he equated with May's "Red Indians." He is also said to have chided his commanders on their timidity in the invasion of France and told them to be more bold, like Karl May!

At the 1987 Plains Conference I gave a talk on the effect that May had on Hitler's thinking and on World War II. I called it "The Role of the Romantic West in Shaping the Third Reich" and delivered it to a standing-room-only audience (they had to wonder, "What the hell is Wood up to now?"). The piece appeared in the *Plains Anthropologist* after an extended review (Wood 1990b). Reviewers found it hard to believe that Hitler would lean on a fictional character for support in a modern war, but skeptics eventually were persuaded that I was not myself writing fiction nor was I trivializing that brutal war.

Karl Bodmer and the Upper Missouri River

In the summer of 1979 I again had no field plans, and Cal Calabrese made an enticing suggestion: that we tour several of the national parks in the West that fell under his archaeological jurisdiction as chief of the Midwest Archeological Center. It was a great idea, bolstered by Cal's suggestion that we do so on motorcycles. He'd recently purchased one, and I could borrow my son Stanley's Kawasaki 500. The trick was to get it in running order, for it needed a variety of repairs to make it roadworthy. I'd invested nearly a thousand dollars to do so before Cal called to tell me that he couldn't make the trip because of scheduling problems. I was left with a motorcycle, a costly investment, and no plans other than to slowly throttle him, though the urge faded quickly. The reason?

Miles Gilbert had contacted me and asked if I'd like to accompany him and a small group that was to canoe down the Upper Missouri River. Miles was an old friend who'd been a member of the American Archaeology Division some years earlier. I jumped at the chance to accompany him when he reminded me that Karl Bodmer's most spectacular paintings of Upper Missouri River landscapes had been made in western Montana, where we'd be floating, and that much of the land was still in a pristine state. I had always been a fan of the work of Bodmer, a young Swiss artist who traveled the Missouri River with Prince Maximilian of Wied-Neuwied in 1833 and 1834 to record its ethnography and natural history. Furthermore, I could recoup the expense of refurbishing the motorcycle by using it to get there and at the same time reclaim my aborted road trip. Having never ridden before, I proceeded to practice with the Kawasaki in the parking lot of a local shopping mall until I felt I was ready.

I rode out of Columbia one bright summer morning and was soon on Interstate 70 carrying a small duffel bag stuffed with field clothes, a kit of necessities, and camera equipment, topped off by a sleeping bag. With the wind whistling in my helmet, I proceeded west, the first time I'd been on the open highway. It was fine going for a time, but when the rain began to spit near Abilene, Kansas, I pulled off the road and, coincidentally, immediately found a Harley-Davidson dealership and bought a pair of gloves. The next day I pulled into a small diner somewhere east of Denver and decided it was a good place to eat because of the number of cars and motorcycles parked outside. Taking off my helmet as I entered, I said "Hi!" to the bikers sitting at a table nearby. They glanced at the helmet I carried in but they said nothing, for I'd been identified as an outsider and a wimp: I wore neither a German helmet nor tattoos, and my Kawasaki was definitely not a Harley.

Passing through four-lane traffic in Denver later that day was a nightmare, but I managed it without incident and soon arrived in Fort Collins. There I took Highway 267, a scenic route over the Laramie Mountains to Laramie. It was dark when I reached Tie Siding, and by the time I arrived in Laramie I was bitterly cold from wind chill. Fortunately, I quickly found a motel on the north side of town with a "Vacancy" sign, and a helpful couple readied my room and checked me in. I thanked them both, and as I left the office, I became aware I'd made the woman's day: she turned to her husband, laughed, and said, "Did you hear that? He thought I was your daughter!"

The next morning I took Highway 130, the scenic road west out of Laramie, toward the snow-capped crest of the Snowy Range, visible in the distance. Past the old territorial prison and the municipal airport, I looked to the south across what I took to be a gigantic valley, but concentrating on driving I neglected to note that there was no stream along its floor. Only later did I learn that it was Big Hollow, a colossal blowout that extends from the airport to the base of the Snowy Range. I stopped for breakfast in the town of Centennial, where the road began twisting upward between Late Pleistocene end moraines as I climbed out of the grassland into the foothills. As I ate, I found that my right hand was so weak from holding down the motorcycle's accelerator that I had to push my fork through my sausage with my left hand. It was a beautiful day and a lovely route, and I drove slowly. It was just as well, for as I rounded one curve I saw that the entire road was filled with sheep, but despite near misses I made it safely through them.

The east face of the Medicine Bow Mountains is a nearly vertical cirque carved by repeated glaciations. It overlooks Lake Marie and numerous protalus ramparts, or ridges of stone parallel to the cirque wall created when rocks cascaded down the cirque face and over giant snowbanks that accumulated at its base during past cold periods. The view in all directions was awesome: to the south, the snow-covered peaks of Rocky Mountain National Park, and to the east, a view of the distant Laramie Range east of

Laramie. The descent to Saratoga is more gradual, for the west side of the range slopes gently from the crest down to the valley of the North Platte River.

Later that day I rode into Rawlins and sought out the house trailer in which one of my graduate students, Steve Chomko, was living. I spent the night there with him, and the following day we drove west of town to do some pistol practice in the isolated reaches of the Great Divide Basin. The basin contains a gigantic dune field, the largest active one in North America and the second-largest active sand dune field in the world. Its name, Killpecker Dunes, derives from the reputed presence of saltpeter in the water nearby. We turned north at a lonesome exchange and drove a few miles to a desolate spot, set up beer cans on a post, and began shooting. As Chomko placed one target, I drew the .357 Magnum he'd loaned me, pointed it toward the ground, and cocked it. Because my hand was so weak from holding down the accelerator on the motorcycle for three days, my thumb slipped off the hammer and the pistol discharged into the ground at my feet, creating a small crater in the sand whose rim undermined the toe of my boot. I'm not sure which of us was the more startled. I was pleased to still have toes on my right foot, but Steve peevishly told me to keep the pistol in its holster until he was away from the target. The next morning as I left town I stopped at a motorcycle shop and wisely bought a cruise control.

I rode west to Rock Springs, turned north, and made my way to Casper, where I visited Ann Johnson, who had obtained her doctorate at Missouri two years earlier (she later became the park archaeologist at Yellowstone National Park). The following day I joined her in investigating a human burial north of town. Later on, I was gassing up the Kawasaki at a station south of Sheridan, Wyoming, when a biker at the next pump said to me, "You're a braver man than I am to drive on a tire like that!" He pointed out that my rear tire was dangerously bald, so when I reached Sheridan I again sought out a motorcycle shop. I couldn't get a new tire mounted until morning, so I contacted one of my mother's sisters and spent the night in her home catching up on family history.

The next morning I took back roads through the Crow Indian Reservation, visiting the reservation headquarters and my friend Margot Liberty (who formerly taught at the University of Missouri), eventually reaching Interstate 90 at Little Bighorn Battlefield National Monument. There I turned north toward Billings and rode west up the valley of the Yellowstone River to Three Forks, whose conjoined waters form the Missouri

River. A few hours later I found myself in Helena, Montana. As I sped up the long, high hill north of town, the motorcycle began sputtering and soon refused to climb higher. I turned around and coasted back to town, where I was fortunate enough to find a motorcycle shop and unfortunate enough to have to leave the bike there for repairs. If I wanted to meet Miles Gilbert on schedule, I had no choice but to take a bus to Fort Benton, hoping the repair would be complete (and affordable) on my return.

I reached Fort Benton the next afternoon and explored the town as I awaited my float partners. Fort Benton is a historic little town, once the largest settlement in Montana. There's a great deal to see there in addition to the ruins (now restored in replica) of the original fur-trading fort. The recently renovated Grand Union Hotel, built in 1882, once the finest such establishment between Chicago and San Francisco, is on the National Register of Historic Places. Not far from its front door is a heroic-sized bronze statue of one of the town's icons: the dog Shep. Farther down the street is another heroic-sized bronze statue, this one of Captains Lewis and Clark, with Sacagawea and her infant son Jean Baptiste (little Pomp) at their feet. Nearby was the decaying keelboat *Mandan*, used in the 1962 motion picture *The Big Sky*. I met Miles, his companion, and Larry Agenbroad the next morning. I'd not seen Larry since I'd visited him at the Hudson-Meng Bison Bonebed; he was teaching geology at Chadron State College, Chadron, Nebraska. We launched our rental canoes into the Missouri at Coalbanks Landing, a few miles below the mouth of the Marias River, and set off on our grand adventure. We were well stocked with food, including a chilled bison loin.

Five miles below Coalbanks Landing we passed the mouth of Little Sandy Creek. At Fort Benton the Missouri River flows through a preglacial valley, where it resembles the Missouri trench as it appears through much of North and South Dakota. Fifty river miles below Fort Benton, however, the valley changes character at the mouth of the Little Sandy. In preglacial times the Missouri River left its present channel and flowed around the north side of the Bearspaw Mountains, then followed the modern valley of the Milk River east to its present channel far downriver. So we now entered a postglacial canyon of the Missouri River.

The valley here is exceptionally youthful, and erosion has created very striking results in the Cretaceous-age Eagle formation, a white sandstone that is both underlain and capped by soft gray shales. Both wind and water have sculpted the river bluffs, and the valley walls are lined for miles with intricately eroded sandstone formations. Terraces are poorly developed, and floodplain forests simply don't exist: timber in this part of the valley is on the canyon walls. Downstream along the Missouri, you'd never be able to point out a given location by saying, "Go to the first tree on the left below the mouth of Arrow Creek." But this description exactly fits the point where in 1833 Karl Bodmer produced his view of a keelboat across the river from a Gros Ventre Indian encampment of 260 tipis.

Eight miles into this canyon we came to what is called the Gates of the Stone Walls. Here the valley narrows between Burned Rock and the cliffs on the opposing wall. For the next twenty-five miles, we passed through the White Cliffs and the Stone Walls of the Upper Missouri River. The White Cliffs are imposing, some of them rising one hundred feet vertically, but they also contain miniature marvels, such as a perfect, door-sized arch atop one of the bluffs (it was later vandalized, or suffered the inevitable effects of erosion). Many of the views along this reach of the river have a grandeur matching if not surpassing that of any of our national parks. Prince Maximilian, not one to engage in flights of prose, said, "Here...you may fancy that you see colonnades, small round pillars with large globes or a flat slab at the top, little towers, pulpits, organs with their pipes, old ruins, fortresses, castles, churches with pointed towers, &c. &c., almost every mountain bearing on its summit some similar structure" (Maximilian in Thwaites 1906:23:78). Meriwether Lewis, in April 1805, described the same scenery in greater detail, concluding, "Those seens of visionary inchantment would never have and end" (Moulton 1987:4:226).

When the Bearspaw Mountains were uplifted millions of years ago, this entire country was severely faulted, and magma (locally named shonkonite) rose through the cracks, where it slowly cooled. When erosion exposes them, these magma-filled cracks, or dikes, weather into blocks that resemble fieldstone walls that stretch across or along the valley. Meriwether Lewis brought himself to the brink of heresy when he observed, "So perfect indeed are these walls that I should have thought that nature had attempted here to rival the human art of masonry had I not recollected that she had first begun her work" (Moulton 1987:4:226).

Karl Bodmer produced many sketches and paintings in this part of the valley, and their locales can be identified today. Some scenes can hardly be missed, such as Castle Rock, Grand Natural Wall, Citadel Rock, and the Seven Sisters. Chapel Rock shows how astonishingly little erosion has taken place in the century and a half since Bodmer was there. These land-

Figure 32. Citadel Rock, in the Upper Missouri River Breaks National Monument. Compare with Karl Bodmer's view of the same scene (in Maximilian 2001:vignette 18). *Author's collection.*

scapes are as photogenic today as they were in his day, and his views are undeniably precise. From the colors in his watercolors it's easy to conclude that he did his painting in the early morning and late evening, at precisely those times when photography is most rewarding because of alpenglow and, of course, at those times when Maximilian's crew was preparing to either make or break camp.

Seventy-five river miles below Fort Benton the White Cliffs begin to disappear and the hills are stark and treeless for miles, though the cliffs briefly reappear at the mouth of Arrow Creek. Farther downriver we began to see, once again, timber along the river bluffs, a signal that the mouth of the Judith River is near. Bodmer captured the image of a beaver den many miles downstream, but I found a perfect analog only a few miles above the mouth of the Judith. Just below its mouth is Judith Landing, where our trip ended. For the last forty-six miles we'd seen only two occupied ranches, and we'd passed through a land that had changed only minutely since the first white explorers made their way up the Missouri nearly two centuries ago.

Miles Gilbert dropped me off at the motorcycle shop in Helena on his way home, and I picked up the Kawasaki. The repair was minor: the air intake had become clogged as I'd traveled the dusty roads on the Cheyenne

Indian Reservation in and around Lame Deer. I stopped to visit an archaeological dig south of Helena the next day and had an educational visit, ending with an evening with archaeologist Steven Aaberg's crew in a local bar. The next morning I headed down the Yellowstone valley past Three Forks, Billings, Pompey's Pillar, and Miles City, then passed into North Dakota near the exit marked "Home on the Range," where I felt compelled to stop for a photograph. I made it to the Knife River Indian villages by dusk. The next day I headed downriver, where it began to rain and I took shelter under a storefront at Fort Thompson, but with no end to the rain in sight, I rode on in perfect misery. When at last I pulled into Calabrese's driveway in Lincoln, I was all but frozen. His warming libations probably saved my life.

I then struck out for home and was back in Columbia that night. Stimulated by the photographs I'd taken of Bodmer's images of the White Cliffs and Stone Walls, I soon found myself enmeshed in the written and pictorial record that Prince Maximilian and Karl Bodmer had left of their tour of the Missouri River. I also began to enlarge on the idea of replicating more of Bodmer's images on film. In recent years repeat photography—the act of going back to the exact site where an early photograph or painting was made and duplicating the view, as I'd learned from geologist Harold Malde—has become popular in a number of fields. Some of the first applications of this process included revisiting sites where early photographers had captured western landscapes. The new photographs revealed the nature and extent of the environmental modification that had taken place: the replacement of grassland by forest cover, decreased grass cover and resulting erosion, and the like. It's been done for photographs taken on the occasion of George Armstrong Custer's visit to the Black Hills, for early photographs of the High Plains taken by Homer Shantz, for pioneering views of the Grand Canyon, and many others.

The approach has other applications. I wanted to see if the technique could give added insight into the precision of views painted by early western artists before the advent of photography. For example, how accurate is Bodmer's work? To what degree can we use his paintings as valid images of the Old West? We had illustrations he'd made of North American Indian artifacts that still exist in museum collections, but for most of his work we can only go on faith. Like others who knew his work, I had great faith in his attention to detail, but rephotography provided an unimpeachable yardstick. Moreover, it was fun, and deductible as well. Minutely detailed

Figure 33. Photographing a scene painted by Karl Bodmer and by Thomas Hart Benton, August 1990. *Author's collection.*

examinations of his paintings demonstrate beyond question that his work is nearly photographic, though the heights of features on the horizon are exaggerated.

Ultimately, I made twelve float trips down the Upper Missouri, usually in August: mosquitoes are less troublesome at that time of the year, and that was the month that Maximilian and Bodmer returned down that reach of the river. This became a near-annual event for a decade for me, and I accumulated a large set of views illustrating Bodmer's landscapes. In about 1980 my friendship with Least Heat-Moon (William Trogden), author of *Blue Highways* and later of *PrairyErth* and *River Horse*, led to a long-term project when he introduced me to Robert M. Lindholm. Lindholm, then a water-quality attorney in the office of the attorney general of Missouri, was an extraordinarily fine photographer. Indeed, he took early retirement to pursue photography as a second vocation. Our association led to a productive collaboration on Bodmer and Prince Maximilian's expedition, discussed below. On three of the floats I was joined by the scientific staff of the Illinois State Museum, and these trips took on the qualities of a Friends of the Pleistocene field trip.

I put together a slide show of my first such float and presented it at the Plains Conference in 1980, using side-by-side views of Bodmer's painting and my photographs. It was a popular talk: by 2010 I'd given it more than thirty times. One of the talks was given at Emporia State University in Emporia, Kansas. Afterward the university's audio-visual department taped the presentation, during which time I was at one time left sitting alone facing the video monitor. Staring at it, I discovered that my face, at perfect rest, presented a hideous visage—I looked angry. Little wonder that some of my students entered my office with trepidation, since I appeared ready to snarl at them; I've tried to be conscious of this appearance ever since.

In about 1980 Bob Lindholm and I decided to collaborate on a book reprising the 1832–1834 expedition of Prince Maximilian and Bodmer in North America, beginning with Bodmer's views of Boston Harbor and continuing through his excursion to Fort McKenzie in present-day western Montana. Bob eventually traveled Maximilian's entire route and obtained photographs of all of Bodmer's landscapes that are identifiable today. I accompanied him to northeastern Nebraska and southeastern South Dakota one June, during which time I was struck by the intense greens of the prairies along the Missouri Valley. In the past I'd been skeptical of the intensity of the greens in many of George Catlin's painted landscapes: I am no longer, even if Catlin did use pure green freshly squeezed from the tube. The greens were especially conspicuous while Bob photographed the vicinity of Grand Tower (today called Old Baldy), the locality where Lewis and Clark captured the "barking squirrel" they sent back to President Jefferson. The nearby town of Lynch, Nebraska, has adopted the prairie dog as its icon, and I'm fond of the saying they print on tourist brochures for the town: "Hang out in Lynch."

We also floated together through the White Cliffs and Stone Walls. I'd noticed something odd there on one of my early trips: circular forms covered the surface of a small delta at the mouth of a gully on the north shore about five miles upstream from the mouth of Arrow Creek. We stopped and Bob took photographs of them for an article I thought would be interesting, for this was the finest group of mud balls I'd ever seen or seen illustrated. Mud balls are formed when a bank of clay caves into a rushing stream and is rolled into balls of varying sizes; they become "armored" by picking up stones that become embedded in their surface. There were literally thousands of these things littering the gully itself and the riverside delta, ranging from the size of golf balls to nearly two feet in diameter. I collected a few of them for analysis, but I was never able to find a geologist or geomorphologist who was interested in this remarkable mud-ball factory and what we called "Gulliver's gonads."

It took more than a decade for Bob to photograph the Bodmer views, and finally, in May 2004, we recruited a publisher; a year later, it defaulted on our contract. In 2006 we obtained the interest of Charles Rankin at the University of Oklahoma Press. Because the press had contracted with Omaha's Joslyn Art Museum to publish translations of the field journals of Prince Maximilian, our book seemed a worthwhile adjunct to that project, though our project remains in limbo because of the high cost of publication. Some years earlier the Joslyn had revived its long-dormant interest in publishing the Maximilian journals, to be produced in three handsome volumes; volumes 1 and 2 appeared in 2008 and 2010. Marsha V. Gallagher headed this project; she brought in Gary Moulton to oversee it and retained numerous specialists to serve as an advisory committee for her and her coeditor, Stephen S. Witte. Raymond J. DeMallie, James P. Ronda, and I served as advisers and prepared material for their notes on history, ethnography, and archaeology (Maximilian 2008–2010).

Sometime about 1995 I visited the Newberry Library to inspect its holdings in maps that predate Lewis and Clark, for I was compiling a second atlas of early maps of the American Midwest. As I was on the point of leaving after concluding my search, I stopped short at the door, for I recalled that the library held a collection of largely unpublished watercolors and sketches by Karl Bodmer. Robert W. Karrow, curator of Special Collections, brought them out for me, and as I inspected them I grew increasingly excited. Although some of them were duplicates of existing originals in the Joslyn Art Museum and some had been published in a German book about the artist that was now out of print, others were new and distinctive. The thing that intrigued me was the contribution they could make to our understanding of how Bodmer used these prototypes to compose the aquatints for Prince Maximilian's atlas. Original field sketches or paintings exist for a few of the engravings, plus sketches and paintings made in the studio, and the final engraved product reveals the varying layers of imagery that went into his productions. I therefore contacted two Bodmer specialists to assist me in publishing these images, historian Joseph C. Porter and art historian David C. Hunt. Together we compiled the intellectual history of the Maximilian-Bodmer expedition, the history of Bodmer's publication of the images, and annotations of the individual works (Wood et al. 2002).

A Sabbatical in Lincoln and New Projects

By 1980 it had been a decade since my first sabbatical, and it was time for another, so I applied for and was granted a year's leave. I spent it in a second home: Lincoln. Since I was to receive only half pay from the university for the year, two of my former students arranged to make up the difference. I was hired by Carl Falk to teach at the University of Nebraska and by Cal Calabrese to conduct research at the Midwest Archeological Center: each institution was to provide one-quarter of my salary. I was invited to live in the home of an old friend, Thomas D. Thiessen, for the duration of my stay. Tom and I were collaborating on the manuscript for what would become our book, *Early Fur Trade on the Northern Plains* (Wood and Thiessen 1985). We spent many hours transcribing early fur trade accounts and preparing an introduction to the book.

In July 1980, just before moving to Lincoln, I decided it would be instructive to follow the route of one of the fur traders whose narrative I was transcribing for our book. In mid-1805 François-Antoine Larocque traveled from Fort Montagne à la Bosse on the Assiniboine River in present-day Manitoba to the Mandan and Hidatsa villages, after which he and two companions accompanied a party of Crow Indians to the Bighorn Mountains and then to a location on the Yellowstone River where Billings, Montana, may be found today. They returned by traveling down the Yellowstone, then down the Missouri to the Mandans and Hidatsas. To track his trail, I first drove to Brandon, Manitoba, and then to the approximate location of Fort Montagne à la Bosse. Following on the ground as carefully as I could, using his narrative and marking his trail on U.S. Geological Survey maps, I traced his route with relative precision from the Assiniboine River to the Knife River, then across western North Dakota and into Wyoming and thence to southeastern Montana. Precision was possible because of the landmarks he mentioned, including the very distinctive mouth of Bighorn Canyon in southern Montana.

The trip allowed me to discuss the events of his route in great detail. For example, as Larocque traveled up the valley of the Powder River in today's Montana, he mentioned seeing some "shiny stones" on the heights of the adjoining hills. To determine what they were, I called the geology department at the University of Montana. The secretary who answered, however, referred me to the geology department at Montana State University in Bozeman, where there was a specialist who knew the area. I called that department and asked the secretary for someone who knew the geology of the Powder River. A few moments later a voice said, "Hello?" I replied, "Hi. My name is Ray Wood and..." I was interrupted by "Hi, Ray. This is John Montagne." John was the treasurer of AMQUA, and he'd assumed I'd called on AMQUA business. But he told me the "shiny stones" were selenite crystals (a form of gypsum), solving my problem. The world is often a very small place, especially in the sciences.

The trip also permitted me to determine the approximate mileage that Larocque traveled. It took his Crow hosts, traveling on horseback with their families, seventy-four days (during twenty of which they did not move) to cover the 480 air miles between the Mandan-Hidatsa villages and their camp on the Yellowstone River. This provides a daily average of about nine miles, though on rare days Larocque recorded that they traveled as much as eighteen miles. Larocque's journal is one of the few accounts that allows us to make such calculations for the movement of an Indian horse caravan. Most of the day would have been spent traveling, for the rapidity with which a tipi could be erected and dismantled is legendary. Much later I read that a good daily march for a large Crow camp was fifteen miles (Leforge 1928:148). I'm constantly surprised when the editor of a travel narrative makes no effort to physically retrace his or her subject's route. There are many benefits in doing so, and it's often challenging, which adds to the spice of the hunt.

During the fall semester at Nebraska I taught "Environment and Archaeology" and over the winter semester a graduate seminar in ethnohistory. The seminar included several highly motivated and professionally talented students, among them John R. Bozell and Lynn M. Snyder. At the Midwest Archeological Center I shared an office with Robert K. Nickel, and I also had space at the university a few blocks away. My obligation to the center was to produce a manual for the remote sensing of sites on the Great Plains as a project for the Cultural Resource Division of the National Park Service. It was quite instructive, for though I'd always used aerial photographs in my work, I was a complete novice in the use of magnetometry and resistivity in archaeology. Bob Nickel, however, specialized in these very topics; he contributed data on them to the study, and one of my Missouri graduate students, David E. Griffin, prepared the sections on the Great Plains landscape and its culture history. The book explored the value of remote sensing in mapping environmental variables, site discovery and documentation, and site mapping and evaluation. I contacted by phone as many Plains archaeologists as I could find who had done any kind of remote sensing and began to compile a draft that I completed before my return to Columbia. The project appeared in print four years later and was immediately reprinted by the J&L Reprint Company (Wood et al. 1984).

When my fiftieth birthday arrived in the spring, I was treated to a magnificent surprise party at Tom Thiessen's home. One of my gifts was a pristine 9-mm Parabellum Luger pistol and holster, obtained from Midwest Archeological Center employee Edward Sudderth, which someone had acquired as a souvenir in the last few days of World War II. Inside the walnut grip was a notation that it was taken at Thale, Germany, on April 18, 1945, just eight days before American troops met advancing Soviet troops at Torgau, on the Elbe River. Inscribed also was the information that one hundred fifty German troops, one colonel, and one general had been captured there. I've as yet been unable to trace the details surrounding this event in U.S. Army unit histories. A few days later I moved back to Columbia.

By the 1980s, reservoir construction in the state of Missouri had ended and I was free to pursue other and older interests. I wasn't enthusiastic about working on problems in Missouri because for the past several years I'd fallen out with Carl Chapman, in large part because of his lack of appreciation for the changes that were taking place in American archaeology, but equally because he continued to treat me as one of his graduate students. We were not comfortable with each other.

Sometime in 1981 I received a phone call from Elden Johnson at the University of Minnesota. Elden was cohosting the UNIC-3 Conference to be held the following February in Minneapolis, and asked if I had any suggestions for a conference theme. (Michael Michlovic informs me that Johnson had said Unic was a Mayan word!) I immediately told him that a conference that explored the relations between the cultures and ecosystems of Minnesota and the Northeastern Plains would be of great interest to me, and most likely to others. After all, several of the "typical" Great Plains nomadic tribes had real or traditional origins in the prairie-forest border of modern Minnesota, and a prevailing view was that many of them had erupted out of the forested regions in Minnesota to become Plains tribes, some of them within a generation. Unfortunately, I didn't tell Elden the rationale for my choice, and he subsequently asked me to give the keynote talk at the meeting, which I did. For the next two days, I sat embarrassed as talk after talk demolished the point of view I'd presented. Friends were gracious enough not to remind me of what I'd said, for I was, after all, repeating what I thought was common knowledge. (I'm reminded here of the bumper sticker that says "Don't believe everything you think.") Needless to say, I eagerly embraced the opportunity to revise my paper in line with what I'd learned before the conference proceedings were published (Wood 1985).

The talks at the conference, especially the one by Elden on the Mdewakanton Dakota, revealed that the tribes that "erupted" from Minnesota came not from the forested regions but from the parkland-savanna and the prairies that make up the southwestern third of the state. The popular view of Minnesota is one of unending forests and lakes, but that stereotype is valid only for the northeastern two-thirds. The Cheyennes, Arapahos, Atsinas, Assiniboines, and various Dakota bands lived either in the forest-prairie border in Minnesota and Manitoba or to the west, in the prairies of Minnesota and in adjacent parts of North and South Dakota, before they moved out onto the plains. These groups did not become "Plains" people in the protohistoric period, for they were already "Plains" Indians well adapted to a grassland habitat, a clear lesson that one must constantly challenge the reigning paradigm.

Writing *Or Go Down in Flame*

Ethnohistorical studies often lead one into oral history. A question that had been in the back of my mind for nearly fifty years led me to investigate the death of my brother in World War II. The War Department had never revealed how he died, and eventually my curiosity about his fate got the better of me. Until my college years I'd sometimes had dreams that he had come home, a common manifestation of post-traumatic stress disorder. As my work in ethnohistory intensified, I began to realize the magnitude of archival material that exists for military events, and in 1983 I decided to research my brother's last bombing mission. His B-17 Flying Fortress, the *Wicked WAAC*, was one of sixty bombers that had been shot down on October 14, 1943. The bombers lost over occupied Europe that day had been sent to bring Hitler's war machine to a grinding halt by destroying the ball-bearing factories in the town of Schweinfurt in central Germany. Without these bearings, German tanks, aircraft, and other machinery simply could not operate. I therefore decided to write the story of his life as best I could reconstruct it. There were many clues to pursue, for after his death my parents had compiled a scrapbook that memorialized his life and told me much about him. One touching memento was a map of the University of Missouri and Stephens College, illustrating where he lived and where his classes had been. But it also showed a dotted line to one of the women's dorms at Stephens College for which he had some attachment.

I first read general histories of the U.S. Army's Eighth Air Force in Great Britain and then began delving into the books and archives they cited. As I continued my research, I was able to find and contact some of his crew members who had survived being shot down—the pilot, the bombardier, a waist gunner, and the ball turret gunner—and I was also able to contact the families of the other waist gunner and the radio operator. I tried to compose a letter to send the survivors asking for information, but it just wouldn't jell. So I bit the bullet and simply called them, introducing myself as the brother of the navigator of their shot-down bomber. The result in each case was the same: astonishment, followed by the story of what had happened to them that day, often including details they'd never shared even with their wives. Eventually, I was able to have face-to-face visits with waist gunner Donald E. Williams (who was a next-door neighbor of Edward Lehner, owner of the Clovis mammoth site in southern Arizona) and with Leland A. Dowden, the bombardier who'd helped my brother bail out of the plane. My contact inspired Leland to write his own book, *One and One Half Missions*, his contribution to the history of the air war over Europe. Leland also graciously agreed to write a foreword for the book I planned to write.

At the time I was composing the manuscript, I was editing *American Antiquity*, a position that became very convenient for my project. As the journal's editor I attended each of the executive committee's business meetings, which were held at the annual meetings of the Society for American Archaeology, but the committee also met semiannually between meetings. Since the bulk of its members then lived in the eastern United States, it was economically sound for us to meet in Washington, D.C., for the three years I was a member. Many of the documents I wanted to consult about my brother's service were in the Modern Military Records Center of the National Archives, so I flew to Washington at the society's expense and then stayed over (at my own expense) to scan the archives. The Records Center was conveniently housed in a facility at Suitland, Maryland, just a few miles east of the downtown offices of the National Archives, and one could ride there free on a shuttle that regularly ran between the units.

One of the archivists, Richard A. Boylin, was especially helpful in suggesting documents for me to inspect. During one session I mentioned that my uncle and namesake had died in World War I and that his body had been returned to the United States for burial in the family cemetery. When he asked me, "Have you ever seen his records?" I admitted I had not, so he said he'd go get them for me, then changed his mind and said, "Come with me." We passed through an ordinary door in the research room into a hall large enough to allow the passage of a sixteen-wheeler and walked past enormous doors that resembled those on garages. Opening one of them, we entered a huge room stacked to the high ceiling with shelves lined with endless rows of Hollinger storage boxes filled with the records of World War I casualties. I was reminded of the last scene in the motion picture *Raiders of the Lost Ark*, in which the ark is being wheeled into a cavernous warehouse. Boylin soon found the right aisle, lifted a Hollinger box from the shelf, and pulled a folder from it that raised the hair on the back of my head, for its label read "Walter Raymond Wood." I returned to the research room and photocopied its contents.

The story of my brother's last mission came together slowly, largely from conversations with his surviving crew. His Individual Deceased File in the Suitland archives provided me with the story of his death and burial in Germany and the return of his body to the United States at the end of the war. But a visit to the locales where he'd served and died was indispensable, and I planned a trip to Europe in October 1988 so I'd be there during the month he was shot down—and perhaps participate in an Oktoberfest (though I was to learn that local Oktoberfests, at least, ended in September). I flew first to Gatwick in England, and I couldn't help contemplating as I stared down at the cold, endless reaches of the gray North Atlantic what my brother must have thought as he'd flown over them forty-five years earlier. I took a bus from Gatwick to a nearby car rental, and it was thrust upon me that I was indeed in a foreign country: I could not understand a single word of the conversation in what I presume was Cockney between the driver and one of the passengers. I did far better in Germany with my rusty German.

Nervously driving away from the rental agency on the "wrong" side of the road, I circled around the congestion of London on Motorway 25, not caring to risk my American-trained driving habits in a metropolitan area, and wended my way to Bedford. I did well driving on the left side of the road, though my very first encounter with a roundabout was confusing; it threw me into a loop, so to speak, from which I eventually escaped. My goal that day was the little town of Oakley, the home of Gordon and

Connie Roberts, local Eighth Air Force enthusiasts, with whom I stayed for my short visit in the locality. They proved to be genial hosts and guides.

My brother's air base was near Thurleigh, a small village a few miles north of Bedford. Access to the base was now restricted, for it had been transformed into a high-security research facility, the Royal Air Establishment (British components of the Concorde supersonic jetliner were developed there), but I was able to tour some of the abandoned buildings remaining around its periphery, and Connie pointed out to me in a pasture the site of a "plague town" that had been decimated during the bubonic plague in the Middle Ages; there may have been crop marks from its former presence, but I saw nothing to indicate its existence in the level field. I spent some time walking about Thurleigh, visiting the ancient St. Peter's Church (surely my brother had visited it), and admired the town's thatched-roof cottages. I also toured the town of Bedford. As an archaeologist I was interested in Bedford Castle, and I found it in a wooded park in the town center. But there was nothing to see, as it had been no more than a wooden tower set on a high mound of earth that left no visible remains, and the stone redoubts built there later had been razed. I was also guided to a number of tourist attractions north of Bedford by retired Royal Navy veteran Cyril Norman, visited the campus of Cambridge University, and made a pilgrimage to nearby Ely Cathedral, constructed in 1081 following the Norman conquest of England. It loomed high over the pancake-flat landscape and the modest architecture in the town around it.

I was unable to spend as much time as I would have liked at the Imperial War Museum at Duxford Airfield, for there was far too much to see. The operations room that dispatched RAF Spitfires and Hurricanes against the marauding German bombers over England during World War II was especially fascinating. *The Battle of Britain*, Harry Saltzman's 1969 documentary war film (of course including a mandatory love story), had been filmed at this airfield, and with its scenes still vivid in my mind, I found it easy to visualize the base as it was during those trying times. In 1943 it had been handed over to the U.S. Army Air Force and became a base for the P-47 Thunderbolts and P-51 Mustangs that flew later that year as escorts for the growing hordes of American heavy bombers over Europe. The motion picture, though generally panned by critics, is one the most authentic war films ever made, having been filmed with the cooperation of the RAF and the British Ministry of Defense, not to mention former officers of the Luftwaffe. Spitfires and Hurricanes that could still fly were obtained from all over the world, and the producers borrowed (and temporarily repainted) planes from the Spanish Air Force to use as the Heinkel bombers flown by the "Germans" in the film.

Cyril Norman also guided me to the beautiful Cambridge American Cemetery and Memorial; most of the 3,811 Americans buried there were members of the Eighth Air Force who died in Great Britain during the war. Anyone who has regrets that a loved one was buried overseas instead of being returned home would find the exquisite setting at Cambridge and other such cemeteries overseas very consoling. The only disconcerting aspect of my travel on some of the rural roads was that I found it impossible to erase from my mind the theme from an old television show, *The Avengers*. It was a constant annoyance, though it abruptly evaporated as mysteriously as it appeared when I drove similar roads in Germany a few days later.

I flew from Gatwick to Frankfurt and rented a car at the airport. Turning on the radio as I left the airport, I found it astonishing that the first song I heard on German radio was the old American ditty "The Red River Valley." I stayed in Frankfurt that evening with Bernd Peyer, whom I'd met earlier at the Newberry Library in Chicago, where he was researching literature written by American Indians. The next day I gave a talk at the Zentrum für Nordamerika Forschung (Center for North American Studies) at the invitation of Professor Dr. Wolfgang Lindig, of the Johann Wolfgang Goethe Universität, giving an overview of the archaeology of the Northern Plains illustrated by my best color slides. There were of course questions from members of the audience in broken and even polished English, and at the end of my talk they enthusiastically pounded the table with their fists for a moment, a form of applause with which I was not familiar. After my lecture Professor Lindig preceded my car out of the maze of streets in Frankfurt and directed me toward Michelbach, where my brother had been buried.

The little town of Michelbach was twenty miles to the east. I checked into a neighborhood inn, the Herrnmuhle Wirthaus, and then called Karola and Reinhard Kaschura, a pleasant German couple who put me up for the remainder of my stay in Michelbach. Karola's father had attended my brother's funeral as a member of the German Army, the Wehrmacht, and she generously took several days of accumulated vacation time from her job at the Alzenau Rathaus (city hall) to act as a guide and translator for my German odyssey and interviews of local eyewitnesses. As my informants talked, Karola translated their comments for me, and I simultaneously tape-recorded everything they said. Karola faithfully translated the conversations, though my tapes later permitted me to pick up some smaller details and nuances.

We were taken to the place where my brother's parachute had landed by a man who'd been there as a child and witnessed its descent; to the cemetery in the middle of Michelbach where he'd been buried; and to the roadside some miles distant where his B-17 had crashed. Everywhere I went I was treated as a long-lost relative, for it was obvious that I was on a friendly mission. When one of the downed B-17's waist gunners, Donald Williams, was awaiting the arrival of Luftwaffe personnel to take him into custody, he'd given a young boy in Michelbach a D-bar (a chocolate ration issued to crewmen). A local Nazi had taken it from the boy, Edgar Handlbichler, telling him, "You shouldn't accept gifts from the enemy." Handlbichler was one of the first residents of the town I met, and when I presented him with the largest Hershey chocolate bar I'd been able to find in Columbia, it set the stage for the friendly acceptance I was to find throughout my trip. Perhaps the strangest element of my trip was my reception by former members of the Wehrmacht, for they were the most helpful and informative of those I interviewed, and showed genuine sympathy for my quest. After all, hundreds of thousands of its former members are still listed as "missing in action" in Russia. Before I arrived, one of them spent nearly a week touring the countryside and interviewing eyewitnesses to the parachute landings of the aircrew and then painstakingly mapping his results. Only the wartime local leader of the Hitler Youth who'd attended Elbert's funeral refused to talk to me: he'd been imprisoned by the Americans after the war and was still bitter.

My brother had been the only member of his crew to die (others had been wounded, some seriously), and Andreas Noll, the *Bürgermeister* of Michelbach, had him buried in the town cemetery with informal military honors. Though Noll had never been in the military, he obviously believed that a deceased soldier, enemy or not, deserved a military funeral, and he'd ordered all the furloughed German soldiers in town to attend the ceremony. In his brief talk he told the soldiers that they might face the same fate as the luckless airman, as indeed some of them did. Noll had been the *Bürgermeister* since 1912, and he ran the town as his private fief, though his concern over the airman's funeral led to mutterings by local Nazis about his loyalty to the Third Reich. I was sorry to learn that he was no longer alive, but I managed to get a good photograph of him for my book. Surprisingly, the wife of one of the veterans who'd attended Elbert's funeral told me that she'd decorated the grave of the "handsome young American" when she visited the adjoining one of her father, telling me she'd thought he looked like motion picture actor James Stewart.

I rented a small plane at the airport at the nearby town of Gelnhausen flown by a former Luftwaffe glider pilot; he was quite friendly until I mentioned that the object of my quest was to photograph the locale where my brother's parachute had landed and the crash site of his B-17, when he became distinctly cooler. But he was a fine pilot and stood the plane on its wing when I pointed out places I wished to photograph. One of my ex-Wehrmacht informants in Michelbach later sent me my brother's fleece-lined flying boots: they'd been taken by the gravedigger, who had worn them for years when he went to cut firewood in the nearby forest. Their quality was unbelievably good, for except for broken zippers and matted fleece, they looked almost new. They're now among the Second Schweinfurt exhibits at the Eighth Air Force Museum in Savannah, Georgia.

I was tape-recoding a conversation during a visit one evening with an informant, enjoying a schnapps and küchen, when I heard a "click." He got up and went to his stereo set to turn over his own tape he was making of our conversation. He'd been a young boy when the plane was shot down, and he'd gone to the top of a hill with a Luftwaffe sergeant to help carry down Leland Dowden, the bombardier, whose leg had been broken in the plane when it was struck by the air-to-air rocket (in reality a mortar mounted under the wings of the aircraft). He'd asked the sergeant, "Why are we treating these people so well when they're bombing our cities?" The sergeant replied that he wanted to be treated the same way were he to be shot down over London. My new friend said that this gave him a new perspective on the war.

On my return to England I took the opportunity to tour London as a typical rubberneck and took a train into Victoria Station. I blundered into Buckingham Palace as the changing of the guard took place and chanced into Westminster Abbey as Polish veterans of World War II were honoring the Tomb of the Unknown Warrior near its entrance. It was a long walk across the River Thames to the Imperial War Museum, though many parts of it I wanted to visit were undergoing renovation and weren't accessible. On my return I visited the subterranean Cabinet War Rooms that provided Winston Churchill and his cabinet protection during the London

Blitz and passed 10 Downing Street. I'd have loved to stop at the British Museum, the Tower of London, St. Paul's Cathedral, and the Sherlock Holmes Museum at 221b Baker Street, but my time was limited. However, I did schedule time to drive south to Worthing-on-Sea, on the English Channel, to visit Terry Harkin, a B-17 waist gunner who had served on two of my brother's earlier "milk run" missions over France. He'd remained in England after the war and had gone into business. I regretted the lack of time that precluded a visit to Stonehenge. Many things remain for my next visit.

My book appeared a decade after I'd begun it: it had taken five years to write and another five years to find a publisher. *Or Go Down in Flame: The Death of a Navigator over Schweinfurt* came off the press only days before the fiftieth anniversary of Elbert's death. Later a summary of the chapter dealing with the recovery of the World War II dead appeared, with the encouragement of William M. Bass III, as a historical contribution in the *Journal of Forensic Sciences*. Another chapter that dealt with the air battle en route to Schweinfurt appeared in an anthology of military exercises titled *Great Raids in History: From Drake to Desert One* (Wood and Stanley 1989; Wood 1993c, 1997).

Elbert had left home before I really had a chance to get to know him, and the book in a small way made up for this loss, and at the same time it provided a small memorial for him, for he no longer remained a mere statistic, an anonymous combatant in a war that had consumed fifty million lives. In October 1993 I attended a meeting in New Orleans of the Second Schweinfurt Memorial Association, at which the survivors of that mission commemorated its fiftieth anniversary. On that date a half century ago many of them were being hospitalized or rounded up by the Luftwaffe for deposition in prison camps. My book had been published so recently that copies of it had to be mailed directly to me at the hotel in which the meeting was held. I'd wondered how these men would feel about an outsider such as myself, but they graciously accepted me, and I nervously waited as some of them read my book. To my intense relief they gave me uniformly favorable comments—they were the only critics whose reviews I cared about.

Two years later I was contacted by the founder of the American World War II Orphans Network (AWON) and asked to give a talk in Seattle. Thousands of American children had lost their fathers in World War II, and now, in middle age, they had the resources to indulge a long-wished-for goal: to find out what had happened to their dads during the war. My book had come to their attention, and I was asked to tell them the story of how I'd researched my brother's death. Richard Boylin, of the National Archives, also spoke on how to investigate such matters using the resources of the Modern Military Records Center. Coincidentally, he had been my mentor and helped me research my brother's records when I'd studied his history at the center several years earlier.

Our messages to the assembled group were identical: be *absolutely* sure that you're prepared for what you will find. Boylin mentioned the death of a tank commander whose comrades had assured his grieving family that he'd been killed instantly by a sniper. The records revealed instead that he'd been roasted alive in a burning tank: there's a reason the War Department leaves such things unsaid. In my case, I'd written the German newspaper that covered the locality where my brother's plane had crashed, and asked for information and copies of any photographs that readers might have of the event, anticipating that someone would have photographed the crash site. Instead, I received a photograph I could have lived forever without having seen: a candid view of my brother's crumpled body lying in the field where his parachute had landed. It had been taken by a local doctor who later examined his body in a makeshift morgue in Michelbach. It was a graphic example of "Be careful what you ask for: you may get it." It was something I never shared with my family.

The close of the AWON meeting coincided with a ceremony to commemorate the fiftieth anniversary of the surrender of the Japanese empire following the atomic bombing of Hiroshima and Nagasaki. AWON members had reserved seats among the thousands who thronged the dockside where the battleship USS *Missouri* was berthed, for its decks had witnessed the surrender ceremony in Tokyo Bay in 1945 and the ship was the focus of the day's commemoration. Sitting beside Boylin at the ceremony, I mentioned how helpful I'd always found every archivist to be; he turned to me and responded with a smile, "We're not all like that."

With the publication of my book and this event, one would think the story ended, for I'd resolved the mystery of my brother's death. Not so, and I continue and conclude his story here. The German fighter that launched an aerial rocket at the B-17 in which my brother was flying struck the left wing and exploded, sending shrapnel into the plane and many of the men inside. Elbert was so badly injured that the bombardier helped him parachute from the plane, hoping the Germans could give him medical attention long before the plane could bomb its target and return to England. The plan failed, for he was dead when his parachute landed near the little town of Michelbach. The stricken plane dived toward the earth, and the remaining men parachuted to safety, but when the plane crashed it exploded. The resulting fireball killed a farmer plowing his field and badly burned a young girl nearby.

In December 2008 I was astonished to receive a letter from one of the Germans who had helped me research the bomber's crash and the events that followed. Residents of the little town of Geiselbach, where the plane exploded, had erected a monument to that crash in the memory of the German farmer who had died, the little girl who was burned, *and* my brother. I was taken aback that these folks would memorialize my brother together with the victims of the crash, for he had, after all, been on a mission to bomb their homeland. The plaque on the monument reads, in German, "On October 14, 1943, an American Air Force B-17 fell here. Geiselbach resident Heinrich Rienecker as well as Lieutenant Elbert S. Wood lost their lives here. Thekla Peter of Geiselbach was severely wounded. This memorial stone is dedicated to the memory of these and all other victims of the war." It is tragic that other peoples around the world cannot resolve old hatreds and conflicts in a like manner and raise humanity to a higher level. Local residents have also erected signs at the points where his parachute landed and where the six bombs exploded that had been jettisoned in open country.

12

Return to the Dakotas, Part Two

Maps in chaotic times supply dignity and precision.
One feels safer with a map, enemy of chaos.

—Thorne Smith, *The Passionate Witch*, 1941

Ethnohistory and Cartography

Donald J. Lehmer suffered a tragic automobile accident in December 1972. He and his family were on their way to visit Bob and Gladys Levis, owners of the Cross Ranch, at their home in Alton, Illinois. His station wagon struck a guard rail over a small stream near Hamburg, Iowa, and his wife, Evelyn, was killed and his three sons were injured, one of them seriously. His secretary at Dana College, Loretta Callahan, called me with the news, and Dick Krause and I drove to Hamburg to see him in the emergency ward. We didn't think he'd live, but he rallied, finally succumbing on June 5, 1975, from complications of his injuries. Bob Levis generously provided a $2,000 subsidy to publish the festschrift that I edited in honor of Don's accomplishments (Wood, ed. 1977b).

I acted as the executor of his professional effects. In 1979 I forwarded his correspondence and other papers relating to his work in the Sonoran Desert and the trans-Pecos area in Texas to the Arizona State Museum, and his Plains materials to the National Anthropological Archives in Washington; and I updated his contribution to the *Handbook of North American Indians*, "Plains Village Tradition: Postcontact" (Lehmer 2001). I also published two volumes in his honor. First, I chose six of his most significant contributions to Plains prehistory and published them in *Selected Writings of Donald J. Lehmer*, together with three of his unpublished papers that I felt should be available for the Plains community. I also organized a symposium in his memory at the 1976 Plains Conference, the proceedings of which appeared the following year as Memoir 13 of the *Plains Anthropologist* (Wood, ed. 1977a, 1977b). He deserved no less.

I was devastated by his death, for Don and I had become very close. Indeed, though he was only fifty-seven years old at the time (I was forty-four), he was never shy about giving me fatherly advice. Don was a friend, mentor, father figure, and role model; only the death of members of my family equaled the sense of loss I felt when he was gone. We got along famously despite his reputation for acid sarcasm, and many people frankly disliked him. But our friendship was based on mutual respect, and we never had an argument or discussion that was not cordial. How much of his personality was shaped by a bitterly unhappy childhood is for others to decide. He was also a fine coauthor, and we collaborated on several Plains Conference talks, passing drafts back and forth until we were both satisfied. At one point Don looked at me after I'd edited one of his drafts and said, "Have you ever thought of working for the *Reader's Digest*?" (I took it as a compliment, though I'm not sure he meant it as such.) Don was a brilliant scholar, and the insightful culture-historical scheme he devised for the Central and Northern Plains in 1954 and later remains remarkably intact despite giant steps in our understanding of the prehistory in both regions over the past half century (Krause 1976; Lehmer 1954, 1971).

Principal among my post-Stanton-Sanger interests was a return to studies in historical cartography. My first atlas, prepared for the Knife River Indian Villages project (published by the Illinois State Museum), was among the first of my cartographic studies of early manuscript maps of the Missouri River and led me to delve deeper into the journals and maps of Lewis and Clark and their predecessors and contemporaries. I frequently ran into problems in researching these charts, and answers to my questions often were not available in the literature. So I began calling researchers who I thought could help me, regardless of their status or seniority, including Donald Jackson and Abraham P. Nasatir. Both were distinguished scholars, but I had no reason to believe that an eager young caller would be brushed off when inquiring about something they'd written; besides, as retirees they'd probably welcome a revival of interest in a subject of mutual concern. Both men responded to my phone call in the most positive fashion and spoke to me for more than an hour: finally, I terminated the calls out of sheer respect for their privacy. I've often told my students, "If you have a question about something that someone has written, call or write or e-mail them." They can't be offended by an interest in their work and in all probability will be thankful for being remembered in their retirement. Of course, the advice holds for scholars of any age. Both Jackson and Nasatir treated me as an old friend when I later met them at meetings of the Western History Association. Both of them clearly fit the appellation "a scholar and a gentleman."

Euroamerican traders were highly instrumental in fostering culture change among the native residents of the Upper Missouri, as they were of course elsewhere in North America. For this reason, Thomas Thiessen and I compiled a narrative account of visits to the Knife River Indian villages by fur traders from Canada, focusing on those who predated the arrival of Lewis and Clark. This project resulted from the fact that the visits of traders from St. Louis to those villages were relatively well known but those from Canada were not. In the course of compiling a calendar of such visits, we discovered several basic sources that had been so badly edited (in one case eviscerated) that we collected, transcribed, and eventually published several of them in *Early Fur Trade in the Northern Plains*, a book that built on the baseline provided by Hubert Smith's study of the explorations of the La Vérendryes (Wood and Thiessen 1985).

Our draft narratives in *Early Fur Trade* were verified in 1979 when I drove to Montreal and picked up Tom at the airport, and we spent a week comparing our transcriptions of photocopies against the originals in the archives of the University of Montreal (where I checked Larocque's Yellowstone journal) and at McGill University Library (where Tom checked McKenzie's and McDonnell's journals). We stayed in a pop-up trailer I'd rented in Columbia and commuted daily into Montreal across the St. Lawrence from our trailer camp in Longueuil. We also made a weekend jaunt down the St. Lawrence to Trois-Rivières, the birthplace of Pierre Gaultier de la Vérendrye, to absorb more of the flavor of the country. Before driving back to Columbia, I spent several days in the Canadian Public Archives in Ottawa checking my transcriptions of David Thompson's visit to the Mandans and Hidatsas in 1797–1798. We also checked the manuscript of Alexander Henry the Younger but omitted it from our book in deference to Barry M. Gough's more comprehensive two-volume edition that was then in preparation (Gough 1992). It was a pleasant vacation overall, for neither of us had spent much time in Canada. One morning as we emerged from our trailer in Montreal we were greeted by an Asian man who introduced himself with the improbable name of Pierre Raddison!

Another project I undertook for the Knife River Indian Villages program was an overview of Hidatsa Indian origins. A summary of traditional and historical accounts, it was first submitted to the Midwest Archeological Center and later published by J&L Reprints (Wood 1986a). It included a chapter by Jeffery R. Hanson, who reviewed aspects of Hidatsa kinship, marriage, and residence as they related to village composition. His chapter laid to rest the often-repeated speculation that the different Hidatsa clans were once residential units that lived in different villages. Not only did the overall work provide useful data, but I am told it is widely read and appreciated by Hidatsa residents of the Fort Berthold Indian Reservation.

A study of the cartographic resources that depicted the vicinity of the Knife River Indian villages, which I also prepared for the Midwest Archeological Center, was subsequently published as part of a longer monograph reporting the work that Lehmer and I had accomplished during our Stanton-Sanger project (Wood, ed. 1986). Because I had now accumulated a vast collection of manuscript and published maps of the Missouri River, I was asked to prepare cartographic overviews for other areas, including Fort Union Trading Post National Historic Site and selected locations along the Oahe and Lake Sharpe Reservoirs. I understand that these reports remain durable and useful documents, though they are still unpublished (Wood 1979a–c).

Still other published studies were by-products of these projects, including a study of a map of traditional Indian village sites and geographic features along the Missouri River that was created in 1907 by Sitting Rabbit (a.k.a. Little Owl), a Mandan (Thiessen et al. 1979). This was truly a collaborative effort: Tom Thiessen investigated the genesis of the document through archival research, I identified the archaeological and topographic features on the ground, and J. Wesley Jones translated the native names that accompanied the English terms on the chart. The map itself is a blend of native and white American imagery, for Sitting Rabbit used a copy of the 1892–1895 Missouri River Commission map of the Missouri River as the basis for his chart. Orin G. Libby, of the State Historical Society of North Dakota, who initiated the project, provided the map for him, though the pictographs that accompanied each feature on the map were distinctively Native American. The accompanying legends provide a native cross-check on early Euroamerican records as well as leads for features for which we should remain alert in the archaeological and historic records. The map will also be useful in providing leads for future archaeological surveys, for much of the Missouri River Valley in North Dakota has never been subjected to a systematic pedestrian archaeological survey. Its value for the Mandan and Hidatsa people and their history is inestimable.

Each of the projects enumerated here built on its predecessors and further enmeshed me in ethnohistorical studies, which I describe later. All of them were professionally and emotionally rewarding, and I began to see that my post-retirement years might well build on this foundation: and they did.

Field Schools in the Dakotas

I conducted two archaeological field schools in South Dakota, in 1996 and 1997. Both were at the request of graduate student Steve J. Dasovich, who used our findings in his 1998 dissertation. We excavated several stone circles (often called "tipi rings") at two sites on the land of Glen Opp northeast of the town of Eureka, in McPherson County. The rings were remarkably sterile of artifacts (only a few such rings contain much in the way of useful specimens), but Steve extracted enough information from our work and from related literature for his dissertation. A reporter from Eureka's newspaper, the *Northwest Blade*, interviewed some of the students who came from outside South Dakota and published some of their comments: "There are lots of rocks here and not many trees." And "I'm used to being around big animals. The only big animals here go 'moo.'" The reporter concluded her article by saying, "With these insights into our community, maybe we can stand back and look at it with renewed appreciation."

Our sites lay along forty-mile-long Spring Creek, one of the rare streams that flow into the Missouri River in this part of its reach. Only a few scattered trees were to be seen along its length, both originally and today; the only trees now seen in the uplands in the entire county are around farmsteads and in towns. Our prehistoric stone-ring builders certainly never lived on that upland or along Spring Creek in the winter: bison chips would never have sufficed as fuel. Years ago one of our students at Missouri, Thomas D. Holland, wrote a paper on the thermal qualities of bison dung (Holland 1984) that I recommend for Plains scholars. He calculated that to keep a three-month winter supply of dung dry would require a shelter 81 percent larger than most tipis to house some 1,300 cubic feet of fuel. Little wonder that the local nomadic peoples sequestered their winter quarters in well-wooded river bottoms.

Randall J. (Randy) Miles, a soil scientist at the University of Missouri–Columbia, joined us in 1997 and was to continue his association with my projects in the Dakotas for the next decade. An enthusiastic researcher and an award-winning teacher, he agreed with me that it is astonishing that we were paid to do such enjoyable work! I often accompanied Randy on his university soils field trips to southwestern Missouri, where I continued to reinforce my knowledge of soil science. Among our stops were the spectacular collapsed karst features and spring in Ha-Ha-Tonka State Park in the Lake of the Ozarks country. On one such trip I wore khaki trousers and a shirt with a Lewis and Clark patch on one shoulder. At the interpretive center a visitor approached me and asked, "How old are the rocks around here?" I replied, "They must be about three hundred million years or so; that's close enough for government work." A little later, on a pond near the spring, another man came up and, pointing over the water, asked, "What kind of duck is that?" I said, "I'm not too good on ducks. But if it quacks like a duck and walks like a duck, it's probably a duck." After he wandered off, Randy turned to me and said, "You know, he thought you were a ranger." I could imagine the two men angrily writing to the park superintendent complaining about his smart-aleck rangers, and the superintendent thinking, "What the hell? I don't have any rangers!" I was henceforth known among the soils students at Missouri as "Ranger Ray."

We were joined in our stone-ring investigations for both summers by the University of South Dakota field school, whose contingent was ably managed by Todd Kapler. Steve Dasovich's wife, Heidi, was from Eureka, and we generally had great relations with the townsfolk, though most of us remained outsiders. One day, as I was shopping for groceries, an elderly man looked at me, smiled, and said, "You're a stranger in these here parts, aren't you?" It was not unusual to hear folks speaking German as you walked down the street, though they'd shift to English as you came closer. We rented houses in town for our crews, but Todd and I shared a suite for both summers at the town's Lakeside Motel. We ate wonderfully in two local restaurants, alternating between them to maintain goodwill in the community. The weather was perfect that first summer: the occasional rainstorms came only during the night, so no hours were lost to the weather for the entire season.

In 1998 I returned to work in North Dakota. The State Historical Society, under chief archaeologist Fern Swenson, had begun a program of archaeologically investigating state historic sites that had been established years earlier, and modern studies were needed so the sites could be better interpreted to the public. Fern, a graduate of the University of Minnesota, had moved to Bismarck in 1986 or 1987 to become the chief archaeologist at the Heritage Center. I was at first disappointed that an individual trained in the Great Plains had not obtained the position, but I was soon disabused of that notion, for she became a most active force there and has created a lasting and positive legacy in preserving the prehistoric resources of the state. When the superintendent of the Heritage Center left to become director of the new D-Day Museum in New Orleans in about 2000, Merlan E. Paaverud Jr., then the director of the Historic Preservation Division, became the new superintendent; Fern moved up into Paaverud's position, and Fern's assistant, Paul R. Picha, became chief archaeologist. Paul had worked for years in various archaeological capacities in the state, and in December 1994 he'd been hired as Fern's assistant. He immediately took leave to attend the University of Missouri, where he obtained a master's degree in 1996, and returned to the society. One could not hope to find a couple more dedicated to the cultural resources of the state, a commitment they pursue with the most modern research tools available.

Fern contracted with Stanley A. Ahler, director of the nonprofit Paleo-Cultural Research Group, based in Flagstaff, Arizona, to excavate and report the findings at Menoken Indian Village National Historic Landmark (32BL2). Stan was admirably qualified to do so, for he'd been working in the Missouri Valley since 1969 at the Lower Grand site, and his knowledge of the prehistory of the region was unsurpassed. I joined the field party that assembled in 1998 at Menoken with my University of Missouri field school, as I also did the following summer. This small (2.5-acre) site was distinctive: it is on the banks of Apple Creek fifteen miles east of the Missouri River and is surrounded by a deep ditch reinforced by four immense bastions. Virtually every other fortified village site along the Missouri is perched on a terrace directly overlooking that stream.

The 1998 and 1999 Missouri field schools at Menoken were superb learning experiences for the students, for it was not a rote excavation project but an integrated, interdisciplinary research program. We were joined by Kenneth L. and Jo Ann Kvamme, of the Archeo-Imaging Lab at the University of Arkansas, who carried out geophysical studies of the entire site: Ken did magnetic gradiometry, and Jo Ann did resistivity. Modern geophysical technology is spectacular, and the Kvammes are so adroit with it that I call them Mr. and Mrs. Merlin (terms they do not find objectionable).

Figure 34. Stanley A. Ahler at the Menoken site, North Dakota, summer 1998. *Courtesy State Historical Society of North Dakota.*

Eventually, they created a geophysical map of the entire site and its archaeological features. The map was invaluable, for it revealed anomalies that turned out to be burned houses, which were not otherwise visible on the ground surface. Guest speakers provided a wide range of expertise for both the program and student education. Students obtained practical experience in geophysical prospecting there and, later that summer, at the prehistoric Huff village. We began digging two houses at Menoken in 1998, completing one that had been marked by a depression and exposing most of another burned dwelling that Kvamme's magnetic survey had revealed. Part of the crew also investigated geophysical anomalies across the site that the Kvammes had detected. Randy Miles described soil profiles at the site and gave lectures on soil science. He still muses about the sign he found in his motel room (Number 8) in the nearby town of Sterling: "Fire extinguisher may be found in Room 13."

Menoken had been nominated to and accepted as a National Historic Landmark site because it was once believed to have been the Mandan village visited by Pierre Gaultier de la Vérendrye in 1738. There had long been doubt about that identification, and our fieldwork quickly dispelled the notion, for nothing about the site spelled "Mandan." The houses we exposed were not Plains earthlodges, though they were earth covered; the pottery did not resemble that of the Mandans; neither cache pits nor agricultural tools were present; and only a few grains of maize were recovered. Furthermore, the small size of the site and the shallow depth of the fortification ditch were wildly different from the descriptions left by Vérendrye (Smith 1980:59). Indeed, the site contained almost exclusively Late Woodland pottery and tools, and when charcoal was radiocarbon-aged, it was found to date to the early thirteenth century. The design of the fortification system and the presence of a few pottery rimsherds and some other artifacts nevertheless register the fact that the inhabitants of the site had been in contact with peoples of the early Middle Missouri tradition farther south on the Missouri River, and it may well figure in the genesis of the Mandan Indians.

The original justification for Menoken's status as a national landmark was thereby obliterated, for the site had been burned and lay in prairie for more than half a millennium before Vérendrye even contemplated visiting the Mandans. Menoken is nonetheless unique among the prehistoric village sites in the Dakotas, and its distinctive content has since led to a revision in its nomination to reflect its new status. We therefore counted our two seasons as eminently successful, though they did not complete as much work as we'd hoped. The State Historical Society supported further work there by Stan Ahler in the summer of 2005, and the second house was fully exposed.

During our first season at Menoken we lived at a farm about ten miles east of the site. The staff lived in a large fixed trailer, and the students initially lived in tents. A storm one evening brought high winds that blew most of them flat, and the promised arrival of alternate housing was eagerly anticipated. It was not long in coming, for the society obtained five Federal Emergency Management Administration (FEMA) house trailers, surplus from the great Red River "flood of the century" at Grand Forks in 1997. Among the tents we retired from service were two of the aging U.S. Army squad tents that had been used by the society since at least 1952. We had lived in them at Like-a-Fishhook Village in 1954, as had Glenn Kleinsasser before us; I used them at Huff in 1960; James E. Sperry used them at the Havens site in 1967 and 1968; and I'm sure they had other use. In 2002 one of them was accessioned into the collections of the society: it had been manufactured only days before the Germans initiated the Battle of the Bulge in mid-December 1944! I wrote up some notes on its history for the archives.

On the afternoon of June 25 I was visited by an acquaintance who worked on the Standing Rock Indian Reservation, and I guided him and his young son around the site. Since it was a workday, I casually asked him if this was his day off, and he replied, "No, it's a reservation holiday." Without thinking, I asked, "What holiday?" I should have expected the answer: "Little Bighorn Day." We confined our investigations to Menoken, but one afternoon Stan Ahler and I were taken to the site of a bison bone bed on Apple Creek some distance upstream that we hoped might be a prehistoric kill site. We found no evidence that it was, but it provided an interesting ecological note: some of the bones were embedded among the sticks in an adjoining beaver dam. From their large size I suspect they were those of an extinct form, but I was in no position to judge which of them. On our way back to camp we noticed a large number of cars parked on an Interstate 90 overpass. Curious, we stopped and a bystander told us to look to the north, saying, "See the cold-air funnel?" We saw, instead, the funnel of the only tornado I've ever witnessed in my many years on the Plains, at a distance that I'd hoped to see one, perhaps twenty miles away.

During our second season at Menoken, in 1999, we occupied a lodge owned by Thomas Ness at a dog-training and bird-hunting farm ten miles south of Menoken, and the students again lived in FEMA trailers. Many of the students had difficulty getting to bed at an appropriate hour, for at this latitude the sun does not set until after nine o'clock, and they were dragging the next day at work. Indeed, from a bluff top or some other high point one may watch the sun pass across the northern night sky as a dim glow on the horizon. This year Darcy F. Morey and his University of Kansas field school students augmented our group, and Elizabeth Prine Pauls joined us to experiment with a field Geographic Information System computer mapping project. We had a cook for most of the summer, a local woman who prepared delicious dishes for us. Her work ethic was unbelievable. One evening she arrived with a young woman who apologized for their lateness and told us that the cook had had a heart attack earlier that day! We forced her into a chair and did not permit her to lift a hand during her stay. Among her recipes was a local German favorite, *Knoephla* soup (minced potatoes, onions, and miniature dumplings in a chicken stock), though thick enough to be classed as a stew. It's a dish I always order when I'm at my favorite family restaurant in Bismarck: the menu at Kroll's Diner orders you, "Sit down and eat!" Another of my local favorite foods is *Fleischküchen* (or *Fleischkeuchle*, "meat pie"), which I would describe as a spicy hamburger in a deep-fried pastry pocket.

Menoken's location posed a problem. We could understand why a group apprehensive of enemies would choose its position, for it adjoins a precipitous bank along the channel of Apple Creek that provided a defensive setting but also allowed ready access to water. Furthermore, according to the 1873 General Land Office survey, it was situated in the only grove of trees to be found in the valley of Apple Creek, trees that would be necessary to erect the stockade that reinforced the bastioned ditch around the site and for building the foundations of the earth-covered houses. Regardless of where people live, however, they must get their groceries, and at first I believed the occupants chose this locale because it was so close to McKenzie Slough, the remnants of late-glacial Lake McKenzie. The lake-bottom topography surrounding the village is as flat as a pool table, and from a slightly elevated position one can see for hundreds of yards, a wonderful setting when one is on the watch for enemies.

McKenzie Slough becomes either a lake or a swamp, depending on the amount of precipitation, and in either case it annually attracts hundreds of thousands of migratory fowl. Apple Creek also contains immense fish, along with snapping turtles a yard in length. Indeed, I saw a snapper fully that size one evening beside a pickup in the parking lot of a local bar; a crowd surrounded it at a respectful distance. Despite these resources, our dig yielded only a few bird bones, and the remains of fish and turtles were uniformly small. On the other hand, bison bones dominated the mammal bones, clearly revealing that they were the major source of protein for the community. Why was it necessary to build a fortified bison-hunting camp with such substantial dwellings a full day's march from the Missouri when they ignored such resources? The question remains unanswered.

The following summer the State Historical Society shifted the focus of its investigation to Fort Clark State Historic Site, which lies on a high terrace overlooking the Missouri River a few miles east of the town of Stanton. Jack L. Hofman and Darcy Morey, of the University of Kansas, joined my field school that year. The first half of the 2000 season was spent at Hofman's Waugh site, a Folsom campsite in extreme northwestern Oklahoma. We camped in a beautiful rural cottonwood grove in the Buffalo city

Figure 35. The author at Fort Clark State Historic Site, North Dakota, summer 2001. *Courtesy Tom Stromme,* Bismarck Tribune.

park at Doby Springs, a few miles west of town. We spent the second four weeks at Fort Clark, when Darcy joined the group, again under the direction of Stan Ahler under contract with the historical society. My 1986 map of the site now began the useful life for which it was designed. Ken and Jo Ann Kvamme joined us again to make a gradiometric and resistivity survey of a strip 400 by 20 meters across the entire village, beginning west of the fortification ditch and extending to the bluff edge, encompassing the plaza of the Mandan village and the Arikara ceremonial lodge that had been built in its center. The transect provided evidence of buried earthlodges that were not visible on the surface, something we'd not expected but certainly reasonable in view of the fact that the Arikaras had rebuilt the village after its destruction by fire in the winter of 1839.

The Kvammes also mapped Fort Clark and its opposition post, Fort Primeau, in preparation for the work we planned for the following summer, producing gradiometric and resistivity maps of both posts as well as the enclosure and earthlodge depression of Pierre Garreau, the Arikara interpreter at Fort Clark. We had a comfortable camp; most of the staff lived near the site entry in a large fixed trailer that also served as an office. An adjoining outbuilding that normally was used to store a tractor and mower was transformed into a kitchen and dining area, and the five FEMA trailers for student housing were parked between the fixed trailer and a newly built latrine. The only drawback of the latter facility was that it was several hundred yards from our excavations. Our summer was productive but tragically marred when Darcy Morey, driving a light pickup truck, collided with a large truck at an intersection near the Missouri River bridge at Washburn. Because of the seriousness of his injuries, he was rushed from the hospital in Bismarck to the Mayo Clinic in Minnesota, spending nearly a month in a coma. He recuperated for many weeks there and in Lawrence and did not return to full-time teaching and research at Kansas for more than a year. Because I had met some of my students and attended a party at the nearby town of Beulah the night before, I went to bed early that night, or I'd have been riding in the death seat beside him, for we were in the habit of going to town nightly to pick up fresh water for camp and having an ice cream bar before heading home. It was a near-brush with death.

In 2001 my field school again joined the State Historical Society at Fort Clark, the goal being to excavate the north blockhouse of Fort Clark itself. The fieldwork was under the direction of William J. Hunt Jr., an archaeologist with the Midwest Archeological Center. Hunt was exceptionally qualified, for he had worked for years with the archaeological remains at Fort Union Trading Post National Historic Site. We exposed the rather flimsy stone foundations of the blockhouse and the adjoining palisade trenches, discovering that the post had been rebuilt twice in its thirty-year history. Paul Picha also investigated an anomaly on the magnetic map that exposed the base of a giant post in the center of the stockade, surely the base of the fort's flagpole. William Hunt and Kenneth Kvamme prepared technical reports on the work at Fort Clark, and a general study of the site and its history and archaeology is scheduled to be published in 2011 (Wood et al. 2011).

In the evenings I reread the journal that director Francis A. Chardon kept at Fort Clark between 1834 and 1839 and was impressed by the number of times he praised the cooking of Toussaint Charbonneau ("Charbonneau gave us a feast" and his "pie was *charming*"). I collected each of Charbonneau's menus (unfortunately, Chardon provided no recipes for any of the dishes) with the idea of having a "Charbonneau dinner" one evening at camp, but the summer slipped by without our doing so. I compensated by putting together a short essay, "Toussaint Charbonneau's Kitchen," for

Figure 36. The author (*left*) and William J. Hunt during the excavation of a blockhouse at Fort Clark, summer 2001. *Author's collection.*

the *Museum of the Fur Trade Quarterly* (Wood 2003c). This museum, a few miles east of Chadron, Nebraska, contains the world's finest collection of mementos from the fur trade in the Far West, and it merits a visit by anyone interested in that era of American history.

The Kvammes also began preliminary geophysics at the Double Ditch village site (32BL8) in preparation for the next season's work. Double Ditch Indian Village State Historic Site is a spectacular Mandan village about twelve miles north of the city of Bismarck. The Mandans abandoned it shortly after the disastrous 1780 smallpox epidemic, which cut down their population so severely that their nine or so villages near Bismarck were reduced to two and the survivors resettled near the Hidatsas upstream near the mouth of the Knife River. William Clark shows Double Ditch on his route map as "Old Mandan village killed by the Soux," and the Mandans knew it as "Yellow Bank Village" (Moulton 1983:1:Map 28). Built on the rim of a high bluff overlooking the river, it was named for the two conspicuous ditches that enclose the lodge depressions and was renowned for its size and for the immense refuse middens that ring the village core. When we began our work, many of us believed the village had been founded about AD 1600 to 1650. Harvard undergraduates George F. Will and Herbert J.

Spinden had dug there in 1905 with the financial support of Clarence H. Moore and the advice and help of Ronald B. Dixon, and their report, published the following year by Harvard University's Peabody Museum, had remained the latest word on the archaeology of the site (Will and Spinden 1906). I've often wondered how many undergraduate reports have been published in such a prestigious outlet! However, the decision to publish it was a good one, for its format still stands as a model for the description and interpretation of archaeological data, however obsolete the field methods and artifact description have become.

At the end of the field season several of our crew (including Kathryn Drennan and Vince Warner, who later married) accompanied me to the Hagen site, near Glendive, Montana. Leslie B. Davis, of Montana State University, was reinvestigating this well-known but poorly understood site that's believed to be a late prehistoric Crow Indian village. We spent two days there as volunteers helping Les test a small part of this very large site. Ann Mary Johnson came up to help from Yellowstone National Park, so the dig became something of a reunion. It was my first visit to this fascinating site, whose interpretation remains enigmatic.

In 2002 the State Historical Society shifted its attention to the Double Ditch site. The Kvammes continued their geophysical work before our arrival, and on the last day of their stay Ken discovered two additional ditches beyond the outer visible one. These two new ditches were invisible on the surface, yet the outermost of them boasted a series of at least ten prominent bastions reminiscent of those at Huff. Only when these outer ditches became known could one see scattered and elusive traces of them on air photographs. These new ditches instantly rendered obsolete the interpretive signs the society had erected only weeks earlier and led to drastic overnight changes in our research design, for we proceeded to test these new features. Cross trenches were dug that verified their presence and depth, revealing that the reason for their surface invisibility was the fact that both had been filled level with earth and trash. We speculate that they were filled in when the village contracted so that enemies would not have protective cover so conveniently close to the new village perimeter.

Fern Swenson found us exceedingly comfortable and convenient field headquarters that year. Paul L. Andahl and Debbie Gronlie made their beautiful new home available to house most of the staff and the Kvammes' geophysical laboratory, and an area north of the house served as a temporary trailer park for the five FEMA trailers that housed the crew and those

Figure 37. Volunteering at Leslie Davis's dig at the Hagen site, Montana, summer 2001. *Author's collection.*

volunteer workers who didn't bring their own tents. An added bonus: the "camp" was less than a mile north of Double Ditch: it was practical to walk to work if one chose, and we drove home daily to have lunch in the oversize garage, which we turned into a kitchen/dining room and storage/laboratory space. It also served as a lounge for evening get-togethers. By any standard our accommodations were luxurious: my private upstairs room was carpeted in white (like the rest of the house), with a comfortable bed, an antique dresser, a ceiling fan, and a television set, plus the ultimate luxury: an adjoining bathroom and shower.

Figure 38. Double Ditch State Historic Site, North Dakota. *Courtesy State Historical Society of North Dakota.*

In 1905 Will and Spinden had dug tests in varying parts of the site and had cross-trenched Mound B, a very large midden on the east side of the village. In 2002 we reopened that trench and found that it was composed largely of earth that had been hauled in from other parts of the site. In the following year we excavated a surface depression that resembled one that would result from the abandonment of a long-rectangular house, but it turned out to be an area of cache pits, which nevertheless yielded a good artifact sample.

In 2003 we focused on fifteen of the prominent refuse middens surrounding the core area of the village, revealing that several of them had been built directly over one or the other of the two outermost ditches. The work this season was again conducted with the assistance of my Missouri field school, and my son Eric joined me for part of the season. One weekend Eric and I attended a powwow at Cannon Ball, my first one for many years, and on another weekend we took in a fur-trade rendezvous at Fort Union. That summer Tommy Ike Hailey, of Northwestern State University, Louisiana, flew a powered parachute over the site and took thermal images of the village that enhanced the geophysical data. Richard Krause also was there, continuing his technological study of the site's pottery begun the

Figure 39. Relaxing in an "on-site recliner," Double Ditch site, North Dakota, 2002. *Author's collection.*

previous year. Excavations in 2004 targeted cache pits in different parts of the village. I visited the site that season with Randy Miles when he and Crystal J. Frey took soil samples across the village for use in Crystal's master's thesis on the site's soils, but I did not otherwise participate in the work. Radiocarbon dates now suggest that the village was first settled in about AD 1450, but analysis of the vast quantities of materials recovered is still in progress. Frey's work will materially assist in understanding what Stanley Ahler termed "planar borrowing" at the site, whereby more than 600 cubic meters of earth were stripped from the village surface and redeposited elsewhere, a feature unknown in any other Plains earthlodge village.

Stanley Ahler had been diagnosed with prostate cancer some years earlier, and for a time it went into remission. But his struggle with it resumed and led to his death in February 2007. At the 64th Plains Conference, the preceding fall, he was presented with the Distinguished Service Award, which he well deserved for his lifelong dedication to archaeology and for his many outstanding contributions to national and Great Plains prehistoric studies. Plains scholarship thereby lost a sterling figure. I treasured my association with him from his graduate student days to his final ones, during which time I learned a great deal from him. I believe the only time he came near violence is when his face turned red on the occasion that I referred to his choice of bluegrass music as "crabgrass."

The Knife River Indian Villages National Historic Site and Historical Cartography

In 1970 Al Johnson, Richard Krause, and I went to Washington, D.C., to testify before the Committee for the Recovery of Archaeological Remains (CRAR), and in 1971 and 1976 I was called to Lincoln, Nebraska, to serve as a consultant in ethnohistory for the Knife River Indian Villages National Historic Site in North Dakota (KNRI), which Congress had authorized in 1974 to preserve and commemorate the history of the Hidatsa and Mandan Indians. In each instance we were appointed National Park Service "collaborators," a term that some of us older folks found discomfiting, given its World War II connotation as a "Quisling." Vidkun Quisling (1887–1945) was a Norwegian politician who collaborated with the Nazis during the German occupation of his country during World War II. The outraged Norwegians tried and executed him after the war.

I embarked on several projects to contribute to the research, for I'd been involved in a study of the locality ever since Don Lehmer and I initiated our Stanton-Sanger project. Part of our original plan had been to test the four Hidatsa earthlodge villages at the mouth of the Knife River: Amahami, Lower Hidatsa, Sakakawea, and Big Hidatsa. The latter three sites were incorporated into KNRI. Don had been a consultant in its planning, but because the Midwest Archeological Center was scheduled to investigate the sites, we did not wish to intrude on that research. By the time the KNRI research program was set up in 1976, the center was under the direction of F. A. Calabrese, who launched a search for an individual to lead these investigations. The choice was my former graduate student, Stanley A. Ahler, who joined the staff of the University of North Dakota and led the research, beginning in 1977. He conducted brilliant archaeological field and interpretive work on them for nearly fourteen years.

Calabrese and Ahler put together an advisory panel to assist them in planning research at KNRI, and I became involved in several projects as a consultant in ethnohistory. I'd taught a seminar in ethnohistory at my university since the winter of 1965, passing on much of what I'd learned of the approach from John Champe and Alan Woolworth. The class led me into many byways and to my own definition of ethnohistory as "the use of historical documents and historical method in anthropological research" (Wood 1990a:81). Many so-called ethnohistorical studies that I'd read had been little more than amateur forays into the rare book room by people who had no real notion how to use historical documents, ignorant of what generations of historians have honed in an approach termed "historical method." Historical method demands a critical analysis of texts and their scrupulous transcription when they are reduced to print. To sharpen my skills in research, I attended a seminar held in the summer of 1981 at the State Historical Society of Wisconsin, on the campus of the University of Wisconsin–Madison. The National Archives and Records Service conducted an annual seminar, informally called "Camp Edit," for the National Historical Publications and Records Commission (NHPRC). It was essentially a program to train historians in the art of transcribing historical documents, but I was able to attend with the support of Gary Moulton. It was an invaluable experience that prepared me for several future projects, and I gained basic knowledge in documentary editing that I transmitted to my students thereafter in my ethnohistory seminar. My tutor and mentor for my project (the journal of Charles Floyd of the Lewis and Clark expedition) was Richard Sheldon, of the National Archives, who supervised Camp Edit from 1979 through 1995.

My first assignment for KNRI was to prepare a plan for ethnographic research in which I reviewed the available resources for the project and offered suggestions for exploiting them (Wood 1977). My initial task was to edit an unpublished manuscript written years before by G. Hubert Smith on the explorations of Pierre Gaultier de la Vérendrye and his sons, for their records document the first visits by Europeans to present-day North Dakota from Canada. These French explorers visited the Mandan Indians between 1738 and 1743 from Fort la Reine, a post they established on the Assiniboine River in today's Manitoba near Portage la Prairie. However, Orin G. Libby, of the State Historical Society of North Dakota, had insisted that they visited not the Mandans but rather the Hidatsas, far upriver near the present town of New Town (formerly Sanish). Because of this belief the National Park Service established Vérendrye National Monument in 1917 near Sanish to commemorate his visit. Since other scholars contested the legitimacy of this location, the National Park Service was considering de-establishing the monument, especially since much of its site was to be inundated by the waters behind Garrison Dam.

Hubert Smith was retained to evaluate the validity of the disputed monument. Every serious scholar since Hubert completed his study in 1951 has agreed with his conclusion that Vérendrye had visited the Mandan villages in the vicinity of Bismarck, for there is no evidence the Hidatsas ever established earthlodge villages as far up the Missouri River as Libby claimed. I too found no reason to question Hubert's conclusions—findings that resulted in the disestablishment of the monument. Hubert was unhappy about this, for he felt that the Sieur de la Vérendrye's explorations deserved recognition, as indeed they do, but in a more appropriate setting. Today the granite boulder that commemorated his exploits at the old monument remains on a prominent hill on the Fort Berthold Reservation opposite the Four Bears Lodge and Casino near New Town, but only four holes and a rectangular outline on the stone's surface mark where a bronze plaque was once attached.

I followed Hubert's manuscript carefully as I edited it, though I updated it with data that had accumulated after it was written and used notations in Hubert's personal copy, which Alan Woolworth kindly loaned me. The end product, published by the University of Nebraska Press, provided a baseline for the first European penetration of the Mandan homeland (Smith 1980). The story of the Vérendryes could nonetheless be more fully understood by further research in the French archives, for surely there are untapped documents that augment those with which we are familiar. In any case, the Vérendrye exercise refreshed my understanding of the techniques of ethnohistory and reinforced a path into the ethnohistory of the Northern Plains that persisted into my retirement.

My second project was to compile a set of early maps, both manuscript and published, that illustrated the growth of knowledge about the upper Missouri River and the Mandan and Hidatsa Indians. In 1942 the Illinois State Museum had published an atlas compiled by pioneer ethnohistorian Sarah (Sally) Jones Tucker that illustrated what was known of the American Indian occupation of the state of Illinois. The atlas proved to be so useful to scholars in the Midwest that it was followed by a supplement prepared by Wayne C. Temple that included some of Tucker's less soundly documented charts. R. Bruce McMillan, director of the museum, agreed to publish my collection (augmented by a number of others to make it more comprehensive), and it appeared in the same format used by Tucker and Temple (Tucker 1942; Temple 1975; Wood 1983a). Their oversize (12 by 16 inches), or folio, dimensions meant that details and wording on the maps can be more readily discerned, as opposed to those at the small scales at which maps are normally published in book form. It had long appeared to me that early charts contained data that supplemented and, indeed, confirmed or refuted information that appeared in narrative documents, yet maps usually were used more as illustrations to break the monotony of dry text than as important documents in their own right.

My most intriguing cartographic study, however, came when I obtained a color photocopy of the original map prepared by Antoine Soulard for use by Mackay and Evans's 1795 expedition up the Missouri River. Three copies of this map had been known for years: one in Spanish, one in French, and the last in English (the one carried by Lewis and Clark). Some years earlier I'd tried to understand the nature of the original by laboriously collating the information on each of the copies, but my friend Robert Karrow, at the Newberry Library, let me know that the original had been found in a private collection in Spain and was about to be auctioned at Sotheby's of London. It was sold to a dealer in Philadelphia, who priced it at $150,000. I finally traced down its final owner at the Karpeles Manuscript Library in Santa Barbara, California, and the owner graciously gave me permission to publish it (Wood 1996), making public at last the original of what has been called the most important eighteenth-century map of the Missouri Valley. The prices in the rare manuscript map market are truly astronomical.

Eventually, I published three atlases through the Illinois State Museum, two of them collections titled "An Atlas of Early Maps of the American Midwest" and a third that contained the maps created by Nicolas Nicollet on his journey up the Missouri River in 1839 and his journey overland to

St. Anthony's Falls on the Mississippi, the present location of Minneapolis (Wood 1983a, 1993e, 2001b). I'd stumbled onto these charts when I was researching other maps in Nicollet's archives in the Library of Congress on one of my trips to Washington. A few of these 1839 maps had been published, but my atlas presented all of those he'd prepared for his tour through the northeastern Plains. These maps provide a unique glimpse into archaeological, historical, and environmental data that are proving useful to a wide range of scholars.

These atlases, together with those prepared by Tucker and Temple, are widely consulted, and the museum has kept each of them in print. My personal collection of copies of early maps eventually came to occupy an eleven-drawer steel map cabinet and one drawer of a vertical steel file. They have served my ethnohistorical studies well, and I've always been happy to share them with colleagues having parallel interests.

13

The Lewis and Clark Bicentennial

Happily for our own time, [the Lewis and Clark] expedition is now going on, under the auspices of an enlightened government, to explore this river to its sources. What gratitude is due from the whole world to those persons who expose themselves to the greatest fatigues, and even to the greatest dangers, to enlarge the circle of human knowledge.

— Antoine Soulard, Surveyor-General of Upper Louisiana, *Descriptive Observations on Certain Parts of the Country in Louisiana*, 1806

The Commemoration Begins

With the approach of the Lewis and Clark Bicentennial in 2004, my involvement in the study of the Corps of Discovery began to accelerate. I'd begun my foray into their activities in the late 1960s when I wrote up the Biesterfeldt site. Knowing nothing of the convoluted history of the expeditionary journals, I consulted the various editions of these important documents in my summary of early Cheyenne history. I'd been interested in these journals for many years—indeed, from the time I worked on Ponca Fort as an undergraduate—for it's impossible to pursue interests in the Missouri River and its Indian residents without being drawn to them as primary sources. The captains' journals had of course mentioned an old Cheyenne village at the mouth of Porcupine Creek, which I'd tried to find in the summers of 1955 and 1956 around Fort Yates, but I've already related my lack of success in locating any such site, much less others mentioned in historic sources.

I began to investigate the content of the journals again after my first float trip down the Upper Missouri through the White Cliffs region, in 1979. At the mouth of Arrow Creek I'd seen the high bluffs over which

Lewis and Clark said vast numbers of bison had been run by the Indians (in what the Blackfeet Indians called a *pishkun*) and had piled up at the foot of the bluffs on the river's bank. When I saw these cliffs, I became suspicious of that interpretation, and some years later I wrote an article, which I later expanded, suggesting that the remains the captains reported were those of float bison that piled up against the shoreline beneath the bluff by the action of flood waters from Arrow Creek (Wood 1982a, 1986b). The remains that Lewis and Clark saw are in a setting unlike that of any other bison drive in the Northern Plains, supporting the idea that when the explorers saw the bison at the foot of the bluff they assumed, naturally enough, that the remains were due to Indian activities. The journals give no source for that identification, but Toussaint Charbonneau was on board to tell them about this practice, for the technique was used by the Mandans and Hidatsas and many other groups in the Northern Plains, and he surely had learned it when he lived with the Hidatsas.

On my way home from my 1979 float trip down the Upper Missouri with Miles Gilbert, I'd stopped in Lincoln to visit Gary E. Moulton, the newly appointed editor of the new edition of the journals of Lewis and Clark, in the Center for Great Plains Studies at the University of Nebraska. Some years earlier Donald Jackson had written a paper called "Some Advice for the Next Editor of Lewis and Clark" (Jackson 1967). Steven F. Cox, executive editor at the University of Nebraska Press, had taken the article to heart and was responsible for initiating the new edition. I'd known Steve for several years (we were in fact scheduled to float down the Upper Missouri together the following summer), and he was familiar with my interest in the early mapping of the Missouri River. So he told me, "You've got to meet Gary Moulton." He also told Moulton of my interests in pre–Lewis and Clark mapping. This being my first visit to Lincoln since that conversation with Steve, I walked into Gary's office and introduced myself. We had a long talk, and on my departure I wondered what impression I'd made on this immaculately dressed professor. I was wearing engineer boots, jeans, and a Levi's jacket and carried my motorcycle helmet. Gary later admitted that he wasn't quite sure just what to make of me. However, when I spent the following year on sabbatical in Lincoln, the two of us had lunch several times a week to discuss the Lewis and Clark atlas he was compiling. It was the beginning of our collaboration on various projects and an enduring friendship. I prepared notes for him concerning archaeological topics that Lewis and Clark mentioned in their text on the Missouri River.

Figure 40. Gary E. Moulton (left) and the author at the Lewis and Clark Trail Heritage Foundation meeting in Sioux City, Iowa, 1996. *Author's collection.*

My participation in what was to become the Lewis and Clark phenomenon was stimulated when I attended my first meeting of the Lewis and Clark Trail Heritage Foundation at the Joslyn Art Museum in Omaha. This was in mid-August 1980, immediately after my return from tracing the route of François-Antoine Larocque across the Northern Plains. Don Lehmer and I had obtained photocopies of William Clark's field maps for the Stanton-Sanger area from Mildred Goosman, the Joslyn's curator of western collections. The maps were archived in the Joslyn's collection of the journals and related material that resulted from the expedition of Prince Maximilian of Wied-Neuwied in North America in 1832–1834. William Clark had given Prince Maximilian these copies of his route maps of the Missouri River above what is today Omaha for the prince's use on his expedition.

These copies are historical treasures, for Clark's original route maps from the mouth of the Missouri to the Mandan and Hidatsa villages have been lost. Because of my interest in and experience with the river, Mildred asked me to give a talk to the group on the prince's copies of the maps. These charts add new dimensions to Lewis and Clark's narratives, and the prince's occasional annotations on them augment the historical record in other ways, for they pinpoint events that took place later in time for which we have no other record. For example, one of the sheets specifies the location of a Yanktonai Indian camp below Fort Clark that we can identify with the Ice Glider archaeological site (Wood, ed. 1986). Mildred also gave Gary and me permission to study the maps in detail, and we collaborated on a paper that brought them to the attention of other scholars (Wood and Moulton 1981). These maps of course became essential elements in Gary's monumental atlas of the journals of Lewis and Clark.

I continued to build on my attachment to the study of early maps, writing a series of articles that examined various aspects of the historical cartography of the Missouri River. The first was a transcription and interpretation of the maps that illustrated the route taken by John Thomas Evans as he ascended the Missouri River in 1796. A copy of his seven-part map was carried by Lewis and Clark "in their glove compartment" and provided an accurate road map for the first full year of their expedition. Evans's map also supplied important clues to the history of the Indians living along its banks, but its content had been compromised by William Clark's annotations. I identified his additions by his handwriting, identifications that were corroborated by the handwriting specialist at the Missouri State Highway Patrol in Jefferson City. This separation permits us to distinguish those elements on the original map from the ones Clark added eight years later. The maps were redrawn in my publication to make them easy to read, for their usually poor reproduction sometimes rendered parts of them illegible. These transcriptions were verified when I checked them against the originals in the Coe Collection at the Beinecke Rare Book and Manuscript Library in the Yale University Library (Wood 1981a).

When I obtained a personal copy of Ernest Osgood's *The Field Notes of William Clark* (1964), I noticed that five of Clark's field entries had been written over crude sketch maps of the lower Missouri River, maps that did not exist in any other form. I transcribed these maps (with the assistance of Gary, who checked my work against the originals at Yale) and published them as "William Clark's Mapping in Missouri" (Wood 1982b). The importance of these charts lay in the fact that not one of Clark's route maps through the present state of Missouri exists today in any other form. Other articles I published on historical cartography include a reexamination of the maps by John Evans and William Clark, a general history of the mapping of the Missouri River, a study of the role of Nicolas de Finiels in the mapping of that river by James Mackay, and a presentation of the original map created by Antoine Soulard in 1795, a chart that in all probability was made for use by the Mackay and Evans expedition (Wood 1983b, 1987a–b, 1996).

An episode illustrating how small the world still is came as I was returning from the first of the two stone-circle sites we'd investigated in South Dakota in 1996. I stopped for the night at a motel in Sioux City, Iowa, and called a good friend, V. Strode Hinds, who came to the motel, where we spent several hours in conversation. Because Strode was an enthusiastic Lewis and Clark buff, we had many interests in common. At one point Strode mentioned that he'd obtained one of the plaster-of-paris casts that was made of Sergeant Floyd's skull before his remains were interred (for a fourth time) in 1900. Sergeant Floyd died as a member of the Lewis and Clark expedition in 1804 and was buried south of modern Sioux City on what came to be called Sergeant's Bluff. After his three previous interments the local Floyd Association reburied Floyd's bones for the last time in 1900. The next year a hundred-foot-high sandstone obelisk was erected over his remains. In October 1966 the monument became the first site to be listed in the National Register of Historic Places. Hiram M. Chittenden, an engineer with the Army Corps of Engineers and renowned historian of the fur-trade era, had designed the obelisk for the Floyd Association and oversaw its construction.

Strode was seeking a forensic facial modeler to create Floyd's image to place on a mannequin that was to greet visitors at the Sergeant Floyd Visitor Center on the riverfront in Sioux City. The visitor center and museum is in a dry-docked Army Corps of Engineers riverboat christened the *Sergeant Floyd*. I promised to help, and on my return to Columbia I called various forensic anthropologists around the country seeking someone to model the skull. Douglas W. Owsley, at the Smithsonian, recommended I contact Sharon Long, a forensic modeler and a good sculptor to boot. I called her one afternoon to see if I could interest her in the project. She wasn't in, but I left a message. That evening I received an excited telephone call from her: yes, she absolutely wanted to do the skull. Sergeant Floyd, as it happened, was her great-great-uncle! Though the mandible had been lost, newspaper photos of the full cranium and skull provided full-front and side views of the remains. Together with the skull cast, the photographs supplied enough information for Sharon to prepare his bust, so today visitors see Sergeant Floyd's likeness as they enter the museum. Using Strode's notes, I completed the story of Floyd's "resurrection" for *We Proceeded On*, a journal devoted to scholarship on Lewis and Clark (Hinds 2001). On October 27, 1997, the plaza surrounding Floyd's Monument was dedicated to Strode's memory.

All these events preceded the bicentennial of the Lewis and Clark expedition, and inevitably I became enmeshed in that hectic commemoration. My involvement also put me in touch with my friend James P. Ronda, whom I'd met earlier in Lincoln when he was just beginning his book, *Lewis and Clark among the Indians*, a study that richly elucidates the background and meaning of the expedition. It's worth noting that the year 2004 was the bicentennial not only of the expedition but also of an event of vastly greater importance than the exploration by the captains: the Louisiana Purchase. Thomas Jefferson's acquisition had doubled the size of the growing United States and made inevitable the eventual expansion of the nation to the shores of the Pacific. But as Peter Kastor observed, its bicentennial was sidelined by the hubris that accompanied the Lewis and Clark commemoration, and the Louisiana Purchase "continued to plod away in relative obscurity" (Kastor 2004:25).

I'd once planned, following retirement, to write a history of the James Mackay and John Evans expedition and the role it played in the story of the Missouri River. When I realized the magnitude of the approaching Lewis and Clark avalanche, I thought, "What on earth are you thinking?" I began to write that story, recognizing that it would serve to point up the significance of the captains' predecessors, who otherwise were being ignored. One evening I heard a prominent eastern historian in a television documentary begin his sound bite with the statement, "When Lewis and Clark went up the unexplored Missouri…," and the comment clinched my resolve to complete that study before the celebration reached a peak; perhaps I could restore some balance to the occasion. I had, after all, been unknowingly working on such a book ever since I was an undergraduate, when I'd investigated Ponca Fort and the activities of the 1795–1797 Mackay and Evans expedition up the Missouri. My studies of pre–Lewis and Clark maps and on-the-ground visits to many of the sites that the two men had visited among the Omahas and Mandans lent further impetus to a labor of love that I published as *Prologue to Lewis and Clark: The Mackay and Evans Expedition* (Wood 2003a).

Without demeaning in any way the accomplishments of the leaders of the Corps of Discovery, I pointed out that the Missouri had been explored for more than a century before them, and that the captains in fact carried with them two highly detailed maps of the Missouri River that covered the first full year of their expedition, created by this duo from Scotland and Wales. The Lewis and Clark expedition did not launch into what was, for white Euroamericans, unexplored territory until it proceeded upriver past the Mandan and Hidatsa villages. The referees the University of Oklahoma Press chose to review the manuscript generally had good things to say about it and recommended its publication, though one of them commented, "There are a few instances of 'fine writing' creeping in, but judicious copy-editing will take care of that." Happily, the copy editor differed and the "fine writing" remained intact.

Near Death on the Missouri

One of my friends is historian James M. Denny, who worked in the Missouri Department of Conservation until his retirement and is the mayor of the hamlet of Lupus (population 39), set on the south bank of the Missouri River not far west of Columbia. Some years ago he discovered Sugar Loaf Rock, a remarkable tower of sandstone on the bank of an old channel of the Missouri a few miles upstream from Jefferson City. It had been visited and recorded by William Clark in 1804 and noted by Prince Maximilian in 1833 and by others; the prince recorded that he'd been told that the Indians said it was the accumulated dung of a race of giant bison. The feature is actually the sand-filled and cemented contents of an ancient sinkhole that formed in the Mississippian-age Burlington limestone.

William Clark climbed to the bluff top behind it on June 4, 1804, where he noted a burial mound, descended into a declivity past some shallow rockshelters, and climbed to the top of this tall, silo-shaped formation. It is one of the few places where it is known that Clark actually stood on his epic journey of discovery. From its flat top he had a commanding view of more than thirty miles of river bottom. Because Jim's discovery was made just before the hullabaloo accompanying the bicentennial, he began efforts to have this scenic vista preserved as a state park. However, before Governor Mel Carnahan would consent to support the appropriation of several million dollars to purchase and develop the land, he insisted on having the rock "authenticated" as a Lewis and Clark locale by a specialist. That specialist was of course Gary Moulton, editor of the new edition of the journals of Lewis and Clark.

I was invited to accompany Denny, Moulton, and Ron Kucera (a deputy director in the Department of Natural Resources) to the site one cloudy afternoon in May 1999. Because it was raining lightly when we arrived, we slid down the muddy slope to its base, then clambered to the top of Sugar Loaf to admire the view that Clark had said had "a prospect of the river for 20 or 30" miles upstream. It was more difficult to climb back up the hill on our return, for the continuing rain made it more slippery by the minute. Gary preceded me up the slope, and at one point he pulled himself up by grasping the base of an immense dead tree. I was immediately behind him, and when I grabbed it, the roots of this twenty-foot-tall behemoth came loose and the whole thing toppled over as I slid backward down the slope; it crashed onto the hillside not a foot from my head. Had it fallen only slightly to one side, my skull would have been crushed flat. When we reached the top of the hill, I noted a sensation on my left elbow and found it had been cut to the bone when I'd slid over a low ledge of limestone. Denny drove me to a hospital in Jefferson City where, coincidentally, one of the doctors who treated me was Dean Breshears, a field hand who had worked with us at Rodgers Shelter when he was in high school, and one of his colleagues named Rodgers also checked my arm.

Moulton agreed with Denny that the locale was indeed the formation that Clark had ascended on that June day in 1804 (Denny 2000). But the story has an unhappy ending: before any action could be taken by the state to purchase it, Sugar Loaf Rock and the surrounding upland was purchased by a local doctor as the site for his home, though it remains safe from further encroachment.

Because the captains returned to St. Louis in September 1806, by 2006 the Lewis and Clark hullabaloo was subsiding. Truly, the commemoration had been, in words of the 1960s, a "happening," eclipsing in activities and enthusiasm, at least in those states bordering the trail, not only the bicentennial of the Louisiana Purchase but that of American independence the nation celebrated in 1976. By this time I'd given dozens of talks from Missouri to North Dakota on the Corps of Discovery, and I was thoroughly tired of the circuit. Many of my friends involved in the commemoration were similarly relieved it was over.

14

Teaching at the University of Missouri

We believe the archaeological record is interesting enough without dressing it up in a mantle of speculation . . . just the facts as we think we know them. We might say, as a recent biographer of Wolfgang Amadeus Mozart phrased it, "this is [an] attempt to cleanse and restore a fresco which has been painted over repeatedly. . . . It is not always a simple task, for the picture is fragile, whereas the materials painted over it are usually quite sturdy."

— Michael J. O'Brien and W. Raymond Wood,
The Prehistory of Missouri, 1998, quoting
Wolfgang Hildesheimer in *Mozart*, 1983

Colleagues and Thoughts about Ethnogenesis

Carl Chapman was director of the American Archaeology Division when I first arrived in Missouri in 1957, and he remained in that capacity until Dale R. Henning took over the position in 1965. Dale was an admirable administrator and provided invaluable assistance for me, especially when I decided to investigate a Nebraska phase house and an Upper Republican lodge in the fall of 1967. His successor was Richard Krause, who held the position between 1968 and 1974, when he resigned to become a faculty member at the University of Alabama. He and Dale were the only members of the department throughout my tenure there who shared my interest in the Plains, and I mourned their leaving. Michael J. O'Brien was appointed director in 1980, and he also served as an associate dean in the College of Arts and Science until he became its dean in 2006. Before his arrival at Missouri, Mike worked with Dale on the Cannon Reservoir project in the Salt River drainage in northeastern Missouri. Henning relinquished that project to O'Brien when Mike was chosen to become a member of our department.

Dale left the University of Missouri in 1968 to accept a position at the University of Nebraska in Lincoln, and in 1971 I collaborated with him on a proposal to the National Science Foundation for a four-year study of the archaeology and paleoecology of the Missouri River Valley between Kansas City and Omaha. Our hearts and minds certainly were in the right place, but our monumental budget and the scope of the work, we suspect, were too much to expect the NSF to support, and it was not funded. The project was never revived, and both of us went on to new ones, though our friendship over the years never flagged.

Because of my four-decade tenure at Missouri, I often received mail addressed to me as chair of the department. But I never once served as chair: I stood for election to that post only one time, in about 1966, but James A. Gavan, our physical anthropologist, won the vote. I've never regretted it, for the position, once largely honorific, has evolved into one more accurately described as horrific. I have, however, served on innumerable college committees, the most interesting of which was the University Research Board. Further service to the state came in 1973 to 1977, when I was appointed by Governor Christopher Bond to serve as a member of the Missouri State Advisory Council on Historic Preservation, a capacity I also filled from 1995 to 1998 at the request of Governor Mel Carnahan. By state law, this council consists of architects, historians, archaeologists, and interested laypersons appointed by the governor to review nominations for placement on the National Register of Historic Places. It was one committee I enjoyed, for unlike the case with many committees, I actually learned a great deal from its diverse membership.

A long-delayed project was finally realized in 1998 with the publication of *Archaeology on the Great Plains* (Wood, ed. 1998). Some ten years earlier, at a Plains Conference, I'd organized a meeting of prospective authors to put together the topical outline for a general book on Plains prehistory. A university press reviewed the proposal, agreed to publish the volume, and issued a contract for it; but so many delays ensued following the revisions called for by outside readers that the press canceled the contract. After the recommended changes were made, the manuscript was submitted to the University Press of Kansas, entailing a second round of outside readers. All this of course improved the text but delayed its publication far beyond what I'd hoped. It was generally warmly reviewed, though as one reviewer (Fox

1999:854) said, it was "unabashedly, a materialist synthesis," and he noted that it overlooked "mobilary and rock art, astronomy, warfare, mortuary, and other ideological realms." It also was criticized for not treating such topics as gender, which had become an important issue over the years the book was in press, and did not do justice to the prehistory of the Canadian Plains. Recent advances in all realms clearly call for a new and expanded synthesis.

In the mid-1990s I collaborated with Michael O'Brien on a book that summarized the prehistory of Missouri (O'Brien and Wood 1998). Such a volume was long overdue, for Chapman's 1975 and 1980 two-volume *Archaeology of Missouri* was becoming increasingly obsolete as field data continued to accumulate, and both of us found that many of his ideas were unacceptable. Concepts likewise were undergoing a change. In 2002 I published a paper called "The Realities of Ethnogenesis," which reflects what I believe is an anthropologically sound approach to the concept of ethnogenesis and archaeological classification, the same approach that Michael and I adopted in the book. I interrupt my narrative to summarize it briefly here.

Every professional and avocational archaeologist has been shown an artifact and asked, "What tribe made it?" It's a question that's raised as often as "How old is it?" Usually, we have to say, "That depends on its context: where it was found and what was found with it." A satisfactory answer might well be an estimate of the rough age of the specimen, but its "tribal identification" invariably remains vague unless it is an ethnographic specimen (an item from a known group of people), and even here we're often on shaky ground because of the widespread trade that took place between American Indians. Using the term "ethnogenesis" here for "tribal origins" may perhaps be misleading, for in this case we are concerned with tracing something that we might better call "tribal genealogies," not "the historical emergence of a people who define themselves in relation to a given cultural heritage." William Sturtevant introduced the concept of ethnogenesis to American anthropologists in his article "Creek into Seminole" (Sturtevant 1971:92), and it later became a fashionable buzzword.

The quest for tribal origins has a long history in the New World. The pioneer work in the scientific investigation of the origin of a tribe on the Great Plains, and still one of the finest integrations of historical, ethnographic, and archaeological data, is the study of the Double Ditch site by George F. Will and Herbert J. Spinden (1906), whose integrated approach became a model for studies of other Plains tribes. As early as 1929 Matthew W. Stirling (1929) was advocating what his Smithsonian colleague Waldo R. Wedel (1938) a decade later would refer to as the direct-historical approach. No one can argue with the logic of that approach, which was not new in the 1930s. Indeed, John Wesley Powell and Cyrus Thomas had adopted it in the 1880s for the Smithsonian Institution's Division of Mound Exploration in its quest to destroy the myth that a race of people separate from American Indians had constructed the thousands of mounds across the eastern United States. The approach comprises two steps. First, one documents the similarities in cultural materials in those evident from ethnographic and ethnohistorical research and those evident archaeologically for a given ethnic group. Second, one assumes that similar materials are temporally and culturally related and constructs a continuous thread, or cultural lineage, from the present into the past. Roland B. Dixon (1913) had espoused just such a strategy in his presidential address to the American Anthropological Association in 1913.

The direct-historical approach has been used in the Great Plains to identify archaeological remains believed to be those of the Pawnee, Kansa, Wichita, Plains Apache, and Cheyenne Indians. However, these were modest claims, extending historically known groups back only a few centuries, and Plains anthropologists have been equally modest in seeking origins for other groups. Until recently, perhaps the best-known "deep derivation" was one by Jack T. Hughes, who made the extraordinary claim that Caddoan groups in the Southern Plains could be traced back to the Archaic period (Hughes 1974). Hughes, of course, was tracing not ethnic identity but elements of material culture into the past, and because of the richness of today's archaeological record, it no longer comes as a surprise to see continuity in the culture content of an area over long periods of time.

William Duncan Strong's classic *Introduction to Nebraska Archeology* (Strong 1935) was the first significant use of ethnohistory and the direct-historical approach in the Plains, and his subsequent essay, "From History to Prehistory in the Northern Great Plains" (Strong 1940), continued the trend. Waldo R. Wedel and Mildred Mott Wedel became and remained dedicated to this approach in their studies of Great Plains groups, and they were the next generation of significant practitioners of studies of tribal origin. Waldo made the direct-historical approach a byword on the Great Plains with his study of the Pawnee Indians (Wedel 1936), although curiously, the approach was not formally defined until a half decade later in *American Antiquity* by Julian Steward (1942). The technique developed in the Plains, leaving us with the question, noted by one anonymous reader of the manuscript of this book, "Why didn't it arise in the Southwest, where connections between ancient and living pueblos are perhaps more clear than that between ancient and living Plains folks?"

In the direct-historical approach in culture-historical studies, as classically defined, one moves from the historic known to the prehistoric unknown. How do we relate a late eighteenth-century village to its ancestors? We begin by using data from an archaeological site known to have been inhabited by a historically documented tribe and seek out consecutively earlier sites until we pass into the realm of prehistory. In some cases the technique has worked well, though it has never successfully penetrated very deeply into the prehistoric record. Often there are a variety of problems, not the least of which is the displacement of traditional American Indian technology by the introduction and acceptance of Euroamerican trade goods. The Osage and Ponca Indians, for example, are known solely from historic sites in which only vestiges of diagnostic native-made pottery and chipped-stone tools are to be found. This severely limits the kind of comparisons that make it possible to search for earlier villages.

But there is a deeper problem that is even more troublesome. The "degree of fit" between ethnic groups and their material remains is far from exact. There are many cases in which different ethnic groups share distinctive elements of subsistence, technology, and lifestyle. Many of these similarities occur because the different groups live near one another and are adapted to the same environment. These elements combine with such social factors as intergroup trade, with the result that neighboring groups often share so many elements of material culture that their archaeological remains are difficult if not impossible to sort out, like those of the Mandans and Hidatsas.

The direct-historical approach is validated by the method of ethnohistory. Ethnohistory has been defined in many ways, but my own minimal definition, as I've said, is "the use of historical documents and historical method in anthropological research" (Wood 1990a:81). "Historical method" has an explicit meaning derived directly from historians and historiography and denotes the ways in which historical documents are gathered, authenticated, critically examined for credibility, and interpreted. There are good manuals explaining the method. My favorite source is Robert J. Shafer's *Guide to Historical Method* (1980); though old, the methodology remains the same. My effort to introduce the method to a wider archaeological audience led me to publish "Ethnohistory and Historical Method" in volume 2 of Michael B. Schiffer's series in archaeological method and theory (Wood 1990a). It drew on my earlier concerns about the validity of "reconstructing" culture history (Wood 1969).

Many years ago at a Plains Conference I stated that although ethnohistory and the direct-historical approach were logical, demanding, and efficient tools for pursuing tribal origins, they were not panaceas and would not solve all our problems in the historical period. Mildred Wedel took sharp exception to my generalization, pointing out that only the surface has been scratched in many archives and that a great deal of work remains to be done in ferreting out still unknown or poorly published sources, ones that will permit us to solve many vexing problems. She was simultaneously right and wrong, for she knew as well as I that only a fraction of the documents that were created still exist, so we can never know everything that was once recorded. Nevertheless, the archives in Europe remain poorly exploited, principally because of the expense of travel and lodging, the length of time necessary to scan the archives, and the need for having a firm grip on not only the language in which they are written but the language at the time the documents were produced, a skill that few of us possess.

Because ethnogenesis has been a favorite pursuit of many of us, and because we are fortunate that late prehistoric Plains village cultures persisted with a high degree of continuity into the historic period, we sometimes overestimate the credibility of some of our associations of historic tribes with archaeological complexes. Even so, few Plains archaeologists are comfortable in assigning tribal names to entities that existed as little as a century before Lewis and Clark. In some cases it is flatly impossible to do so. For example, every known Osage Indian village site is fully historic, and not one of them contains a good roster of native-made artifacts. The Osage appear in southwestern Missouri suddenly, without known antecedents (Henning 1998:361, 402–403).

In the past, when American archaeologists were dealing with only a few widely scattered sites, the "periodization" of their sites was inevitable, with major permutations in artifacts and inferred activities being defined as marking period boundaries. No such simple periodization is rational today. The basic features of the Woodland period in eastern North America, for example, can be traced back to Late Archaic food experimentation, burial-mound interment, and pottery making. Furthermore, today we know that the elaborate cultures of the Mississippi River Valley are not based on ideas imported from Mesoamerica but an indigenous North American development founded on preexisting Woodland and other local elements. That is, continuity is becoming increasingly evident as our archaeological data bank continues to expand. So how far can we hope to trace historic groups back in time? The answer is, not very far, and for two very sound reasons. First, there is a high probability that the first European-introduced diseases massively disrupted traditional cultures across the entire North American continent, and second, we cannot assume isomorphism between ethnic groups and their material culture.

Let me turn first to smallpox and other diseases. There has been an expanding realization of the effects that smallpox and other introduced diseases had on American Indian cultures ever since Henry F. Dobyns jarred American anthropologists and historians into the realization that those diseases played a far more significant role in modifying native cultures than previously realized. Disease had much more dramatic consequences than simply reducing population, drastic as that might have been. A loss of population of more than 95 percent was a common figure in many epidemics. Such depopulation would have led to changes in every aspect of life, and there were repeated epidemics in the centuries following the first major smallpox epidemic in Mexico. Smallpox epidemics began when a Spanish ship carrying smallpox-infected passengers arrived in the Caribbean in 1516, and the disease spread to Mexico three years later when Cortez attacked and destroyed the Aztec empire. According to Dobyns, the most lethal of all pandemics, the very first on the continent, swept over North America between 1520 and 1524 from Mexico. The Spaniards reported that half the natives in Mexico died, a figure that almost certainly is underestimated (Dobyns 1983:336–344).

Anthropologists have long assumed that late prehistoric American Indian people led lifeways closely paralleling those that are described historically. But epidemics raced far ahead of the frontier. In fact, it may be no exaggeration to say, as Dobyns has, that native lifeways in North America ended with large-scale depopulation between 1520 and 1524, when cultures across the continent were shattered by disease-induced population losses. Between about 1600 and 1780, for example, the Mandans were reduced from some 12,000 individuals to perhaps 1,500. Most of this 80 percent reduction in population came before the first significant face-to-face contact with Europeans and before Mandan culture was described in any detail. The 1837 epidemic further reduced the Mandans to no more than about 125 people or so, an overall reduction of about 96 percent.

Dissenting voices nonetheless dispute the breadth and magnitude of the depopulation envisioned by Dobyns. For example: "Physical and social barriers, however, separated individual communities and, especially, more inclusive social groups such as the southeastern chiefdoms. Such gaps in population distribution, including social impediments to contact among traditional enemies, produced far less than Dobyns' [1983:324] essentially uniform dissemination of diseases across vast regions—his single 'epidemic region'" (Milner et al. 2001:16). Nevertheless, we cannot assume that any given community escaped the ravages of disease, and we must assume, at least as a working hypothesis, that it may have undergone massive change in every sphere of life, from social structure to technology. The result of disease often was the telescoping of villages of only a few survivors into larger units that were capable of self-maintenance. The resulting depopulation sometimes was so severe that it probably is impossible to draw accurate archaeological inferences for a group from the ethnographic data, clearly a barrier to the successful use of the direct-historical approach (Dobyns 1983:338).

The lack of ethnic isomorphism is a more serious problem. Since the time of Franz Boas in the early twentieth century, anthropologists have emphasized the use of empirical data to support the construction of culture histories and to avoid speculation, however convincing or emotionally satisfying it might be. Boas demonstrated there was no necessary correlation among biology, language, and culture. The most egregious recent example that flouts a century of anthropological research in this vein is the final chapter in the book *Plains Indians, ad 500–1500*, by Karl H. Schlesier (1994). In that chapter Schlesier claims to have pushed the ethnic identities of every single historic Plains group back as much as a millennium or more. We have every reason to be dubious, as any serious anthropologist would dismiss such nonsense out of hand. Conclusions based on such assertions can only be spurious.

Schlesier believes that an archaeological phase represents something that is "real." Phases are, of course, useful constructs for some purposes and serve as convenient labels for discussing a particular set of sites or components in a general treatise or an introductory class. However, their credibility is on a par with that of the culture area, a concept introduced formally into anthropology by Clark Wissler (1914), although its roots extend back to archaeologists working in the U.S. National Museum and the Bureau of American Ethnology in the late nineteenth century. My former professor, John L. Champe, once said that culture areas perform the useful task of breaking down continent-wide variation so that general works can summarize a massive amount of detail (such as in talks to the local Rotary Club), but as intuitively derived entities they are scientifically useless.

The phases established by Willey and Phillips in 1958 are therefore of limited utility. Often they are defined on the basis of the contents of a single site that may be augmented by adding other "sufficiently similar" sites. The resulting construct is purely intuitive, selected as it is from among the vast array of sites that exist in any area. That is, a phase is an entity composed of arbitrarily defined attributes, particularly of pottery and projectile point types (O'Brien and Wood 1998:28). Nevertheless, phases often have assumed a life of their own, and some archaeologists use them as if they were entities that live and die and even mate and have offspring. Tracing a dynamic social entity such as a "tribe" into a past that is populated by such "phases" is rank speculation.

Let us realize we're not capable of tracing tribal histories very far into the past, sad as that might be. Prehistoric cultures that have similar artifact contents share some sort of historical or cultural relation, but those relations are not necessarily genetic. Rather, what we trace into the past is a cultural tradition, best defined as "a socially transmitted cultural form which persists in time" (Haury 1956:39). We must remember that, as archaeologists, we deal with the development of material culture and its consequences, not with the development of individuals or of societies.

Classes and Seminars

When I returned to Missouri in 1963, it was as a member of the American Archaeology Division of the Department of Sociology and Anthropology. Carl Chapman hired me without the advice, consent, or even the knowledge of other members of the anthropology faculty, a fact that led to embarrassing relations with the rest of the department until I'd established my credentials with them and demonstrated competence as a professional. When I arrived as the fifth member of the department, the faculty was diminutive, consisting of Chapman; H. Clyde Wilson, a cultural anthropologist who had studied the Jicarilla Apaches for his dissertation; Robert

F. G. Spier, son of the renowned Leslie Spier and also a cultural anthropologist; and Robert T. Bray, who became a preeminent historic-sites archaeologist in the Midwest. Other faculty followed in 1965, including Margot Liberty, Dale R. Henning, and Richard A. Krause, among others who moved on. A later addition was physical anthropologist Robert F. Benfer, who was part of a team that forensically authenticated the skeleton of Francisco Pizarro; Bob had to purchase an airline ticket to transport the Spaniard's bones from Peru to Columbia for study. In 1966 the department was granted autonomy, and we separated from the Department of Sociology and Anthropology.

I began teaching the course in introductory anthropology the second semester I arrived. This was my first-ever teaching experience, for my only previous such contact with students was when I was a laboratory instructor for John Champe in physical anthropology; in that case the class was learning the human skeleton, and there were just questions and answers, no lectures. In contrast, the introductory course required a great deal of preparation and was a terrifying experience. It was several years before I became comfortable in front of a large class, but I never did enjoy the course, though sometimes I was able to lighten the lecture with personal anecdotes. One day as I stepped out the back door of Swallow Hall on my way to class, I stopped momentarily to say hello to the mail carrier. I'd just done so when a plump red squirrel dropped from the heights of a giant elm tree above me and struck the sidewalk (instead of the top of my head) with a resounding smack; it quickly died. Coincidentally, I was to talk that day about the arboreal nature of early primates, but when I mentioned the death of the squirrel and stressed the importance of binocular vision in arboreal animals, they considered the anecdote a joke.

I always enjoyed campus life: indeed, except for the brief time I lived in Bismarck, I've spent my entire adult life in a university town. You never knew what you'd see as you crossed the campus—or hear, for that matter, from snippets of conversations in unfamiliar languages to indecipherable fragments by physics professors to occasional "keepers" that stand out in my memory. One day I passed a young man whose long hair was held by a headband and who wore ragged trousers and a tie-dyed T-shirt: he stared at the sidewalk as he shuffled along in sandals. As we passed, I heard him mutter, "Even Adolf Hitler wanted the best for his children." I desperately wanted to turn and follow him to hear more of his monologue, but I'd have been late for class. Another time, again as I was hurrying to class, I passed two co-eds as one said to the other: "And my mother agrees with me. No one who weighs three hundred pounds has any business teaching a course in nutrition!"

Eventually, I was to teach only 136 courses (including field schools) during my career, for I remained a half-time researcher in the American Archaeology Division for my entire tenure at Columbia. Initially, I was required to obtain half of my salary from research contracts, but after a few years the department picked up the other half, resulting in a far less stressful situation. Promotion came steadily, though I'm surely the only member of the faculty to have been demoted. There was a typographical omission in the paperwork the year I was to be promoted to associate professor, and I was elevated instead to a full professorship, omitting the step of associate. One day H. Clyde Wilson, the department chair, approached me with a smile, saying, "I'm not sure how to tell you this, Ray, but I'm going to have to demote you." But full professorship came a few years later.

For a time I taught Primitive Political Organization, but I soon settled into a routine of teaching Introduction to Archaeology, North American Archaeology, North American Indian Culture, and a variety of seminars. I enjoyed North American Indian Culture. My familiarity with Indians as a child in Cody and in the years I worked with Alan Woolworth on reservations in the Dakotas had given me sympathy for them, though my only "ethnographic" fieldwork was to collect a kinship schedule from an elderly Hunkpapa Sioux in Fort Yates to satisfy a delayed grade for a class in cultural anthropology taught by John M. Roberts in Lincoln. One day in class I recounted my familiarity with Blue Horse, a Sioux Indian I'd known in Cody who'd been a member of Buffalo Bill's Wild West Show. One of the older students, originally from Connecticut, came up to me after class and asked, "Dr. Wood, just how old *are* you?" History obviously is much "older" in Connecticut than it is in western Nebraska! Another student accosted me after I'd carelessly mentioned that the class's parents probably had been influenced in their perceptions of the West by attending Buffalo Bill's performances. She said, "My mom's *really* mad at you. She said *Grandmother* had seen them." I'd foolishly forgotten the generational gap that separated us. After I retired, I transformed my notes for that class into an article I prepared for Robert M. Utley's *Story of the West* (Wood 2003b).

My third semester in Columbia I team-taught with Carl Chapman the introductory archaeology course and a seminar in ethnohistory, the latter a disastrous experience that I swore that I'd never repeat, for we had very different approaches to teaching. I was never required to teach more than one course a semester because of my half-time status, but usually I taught a seminar of my choice at least once a year. I began with one in ecological adaptation, and over the years I directed a variety of seminars, for my half-time status gave me great flexibility. I was once asked, "How do you manage to publish so much?" Since I was then a half-time researcher, my response was, "That's what I'm paid to do."

Given the fact that all of us are prone to forgetfulness, at least at times, I'm proud that only once in my thirty-nine years of teaching did I forget to go to class—totally forgot, only to remember an hour later. I've been late a few minutes, to be sure, but never so late that the class decided I wasn't coming. But anyone can be forgetful, if not stupid. One afternoon I purchased a new set of black walking shoes at Sears; one of them was a bit snug at the store, but I expected that in a new pair. The next evening I hobbled home after having worn them all day: my right foot was in pain. In the morning I took the pair to a shoe shop just off campus and asked if the shoe could be stretched, but the cobbler told me, "You can't stretch this kind of shoe." As he spoke, he reached into the offending shoe and pulled out of its toe a wad of tissue paper the size of my fist and said with a smile, "There'll be no charge." Another customer in the shop nearly collapsed laughing.

Beginning in about 1983 I participated for ten years in the Bianchi International Pistol Tournament, held at the Chapman Academy of Practical Shooting a few miles north of Columbia. The tournament was held every May, sponsored by Bianchi International, a manufacturer of leather goods and holsters used by many police departments nationwide. It provided a welcome and dramatic change from my general inactivity. I acted in various capacities to score pistol-shooting events by a wide variety of participants, many with national and international reputations. This invitational meet drew men and women from all over the globe, from South Africa to Japan. The Japanese shooters were very good, especially since they could not practice in Japan because of its prescription against firearms, so they had to fly to Hawaii to practice! I was given the opportunity to shoot on the range after the events were over using my Luger pistol, but my hand was not steady enough and I never did hit the target. After a time the tournament lost its novelty and I retired from it; my son Stanley replaced me for a time.

In the fall of 1967 I began a series of seminars in which students analyzed the materials from an unstudied archaeological site and wrote up varying sections of the final report. It proved to be a rewarding academic experiment for everyone involved. I'd never had the opportunity to work in either an Upper Republican or a Nebraska phase site, and both entities interested me. This curiosity was the genesis of a project I undertook between September 5 and 18, in the weeks before the opening of the fall semester. Graduate student volunteers joined me in the excavation of two house sites in the Central Plains: at the Nebraska phase Nuzum site (14DP10) in northeastern Kansas, and at the Upper Republican Mowry Bluff site (25FT35) in Frontier County, in southern Nebraska. We rented motel rooms in Hiawatha for the Nuzum site, and in the town of Cambridge while we dug Mowry Bluff. We essentially worked from dawn to dusk, for our time was limited, but no one seemed to mind: it was a busman's holiday.

Alfred Johnson, from the University of Kansas, kindly led us to the Nuzum site, which he'd arranged for us to dig. The site was atop a high bluff overlooking the Missouri River about three miles southeast of the little town of White Cloud, in Doniphan County. We dug one of the two house depressions that capped the bluff, the other having been investigated in about 1915 by amateur M. E. Zimmerman. A bulldozer was summoned to strip nearly four feet of loess from above the house floor. The structure yielded a small but representative group of artifacts, though we never successfully traced its floor plan. On the other hand, we fully excavated the Mowry Bluff house by hand, exposing a well-defined four-post lodge of typical Upper Republican construction. The only anomaly was the discovery by student Kerry Lippincott of a five-centimeter-long Scottsbluff point in the fill of a bell-shaped pit in the house floor. Clearly, it was an aboriginal collector's item.

That fall the participants enrolled in a seminar to write up the sites. Technical details we could not handle were prepared by outside scholars. For example, David A. Baerreis, of the University of Wisconsin, analyzed the gastropods, and Hugh C. Cutler and Leonard W. Blake identified the maize. Al Johnson published the seminar's deliberations as *Two House Sites in the Central Plains: An Experiment in Archaeology*, Memoir 6 of the *Plains Anthropologist* (Wood, ed. 1969). In the monograph we offered fresh interpretations provided by new near-total recovery and analytical techniques, a reexamination of taxonomic problems by Richard Krause, and my own inferences relating to social organization and cultural ecology. The study, in brief, was an experiment in extracting as much information as possible from a limited field project. Empirical data supported some assumptions that were largely intuitive in the past, and challenged other assumptions. It was indeed a provocative experiment.

The work, however, inspired a long and acrimonious attack by Waldo Wedel (1970) in *Nebraska History* magazine, some of it justified because I'd incorrectly used a number of words without realizing their connotation (I've been far more careful since). However, most of his criticism was misdirected, at least to my mind and that of many others, for Waldo remained very much a traditionalist at a time when many in our profession were becoming processualists, or "New Archaeologists." It probably didn't help that I'd dedicated the study to his enemy, John Champe. (Other reviewers were more kind.) I'd read, appreciated, and reviewed Lewis and Sally Binford's 1968 book, *New Perspectives in Archeology* (Wood 1970), though I never became a processualist as such, or any other kind of "ist" other than a traditionalist. However, I never discouraged the use of any approach by my students if it meant an advance in knowledge. On the other hand, I wholeheartedly agreed with Jesse Jennings when he wrote that our discipline "owes much more to the improved, and more detailed, insights into the prehistoric cultures provided by the many ancillary additions to the arsenal of field procedures and general concepts than to either theory or 'science'" (Jennings 1994:268). Far too many "Mickey Mouse laws" were "demonstrated" at the time for New Archaeology to survive the messianic efforts by its initial proponents, though it enriched the profession by insisting that a hypothesis be investigated in all fieldwork.

The second seminar, in 1973, investigated Fay Tolton (39ST11), a fortified Initial Middle Missouri village site in central South Dakota. A party from the MRBS had excavated two long-rectangular houses at the site in 1957, but the remains had never been studied. I borrowed the material from the Midwest Archeological Center in Lincoln and carried it home to Columbia. The site contained graphic evidence of violent prehistoric warfare, for one of the dwellings had burned and collapsed over the remains of three young women lying in one corner of the house, and in the back of the structure were the remains of a mature male kneeling in a pit. The fragmented nature of the skulls of the three young women suggests that blows to the head had killed them, though the skull of the male was intact. In another house the skull of a young male was missing, surely having been taken as a trophy. The report augmented our meager understanding of the

Initial Middle Missouri variant, as well as providing concrete information on warfare practices of the time. We published our collected papers in the research series of the Missouri Archaeological Society (Wood, ed. 1976).

A third productive seminar followed in 1975. In it we wrote up the Loftin site (23SN42), the Caddoan mound and village site in southwestern Missouri where I'd dug in 1957 and 1958. Richard Marshall and I prepared a preliminary manuscript on the site for the National Park Service following our work, but no formal report was ever published because there was a fire in the building where the material was stored. Some of the artifacts were impregnated by smoke, and others were destroyed. The notes, filed separately, had not suffered, and we were able to rescue most of the necessary information from the uncharred but damaged remains and from our preliminary manuscript. Timothy K. Perttula provided an in-depth interpretation of the remains and their place in western Ozark prehistory; Loftin offered new information for Caddoan studies, being the northeasternmost known mound and village center, dating to about AD 1000–1180 (Wood, ed. 1983).

My 1979 seminar was devoted to an analysis of the Ice Glider site, on Cross Ranch property adjoining the Missouri River opposite the town of Washburn, North Dakota. Bob Levis plowed this bottomland site for the first time in 1971, and when he looked down on it from a high terrace, he saw dozens of orange spots (they were hearths) scattered across the field. He promptly called Don Lehmer, who quickly flew to North Dakota and plotted 255 hearths on his map of the field. However, nothing further was done there until 1976, when Bob called to tell me that the site had been plowed a second time: would I come and take a look at it? I flew to Bismarck, rented a car, and assembled a group of thirteen volunteers. Artifacts were thinly scattered over the terrace, and we collected everything we could find. We also tested, without result, one of the hearths. We neither expected nor found postholes, for no suggestions of depressions were ever visible there, so obviously we were dealing with a surface site.

The site was named for the large number of bison-rib ice gliders we recovered, game pieces that were used in a winter sport that was popular among many Northern Plains groups. The artwork engraved on some of the gliders was especially intriguing and included bison, birds, snakes, and at least one anthropomorphic figure. We dated the site to between 1830 and 1860 on the basis of the age of the Euroamerican goods, and concluded that the remains belonged to a Yanktonai Indian encampment that Prince

Maximilian had mentioned as he made his way up the Missouri River on June 17, 1833. At this point on the river the prince noted on his copy of William Clark's route map, "Zusamm Kunft mit dem Yanktonan," and wrote in his diary that these Indians were living in a camp of three hundred tipis in the bottomlands nearby. This clearly was territory the Yanktonai exploited in Maximilian's time, though generally they lived near Devil's Lake, on the Minnesota River, and on the Sheyenne River, a tributary of the Red River of the North. Maximilian reported that their chief, Tatanka-Kta (Dead Buffalo), had an expressive face and was dressed in a red uniform; his hair was knotted above his forehead, and he carried an eagle wing fan in his hand (Maximilian in Thwaites 1906:22:342–343; Wood, ed. 1986). This congruence of archaeological data and historical reference gives the site a breath of life that is rarely possible in archaeology.

In 1996 I obtained from the State Historical Society of North Dakota the material from the Tony Glas site, an Extended Middle Missouri site on the Missouri River in southern North Dakota. Its excavator, James H. Howard, had written it up cursorily, and it was deserving of more intensive study. Howard was an astute and productive ethnographer of Northern Plains cultures, but his archaeological work left a great deal to be desired. Jim was known to some of us, irreverently, as "Howard Handsome Dog." He was accomplished at performing Indian dances, for which he wore a magnificent Indian costume, and sometimes he took prizes at Indian powwows. One day Steve Sigstad overheard him say, as he looked into a mirror after he'd finished dressing and painting himself for a dance, "Howard, you handsome dog." It stuck. Jim was married to Elfriede, a German war bride, and they adopted two Indian children.

The seminar's final product appeared as *The Tony Glas Site, 32EM3* in *North Dakota Archaeology*, journal of the North Dakota Archaeological Association (Wood, ed. 1999). The village had long been thought to be a Terminal Middle Missouri site because of its rectangular fortification ditch, but our study confirmed it as an Extended Middle Missouri community that dated between about AD 1200 and 1400. The discovery by the excavator of numerous shell thunderbird effigies and highly fragmented human skeletal elements in the houses surely relates to community belief systems and warfare in a manner we have yet to understand.

My final seminar was held in the winter of 2001. We obtained from the Archaeology Laboratory of the South Dakota Historical Society, Rapid City, the remains from the Dirt Lodge Village site (39SP11). The village was on the east bank of the James River in east-central South Dakota and was occupied by Yanktonai Indians at about the time of the Civil War. Highway salvage excavations at this site in 1980 and 1981 had yielded two components: a Late Woodland one and the historic Dakota one, which, according to historical records, consisted of about fifteen earthlodges. The Late Woodland material had been written up by the excavator, Thomas W. Haberman, but because of his untimely death, the Dakota component remained unanalyzed. We are so used to thinking of the Dakota as tipi-dwelling peoples that we often overlook the fact that the Yanktonais sometimes lived in Arikara-style earthlodges and grew corn in their gardens. The final report of this seminar appeared in *South Dakota Archaeology*, published by the South Dakota Archaeological Society. It essentially consists of the master's thesis of Kathryn Drennan Warner, who drew together the data from several previously unpublished Yanktonai earthlodge components, including two lodges a few miles north of Fort Yates, North Dakota. Daniel Scheans excavated them in 1957 on the Standing Rock Indian Reservation for the State Historical Society of North Dakota. The Yellowlodge and Young Sites were erected in the early years of Yanktonai reservation life (Warner 2011). The earthlodge lifestyle of these and related Yanktonais merit them a marginal position in the Plains Village tradition.

These seminars were popular with students for several reasons. In addition to obtaining graduate hours, the students improved their skills in practical laboratory techniques, library research, and writing. The experience of writing a technical report that had to articulate with the findings of others reinforced an integrated if not an interdisciplinary approach, and a respectable publication resulted instead of a term paper that eventually ended up in a wastebasket. Often the students gave their papers at conferences, further enhancing the professional learning experience. This teaching device has been replicated many times since.

15

Retirement, 2002

You can't drown your troubles, not the real ones,
because if they are real they can swim.

— William Manchester, *Goodbye Darkness*, 1979

I Leave Teaching

I retired from teaching after thirty-nine years of service at the University of Missouri following my final field school at the Double Ditch site. The move was effective September 1, 2002, and the department and college awarded me emeritus status. There was no mandatory retirement age, but as a citizen born before the middle of the preceding century, I felt it was time to go. I'd become bored with repeatedly teaching some of my classes, for it was increasingly difficult to come up with original examination questions, and I despised grading exams in the first place. Furthermore, I'd served on 150 master's and doctoral committees, having chaired 36 of the former and 22 of the latter. On May 10 Mary I. Porter and A. Gail Lawrence, our wonderful departmental staff, hosted a magnificent retirement reception for me: perhaps two hundred people traveled from as far away as North Dakota, Texas, Illinois, and Nebraska. Another retirement party was held for me at the Plains Conference that October in Oklahoma City. Todd L. VanPool, a gifted southwestern and Mesoamerican archaeologist, soon filled my departmental position.

In mid-January 2002 Carolee and I, along with son Stanley and some of his friends, celebrated my retirement with a trip to the Caribbean. It was our first cruise, and only my third trip overseas. (Years earlier I'd flown to Bimini Island in the Bahamas on an AMQUA field trip, and later I visited Europe when I was researching my brother's death.) We flew to Fort Lauderdale and sailed on the Celebrity cruise ship *Century* to Puerto Rico,

Figure 41. Swallow Hall, University of Missouri, my home away from home for nearly forty years. My office was on the second story of the tower. *Author's collection.*

St. Thomas, St. Maarten, and Nassau. It was a magnificent five-day outing in perfect weather, giving us much to see at our stops and plenty of time to read during the days we spent at sea. I reread one of the most interesting books I'd read in recent decades, *The Song of the Dodo*, by David Quammen. It's a history of island biogeography and its significance for the modern world, and I recommend it to anyone with an ecological conscience. I'm grateful that Larry Agenbroad insisted I buy it when I stopped by the Mammoth Site in Hot Springs, South Dakota, on my way home from a season in North Dakota. When I tired of reading, I found a comfortable and shaded place on the ship's stern where I could watch the receding white-foamed wake of the ship bisect the jade-green ocean as the horizon slipped behind us. We also got our exercise. The ship was larger than the RMS *Titanic*, and whereas our cabin was somewhere near the anchor, the dining room overlooked the ship's stern, an eight-hundred-foot hike to another deck.

We took a second cruise in August 2005, this time to the Mediterranean: it began when I went to a travel agency to redeem an airline ticket that Carolee hadn't used when she became too ill to attend the Plains Conference in Billings the previous fall. Matters got out of hand, and we soon found ourselves on a twelve-day cruise on the Princess line's *Grand Princess*, following a flight into the Marco Polo airport in Venice, a remarkably appropriate name for that mecca of Renaissance and modern travelers. Of course, we took a gondola ride, then sailed to Athens (and saw the Acropolis), the island of Mikonos, Istanbul (we toured the Bosporus), Ephesus (where the Virgin Mary is said to have spent her last days), Naples (and Pompeii, of course), Rome (the Coliseum and the Vatican), Florence (Michelangelo's *David*), and Marseilles, by which time we were too tired to go on another tour. I deeply regretted not having paid more attention in the past to classical archaeology. However, the flight that took us over the heart of the Alps to Venice was a high point; from my window I could see Alpine villages tucked between snowfields and, much higher, an occasional glacier. I'd often tried to visualize glaciers in the Rockies, and here glacial geology was brought to life. It was a delightful grand tour of the Mediterranean, but there was much of the old saying about it: "If it's Rome, it must be Tuesday." We have yet to find another tour that matches this one and likely will take it again, for there is much more to see.

I returned home in time to have a rotten gall bladder removed, an operation so simple nowadays that I was home in my own bed that evening and was never off my feet, though it certainly slowed me down. I've been fortunate in my health to date, having had only one previous operation, to repair a hernia, which I blame on wrestling my son's motorcycle into the bed of a pickup to take it for repairs for my 1979 Missouri River float trip. Nor had I suffered any broken bones until I broke two ribs on an AMQUA field trip to the Snowy Range in August 2010. As far as I know, my childhood diseases were confined to the mumps, which erupted the night before I was to accompany my family to visit my sister Marjorie in California. I keep my fingers crossed for the future.

In retiring I lost my magnificent university office complex in Swallow Hall to another faculty member, paleoanthropologist Carol Ward, who had an abundance of graduate students with whom to populate it, for by now I had only a few remaining advisees to see through their degrees, and most of them were off campus. I moved into a smaller office down the hall. It was no hardship, and I disposed of those books I'd been using for teaching general courses, donated a large number of others to colleagues, and got rid of furniture for which I had no need. I was granted the option of teaching one class a year—my two favorites, on environment and archaeology and my seminar in ethnohistory—and retained my office privileges. Life went on as usual, except that I didn't have to teach. I had enough research projects to keep me busy, and I continued going to my campus office every workday, perpetuating a four-decade-long schedule, somehow finding new projects when old ones were completed. Carolee often smiles when she's asked how I enjoy my retirement, responding only, "What retirement?"

Still later, as new faculty replaced the old, I moved my office to the Museum of Anthropology's Support Center, about a mile off campus. It removed me from the center of activity, but my new room was luxurious: it was climate controlled, had a carpeted floor that did not squeak, and was across the hall from the men's room, a water cooler, a fully equipped kitchen, and a recycling bin. Furthermore, I could park in front of the building and no longer had to climb the thirty-two six-and-a-half-inch steps it took to get to the second floor of Swallow Hall. Over the years, getting to my office translated into climbing some 155 miles, well above the earth's stratosphere into a zone now occupied by satellites.

An obligation that continued into retirement was one I'd assumed in 1990: editing the *Missouri Archaeologist*, a task I took over from its retiring editor, Robert T. Bray. As of 2010, I've edited volumes 50 through 70. The initial associate editor and compositor, Melody Galen, made issuing the journal nearly painless and a genuine pleasure. Since it is published annually, it takes far less time than any editorial commitment I'd undertaken in the past, and this time I had no trouble choosing appropriate referees. I remained editor even after the offices of the Missouri Archaeological Society moved to Missouri State University in Springfield with the appointment of Neal Lopinot as secretary of the society.

New Projects

Ethnohistory and western history continued to hold my interest. In 2003 I embarked on a project to edit the journal and letters of Henry A. Boller. Young Boller entered the Upper Missouri River fur trade in the spring of 1857 as a clerk for Frost, Todd and Company and was assigned a post at Fort Atkinson, Dakota Territory. The newly built fort was on the south side of Like-a-Fishhook Village, where it operated in competition with Fort Berthold, one of the principal posts of the monopolistic American Fur Company. Boller interacted closely with his fur-trading competitors and with the Hidatsa and Mandan residents of the village for the next two years. He left a rich store of historic and ethnographic notes in his letters, journals, and a book, *Eight Years among the Indians*, which he published in 1867. His original letters and journals, written between 1857 and 1860, are held in the archives of the State Historical Society of North Dakota.

Hubert Smith had excavated the site of Fort Atkinson for the MRBS in 1952, and its ruins still lay open when I worked on the site of Fort Berthold with Alan Woolworth in the summer of 1954. Editing Boller's reminiscences was in many ways a return to my years as a beginning archaeologist. I'd lived on the site of Like-a-Fishhook Village for the better part of a summer; I'd hiked the surrounding countryside; and I was familiar with the surviving artistic renditions of the post and the photographic record made of it, so I could easily envision the surroundings of the activities that Boller described in his narratives. Indeed, I could "see" the background detail as I read the accounts almost as though I was watching a film. The resulting manuscript and my introduction to Boller's text appeared as *Twilight of the Upper Missouri River Fur Trade: The Journals of Henry A. Boller*, published by the State Historical Society of North Dakota (Wood, ed. 2008).

This project led immediately to another and related one. In choosing illustrations for *Twilight*, I had come across the journal and artwork of General Régis de Trobriand. De Trobriand, a Union hero of the Civil War, had been sent to Dakota Territory by the U.S. Army as the first commander of Fort Stevenson. The fort, still under construction when he arrived in 1867, was only twenty miles down the Missouri River from Fort Atkinson (by this time it had been renamed Fort Berthold II). This talented French artist and writer left a detailed narrative of Dakota military life that overlapped in personalities with the residents of Like-a-Fishhook Village, though it provides a picture of life a decade later than Boller's text. These two accounts offer rich and interrelated detail on Indian-white relations in the years immediately preceding the establishment of the Fort Berthold Reservation. De Trobriand's numerous sketches and oil paintings of the region's forts, landscapes, and Indians significantly augment his narrative (and that of Boller as well), but since they had been published piecemeal, I was encouraged to collect them and publish them under one cover, appropriately annotated. This project was published as a full issue of *North Dakota History* (Wood 2006b).

In 2007 I contracted with the State Historical Society to prepare a book on the history and archaeology of Fort Clark State Historic Site. One of the most significant historical sites in the state, it contains the remains of two fur-trading posts and the two Indian villages they served, the Mandan village of Mih-tutta-hang-kusch and the subsequent Arikara village. Despite its importance to the history of the two tribes, and the significance of the two forts to fur trade history, this complex site has never received a full-length treatment. I had participated in some of the fieldwork the society had sponsored there, directed by Stanley A. Ahler, but Stan passed away before any general work could be prepared. This work is to be published in 2011 under the title *Fort Clark and Its Indian Neighbors: A Trading Post on the Upper Missouri River.*

As I compiled the manuscript for that book, I became deeply intrigued with the story of the Canadian trader who had built the post, James Kipp. He was arguably the most important of the numerous agents of the Columbia and American Fur Companies on the Upper Missouri River in the nineteenth century. Builder of at least five of these companies' trading posts and probably the architect of the remaining ones, he was a corresponding member of the Academy of Science of St. Louis, the host and translator for George Catlin and Prince Maximilian at Fort Clark, a consultant for the Smithsonian Institution's evaluation of the paintings of the Mandan Okipa by George Catlin, and a participant in the revision of the Fort Laramie Treaty of 1851. He was also the husband of two white wives (one in Canada, the other in Missouri) and two Mandan "country wives." The first was an unnamed Mandan woman at Fort Clark, and the second was the daughter of Mató-Tópe, or Four Bears, second chief of the Mandans at Mih-tutta-hang-kusch. Four Bears' daughter, Earth Woman, bore him a son, Joseph Kipp, who became a major player in the late fur trade and early history of western Montana. The lives of James Kipp, Earth Woman, and Joseph's family encapsulate the history of the entire Upper Missouri River between 1822 and the statehood of North Dakota and Montana. Telling this story was one of the most fascinating tasks I ever set out to do. It carried me via the Internet and telephone to archives and sources from coast to coast, and to some of Kipp's living descendants on the Blackfoot Indian Reservation in Montana. I completed the biography in 2010 (Wood 2011).

In the fall of 2003 I attended the 62nd Plains Conference in Fayetteville, Arkansas: it was my fiftieth such meeting—I had missed only four of them since 1950. At the banquet the officers of the Plains Anthropological Society presented me with an exquisite bowl made by a local artist and embellished with the design of a multiheaded snake that had been found on an artifact at Spiro, Oklahoma. It has a place of honor in my office on campus; at home I cherish the Distinguished Service Award I received at the 1995 Plains Conference in Laramie, Wyoming. I was about to skip the banquet that year, but Cal Calabrese insisted that I go and somehow acquired a ticket for me. At that time the award was held secret until the banquet presentation, and I was so surprised that I was speechless, and able to stammer only a few words of thanks. I was, however, far more astonished to receive the Distinguished Service Award from the Missouri State Historical Society in 2009, no less than the one from the American Quaternary Association at its biennial meeting in June 2008. The latter one was based on the interdisciplinary program I'd initiated in the Pomme de Terre valley in the 1960s. I was equally humbled by the establishment in 1995 of the "W. Raymond Wood Opportunities for Excellence Fund" in the anthropology department at the University of Missouri, a fund that was spearheaded by Cal Calabrese, and the publication of a festschrift in 2007 by the University of Utah Press, *Plains Village Archaeology*, edited by Stanley Ahler and Marvin Kay (2007). But I also cherish two unintended compliments. When a friend asked a visitor in town if he knew someone in Columbia whom he'd like to have join them for dinner, the visitor mentioned my name. The response was, "What? Is he still alive?" On a later occasion, after I'd decided to retain a permanent beard, I was in a grocery store when I overheard a small girl whisper loudly to her mother, "Mommy, look! There's Indiana Jones's daddy!" This was superior in my mind to being mistaken for the Galloping Gourmet, as I once was on the steps of a cabin in Yellowstone National Park.

By 2010 a long-standing investigation of early maps of the American Midwest led me to compile, from those maps and from historical and ethnographic sources, an overview of tribal movements in the Northern Plains at the time of the 1780–1781 smallpox epidemic. Canadian fur trader Donald Mackay had visited and left a description of the Mandans and Hidatsas on the Missouri River in 1781, six years before James Mackay, generally credited with being the first Canadian trader to do so since visits by the La Vérendryes in the mid-1700s. Information from Donald Mackay's visit was incorporated into the Edward Jarvis and Donald Mackay map of 1791. The epidemic destroyed thousands of village and nomad Indians alike and led to a drastic change, indeed a reversal, of the power of the villagers vis-à-vis that of the Lakota Sioux, who were then engulfing the villagers' seat of power on the Missouri River. In that work I hypothesized that the mysterious "Shevitoon" Indians on the Northern Plains were the Sutaio, a group that historically merged with the Cheyenne nation about the time the Cheyennes migrated west of the Missouri River (Wood 2010b).

Because I taught half time and did research half time for my entire career at Missouri, I had sufficient opportunity to write up all my fieldwork, and I retired with no backlog of unreported sites save for my report on the Crenshaw site, now hopelessly obsolete, which resides in the files of the

Arkansas Archeological Survey in Fayetteville. Indeed, I published my last unreported sites in 2000, two years before my retirement (Wood and Brock 2000), so I was able to devote my "reclining" years to the pursuit of fresh research projects that genuinely interested me. None of them was strictly archaeological, and some were far removed indeed from past activities.

In June 2006 I attended the 52nd Midwest Friends of the Pleistocene Field Conference in North Dakota, hosted by the North Dakota Geological Survey. There I firmed up my plans to assist John W. Hoganson, geologist and state paleontologist with the survey, as a volunteer in the excavation of a mosasaur (*Platecarpus*) in the Cretaceous-era Pierre Shale formation in the fossil-rich Little Missouri badlands near Marmarth (the second *r* is silent), in extreme southwestern North Dakota. The overlying Hell Creek formation consists of the deposits that yielded Sue, the *Tyrannosaurus rex*, as well as ankylosaurs, pachycephalosaurs, and hadrosaurs. I was given grief by some of my colleagues for contributing to the false impression that "archaeologists do dinosaurs." Having been intrigued by these beasts since my preteen years, however, I ignored their petty complaints and permitted the child in me to assert itself. In any case, mosasaurs were not dinosaurs but marine reptiles related to snakes and the Komodo dragon (they had the same hinged jaws that permitted them to swallow things larger than their heads).

Marmarth is a small town (population 128, though once it could boast nearly 2,700) that provides few amenities besides the Pastime Club, a typical western bar. Nonetheless, its back rooms feature a gourmet restaurant that people come all the way from Bismarck, a two-and-a-half-hour drive, to patronize. The weather was miserable, with the temperature hovering just under 100 degrees, and there was not a tree within miles; but I had a glorious time using familiar archaeological techniques on vastly older specimens. We assisted Tyler Lyson in the dig; he is the director of the Marmarth Research Foundation, an organization dedicated to understanding the terrestrial and marine Cretaceous deposits in the badlands carved by the Little Missouri River. Volunteer excavators from Texas, Illinois, New Jersey, and New York joined us (the New Yorker was a bartender in Brooklyn!). Lyson is the paleontologist who discovered "Dakota," the "mummified" *Hadrosaurus*, when he was a sophomore in high school.

The following June I rejoined Hoganson in excavating a second mosasaur (but much larger, perhaps forty feet in length) near the little town of McCanna, in northeastern North Dakota not far from Devil's Lake. My son Eric accompanied me; he must have inherited an urge that leads him to enjoy digging almost as much as I do. This specimen of *Hainosaurus* or *Tylosaurus* was in Cretaceous-age Pierre shale deposits about eighty million years old. The summer weather was perfect; neither heat nor humidity bothered us, though there was a constant threat of rain.

My only enduring social membership for years was with Westerners International, an international group of western history buffs that has "corrals" headed by "sheriffs" scattered across the United States, Europe, and Asia. I gave the very first talk to the Columbia group, the John G. Neihardt Corral, in November 1978. Though Neihardt is famed as Nebraska's poet laureate, he taught literature at the University of Missouri during my early years in Columbia. I have enjoyed participating in the Westerners ever since. Though I've never been a joiner, in 2010 I also joined Columbia's Optimists Club, a group that is dedicated to helping children weather these difficult times.

One of the inevitable consequences of having spent so many years in a career is being asked to give talks about the "olden times" and to write book forewords, endorsements, and reviews. This last request forces one to keep abreast of the book's topic, for a review necessitates a careful reading of the volume. I'd never read a book about Colonel George Armstrong Custer and his demise, but I did read Richard A. Fox's *Archaeology, History, and Custer's Last Battle* in my capacity as an archaeologist to prepare to write its foreword. (But I do recommend that Plains specialists read Colonel Custer's *My Life on the Plains.*) When I visited the museum at the Presidio in San Francisco shortly after Fox's book came out, I began a conversation with a young ranger at the door. When he said he was reviewing Fox's book, I mentioned that I'd written its foreword. He almost went pale and gasped, "Just who *are* you?" I replied that I was no one he'd ever heard about, or would ever hear about again, but his reaction to Colonel Custer seems characteristic of the fanatics who fawn over him.

By this time I'd begun to witness an accelerating parade of retirements among my colleagues and students. Dale Henning retired in 2003 and moved to Santa Fe (and then back to Iowa), where he began to complete some of his unfinished projects from an outstanding career. In 2006 he was awarded the Distinguished Service Award at the 63rd Plains Conference. In 2005, three years after my own retirement, Bruce McMillan retired as director of the Illinois State Museum. After years of dedicated and inspired direction of the museum and its Quaternary research program, he was finally able to turn to full-time research. I was ecstatic when Bruce decided to retire in Columbia, and he obtained office space in the Museum Support Center just down the hall from me. After being expunged together with other anthropology emeriti from Swallow Hall, my residence for thirty-nine years, I am delighted to have such an amiable colleague under the same roof. Well-deserved accolades were showered on both Dale and Bruce on their retirement.

As I watched other of my colleagues slowly succumb to age and infirmities, I decided to begin disposing of those elements of my research resources I'd not used for years. This was in part prompted by the fact that I'd been the "academic executor" for Don Lehmer after his death, when I placed his correspondence and research material in the most appropriate archives. Later I began delivering some of my own material to the State Historical Society of North Dakota, the Archaeology Laboratory of the South Dakota State Historical Society, and other repositories. If you don't do it yourself (or specify what's to be done with it in a will), someone else will do it for you, and precious data might be lost.

Over the past four decades I've been blessed by a succession of outstanding students. They've had three qualities necessary for good science: an insatiable curiosity, an enviable work ethic, and the highest degree of professionalism. It's a good day when a new student walks into your office and tells you, "I want to learn about paleoecology and Plains archaeology," and it's gratifying to watch that student develop in precisely those areas. One's own children rarely follow in one's footsteps, but students do, and I'm inordinately proud of them. All of us are secretly pleased when a project is finally done and in print. Those who say they're indifferent to seeing a final publication bearing their name are simply not being honest with you (or themselves). It's an even greater pleasure to see articles by former students, whether in the *Plains Anthropologist*, *American Antiquity*, or *Science*, especially if they're building on something you've written or taught. I feel an even deeper pride when they criticize or correct something I've done (at least after that initial twinge), for this is how knowledge advances, one step and one correction at a time. There's added pride, too, when the publication is by an administrator who is not paid, or even encouraged, to do research. I've learned a lot from my students, but this is only common knowledge: any honest professor will readily acknowledge its truth.

I've seen many changes in my profession over the past half century; there have been major shifts in the paradigms of virtually all the sciences, shifts that often led to methods and techniques that found their way into archaeology. Our field became greatly enhanced by such innovations as radiocarbon dating (which entered the field about the same time I did) and geophysical prospecting and investigation (which became ever more precise as my teaching career neared its end), not to mention a host of other techniques used to understand, find, date, and validate archaeological discoveries. We survived the excesses of the "New Archaeology" advocated by Lewis Binford and his cohorts, though processual archaeology successfully reinforced the necessity for hypothesis-driven field research. I saw Binford's program as a means of understanding human behavior (as opposed to human history), for I'd reviewed Binford and Binford's *New Perspectives in Archaeology*, though I felt it unnecessary to burden our hypothesis-driven and interdisciplinary reports on the Pomme de Terre research with its terminology. In our program, however, we embraced and used ecological concepts to our advantage, treating "ecology" as the dynamic concept it is, not as a substitute for "environment," in our effort to understand the interplay of human behavior and the environment. My own contribution to processual archaeology was in the dynamics of site formation, in the paper that geographer Donald Lee Johnson and I coauthored on pedoturbation, or soil disturbance (Wood and Johnson 1978).

I never embraced any aspect of post-processual archaeology in its many forms, in large part perhaps because it essentially began in the 1980s, at a time when my archaeological interests were fading even as my interest in ethnohistory was growing. Because most post-processualists believe we cannot accurately reconstruct the past, they assert that there is no point in doing so, some of them even creating historical fantasies. Frankly, much of their work is reminiscent of "New Age" mysticism (though lacking crystals) and appears to be a nonscientific, negative reaction to scientific inquiry. Perhaps they will outgrow it. The past decade has seen the arrival of yet another approach that challenges traditional theory: the application of Darwinian theory in the field of evolutionary archaeology. It is still being evaluated, together with the emerging field of landscape archaeology. There is of course a groundswell of interest in creating alternatives to culture history: that's fine, but don't throw out the baby with the bath. I am in perfect agreement with my colleague Richard Krause when he says that "neo-evolutionists, processualists, post-processualists and landscape archaeologists all use the analytical, descriptive, classificatory and sequencing practices developed by prehistorians for the study of culture history"

(Krause 2010:252). Culture history is the basis for so much of what we do as archaeologists that their criticism of it is frankly absurd. Surely we can have multiple paradigms without having to select only the one that favors our personal biases! My first fieldwork was in the Plains, and that great grassland remains the area most emotionally charged for me. It's been a privilege and joy to work in it and to travel its breadth. Except for summer jobs and temporary assignments with the MRBS, my first professional position after graduation was as Alan Woolworth's assistant between 1954 and 1956. I've returned to North Dakota many times since, always with a sense of homecoming. There also was the attraction of having grown up in the Sandhills of northwestern Nebraska in "Old Jules Country," made famous in the 1935 biography of Jules by his daughter, Mari Sandoz (though my parents had known him and, like most of their contemporaries, had a very low opinion of him—read her book and you'll understand why).

My entry into archaeology was initially prompted by simple curiosity about the past, reinforced by the excitement of unearthing something new, something that had lain dormant in the earth for hundreds or even thousands of years. With the experience and insights I gained through our work in the rich paleoenvironmental setting at Rodgers Shelter and the spring bogs, my enthusiasm for the field increased manyfold, for there we embarked on a new intellectual adventure. But the archaeological record is not only an account of our past; it's also an integral part of the record of the recent history of our planet. Through the efforts of Quaternary scientists of all kinds, the record of the earth's past is slowly being pieced together. Its many glacial and interglacial periods, climatic optima, and other climatic changes are beginning to provide us with a means to judge the rate and degrees of climate change, which will have dramatic effects not only on humans but on all organisms in the future.

Our knowledge of the planet's history is shaped by developments in the natural sciences. As Richard Foster Flint said many years ago, Darwin's ideas on natural selection and its role in shaping biological diversity solved a critical part of the problem of how species evolve. Similarly, knowledge of plate tectonics explained the movements of continents and the making of mountain chains—in short, the creation of the physical world we see around us today. Nevertheless, a major component of that complex story still eludes us: there is no general theory of the atmosphere. Of course, we understand what is happening climatically, but we do not understand why.

Some years ago a television weather program called on an atmospheric scientist to explain what was happening during a bitterly cold blast that was affecting most of the Midwest. He could say that the chilly spell was due to an unusually southerly sweep of the cold, northerly winds accompanying the jet stream, but he couldn't tell us why the jet stream was sweeping farther south than usual. It will take considerably more research to reveal the "why" of such things.

Much of our understanding of the atmosphere will come, as Quaternary scientists know, not from going up in balloons but from digging into the earth. Archaeology, in concert with other disciplines, plays a role in our knowledge of the atmosphere and how it has affected plants, animals, and humans throughout our planet's history. Archaeological work during the 1970s in the lower Pomme de Terre River valley, for example, richly augmented by other studies, not only yielded one of the longest and most detailed archaeological sequences in Missouri but also revolutionized our knowledge of the vegetational and geological history of the state. Today students of the past are not lone adventurers investigating an esoteric spectrum of scholarship but scientists attempting to produce a coherent theoretical framework that promotes what has been called a "seamless interdisciplinary integration" of knowledge of how the earth arrived at its present condition. We will of course continue to use archaeology to learn about prehistoric stone-tool users, but that is only one part of the story. The archaeological record is a major component of the broad field of natural history: not only is it fascinating in its own right, but it is a vital cog in the ongoing study of our planet's past (O'Brien and Wood 1998:365).

I always experience a feeling of awe on crossing that vast open pasture called the Great Plains, not to mention the "Wide Missouri," and despite a lifetime of exposure to it, I've never lost my sensitivity to the hypnotic effect of the treeless, ocean-like expanse of mixed and short-grass plains. It has been a tremendous pleasure to look over a site such as Fort Clark and, through my research and imagination, visualize it as a living and active community, seeing people in motion, children playing, a Mandan war party returning from its quest for scalps or horses, bison grazing on the adjoining hills, and a steamboat plowing up the Missouri River to dock at the foot of the fort, the traders and villagers alike streaming to the riverbank to greet its arrival. There are indeed ghosts in our world, awaiting those with curiosity enough to bring them to life.

Looking back over my life, I realize I was favored by possessing loving and supportive parents, a shining sibling role model, and an insatiable curiosity. Furthermore, I've unconsciously managed to be in the right place at the right time for a successful career, and as far as I'm aware, all the problems I've faced throughout life have been of my own making. I'm truly envious that General James H. Doolittle, the renowned commander of the World War II Army Air Force, preempted me with the title to his 1991 autobiography, *I Could Never Be So Lucky Again*.

APPENDIX

Résumé

Professional and Field Experience

1950–53 Field hand for Smithsonian Institution, River Basin Surveys: Survey and excavation in Montana, Wyoming, North and South Dakota, Nebraska, and Kansas.

1952 Assistant Archeologist, Smithsonian Institution, River Basin Survey party at the Buffalo Pasture and other sites, Oahe Reservoir, South Dakota.

1954–57 Staff Archaeologist, State Historical Society of North Dakota, codirecting excavations at the Fort Berthold I, Grandmother's Lodge, Paul Brave, and Demery sites, Garrison and Oahe Reservoirs, North and South Dakota.

1955–56 Assistant Instructor in Anthropology (in prehistory and physical anthropology), University of Nebraska–Lincoln.

1957–58 Research Associate in Anthropology, University of Missouri–Columbia, directing survey and excavations in the Pomme de Terre and Table Rock Reservoirs, Missouri.

1959–61 Research Assistant in Anthropology, University of Oregon–Eugene, participating in the Wildcat Canyon site project, John Day Reservoir, Oregon.

Staff Archaeologist, State Historical Society of North Dakota, directing excavations at the Huff site, North Dakota.

1961–63 Curator of Anthropology, University Museum, University of Arkansas–Fayetteville, directing excavations at the Denham and Crenshaw Mounds and Bushwhack and Breckenridge Shelters, Arkansas.

1963–64 Instructor in Anthropology, Research Associate, and Director of River Basin Archaeology, University of Missouri–Columbia, directing excavations in the Kaysinger Bluff (later Harry S. Truman) Reservoir, Missouri.

1964–68 Assistant Professor of Anthropology and Director of River Basin Archaeology, University of Missouri–Columbia, directing excavations in the Harry S. Truman and Stockton Reservoirs, Missouri.

1968–71 Associate Professor of Anthropology and Research Professor, University of Missouri–Columbia, directing work in the Truman Reservoir under National Science Foundation grants at Rodgers Shelter and various spring sites, Missouri, and at Plains village sites in the Oahe Reservoir, South Dakota.

Directed the University of Missouri–Columbia archaeological field school at the Old Fort site, Saline County, Missouri.

1970–71 Visiting Professor of Anthropology, Department of Anthropology, and Research Associate, University of Colorado Museum, Boulder, on sabbatical leave.

1971–77 Professor of Anthropology and Research Professor, Division of American Archaeology, University of Missouri–Columbia, directing the survey of the Truman Reservoir for the U.S. Army Corps of Engineers.

1973 Visiting Professor of Anthropology, University of Wyoming, Laramie (summer).

1980–81 Visiting Professor of Anthropology, University of Nebraska–Lincoln, and Archeologist, Midwest Archeological Center, National Park Service, Lincoln, Nebraska, on sabbatical leave.

1981 Attended National Historic Publications and Records Commission, Institute for the Editing of Historical Documents, Madison, Wisconsin (July).

1985–86 Directed remote sensing and mapping fieldwork at Fort Clark State Historic Site, North Dakota.

1992 Attended workshop on Geophysical Techniques in Archeology at the Piñon Canyon Maneuver Site, Colorado, June 11–13 (National Park Service training program).

1995 Research leave, winter semester, to write/compile Part II of *An Atlas of Early Maps of the American Midwest.*

1996–97 Codirected, with Todd Kapler, the joint University of Missouri–Columbia and University of South Dakota archaeological field school at stone-ring sites in McPherson County, South Dakota.

1998–99 Directed the University of Missouri–Columbia archaeological field school at Menoken Indian Village State Historic Site, North Dakota.

2000 Directed the University of Missouri–Columbia archaeological field school at the Waugh site, Oklahoma, and Fort Clark State Historic Site, North Dakota.

2001 Directed the University of Missouri–Columbia archaeological field school at Fort Clark State Historic Site, North Dakota.

2002 Directed the University of Missouri–Columbia archaeological field school at the Winger site, Kansas, and at Double Ditch State Historic Site, North Dakota.

2002 Retired: Appointed Professor Emeritus

2003 Directed the University of Missouri–Columbia archaeological field school at the Double Ditch State Historic Site, North Dakota.

2004 Participated in the archaeological and pedological investigation of Double Ditch State Historic Site, North Dakota.
2005 Lecturer at William Woods University, Fulton, Missouri, fall semester.
2006–7 Assisted John Hoganson, North Dakota Geological Survey, in the summer excavation of Cretaceous mososaurs at Marmarth and McCanna, North Dakota.

Honors

Alumni Achievement Award: College of Arts and Sciences, University of Nebraska–Lincoln, March 31, 1988.
Byler Distinguished Professor: College of Arts and Sciences, University of Missouri–Columbia, April 15, 1991.
Second Plains Anthropological Society Distinguished Service Award and Founder's Award: 50th Plains Conference, Lincoln, Nebraska, November 13, 1992.
W. Raymond Wood Fund for Excellence in the Teaching of Archaeology: Established by alumni, Department of Anthropology, University of Missouri–Columbia, 1997.
Heritage Profile Honor Award: 14th Governor's Conference on North Dakota History, State Historical Society of North Dakota, Bismarck, November 15, 2002.
Honoring W. Raymond Wood's Legacy: Quaternary Ecology, Archaeology, and Ethnohistory of North America's Heartland. Symposium at the 69th annual meeting of the Society for American Archaeology, Montreal, Canada, April 1, 2004.
First Gerard B. Fowke Award for Career Contributions to the Archaeology of Missouri: Missouri Association of Professional Archaeologists (MAPA), Columbia, April 30, 2005.
South Dakota Archaeological Society Achievement Award: Aberdeen, September 10, 2005.
Publication of *Plains Village Archaeology: Bison-Hunting Farmers in the Central and Northern Plains*: Dedicated to W. Raymond Wood, edited by Stanley A. Ahler and Marvin Kay (Salt Lake City: University of Utah Press, 2007).
American Quaternary Association (AMQUA): Distinguished Service Award for 2007, University Park, Pennsylvania, June 6, 2008.
North Dakota History: Editor's Award for Outstanding Contribution of the Year 2007 [De Trobriand issue]: 20th Governor's Conference on North Dakota History, Bismarck, November 7, 2008.
Plains Anthropologist, "W. Raymond Wood: A Celebration": Volume 54, No. 210, 2009.

William Duncan Strong Memorial Award: Nebraska Association of Professional Archeologists (NAPA), Lincoln, August 6, 2009.

Distinguished Service Award: State Historical Society of Missouri, Columbia, October 31, 2009.

75th Anniversary Award for Exemplary Service: Missouri Archaeological Society, Excelsior Springs, March 20, 2010.

2011 Society for American Archaeology Lifetime Achievement Award, April 1, 2011.

Editorships

1972–74 *Plains Anthropologist*, volumes 17–19 (Nos. 55–66).

1972–79 *Plains Anthropologist Memoirs*, Nos. 9–13, 15.

1969–80 Missouri Archaeological Society, *Research Series*, Nos. 6–15.

1987–90 *American Antiquity*, volumes 52(3)–55(2).

1990– *Missouri Archaeologist*, volumes 50–.

References

Ahler, Stanley A.

1971 *Projectile Point Form and Function at Rodgers Shelter, Missouri.* Missouri Archaeological Society, Research Series No. 8. Columbia, Missouri.

Ahler, Stanley A., editor

2003 *Archaeological Investigations at Fort Clark State Historic Site, North Dakota: Through 2003.* PaleoCultural Research Group, Flagstaff, Arizona. Submitted to the State Historical Society of North Dakota, Bismarck.

Ahler, Stanley A., and Marvin Kay, editors

2007 *Plains Village Archaeology: Bison-Hunting Farmers in the Central and Northern Plains.* University of Utah Press, Salt Lake City.

Antevs, Ernst

1955 Geologic-Climatic Dating in the West. *American Antiquity* 20(4):317–335.

Baerreis, David A.

1961 The Ethnohistoric Approach and Archaeology. *Ethnohistory* 8(1):49–77.

Bamforth, Douglas B.

1988 *Ecology and Human Organization on the Great Plains.* Plenum Press, New York.

Barrett, Samuel A.

1933 *Ancient Aztalan.* Bulletin of the Public Museum of the City of Milwaukee, Vol. 13. Milwaukee.

Bell, Christopher J., Ernest L. Lundelius Jr., Anthony D. Barnosky, Russell W. Graham, Everett H. Lindsay, Dennis R. Ruez Jr., Holmes A. Semken, S. David Webb, and Richard J. Zakrzewski

2004 The Blancan, Irvingtonian, and Rancholabrean Mammal Ages. In *Late Cretaceous and Cenozoic Mammals of North America: Biostratigraphy and Geochronology,* edited by Michael O. Woodburne, pp. 232–314. Columbia University Press, New York.

Bell, Earl H.

1936 Introduction to *Chapters in Nebraska Archaeology.* University of Nebraska, Lincoln.

Blakeslee, Donald J.

1975 *The Plains Interband Trade System: An Ethnohistoric and Archaeological Investigation.* Ph.D. dissertation, University of Wisconsin–Milwaukee. University Microfilms International, Ann Arbor, Michigan.

Bleed, Peter

1989 Objectivity, Reflection and Single Case Studies: Comments on Hassler's "The Effects of CRM. . . ." *Plains Anthropologist* 34(124, Pt. 1):111–128.

Bowers, Alfred W.

1948 A History of the Mandan and Hidatsa. Unpublished Ph.D. dissertation, University of Chicago.

Brown, James A.

1983 Summary. In *Archaic Hunters and Gatherers in the American Midwest*, edited by James L. Phillips and James A. Brown, pp. 5–10. Academic Press, New York.

Bryson, Reid A., and Wayne M. Wendland

1970 The Character of Late-Glacial and Post-Glacial Climatic Changes. In *Pleistocene and Recent Environments on the Central Great Plains*, edited by Wakefield Dort Jr. and J. Knox Jones Jr., pp. 53–74. University Press of Kansas, Lawrence.

Calabrese, F. A.

1972 *Cross Ranch: A Study of Variability in a Stable Cultural Tradition*. Memoir 9. *Plains Anthropologist* 17(58, Pt. 2).

Catlin, George

1841 *Letters and Notes on the Manners, Customs, and Condition of the North American Indians*. 2 vols. London.

Champe, John L.

1946 *Ash Hollow Cave: A Study of Stratigraphic Sequence in the Central Great Plains*. University of Nebraska Studies, new series, No. 1. Lincoln.

1948 A is for Apple. *Plains Archeological Conference News Letter* 1(3). Reprinted in 1961 volume, pp. 45–48, Lincoln, Nebraska.

1949 White Cat Village. *American Antiquity* 14(4):285–292.

Chomko, Stephen A., and Gary W. Crawford

1978 Plant Husbandry in Prehistoric Eastern North America: New Evidence for Its Development. *American Antiquity* 43(3):405–408.

Chomko, Stephen A., and W. Raymond Wood

1973 Linear Mounds in the Northeastern Plains. *Archaeology in Montana* 14(2): 1–19.

Coe, Michael D.

2006 *Final Report: An Archaeologist Excavates His Past*. Thames and Hudson, London.

DeMallie, Raymond J., editor

2001 *Plains*. Handbook of North American Indians, Vol. 13, Pts. 1–2. William C. Sturtevant, general editor. Smithsonian Institution, Washington, D.C.

Denny, James M.

2000 Lewis and Clark in the Boonslick. *Boone's Lick Heritage* 8(1–2):3–26. Boonville, Missouri.

Dickson, Jim
1996 Buffalo 4, Bulls 0. *Plains Anthropologist* 41(158):401–403.
Dixon, Roland B.
1913 Some Aspects of North American Archeology. *American Anthropologist* 15:549–577.
Dobyns, Henry F.
1983 *Their Number Become Thinned.* University of Tennessee Press, Knoxville.
Dort, Wakefield, Jr., and J. Knox Jones Jr., editors
1970 *Pleistocene and Recent Environments of the Central Great Plains.* University Press of Kansas, Lawrence.
Dumond, Don E., and Rick Minor
1983 *Archaeology in the John Day Reservoir: The Wildcat Canyon Site, 35-GM-9.* Anthropological Papers No. 30. University of Oregon, Eugene.
Ewers, John C.
1968 The Indian Trade of the Upper Missouri before Lewis and Clark. In *Indian Life on the Upper Missouri,* pp. 14–33. University of Oklahoma Press, Norman.
Falk, Carl R., and F. A. Calabrese
1973 Helb: A Preliminary Statement. *Plains Anthropologist* 18(62, Pts. 1–2): 336–343.
Fletcher, Alice C.
1904 The Hako: A Pawnee Ceremony. *Annual Report of the Bureau of American Ethnology* 22(2):5–372. Washington, D.C.
Fox, Richard A.
1999 Review of *Archaeology on the Great Plains*, edited by W. Raymond Wood. *American Anthropologist* 101(4):853–854.
Friends of the Pleistocene
1975 Quaternary Paleoenvironmental History of the Western Missouri Ozarks. *Guidebook for the 23rd Annual Meeting, Midwest Friends of the Pleistocene.* Columbia/Rolla, Missouri, and Springfield, Illinois.
Frison, George C.
1973 The Plains. In *The Development of North American Archaeology,* edited by James E. Fitting, pp. 151–184. Anchor Books, Garden City, New York.
Glenn, James R.
1994 The River Basin Surveys Program. *North Dakota Archaeology* 5:5–14.
Gough, Barry M., editor
1992 *The Journal of Alexander Henry the Younger, 1799–1814.* 2 vols. Champlain Society, Toronto.
Graham, Russell W., C. Vance Haynes, Donald Lee Johnson, and Marvin Kay
1981 Kimmswick: A Clovis-Mastodon Association in Eastern Missouri. *Science* 213:1115–1117.

Grant, H. Roger

1994 Living in the Depot: The Two-Story Railroad Station on the Northern Plains. *Great Plains Quarterly* 14(2):117–128.

Griffin, David E.

1977 *Timber Procurement and Village Location in the Middle Missouri Subarea.* Memoir 13. *Plains Anthropologist* 22(78, Pt. 2):177–185.

Grinnell, George Bird

1923 *The Cheyenne Indians: Their History and Ways of Life.* 2 vols. Yale University Press, New Haven.

Gunnerson, James H.

2006 Archaeological Reminiscences: From the Plains and Back Again. In "Plains Archaeology's Past: A Collection of Personal Narratives." *Plains Anthropologist* 51(200):615–632.

Hassler, Robert

1989 The Effects of CRM: A Sociohistorical Perspective of the Development of Anthropology, University of Nebraska at Lincoln. *Plains Anthropologist* 34(124, Pt. 1):111–128.

Haury, Emil W.

1956 An Archaeological Approach to the Study of Cultural Stability, chaired by Emil W. Haury. In *Seminars in Archaeology: 1955*, edited by Robert Wauchope, pp. 31–57. Memoir 1. Society for American Archaeology, Salt Lake City.

Hawley, Marlin F.

2006 Introduction to "Plains Archaeology's Past: A Collection of Personal Narratives." *Plains Anthropologist* 51(200):487–520.

Hawley, Marlin F., and Virginia A. Wulfkuhle, editors

2006 Plains Archaeology's Past: A Collection of Personal Narratives. *Plains Anthropologist* 51(200).

Heaney, Seamus

2000 *Beowulf: A New Verse Translation.* Farrar, Straus and Giroux, New York.

Henning, Dale R.

1998 The Oneota Tradition. In *Archaeology on the Great Plains*, edited by W. Raymond Wood, pp. 345–414. University Press of Kansas, Lawrence.

Hinds, V. Strode

2001 Reconstructing Charles Floyd. *We Proceeded On* 27(1):16–19.

Holland, Thomas D.

1984 A Pilot Study in the Thermal Properties of Buffalo Chips. *Plains Anthropologist* 29(104):161–165.

1987 How to Create Professional-Looking Photographic Plates. *Missouri Archaeological Society Quarterly* 4(1):12–15.

Hughes, Jack T.
1974 *Prehistory of the Caddoan-Speaking Tribes*. Garland, New York.
Hunt, William J., Jr.
1994 Fort Floyd: An Enigmatic Nineteenth-Century Trading Post. *North Dakota History* 61(3):7–20.
Hurt, Wesley R., Jr.
1953 *Report of the Investigation of the Thomas Riggs Site, 39HU1, Hughes County, South Dakota, 1952*. Archaeological Studies, Circular No. 5. South Dakota Archaeological Commission, Pierre.
Jackson, Donald
1967 Some Advice for the Next Editor of Lewis and Clark. *Missouri Historical Society Bulletin* 24(1):52–62.
Jantz, Richard L.
1974 The Redbird Focus: Cranial Evidence in Tribal Identification. *Plains Anthropologist* 19(63):5–13.
Jantz, Richard L., and Douglas W. Owsley
1994 White Traders in the Upper Missouri: Evidence from the Swan Creek Site. In *Skeletal Biology in the Great Plains: Migration, Warfare, Health, and Subsistence*, edited by Douglas W. Owsley and Richard L. Jantz, pp. 189–201. Smithsonian Institution Press, Washington, D.C.
Jennings, Jesse D.
1948 Plainsmen of the Past: A Review of the Prehistory of the Plains. Mimeographed. Region 2, National Park Service, Omaha, Nebraska.
1954 The Archeology of the Plains: An Assessment. Region 2, National Park Service, Omaha, Nebraska.
1985 River Basin Surveys: Origins, Operations, and Results, 1945–1969. *American Antiquity* 50(2):281–296.
1994 *Accidental Archaeologist: Memoirs of Jesse D. Jennings*. University of Utah Press, Salt Lake City.
Johnson, Alfred E., and W. Raymond Wood
1980 Prehistoric Studies on the Plains. In *Anthropology on the Great Plains*, edited by W. Raymond Wood and Margot Liberty, pp. 35–51. University of Nebraska Press, Lincoln.
Johnson, Craig M.
2007 *A Chronology of Middle Missouri Plains Village Sites*. Smithsonian Contributions to Anthropology No. 47. Smithsonian Institution Scholarly Press, Washington, D.C.
Johnston, Richard B.
1982 *Archaeology of the McClure Site (39HU7) and the Protohistoric Period in the Big Bend Region of South Dakota*. Memoir 18. *Plains Anthropologist* 27(98):1–53.

Kastor, Peter J.

2004 Gateways and Guardians: Lewis and Clark and the Louisiana Purchase. In *Finding Lewis and Clark: New Trails, New Directions*, edited by James P. Ronda and Nancy Tystad Koupal, pp. 25–44. South Dakota State Historical Society Press, Pierre.

King, James E.

1973 Late Pleistocene Palynology and Biogeography of the Western Missouri Ozarks. *Ecological Monographs* 43:539–563.

Klepinger, Linda, and Dale R. Henning

1976 The Hatten Site: A Two-Component Burial Site in Northeast Missouri. *Missouri Archaeologist* 37:92–170.

Krause, Richard A.

1976 Donald Jayne Lehmer, 1918–1975. *Plains Anthropologist* 21(71):73–76.

1998 A History of Great Plains Prehistory. In *Archaeology on the Great Plains*, edited by W. Raymond Wood, pp. 48–86. University Press of Kansas, Lawrence.

2010 Review of *Archaeological Landscapes on the High Plains*, edited by Laura L. Schieber and Bonnie J. Clark. *Journal of Archaeological Sciences* 35(2): 249–252.

Kroeber, Alfred L.

1947 *Cultural and Natural Areas of Native North America*. Publications in American Archaeology and Ethnology, Vol. 38. University of California, Berkeley.

Leforge, Thomas H.

1928 *Memoirs of a White Crow Indian, as told by Thomas B. Marquis*. Century, New York.

Lehmer, Donald J.

1952 The Fort Pierre Branch in Plains Prehistory. Unpublished Ph.D. dissertation, Department of Anthropology, Harvard University, Cambridge.

1954 *Archeological Investigations in the Oahe Dam Area, 1950–51*. River Basin Surveys Papers No. 7. Bulletin No. 158, Bureau of American Ethnology, Smithsonian Institution, Washington, D.C.

1966 *The Fire Heart Creek Site*. Smithsonian Institution, River Basin Surveys. Publications in Salvage Archeology No. 1. Lincoln, Nebraska.

1970 Climate and Culture History in the Middle Missouri Valley. In *Pleistocene and Recent Environments of the Central Great Plains*, edited by Wakefield Dort Jr. and J. Knox Jones Jr., pp. 173–184. University Press of Kansas, Lawrence.

1971 *Introduction to Middle Missouri Archeology*. Anthropological Papers No. 1. National Park Service, Washington, D.C.

2001 Plains Village Tradition: Postcontact. In *Plains*, edited by Raymond J. DeMallie, pp. 245–255. Handbook of North American Indians, Vol. 13, Part 1, William C. Sturtevant, general editor. Smithsonian Institution, Washington, D.C.

Lehmer, Donald J., and Warren W. Caldwell

1966 Horizon and Tradition in the Northern Plains. *American Antiquity* 31(4): 511–516.

Lehmer, Donald J., and David T. Jones

1968 *Arikara Archeology: The Bad River Phase.* Smithsonian Institution, River Basin Surveys. Publications in Salvage Archeology No. 7. Lincoln, Nebraska.

Lehmer, Donald J., W. Raymond Wood, and C. L. Dill

1978 Knife River Phase. Department of Sociology and Anthropology, Dana College, Blair, Nebraska, and American Archaeology Division, University of Missouri, Columbia. Submitted to the National Park Service, Interagency Archeological Services, Denver.

Liberty, Margot, W. Raymond Wood, and Lee Irwin

2001 Omaha. In *Plains*, edited by Raymond J. DeMallie, pp. 399–415. Handbook of North American Indians, Vol. 13, Part 1, William C. Sturtevant, general editor. Smithsonian Institution, Washington, D.C.

Lowie, Robert H.

1912 Some Problems in the Ethnology of the Crow and Village Indians. *American Anthropologist* 14(1):60–71.

1982 *Indians of the Plains.* Preface by Raymond J. DeMallie. University of Nebraska Press, Lincoln.

Luttig, John C.

1920 *Journal of a Fur-Trading Expedition on the Upper Missouri, 1812–1813.* Edited by Stella M. Drumm. Missouri Historical Society, Saint Louis.

Madsen, David B.

1973 Quaternary Paleoecology in the Southeastern Great Basin. Unpublished Ph.D. dissertation, Department of Anthropology, University of Missouri, Columbia.

Mandel, Rolfe D., editor

2000 *Geoarchaeology in the Great Plains.* University of Oklahoma Press, Norman.

Mann, Donna J.

1971 *Valley of the Mastodons.* Privately printed, Warsaw, Missouri.

May, David W.

2000 Geoarchaeological Research in Nebraska: A Historical Perspective. In *Geoarchaeology in the Great Plains*, edited by Rolfe D. Mandel, pp. 166–198. University of Oklahoma Press, Norman.

Maximilian of Wied, Prince
2001 *Travels in the Interior of North America.* Taschen, Cologne, Germany.
2008–2010 *The North American Journals of Prince Maximilian of Wied, May 1832–April 1833*, Vols. 1 and 2. Edited by Stephen S. Witte and Marsha V. Gallagher. University of Oklahoma Press, Norman.

McKern, William C.
1939 The Midwestern Taxonomic Method as an Aid to Archaeological Study. *American Antiquity* 4(4):301–303.

McMillan, R. Bruce
1970 Early Canid Burial from the Western Ozark Highland. *Science* 167: 1246–1247.
2010 The Discovery of Fossil Vertebrates on Missouri's Western Frontier. *Earth Sciences History* 29(1):26–51.

Mehl, Maurice G.
1962 *Missouri's Ice Age Mammals.* Educational Series No. 1. State of Missouri, Division of Geological Survey and Water Resources, Rolla.
1966 *The Grundel Mastodon.* Report of Investigations No. 35. Division of Geological Survey and Water Resources, Rolla, Missouri.

Mehringer, Peter J., Jr., James E. King, and Everett H. Lindsay
1970 A Record of Wisconsin-Age Vegetation and Fauna from the Ozarks of Western Missouri. In *Pleistocene and Recent Environments of the Central Great Plains,* edited by Wakefield Dort Jr. and J. Knox Jones Jr., pp. 173–184. University Press of Kansas, Lawrence.

Mehringer, Peter J., Jr., Charles E. Schweger, W. Raymond Wood, and R. Bruce McMillan
1968 Late-Pleistocene Boreal Forest in the Western Ozark Highlands? *Ecology* 49(3):567–568.

Miller, Carl F.
1963 Archeological Manifestations in the Toole County Section of the Tiber Reservoir Basin, Montana. River Basin Surveys Papers No. 3. Bulletin No. 185, pp. 235–255, Bureau of American Ethnology, Smithsonian Institution, Washington, D.C.

Milner, George R., David G. Anderson, and Marvin T. Smith
2001 The Distribution of Eastern Woodlands Peoples at the Prehistoric and Historic Interface. In *Societies in Eclipse: Archaeology of the Eastern Woodland Indians, ad 1400–1700*, edited by David S. Brose, C. Wesley Cowan, and Robert C. Mainfort Jr., pp. 9–18. Smithsonian Institution Press, Washington, D.C.

Moorehead, Warren K.
1922 *The Hopewell Mound Group of Ohio. Fieldiana* 6(5). Field Museum of Natural History, Chicago.

Mosiman, James, and George B. Rabb
1963 The Herpetology of Tiber Reservoir Area, Montana. *Copeia*, No. 1.
Moulton, Gary E., editor
1983– *The Journals of the Lewis and Clark Expedition*. 13 vols. University of
2001 Nebraska Press, Lincoln.
Mulloy, William
1958 *A Preliminary Historical Outline for the Northwestern Plains*. University of Wyoming Publications, Vol. 8, Nos. 2–3. Laramie.
Nasatir, Abraham P.
1952 *Before Lewis and Clark: Documents Illustrating the History of the Missouri, 1785–1804*. 2 vols. St. Louis Historical Documents Foundation, Saint Louis, Missouri.
Neuman, Robert W.
1975 *The Sonota Complex and Associated Sites on the Northern Great Plains*. Publications in Anthropology No. 6. Nebraska State Historical Society, Lincoln.
Newman, Thomas M.
1959 Tillamook Prehistory and Its Relation to the Northwest Coast Culture Area. Unpublished Ph.D. dissertation, Department of Anthropology, University of Oregon, Eugene.
O'Brien, Michael J.
1996 *Paradigms of the Past: The Story of Missouri Archaeology*. University of Missouri Press, Columbia.
O'Brien, Michael J., and W. Raymond Wood
1998 *The Prehistory of Missouri*. University of Missouri Press, Columbia.
Osgood, Ernest S.
1964 *The Field Notes of Captain William Clark, 1803–1805*. Yale University Press, New Haven.
O'Shea, John, and John Ludwickson
1992 *Archaeology and Ethnohistory of the Omaha Indians: The Big Village Site*. University of Nebraska Press, Lincoln.
Raffel, Burton
1963 *Beowulf*. Mentor Books, New York.
Ray, Jack H.
2007 *Ozarks Chipped-Stone Resources*. Special Publication No. 8. Missouri Archaeological Society, Springfield.
Reeves, Brian O. K.
1973 The Concept of an Altithermal Cultural Hiatus in Northern Plains Prehistory. *American Anthropologist* 75:1221–1253.
Roberts, John M.
1951 *Three Navaho Households: A Comparative Study in Small Group Culture*.

Papers of the Peabody Museum of American Archaeology and Ethnology, Vol. 40, No. 8. Harvard University, Cambridge.

1964 The Self-Management of Cultures. In *Explorations in Cultural Anthropology: Essays in Honor of George Peter Murdock*, edited by Ward Goodenough, pp. 433–454. McGraw Hill, New York.

Rooney, Andy

1995 *My War.* Times Books, New York.

Roper, Donna C.

1990 Artifact Assemblage Composition and the Hunting Camp Interpretation of High Plains Upper Republican Sites. *Southwestern Lore* 56(4):1–19.

Sandoz, Mari

1935 *Old Jules.* Little, Brown, Boston.

Saunders, Jeffrey J.

1977 *Late Pleistocene Vertebrates of the Western Ozark Highland, Missouri.* Reports of Investigations No. 33. Illinois State Museum, Springfield.

Schlesier, Karl H.

1994 *Plains Indians, ad 500–1500: The Archaeological Past of Historic Groups.* University of Oklahoma Press, Norman.

Schwartz, Douglas W., David A. Baerreis, Jesse D. Jennings, and W. Raymond Wood

1968 River Basin Surveys. Report to the Director, Museum of Natural History, Smithsonian Institution, April 4. Washington, D.C.

Sellers, Mary

1973 The Secret Notebook for the Practicing Archaeologist: With Preliminary Notes Toward an Ethno-Science of Archaeology. *Plains Anthropologist* 18(60):140–148.

Shafer, Robert J., editor

1980 *A Guide to Historical Method.* 3rd ed. Dorsey Press, Homewood, Illinois.

Shotwell, J. Arnold

1955 An Approach to the Paleoecology of Mammals. *Ecology* 36:327–337.

Smith, Bruce D.

2006 Eastern North America as an Independent Center of Plant Domestication. *Proceedings of the National Academy of Sciences of America* 1–3: 12223–12228.

Smith, Carlyle S.

1959 Reconstructing a Plains Indian Earth Lodge. In *The Archaeologist at Work*, edited by Robert F. Heizer, pp. 131–133. Harper and Brothers, New York.

Smith, G. Hubert

1972 *Like-a-Fishhook Village and Fort Berthold: Garrison Reservoir, North Dakota.* Anthropological Papers No. 2. National Park Service, Washington, D.C.

1980 *The Explorations of the La Vérendryes in the Northern Plains, 1738–43*. Edited by W. Raymond Wood. University of Nebraska Press, Lincoln.

Smith, G. Hubert, and John Ludwickson

1981 *Fort Manuel: The Archeology of an Upper Missouri Trading Post of 1812–1813*. Special Publication No. 7. South Dakota Archaeological Society, Vermillion.

Speer, Albert

1976 *Spandau: The Secret Diaries*. Translated by Richard and Clara Winston. Macmillan, New York.

Stanford, Dennis J.

1978 The Jones-Miller Site: An Example of Hell Gap Bison Procurement Strategy. In *Bison Procurement and Utilization: A Symposium*, edited by Leslie B. Davis and Michel Wilson. Memoir 14. *Plains Anthropologist* 23(82, Pt. 2):90–97.

Stephenson, Robert L.

1954 Taxonomy and Chronology in the Central Plains–Middle Missouri River Area. *Plains Anthropologist* 1(1):15–21.

Steward, Julian H.

1942 The Direct Historical Approach to Archaeology. *American Antiquity* 7:337–343.

Stirling, Matthew W.

1929 Comments on Mr. Hodge's Paper. In *Report of the Conference on Midwestern Archaeology, Held in St. Louis, Missouri, May 18, 1929*. National Research Council, Bulletin No. 74:4–28.

Strong, William Duncan

1933 The Plains Culture Area in the Light of Archaeology. *American Anthropologist* 35:271–287.

1935 *An Introduction to Nebraska Archeology*. Smithsonian Miscellaneous Collections 93(10). Washington, D.C.

1940 From History to Prehistory in the Northern Great Plains. In *Essays on the Historical Anthropology of North America in Honor of John R. Swanton*. Smithsonian Miscellaneous Collections 100:353–394. Washington, D.C.

Sturtevant, William C.

1971 Creek into Seminole. In *North American Indians in Historical Perspective*, edited by Eleanor Leacock and Nancy Lurie, pp. 92–128. Random House, New York.

Taylor, Colin F.

2003 *The People of the Buffalo*, vol. 1. Tatanka Press, Wyk auf Foehr, Germany.

Taylor, Walter W.

1948 *A Study of Archaeology*. Memoir 69. American Anthropological Association, Menasha, Wisconsin.

Temple, Wayne C.

1975 *Atlas: Indian Villages of the Illinois Country; Supplement*. Scientific Papers No. 2, Part 1. Illinois State Museum, Springfield.

1977 *Indian Villages of the Illinois Country*. Scientific Papers No. 2, Part 2. Illinois State Museum, Springfield.

Terry, Keith

2009 *Nebraska's Cowboy Rail Line*. Arcadia Publishing, Charleston, South Carolina.

Thiessen, Thomas D.

1999 *Emergency Archeology in the Missouri River Basin*. Special Report No. 2. Midwest Archeological Center, Lincoln, Nebraska.

Thiessen, Thomas D., W. Raymond Wood, and A. Wesley Jones

1979 The Sitting Rabbit 1907 Map of the Missouri River in North Dakota. *Plains Anthropologist* 24(84):145–167.

Thompson, Ralph Stanton

1961 The Final Story of the Deapolis Mandan Indian Village Site. *North Dakota History* 28(4):143–153.

Thwaites, Reuben Gold, editor

1906 Maximilian, Prince of Wied, Travels in the Interior of North America, 1832–1834. In *Early Western Travels, 1748–1846*, vols. 22–25. Arthur H. Clark, Cleveland, Ohio.

Tucker, Sarah Jones

1942 *Atlas: Indian Villages of the Illinois Country*. Scientific Papers No. 2, Part 1. Illinois State Museum, Springfield.

Voegelin, Erminie W.

1954 A Note from the Chairman. *Ethnohistory: The Bulletin of the Ohio Valley Historic Indian Conference*, No. 1:1–3.

Warner, Kathryn Drennan

2011 An Overview of Yanktonai Archaeology in the Dakotas. *South Dakota Archaeology* 27.

Wedel, Waldo R.

1934 Preliminary Classification for Nebraska and Kansas Cultures. *Nebraska History* 15(3):251–255.

1936 *An Introduction to Pawnee Archeology*. Bulletin No. 112. Bureau of American Ethnology, Smithsonian Institution, Washington, D.C.

1938 *The Direct-Historical Approach in Pawnee Archeology*. Smithsonian Miscellaneous Collections 97(7). Washington, D.C.

1940 Culture Sequence in the Central Great Plains. In *Essays on the Historical Anthropology of North America in Honor of John R. Swanton*. Smithsonian Miscellaneous Collections 100:291–352. Washington, D.C.

1961 *Prehistoric Man on the Great Plains.* University of Oklahoma Press, Norman.
1970 Some Observations on "Two House Sites in the Central Plains: An Experiment in Archaeology." *Nebraska History* 51(1–28):225–252.
1981 Toward a History of Plains Archeology. *Great Plains Quarterly* 1(1):16–38.

Weltfish, Gene
1965 *The Lost Universe.* Basic Books, New York.

Wendorf, Fred, and Raymond H. Thompson
2002 The Committee for the Recovery of Archaeological Remains. *American Antiquity* 67(2):317–330.

Wheeler, Richard Page
1996 *Archeological Investigations in Three Reservoir Areas in South Dakota and Wyoming: Part II; Keyhole Reservoir.* J&L Reprint Company, Lincoln, Nebraska.

White, Theodore E.
1956 The Study of Osteological Material in the Plains. *American Antiquity* 21(4):401–404.

Will, George F., and Thad. C. Hecker
1944 The Upper Missouri River Valley Aboriginal Culture in North Dakota. *North Dakota Historical Quarterly* 11(1–2).

Will, George F., and Herbert J. Spinden
1906 *The Mandans: A Study of Their Culture, Archaeology and Language.* Papers of the Peabody Museum of American Archaeology and Ethnology, Vol. 3, No. 4:81–219. Harvard University, Cambridge.

Willey, Gordon R.
1966 *An Introduction to American Archaeology: North and Middle America.* Prentice-Hall, Englewood Cliffs, New Jersey.

Willey, Gordon R., and Philip Phillips
1958 *Method and Theory in American Archaeology.* University of Chicago Press, Chicago.

Wilson, Gilbert L.
1921 *Waheenee: An Indian Girl's Story.* Webb Publishing, Saint Paul, Minnesota.

Wissler, Clark
1909 *The Indians of Greater New York and the Lower Hudson.* Anthropological Papers Vol. 3. American Museum of Natural History, New York.
1914 Material Cultures of the North American Indians. *American Anthropologist* 16:447–505.
1917 *The American Indian.* McMurtie, New York.
1948 *North American Indians of the Plains.* 3rd edition. Handbook Series No. 1. American Museum of Natural History, New York.

Wood, Simeon
1920 *A History of Hauppauge, Long Island.* Charles J. Werner, New York.
Wood, W. Raymond
1955a Historical and Archeological Evidence for Arikara Visits to the Central Plains. *The Plains Anthropologist*, No. 4:37–49.
1955b Pottery Types from the Biesterfeldt Site, North Dakota. *The Plains Anthropologist,* No. 3:3–12.
1957a Notes on a Burned Earth Lodge at the Ward Site, North Dakota. *The Plains Anthropologist*, No. 8:41–42.
1957b Perforated Elk Teeth: A Functional and Historical Analysis. *American Antiquity* 22(4):381–387.
1959 Notes on Ponca Ethnohistory, 1785–1804. *Ethnohistory* 6(1):1–27.
1960a *Nánza, the Ponca Fort.* Archives of Archaeology No. 3. Society for American Archaeology, Madison, Wisconsin.
1960b The Boundary Mound Group: An Eastern Woodland Complex in North Dakota. *Plains Anthropologist* 5(10):71–78.
1961 The Pomme de Terre Reservoir in Western Missouri Prehistory. *Missouri Archaeologist* 23:1–131.
1962 A Stylistic and Historical Analysis of Shoulder Patterns on Plains Indian Pottery. *American Antiquity* 28(1):25–40.
1963a Breckenridge Shelter: An Archeological Chronicle in the Beaver Reservoir Area. *Arkansas Archeological Society, Arkansas Archeology: 1962*, pp. 67–96. Fayetteville.
1963b *The Denham Mound: A Mid-Ouachita Focus Temple Mound in Hot Spring County.* Anthropology Series No. 1. University of Arkansas Museum, Fayetteville.
1963c A Preliminary Report on the 1962 Excavations at the Crenshaw Site. *Arkansas Archeological Society, Arkansas Archeology: 1962*, pp. 1–4. Fayetteville.
1965a *The Redbird Focus and the Problem of Ponca Prehistory.* Memoir 2. *Plains Anthropologist* 10(28).
1965b Bushwhack Shelter, 3BE2: An Ozark Bluff-Dweller Site in Northwest Arkansas. *Arkansas Archeologist* 5(8–9):151–171.
1967a The Fristoe Burial Complex. *Missouri Archaeologist* 29.
1967b *An Interpretation of Mandan Culture History.* River Basin Surveys Papers No. 39. Bulletin No. 198, Bureau of American Ethnology, Smithsonian Institution, Washington, D.C.
1967c An Archaeological Appraisal of Early European Settlements in the Senegambia. *Journal of African History* 8(1):39–64.
1968 Mississippian Hunting and Butchering Patterns: Bone from the Vista Shelter, 23SR20, Missouri. *American Antiquity* 33(2):170–179.

1969 The Middle Missouri Region: Typology and Concepts. *Plains Anthropologist* 14(44):144–148.

1970 Review of *New Perspectives in Archaeology*. *Plains Anthropologist* 15(49): 229–231.

1971a *Biesterfeldt: A Post-Contact Coalescent Site on the Northeastern Plains.* Smithsonian Contributions to Anthropology No. 17. Smithsonian Institution Press, Washington, D.C.

1971b Pottery Sites near Limon, Colorado. *Southwestern Lore* 37(3):53–85.

1971c A Protohistoric Mandan or Hidatsa Bundle. *Archaeology in Montana* 12:1–7.

1971d Contrastive Features of Native North American Trade Systems. *University of Oregon Anthropological Papers* 4:153–169.

1973 Culture Sequence at the Old Fort, Saline County, Missouri. *American Antiquity* 38(1):101–111.

1974 Northern Plains Village Cultures: Internal Stability and External Relationships. *Journal of Anthropological Research* 30(1):1–16.

1976 Vegetational Reconstruction and Climatic Episodes. *American Antiquity* 41(2):206–208.

1977 Historical Resources of the Knife River Indian Villages National Historic Site. Planning document prepared for the Midwest Archeological Center, Lincoln, Nebraska.

1979a Notes on the Historical Cartography of the Fort Union Trading Post National Historic Site. Review document prepared for the Midwest Archeological Center, Lincoln, Nebraska.

1979b Notes on the Historical Cartography of the Oahe Reservoir Area. Review document prepared for the Department of Anthropology, University of Nebraska, Lincoln.

1979c Notes on the Historical Cartography of the Lake Sharpe Area. Review document prepared for the Department of Anthropology, University of Nebraska, Lincoln.

1979d John Leland Champe, 1895–1978. *American Anthropologist* 81(2):338–341.

1980 Plains Trade in Prehistoric and Protohistoric Intertribal Relations. In *Anthropology on the Great Plains*, edited by W. Raymond Wood and Margot Liberty, pp. 98–109. University of Nebraska Press, Lincoln.

1981a The John Evans 1796–97 Map of the Missouri River. *Great Plains Quarterly* 1(1):39–53.

1981b *The Poole Site, 3GA3*. Foreword and summary by Ann M. Early. *Arkansas Archeologist* 22:7–65.

1982a Lewis and Clark and Middle Missouri Archaeology. *Quarterly Review of Archaeology* 3(4):3–5.

1982b William Clark's Mapping in Missouri, 1803–1804. *Missouri Historical Review* 76(3):241–252.

1983a *An Atlas of Early Maps of the American Midwest*. Scientific Papers Vol. 18. Illinois State Museum, Springfield.

1983b John Thomas Evans and William Clark: Two Early Western Explorer's Maps Re-examined. *We Proceeded On* 9(1):10–16.

1985 The Plains-Lakes Connection: Reflections from a Western Perspective. In *Archaeology, Ecology and Ethnohistory of the Prairie-Forest Border Zone of Minnesota and Manitoba*, edited by Janet Spector and Elden Johnson, pp. 1–8. J&L Reprint Company, Lincoln, Nebraska.

1986a *The Origins of the Hidatsa Indians: A Review of the Ethnohistorical and Traditional Data*. J&L Reprint Company, Lincoln, Nebraska.

1986b Slaughter River: Pishkun or Float Bison? *We Proceeded On* 12(2):11–14.

1987a Mapping the Missouri River through the Great Plains, 1673–1895. In *Mapping the North American Plains*, edited by Fred C. Luebke, F. W. Kaye, and Gary E. Moulton, pp. 27–40. University of Oklahoma Press, Norman.

1987b Nicolas de Finiels: Mapping the Mississippi and Missouri Rivers, 1797–1798. *Missouri Historical Review* 81(4):387–402.

1990a Ethnohistory and Historical Method. In *Advances in Archaeological Method and Theory*, Vol. 2, edited by Michael B. Schiffer, pp. 81–110. University of Arizona Press, Tucson.

1990b The Role of the Romantic West in Shaping the Third Reich. *Plains Anthropologist* 35(132):313–319.

1991 Ecology and Great Plains Studies. *Review of Archaeology* 12(2):30–34.

1993a *Nánza, the Ponca Fort*. 2nd edition. J&L Reprint Company, Lincoln, Nebraska.

1993b Some Views on Great Plains Prehistory. *Review of Archaeology* 14(1):21–24.

1993c *Or Go Down in Flame: The Death of a Navigator over Schweinfurt*. Sarpedon, New York, and Greenwood Press, London.

1993d Integrating Ethnohistory and Archaeology at Fort Clark State Historic Site, North Dakota. *American Antiquity* 58(3):544–559.

1993e *Joseph N. Nicollet's 1839 Manuscript Maps of the Missouri River and Upper Mississippi Basin*. Scientific Papers Vol. 24. Illinois State Museum, Springfield.

1995a The Missouri River Basin Surveys: Archaeology without the Middle "A." *Kansas Anthropologist* 16(2):1–13.

1995b Fort Charles, or "Mr. Mackey's Trading House." *Nebraska History* 76(1):2–7.

1996 The Missouri River Basin on the 1795 Soulard Map: A Cartographic Landmark. *Great Plains Quarterly* 16(3):183–198.

1997 Second Schweinfurt. In *Great Raids in History: From Drake to Desert One*, edited by Samuel A. Southworth, pp. 222–233. Sarpedon, New York.

1999 The Jaguar Gorget: "The Missouri State Artifact." *Missouri Archaeological Society Quarterly* 16(2):8–11.

2001a Plains Village Tradition: Middle Missouri. In *Plains*, edited by Raymond J. DeMallie, pp. 186–195. Handbook of North American Indians, Vol. 13, Pt. 1, William C. Sturtevant, general editor. Smithsonian Institution, Washington, D.C.

2001b *An Atlas of Early Maps of the American Midwest, Part 2*. Scientific Papers Vol. 29. Illinois State Museum, Springfield.

2002 The Realities of Ethnogenesis. *Missouri Archaeologist* 63:71–82.

2003a *Prologue to Lewis and Clark: The Mackay and Evans Expedition*. American Travel and Exploration Series No. 79. University of Oklahoma Press, Norman.

2003b The West before Columbus: Prehistory to AD 1500. In *The Story of the West*, edited by Robert M. Utley, pp. 8–53. DK Publishing, New York.

2003c Toussaint Charbonneau's Kitchen. *Museum of the Fur Trade Quarterly* 39(4):2–5.

2006a The Missouri River Basin Surveys: Archaeology without the Middle "A." In "Plains Archaeology's Past: A Collection of Personal Narratives." *Plains Anthropologist* 51(200):671–682.

2006b The North Dakota Artwork of General Régis de Trobriand. *North Dakota History* 74(3–4):2–30.

2010a Folk Art on the Northern Plains: The Case of the Prairie Dinosaurs. *Plains Anthropologist* 55(215):235–240.

2010b The Earliest Map of the Mandan Heartland: Notes on the Jarvis and Mackay 1791 Map. *Plains Anthropologist* 55(216), in press.

2011 James Kipp: Upper Missouri River Fur Trader and Missouri Farmer. *North Dakota History* 77(1–2), in press.

Wood, W. Raymond, editor

1969 *Two House Sites in the Central Plains: An Experiment in Archaeology*. Memoir 6. *Plains Anthropologist* 14(44, Pt. 2).

1976 *Fay Tolton and the Initial Middle Missouri Variant*. Research Series No. 13. Missouri Archaeological Society, Columbia.

1977a *Selected Writings of Donald J. Lehmer*. J&L Reprint Company, Lincoln, Nebraska.

1977b *Trends in Middle Missouri Prehistory: A Festschrift Honoring the Contributions of Donald J. Lehmer*. Memoir 13. *Plains Anthropologist* 22(78, Pt. 2).

1983 The Loftin Component, 32SN42. *Missouri Archaeologist* 44:1–74.

1986 *Ice Glider, 32OL110: Papers in Northern Plains Prehistory and Ethnohistory*. Special Publication No. 10. South Dakota Archaeological Society.

1998 *Archaeology on the Great Plains*. University Press of Kansas, Lawrence.

1999 The Tony Glas Site, 32EM3. *North Dakota Archaeology* 7:9–12.

2008 *Twilight of the Upper Missouri River Fur Trade: The Journals of Henry A. Boller*. State Historical Society of North Dakota, Bismarck.

Wood, W. Raymond, and Sharon L. Brock

1984 The Bolivar Burial Complex of Southwestern Missouri. *Missouri Archaeologist* 45.

2000 Six Late Prehistoric Burial Mounds in Southwestern Missouri. *Missouri Archaeologist* 61.

Wood, W. Raymond, and J. J. Hoffman

1995 Reminiscences of Two Missouri Basin Shovel Bums. In "40 Something: The River Basin Surveys." *North Dakota Archaeology* 5:221–229.

Wood, W. Raymond, William J. Hunt Jr., and Randy H. Williams

2011 *Fort Clark and Its Indian Neighbors: A Trading Post on the Upper Missouri River*. University of Oklahoma Press, Norman, in press.

Wood, W. Raymond, and Lee Irwin

2001 Mandan. In *Plains*, edited by Raymond J. DeMallie, pp. 349–364. Handbook of North American Indians, Vol. 13, Pt. 1, William C. Sturtevant, general editor. Smithsonian Institution, Washington, D.C.

Wood, W. Raymond, and Ann Mary Johnson

1973 High Butte, 32ME13: A Missouri Valley Woodland-Besant Site. *Archaeology in Montana* 14(3):35–83.

Wood, W. Raymond, and Donald Lee Johnson

1978 A Survey of Disturbance Processes in Archaeological Site Formation. In *Advances in Archaeological Method and Theory*, vol. 1, edited by Michael J. Schiffer, pp. 315–381. Academic Press, New York.

Wood, W. Raymond, and Margot Liberty, editors

1980 *Anthropology on the Great Plains*. University of Nebraska Press, Lincoln.

Wood, W. Raymond, and R. Bruce McMillan, editors

1976 *Prehistoric Man and His Environments: A Case Study in the Ozark Highland*. Academic Press, New York.

Wood, W. Raymond, and Gary E. Moulton

1981 Prince Maximilian and New Maps of the Missouri and Yellowstone Rivers by William Clark. *Western Historical Quarterly* 12(4):373–386.

Wood, W. Raymond, Robert K. Nickel, and David E. Griffin

1984 *Remote Sensing: The American Great Plains*. Supplement No. 9 to *Remote Sensing: A Handbook for Archeologists and Cultural Resource Managers*. National Park Service, Washington, D.C. Reprinted 1984 by J&L Reprint Company, Lincoln, Nebraska.

Wood, W. Raymond, Joseph C. Porter, and David C. Hunt
2002 *Karl Bodmer's Studio Art: The Newberry Library Bodmer Collection*. University of Illinois Press, Urbana.
Wood, W. Raymond, and Lori Ann Stanley
1989 Recovery and Identification of World War II Dead: American Graves Registration Activities in Europe. *Journal of Forensic Sciences* 34(6): 1365–1373.
Wood, W. Raymond, and Thomas D. Thiessen
1985 *Early Fur Trade on the Northern Plains: Canadian Traders among the Mandan and Hidatsa Indians, 1738–1818*. American Travel and Exploration Series No. 68. University of Oklahoma Press, Norman.
Wood, W. Raymond, and Alan R. Woolworth
1964 The Paul Brave Site (32SI4), Oahe Reservoir Area, North Dakota. River Basin Surveys Papers No. 33:1–66. Bulletin No. 189, Bureau of American Ethnology, Smithsonian Institution, Washington, D.C.
Woodward, John A.
1986 Prehistoric Shipwrecks on the Oregon Coast? Archaeological Evidence. In *Contributions to the Archaeology of Oregon, 1983–1986*, pp. 219–254. Occasional Papers No. 3. Association of Oregon Archaeologists, Salem.
Woolworth, Alan R.
1956 Archeological Investigations at Site 32ME59 (Grandmother's Lodge). *North Dakota History* 23(2):78–102.
2006 Adventures of a Plains Anthropologist-Historian. In "Plains Archaeology's Past: A Collection of Personal Narratives." *Plains Anthropologist* 51(200):649–670.
Woolworth, Alan R., and W. Raymond Wood
1960 The Archeology of a Small Trading Post (Kipp's Post, 32MN1) in the Garrison Reservoir, North Dakota. River Basin Surveys Papers No. 20: 239–305. Bulletin No. 176, Bureau of American Ethnology, Smithsonian Institution, Washington, D.C.
1964 The Demery Site (39CO1), Oahe Reservoir Area, South Dakota. River Basin Surveys Papers No. 34:67–138. Bulletin No. 189, Bureau of American Ethnology, Smithsonian Institution, Washington, D.C.

Index